*Charles Johnson in Context*

# CHARLES JOHNSON
## in Context

*Linda Furgerson Selzer*

UNIVERSITY OF MASSACHUSETTS PRESS

*Amherst*

LC 2008053930

ISBN 978-1-55849-723-8 (paper); 698-9 (library cloth)

*Designed by Steve Dyer*

*Set in Sabon by House of Equations, Inc.*

*Printed and bound by The Maple-Vail Book Manufacturing Group*

LIBRARY OF CONGRESS CATALOGING-IN-PUBLICATION DATA

Selzer, Linda F.

Charles Johnson in context / Linda Furgerson Selzer.

p. cm.

Includes bibliographical references and index.

ISBN 978-1-55849-698-9 (alk. paper)—

ISBN 978-1-55849-723-8 (pbk. : alk. paper)

1. Johnson, Charles Richard, 1948–    —Criticism and interpretation.

2. African Americans in literature.   I. Title.

PS3560.03735Z85 2009

813'.54—dc22

2008053930

*British Library Cataloguing in Publication data are available.*

*For my mother,*
*Thelma Louise Furgerson*
*and*
*in memory of my father,*
*Truman Allison Furgerson, Sr.*

# CONTENTS

# ILLUSTRATIONS

# ACKNOWLEDGMENTS

I wish to thank the Africana Research Center of Penn State University for supporting my research with a generous travel grant. The College of the Liberal Arts and the Department of English at Penn State also provided helpful assistance. I owe a special debt of gratitude to Bernard Bell and Aldon Nielsen for their insightful comments on earlier versions of the entire manuscript. Philip Jenkins also made helpful suggestions, and many others provided useful provocations along the way, including Deb Clarke, Ann Hostetler, Keith Gilyard, Janet Lyon, Robert Caserio, Robin Schulze, Marie Secor, Bob Secor, and George Yancy. Charles Johnson responded unfailingly to my many requests for information. I also benefited from the professionalism of the University of Massachusetts Press, especially the counsel of senior editor Clark Dougan and the attentions of copy editor Amanda Heller.

Some of the material included in this book was presented in earlier forms at conferences, and I would like take this opportunity to thank the African American Literature and Culture Society, the American Literature Association, the American Studies Association, the College English Association, MELUS, MLA, and the Charles Johnson Society for providing the organizational structures and intellectual community that enabled me to develop my work. I am especially indebted to Don Bialostosky (without whose confidence in the project this book would not have been written).

For their love and patience over the past few years, I thank my daughters, Maggie and Molly, and my mother, Thelma. Jack's steadfastness and sense of humor sustain us all.

Portions of this book appeared in earlier form as "The Genesis of Charles Johnson's Philosophical Fiction," in *Charles Johnson: The Novelist as Philosopher*, edited by Marc C. Conner and William R. Nash (Jackson: University of Mississippi Press, 2007), and in the introduction to *New Essays on the African American Novel*, edited by Lovalerie King and Linda F. Selzer (New York: Palgrave Macmillan, 2008). I thank the publishers for permission to reuse this material here.

*Charles Johnson in Context*

# 1

## From Philosophy to Black Philosophical Fiction

> Art does not happen outside history. Art is always forged in the tempestuous crucible of a particular historical moment. It is a specific hour in cultural history, in the enveloping society, and in the state of one's profession at a moment in time, which define and determine the real creative and imaginative possibilities for the work of any artist, scientist, educator, or scholar. His methods, the styles the artist selects from, even the questions he will ask—all these are shaped by the specific cultural and historical forms in play . . . especially during his years of apprenticeship or when he is a student.
>
> *Charles Johnson, "The Katz Lecture"*

Aᴛ ᴏɴᴇ ᴛʜᴏᴜɢʜᴛ-ᴘʀᴏᴠᴏᴋɪɴɢ ᴍᴏᴍᴇɴᴛ ɪɴ Cʜᴀʀʟᴇꜱ Jᴏʜɴꜱᴏɴ'ꜱ second novel, *Oxherding Tale* (1982), the protagonist, Andrew Hawkins, comes upon a wood carving of himself that has been sculpted by the master artisan Reb, the African American slave and descendant of the fictional Allmuseri tribe that so often figures creatively in Johnson's fiction. As Andrew reflects on the four-sided figure, he is fascinated by the representation of his earlier life that he sees chiseled there and puzzled by the fourth side of the sculpture, which remains blank—an unmarked surface that hints both at the possibilities that lie latent in Andrew's unrealized future and at Johnson's characteristic faith in the phenomenological abundance of life. Reb's sculpture of Andrew and Johnson's approach to writing fiction remind us that individual perspectives never give us the entire thing itself but instead offer individual profiles and angles of vision. As Johnson emphasizes in "Philosophy and Black Fiction" (first published in *Obsidian* in 1980), even true perceptions are "partial, one-sided, and badly in need of completion" (82). Comprehensive vision therefore requires multiple perspectives.

In this volume I seek to delineate new perspectives on Charles Johnson's art.[1] Specifically, the chapters that follow analyze Johnson's literary production in relation to the critical issues raised by the emergence of three black intellectual and cultural formations in the late-twentieth and early-twenty-first centuries: black philosophers, black Buddhists, and "new" black public intellectuals.[2] By placing Johnson's fiction in context—in detailed historical and conceptual relation to these three groups—I tie Johnson's artistic achievements to the larger projects of those working to reform the practice of American academic philosophy in the post–World War II era, those seeking to translate an ancient religious practice into an African American idiom, and those attempting to redefine cosmopolitan thought in order to make it a more effective tool for social justice. Johnson's participation in all three of these endeavors deepens the historical import, social consequence, and conceptual depth of his art. At the same time, the social history of each of these groups is exciting in its own right and constitutes a notable development in the black public sphere since the 1960s. While Johnson's characteristic fusion of literature, Buddhism, and philosophy is remarkably original—and may strike readers as highly idiosyncratic—his creative work vigorously participates in, advances, and helps to define larger directions in American intellectual life.

Johnson's troubled relation to the Black Power and Black Arts movements has been the focus of the most extensive historical criticism on Johnson's work to date.[3] As important and highly visible social projects during the period of Johnson's writing apprenticeship, the Black Power and Black Arts (BAM) movements have been justifiably analyzed in relation to the development of Johnson's art—from their role in the creation of the cartoon books he drafted while he was still an undergraduate, to their influence on the evolution of the neo-slave narrative genre to which Johnson has contributed two major novels (*Oxherding Tale* and *Middle Passage*), to their impact on specific characters in Johnson's fiction, and to Johnson's polemical representations of these movements as cultural wrong turns in his various prose essays on the current condition of black Americans. Indeed, the very visibility of the Black Power and Black Arts movements in the last half of the twentieth century ironically contributed to the difficulty of distinguishing other social developments that have been less visible—but equally important—to Johnson's writerly project. Recovering these contexts provides a richer, more finely detailed, and more intellectually complete picture of the cultural backgrounds that influenced Johnson's aesthetic project of writing "philosophical fiction."

While scholarship on the Black Arts movement has evolved through a number of stages, recovery work is just getting under way on the social history of the generation of black students who entered graduate programs in philosophy in the post–World War II period, on the African Americans who were drawn to the dharma in the second half of the twentieth century, and on what has been called the "rise" of new black public intellectuals around the turn of the millennium. As Tommy Lott points out, African American philosophy has only recently entered its period of "canonization" (Yancy, *African* 198).[4] Similarly, the emergence of what the Buddhist publication *Tricycle* calls "Black Dharma" went largely unaccounted for until black Buddhists themselves began to speak out about their practice in the 1980s and 1990s. Although a new generation of black public intellectuals burst onto the national stage to some fanfare in the last decade of the twentieth century — and although scholars such as Hortense Spillers have emphasized that the social implications of this phenomenon are "massive" (91)—their cultural history is still unfolding. Therefore, while Johnson has contributed to different degrees to each of these groups, his work has not yet received extended analysis from the specific perspectives their cultural histories provide.

Johnson's philosophical fiction is commonly interpreted in terms of the philosophical ideas that can be found "in" his literary productions. Alternatively, in this chapter I trace the genesis of that fiction to the unique challenges and opportunities encountered by the small group of black students who entered graduate programs in philosophy in the 1960s and 1970s, a time that has been identified as a moment of "crisis" in the discipline. Like those of other black students, Johnson's early experiences in philosophy reveal both a deeply felt passion for intellectual pursuits and a self-conscious awareness of the singular status of blacks in relation to the discipline's intellectual and disciplinary norms. Not surprisingly, as black students entered philosophy programs across the nation, they frequently sought out alternatives to the dominant Anglo-American approaches that emphasized abstract logic and linguistic analysis at the expense of ethics and moral philosophy. Against narrowly conceived intellectual preoccupations that seemed divorced from social reality, students such as Lucius Outlaw, Cornel West, Howard McGary Jr., Leonard Harris, and Tom Slaughter—Johnson's teacher at Southern Illinois University (SIU) and fellow graduate student in philosophy at SUNY Stony Brook—sought a new intellectual grounding in approaches such as neo-Marxism and phenomenology. Contemporary efforts to infuse academic philosophy with a new social and phenomenological immediacy were a significant factor in the development of Johnson's aesthetic practice. By engaging philosophical questions in a literary mode, Johnson sought to invigorate philosophy, as he emphasizes, by putting "flesh" back on its "abstract bones" (Ghosh 374). Because Johnson was an undergraduate and master's degree student in philosophy at SIU (1966–1973) and a Ph.D. student in philosophy at Stony Brook (1973–1976), his work as a philosophy student and the fiction that grew out of that experience are justly considered part of the history of this generation of philosophers. In the process of legitimating their philosophical interests in the 1960s and 1970s, blacks investigated old philosophical questions from a new perspective, raised new questions, and sought to reform the practice of philosophy itself. By boldly claiming the literary as an important site for black philosophical agency, Johnson's fiction makes its own powerful contribution to a vital moment in the history of American philosophy.

While this chapter focuses on the disciplinary context for the genesis of Johnson's aesthetic project, chapter 2 extends the analysis of Johnson's relationship to philosophy by analyzing the manner in which his first published novel, *Faith and the Good Thing* (1974), joined in a contemporary discussion about neo-Marxism, one of the alternative philosophies—and perhaps the leading one—that proved attractive to black philosophy students of Johnson's generation (and, of course, to others). From a vantage point in the twenty-first century, after the collapse of the Soviet Union and a restructuring of the economy in a number of former communist and socialist countries, it can be hard to appreciate the excitement that was generated by the dissemination of Marxist thought on the nation's campuses when Johnson arrived at Southern Illinois University in the fall of 1966, a year and a half before the Prague Spring and the French May. Chapter 2, "From Marx to Marcuse in *Faith and the Good Thing*," demonstrates that Johnson's encounter with Marxist philosophy as a student—especially as it is reflected in his unpublished and largely overlooked master's thesis—provides an essential framework for understanding his first published novel. Johnson began his study of Marx as a sophomore, at a time when neo-Marxist critique was an energizing presence in American universities and when Marxist principles increasingly provided conceptual frameworks for black and student social protest in the United States. The black students who were studying philosophy in the 1960s and 1970s found in neo-Marxism a fascinating tool for understanding their situated position as black Americans. Cornel West has asserted that "black intellectuals must pass through [Marxism], come to terms with it, and creatively respond to it if black intellectual activity is to reach any recognizable level of sophistication and refinement" ("Dilemma" 79). Johnson's master's thesis and his novel *Faith and the Good Thing* constitute his own intellectual and creative responses to Marxist thought. If after 1974 the trajectory of Johnson's philosophical interests would move away from Marxist philosophy toward an increasing interest in phenomenology— and an increasingly profound engagement with Buddhism—Johnson's early immersion in neo-Marxism, and especially his introduction to a liberating conception of productive subjectivity, would have a lasting impact on his practice of fiction.

Like the social history of black philosophers, the history of black Buddhists in the United States has also remained unwritten. And like the black philosophers who are revising Western philosophical practices, contemporary black Buddhists are also engaged in a larger revisionist task: the translation of an ancient Eastern religion into a contemporary African American idiom. As a philosophical religion that encourages the intellectual critique of inherited dogma, Buddhism is known for embodying a "tradition of originality." Black Buddhists like Charles Johnson, bell hooks, Jan Willis, and Angel Kyodo Williams (as well as fellow travelers such as Alice Walker) represent the latest moment in that long history of innovation. Deeply influenced both by the growing globalization of values that is one characteristic of postmodernity and by their experiences as black Americans, black practitioners interpret their adopted religion from a singular cultural location. Johnson, hooks, and Willis belong to a generation of African Americans who matured as Dr. Martin Luther King Jr.'s nonviolent approach to reform became increasingly disparaged as insufficiently radical—as "Uncle Tomism." As their writings demonstrate, Buddhism provides them with an intellectual and spiritual path back to King's ethic of nonviolence. At the same time, King's emphasis on the importance of direct social action motivates them to promote a form of "engaged" Buddhist practice that moves beyond a focus on personal enlightenment to advocate for social reform. Drawing on Buddhist magazines such as *Turning Wheel, Tricycle,* and *Shambhala Sun*; on scholarly studies of Western Buddhism such as Christopher S. Queen's *Engaged Buddhism in the West* (2000); and on the writings of black Buddhists published in books such as Willis's *Dreaming Me: An African American Woman's Spiritual Journey* (2001) and Johnson's *Turning the Wheel* (2003), chapter 3, "The Emergence of Black Dharma and *Oxherding Tale*," derives a critical apparatus for understanding the relationship between personal enlightenment and civic engagement in Johnson's fiction. By increasingly engaging his Buddhist practice in his prose and fiction since the 1980s, Johnson joins with others in translating ancient teachings into an African American idiom and makes his own contribution to the development of an innovative form of Western Buddhism.

Johnson also matured as a writer and a thinker alongside a rising generation of black intellectuals, many of whom, like Johnson himself, gained a new national prominence in the 1990s. In an important 1993 *Boston Review* forum Randall Kennedy grouped Johnson with other black public intellectuals—including Cornel West, Henry Louis Gates Jr., Toni Morrison, Orlando Patterson, Steven Carter, and Derrick Bell—as representing something "entirely new in . . . national life": the growing numbers of black people who "have access to institutions, to media, to audiences, to recognition" ("The Responsibility of Intellectuals"). As more people of color attained the status of public intellectuals across a wide spectrum of fields in the 1990s, the position, opportunities, and responsibilities of black intellectuals were debated with special urgency in the nation's leading newspapers and magazines as well as in academic journals and scholarly studies. Although this debate has long historical roots reaching back at least to W. E. B. Du Bois's arguments for the influential contributions that a "talented tenth" would make to black uplift, the rise of new black intellectuals in the late twentieth century was an important social development that differed in several respects from earlier models of black intellectualism in the nation's history. Changing educational, economic, and social conditions—including the explosion of novel forms of media—prompted black intellectuals to renegotiate their relationship to celebrity, to black communities, and to the nation at large. Most important, as I emphasize in chapter 4, "The Rise of the New Black Intellectual and the Varieties of Cosmopolitanism in *Middle Passage*," these intellectuals set out to revise the conceptual boundaries of cosmopolitan thought. Although cosmopolitanism has been frequently identified with the privileged mobility of the elite, one of the most significant features of the recent theorization of cosmopolitanism has been the effort to rethink its relation to non-elites, including the poor and the enslaved. Critical debate has focused especially on whether or not the cosmopolitan appeal to universal norms promotes abstract loyalties at the expense of actually existing ethnic, geographical, and national communities. By means of his prose writings on black intellectualism, and by putting into play on a single ship multiple forms of cosmopolitanism that interrogate one another in *Middle Passage* (1990), Johnson joins the efforts of contemporary thinkers such as Kwame Anthony Appiah and Henry Louis Gates Jr. to expand the conceptual borders of cosmopolitan thought by articulating a "situated," "patriotic," or "rooted" cosmopolitanism.

Like the separate depictions on Reb's multisided statue of Andrew, each of the chapters in this book is specifically designed to bring into sharp relief an individual—but significant—profile of Johnson's art. In a 2002 article in which he describes his use of phenomenological variation as an intellectual tool and writerly practice, Johnson emphasizes that "every disclosure that renders something visible simultaneously brings about a concealment that renders something else invisible" ("Novel" 19–20). Every profile, therefore, both reveals *and* conceals. Because the emergence of each of these groups raises different historical and conceptual issues, each resonates with Johnson's fiction in distinctive ways. As a writer whose career has spanned a period of several decades, it is not surprising that Johnson has developed a number of intellectual and cultural interests, or that the concerns left unanswered by one pursuit have sometimes been addressed by his immersion in another. By analyzing Johnson's representation of King's social legacy, however, chapter 5, "The Return of the King and the Logic of Conversion in *Dreamer*," unifies and completes this study's depiction of Johnson's development in two important ways. First, it brings issues raised in each of the previous chapters together in a single cultural debate about the lasting significance of King's legacy to the nation. After King's death some black thinkers—including some of the black philosophers discussed in chapters 1 and 2—established a particular reading of King as being insufficiently radical in his methodology and too closely aligned with whites. Later in the century, however, many black thinkers (such as Michael Eric Dyson, Cornel West, and Charles Johnson) set out consciously to recover aspects of King's legacy that they believed were missing from that earlier interpretation—and the debate over King's legacy entered a distinctively new stage. This larger recovery project, as chapter 5 demonstrates, is an important cultural context for understanding Johnson's 1998 novel *Dreamer*.

Second, I argue in chapter 5 that by joining the larger cultural conversation about King's legacy, Johnson developed a specific resolution to a tension between personal enlightenment and social engagement that is evident from the first in his fiction. His participation in the larger projects of black philosophers, Buddhists, and public intellectuals helps to clarify a problem of central and recurring concern to Johnson, and one that has been the subject of considerable critical debate: How do personal growth, education, and conversion—or in Johnson's Buddhist-inspired term, "enlightenment"—relate to civic action? Each of the groups to which Johnson contributes suggests a different way of framing this question and thereby provides, as the chapters that follow demonstrate, a specific conceptual architecture for one of his first three novels. As he participates in the larger cultural debate about King's legacy, Johnson's various intellectual, spiritual, and cultural interests become crystallized and powerfully focused. He then develops in *Dreamer* a particular resolution to the question of how private conversion relates to civic action in his depiction of King as a "transformed nonconformist." This trope, which Johnson takes from a sermon by King, centers precisely on the question of the requirements for effective action in the civic arena. King offers the transformed nonconformist as a regulative ideal that enables him to critique both a citizenship of conformity which fails to challenge the nation to improve and a citizenship of indulgent nonconformity which easily degenerates into mere self-expression. Nonconformity becomes constructive, King asserts—and Johnson agrees—precisely when it is "controlled and directed by a transformed life" or "embraces a new mental outlook" ("Transformed" 15). In other words, citizens *require* enlightenment in order to take effective action in the social sphere. By participating in a larger cultural debate about

King's legacy and by coming to understand King as a transformed non-conformist, Johnson develops a sophisticated account of how personal conversion and civic action are related and presents in *Dreamer* his most powerfully realized social vision.

Because the chapters that follow provide new research on intellectual and cultural groups that are significant in their own right as well as important social contexts for an understanding of Johnson's art, the focus of this study is necessarily dual. Each of the following chapters offers substantial research (both original recovery work and fresh syntheses of existing research) into the critical issues that are raised by the emergence of one of these groups of black Americans and considers how those critical issues animate a single Johnson novel. Illustrating this structure in miniature, this chapter examines the disciplinary issues raised by a critical moment in academic philosophy and then demonstrates through an analysis of a single Johnson short story how those issues contributed to the development of Johnson's chosen aesthetic practice of writing philosophical fiction. Readers with an interest in African American intellectual and cultural history will find the contextual research provided by this interdisciplinary approach especially compelling. All readers should gain a new appreciation for the difficulties these groups of black Americans encountered, for the critical issues that they raise, for the opportunities they represent, and—most important—for the ways in which they enrich an understanding of Johnson's complex and multisided art.

## The Writer as Philosophy Student

> The thing about movements is that accounts of them tend to be written after they are over. So, we'll have to wait to see the historical accounts . . . regarding our efforts on behalf of African American philosophy.
>
> *Lucius Outlaw, "Interview"*

In 1994 Charles Johnson—a native son of Evanston, Illinois, and by that time also a college professor at the University of Washington and an internationally recognized author—was invited to serve as commencement speaker by Northwestern University, the elite institution of higher education located only five miles from his boyhood home on Dodge Avenue in a predominantly black neighborhood of Chicago's prosperous northern suburb. At the graduation, Northwestern awarded Johnson an honorary degree, which he accepted in honor of his mother, Ruby Elizabeth Jackson Johnson, and his grandmother Beatrice Jackson. To the family members and friends who attended the ceremony, the writer's tribute to his maternal ancestors must have seemed especially meaningful. Johnson's mother, who had always supported her son's various artistic and intellectual interests, had been prevented from realizing her own dreams of becoming an educator by health complications stemming from asthma. She died in 1981, thirteen years before Johnson's address. Furthermore, Johnson's status at the graduation ceremony as a local product of the tight-knit black community in Evanston who had made good as a celebrated author was both complicated and intensified by his family's personal history with Northwestern University, for during the early 1960s Johnson's grandmother had worked regularly as a cook and his mother intermittently as a cleaning lady for the Gamma Phi Beta sorority house on Northwestern's campus. There his mother once heard the all-white sorority chapter declare that no blacks would "ever be admitted into its ivied halls" (Johnson, "Charles" 226).[5]

One can only speculate on the mixed emotions that Johnson experienced when he was honored at the graduation ceremonies on that day in 1994, or some years before when, in 1990, he was offered a chair in the humanities at Northwestern—an offer he declined in order to remain in Seattle.[6] But he was certainly aware of the irony in his return to Northwestern as commencement speaker, for the sisters of Gamma Phi Beta sorority had unwittingly contributed to his own education in a very tangible fashion. At the end of each semester, Johnson explained, the young sorority women would leave discarded books in the chapter house when they left for home. Johnson's mother would gather up the books—"boxes and boxes of them"— and bring them home to her son ("Northwestern" 142). These college-level texts, which included among other works the tragedies of Shakespeare and Mary Shelley's *Frankenstein*, accounted for much of Johnson's reading during his middle school years. Later he would reflect with some amusement on the unsuspecting sources of his personal library, explaining that as a young man he had "devoured" the sorority members' cast-off books with "the pleasure, the delight, the wicked knowledge that the girls of Gamma Phi Beta would never be able to say they knew something their cleaning woman's son didn't know" (142).

The efforts of Johnson's mother and grandmother on behalf of their son and grandson resonate with the subversive tactics used by many blacks under nineteenth-century plantation slavery to claim the education that was denied them, stratagems summarized by Frederick Douglass in his famous *Narrative*. Those efforts also speak to the black community's long-held belief in the value of education as a path to individual and social progress, a value that Johnson's own family and local community strongly endorsed. A self-described "voracious" reader of everything from classics to comic books, Johnson as a boy was inspired and supported in particular by his mother, who gave him a blank book as a present when he was twelve, leading him to a lifelong daily habit of keeping journals and writer's notebooks, and, he

says, "seducing him" with the "beauty of blank pages" ("I Call" 8). On his
paternal side, Johnson's great-uncle Will encouraged him early and often to
get an education, a recommendation that carried considerable weight owing
to William Johnson's status in the community as founder and owner of Johnson's Construction Company, a business started after the Great Depression
which at times employed several of Charles Johnson's relatives, including his
father. The strong sense of community among the black families in Evanston,
where everyone looked out collectively for the well-being of the neighborhood children, also fostered an environment conducive to Johnson's academic success. That community included Dr. Elizabeth Hill, one of the area's
first black physicians. After watching some of her patients die while in tran-
sit to a hospital on the South Side of Chicago that would treat blacks, Dr. Hill
lobbied for an all-black community hospital in Evanston. She delivered
Charles Johnson there on April 23, 1948. Johnson's interest in a variety of
subjects—especially art and literature—was further stimulated by the education he received at Evanston Township High School. Unusual for its long
history of integration—Johnson's mother graduated from the school as early
as the 1930s—it had a black population of approximately 11 percent when
Johnson attended ("I Call" 10). With the same pleasure that he demonstrated
in learning from the books gathered from Gamma Beta Phi, Johnson took
advantage in high school of the specialized classes in art, photography, and
creative writing that were offered by the well-heeled suburban institution,
programs that were funded largely, he would later come to recognize, by well-
to-do white parents eager to pay for a "first-rate" education for their children
("Charles" 229).

But if Johnson's invitation to address Northwestern's commencement exercises speaks to a communal, familiar, and individual commitment to education, it also points to changes in the nation at large in the decades after
World War II, when several groups—including minorities, women, and
working-class youth—enjoyed expanding access to higher education.
Enrollment in American colleges and universities, which stood at 1,101,000
in 1930, rose to a figure of 7,136,000 by 1970 (Farber and Bailey 346).
During the thirty-year period from 1940 to 1970, the number of blacks en-
rolled in higher education increased an astounding 1,000 percent. Johnson's
arrival on the campus of Southern Illinois University in the fall of 1966 was
therefore both an individual achievement and an event representative of
broader changes in the nation at large. As an undergraduate majoring in journalism and minoring in philosophy from 1966 to 1971, Johnson attended an
institution that, like many others across the nation, was rapidly expanding
to meet a new influx of students. During a single five-year period overlapping
with Johnson's arrival, the university in fact hired no fewer than two hundred
new faculty members to meet the demands of its growing student population

and expanding programs (Harper 218). After completing his undergraduate degree, Johnson immediately began work on a master's degree at SIU in philosophy, which he completed in 1973. In the same year he received an assistantship to enroll in the Ph.D. program in philosophy at SUNY Stony Brook, another public institution undergoing expansion, and one that had recently made substantial enhancements in the area of graduate education. Johnson studied at Stony Brook until 1976, two years after *Faith and the Good Thing*, his first published novel, appeared to reviews in both the *New York Times* and *Black World*, when he left to accept the position of acting assistant professor at the University of Washington.[7]

A member of a postwar generation that benefited from the increased educational opportunities that resulted from the expansion of the university system across the nation, Johnson made of those opportunities a rather spectacular rise within the academy and in national letters: at the University of Washington he moved quickly through the academic ranks, rising from acting assistant professor to full professor of English in a mere six years (1976–1982). In the next decade Johnson would earn numerous scholarly and literary awards—including such prestigious honors as a Guggenheim Fellowship (1988), the National Book Award (for *Middle Passage* in 1990), and a MacArthur Fellowship (1998)—and would establish himself as an internationally respected literary figure; his award-winning novel *Middle Passage* has been translated into seven languages. In 1990 Johnson was named S. Wilson and Grace M. Pollock Professor at Washington, and in 2003 he was elected to the American Academy of Arts and Letters. Johnson published four novels, *Faith and the Good Thing*, *Oxherding Tale*, *Middle Passage*, and *Dreamer*; three short story collections, *The Sorcerer's Apprentice* (1986), *Soulcatcher* (2000), and *Dr. King's Refrigerator* (2004); a revised version of his dissertation for the Ph.D. in philosophy, *Being and Race* (1988); and a number of screenplays for television and film, including *Booker* (1984). He has published two books of cartoons, *Black Humor* (1970) and *Half-Past Nation Time* (1972); contributed to a photo-biography of Martin Luther King Jr. (*King: The Photobiography*, 2000); co-edited an anthology of literature about the experience of African American males in America, *Black Men Speaking* (1997); and written introductions for works as diverse as the *Selected Writings of Ralph Waldo Emerson* (2003), Harriet Beecher Stowe's *Uncle Tom's Cabin* (2002), and *Humor Me* (2002), an anthology of humor by writers of color. In addition, he has been a regular contributor to Buddhist publications such as *Shambhala Sun* and *Tricycle: The Buddhist Review*. Since 1977, the year when he published a review of Richard Wright's *American Hunger* for the *American Book Review*, Johnson has also been active as a book reviewer, publishing over fifty reviews in outlets such as the *New York Times*, *The Times* of London, the *Washington Post*, the *Los Angeles*

*Times,* and the *Times Literary Supplement.* By any measure, Johnson's career both as academic and as practicing writer has been a stunning success.

Providing a striking example of individual achievement through access to education, Johnson's academic accomplishments also resonate with several questions that have been debated with special urgency since the 1990s concerning the unique position of black intellectuals in national life. Unfolding in the pages of newspapers and magazines such as the *New York Times,* the *New Yorker,* the *New Republic,* the *Los Angeles Times,* the *Atlantic Monthly,* the *Village Voice,* and *Boston Review,* as well as in more specialized academic journals such as *Critical Inquiry,* and in a number of book-length studies that focused explicitly on the black intellectual, the debate has sparked a wide range of opinion.[8] Some voices in the discussion have been optimistic about the social meaning of the increased emergence of black scholars and largely sympathetic to the special demands such intellectuals face as they are expected to distinguish themselves in their respective fields while also being asked to be responsible for additional social burdens not required of white intellectuals. Randall Kennedy, for example, describes a current "renaissance" in black intellectual thought that speaks to a "tremendous advance on the cultural front" ("Forum"). Others, however, criticize black intellectuals in a manner reminiscent of Harold Cruse's influential 1967 study of postwar black leaders, *The Crisis of the Negro Intellectual,* which indicted an earlier generation of black leaders as "petit bourgeois" who were removed from the interests of the black community. Today black intellectuals may find themselves criticized from several different directions: by those who worry that success beyond the black community entails an alienation from that community (some of whom levy charges that black intellectuals are not being "black enough"); by Afrocentrists who charge that those who succeed in white institutions are necessarily co-opted by those institutions (some of whom argue for a complete rejection of Western educational traditions); and by commentators from the right (some of whom judge black intellectuals not to be, in the final analysis, "true" intellectuals at all).[9]

From the perspective of such criticism, Johnson's educational success and even his experience with the sisters of Gamma Beta Phi acquire meanings different from those of subversive tricksterism and communal uplift—meanings more suggestive of an alienation from black culture and acculturation to a white one—an acculturation reflected, perhaps, in the authors of some of the sorority sisters' cast-off books, Shakespeare and Shelley. Raised in the well-to-do suburb of Evanston instead of the poorer—and blacker—communities within Chicago's city limits (and especially its South Side), the only child of a stable two-parent household, educated at primarily white institutions, Johnson would seem to enjoy a status of relative privilege that reverberates with many of the concerns raised by the critics of contemporary black intellectuals. Reading Johnson simply as a son of suburban privilege, however, has its own dangers, and serves to illustrate in miniature some of the complicated historical and conceptual issues encountered in any attempt to "place" black thinkers as public intellectuals.

For example, the easy juxtaposition of an essentialized black urban identity against an inauthentic suburban one has received scholarly attention in studies of black suburbanization that emphasize the complex social relations which have characterized integrated suburbs in post–World War II America and the invisible "race gap" that endures even in affluent suburbs like Evanston.[10] To judge the black communities that established themselves around urban centers simply as having been "acculturated" into white suburbs in fact de-racializes the complex social relations through which such suburbs were stratified, ignores the specific history of blacks as contributors to the development of those communities, and tends to oversimplify especially the conditions of black labor within those suburbs, such as the common necessity for blacks to work *for* the whites who lived in the same area (as did Johnson's maternal grandmother) or the need for blacks to hold down two or more jobs for the "privilege" of suburban living. (Johnson's father, for example, sometimes held three jobs in order to make ends meet.) To subsume black suburbanites into their white counterparts in fact erases the strong black working-class roots—and accomplishments—of the majority of black families who struggled at some personal cost to provide safe environments and access to a good education for their children in suburbs that sometimes failed to provide social services for their needs; and to do so in fact adds little to a concrete understanding of the specific historical situation of black families like Johnson's who lived in primarily white suburbs.[11] Johnson's own work hauling trash for the Chicago sanitation system in order to contribute to his college expenses suggests how relative charges of privilege can prove to be.

Today the complex role of suburbanization in black life has become increasingly significant as growing numbers of blacks move from city centers to suburbs. In 1970 one-sixth of the black population of the United States lived in suburbs; during the period from 1970 to 1995, more than 7 million moved there, a staggering migration that, as Sheryll Cashin points out, is *larger* than the exodus of 4.4 million from South to North during the thirty-year period from 1940 to 1970 ("Middle Class" 4). As growing numbers of Hispanic immigrants have moved into historically black neighborhoods, blacks have increasingly followed the movement from city to suburb previously followed by European American immigrants—a movement open to large numbers of African Americans only after the passage of the Civil Rights Act of 1964 and the Fair Housing Act of 1968. Unracialized understandings of suburban life, simplistic notions about the unbridgeable divisions between black suburban and black urban communities (Johnson's wife, Joan New, is from Atgeld Gardens, a housing project on the southeast side of Chicago), the lack of scholarly attention paid to the ways in which a black presence re-shapes suburbs as well as being shaped by them (Johnson's great-uncle William Johnson built Springfield Baptist Church and many other buildings in Evanston), and the lingering effects of a "race gap" in even the most afflu-ent neighborhoods all challenge any simplistic judgments about the "accul-turation" of blacks in middle-class suburbs and their educational institutions. The two ways of reading Johnson's experience with Sigma Phi Gamma—as a tale of transgressive tricksterism or as one of acculturation—thus suggest some of the contradictions encountered in any attempt to "fix" the status of contemporary black artists and intellectuals.

Johnson's own status is further complicated by the strikingly eclectic nature of his creative work and intellectual interests. Given the diversity of traditions—both literary and philosophical—from which he draws inspira-tion, and given the range of his stylistic experiments, readers of his fiction are apt to find themselves in a situation analogous to one faced by the narrator of his 1981 novel *Oxherding Tale*, who enters his tutor's small rooms to dis-cover himself surrounded by an overwhelming "catastrophe of books" drawn from all over the world (29). With philosophical interests that range from the Presocratics to Hegel, Marx, Husserl, Frantz Fanon, Merleau-Ponty, Martin Luther King Jr., and Thich Nhat Hanh—to name only a few of the philoso-phers Johnson engages—and with an interest in literary form that stretches from classical fabliaux to the *Bildungsroman* to African American folktales to deconstructive fiction, Johnson's work is notoriously difficult to categorize. Further complicating the task is the fact that Johnson is active in a number of genres, as the brief overview of his career given earlier suggests. More im-portant, the aesthetic, moral, and political positions Johnson endorses can appear at times puzzlingly paradoxical—even after taking into account the natural evolution of thought that one would expect to find in work produced by a writer whose career spans a period of over thirty years. How does one categorize a writer who frequently employs what appears to be a post-modern critique of identity politics, but who just as frequently defends claims of "universality"? Or a cartoonist who defends a high-art aesthetic? (Al-though Johnson served on the committee that awarded Art Spiegelman's *Maus* a Pulitzer Prize in 1992, he also asserts, "I do think that art is elitist. It is an elitist activity" [Little, "An Interview" 121].) How should one evaluate a literary critic who calls eloquently for the increased inclusion of women's voices in fiction but who also criticizes the work of leading women writers, calling, for example, Toni Morrison's *Beloved* "an interesting, middlebrow book" (Little, "Interview" 107)? Not surprisingly, critics of Johnson's work have argued that his fiction is characteristically informed by recurrent aesthetic and conceptual tensions. Jonathan Little suggests that Johnson's fiction fulfills "certain Black Aesthetic critical expectations," while simultaneously rejecting "essentialist modes of thinking" (*Charles* 68). Ashraf Rushdy points to "persistent tensions" in Johnson's fiction and to the way his work "treads on the borders of a conservative and an oppositional aesthetic" (*Neo-Slave* 184). And William Nash focuses on the friction that is created in Johnson's work by a "transcendent approach to racial questions" (*Charles* 5). No wonder Nash, with William Gleason, has suggested that as a black intellectual, Johnson might most appropriately be placed in the paradoxical-sounding category of "anti-race race man," as defined by Ross Posnock in *Color and Culture*.[12]

In this chapter I analyze Johnson's status as a black intellectual from a different cultural and historical perspective by examining his work in relation to the disciplinary pressures encountered by the generation of black scholars who took advantage of expanding postwar access to higher education in order to pursue graduate work in philosophy during the 1960s and 1970s. In *On Race and Philosophy*, Lucius T. Outlaw identifies the group of black philosophers "working to define a place" for themselves within the discipline of philosophy at the time as including Howard McGary Jr., Leonard Harris, Bernard Boxill, William Jones, Robert C. Williams, Joyce Mitchell Cook, Ifeanyi Menkiti, Robert Chemooke, Albert Mosley, John Murungi, Tom Slaughter, Laurence Thomas, Cornel West, Bill Larson, George Garrison, Blanche Radford-Curry, and Johnny Washington (xxix).[13] Together with other, mostly younger black and mixed-race philosophers (such as Adrian Piper, Anita Allen, Lewis Gordon, Tommy Lott, John Pittman, Charles Mills, George Yancy, and Naomi Zack), these scholars would reshape American academic philosophy at the end of the twentieth century by ensuring that issues of interest to black people were at the forefront of philosophical consideration. Approaching Johnson from this particular perspective is not an attempt to explain away the tensions in his work but rather an effort to understand them in relation to certain *disciplinary* pressures encountered by those who took up the task of applying Western philosophical insights to the experiences of black people in America — disciplinary pressures that helped to shape Johnson's early intellectual evolution as well as the complex practice of his "philosophical fiction."

Of course, the generation of young black men and women who studied philosophy at institutions of higher education in the sixties and seventies were not the first who sought to analyze the social, psychological, and political dimensions of race and racism or to attempt to specify the philosophical problems generated by what Gordon terms "experience in black" (the title of his 1997 collection of essays on the black existential tradition). The names of many of the earliest mixed-race and African

American philosophers, such as Patrick Francis Healy, Gilbert Haven Jones, and Thomas Nelson Baker, are not well known.[14] More famously, W. E. B. Du Bois studied philosophy with William James, Josiah Royce, and George Santayana at Harvard. Partly as a result of his disagreements with these thinkers, Du Bois developed—among his other achievements as sociologist, historian, and political thinker—a social philosophy of interdependence that some believe anticipated Charles Hartshorne's theory of reality as a social process.[15] Alain Locke majored in philosophy at Harvard College from 1904 to 1906—and studied it as the first black Rhodes Scholar at Oxford from 1907 to 1910 and at Berlin from 1910 to 1911—before he developed his own analysis of the "lived experience of values." Locke's long career at Howard University (1912–1953) is, moreover, part of a tradition of black philosophical thought that was established at historically black institutions before white institutions of higher education entered broadly into the field, a tradition to which Harris pays tribute in the first collection of essays devoted entirely to African American philosophy, *Philosophy Born of Struggle* (1983).[16] From Thomas N. Baker, who received his doctorate in philosophy from Yale in 1903, to Joyce Mitchell Cook—the first African American woman to receive a Ph.D. in philosophy, also from Yale, in 1965—and from institutions as different as Howard and Harvard, the twentieth century charts the growing appropriation and application of Western philosophy to the concerns of people of African descent in the United States.

Similarly, Johnson is not the first black creative writer whose work is informed by an engagement with Western philosophy, as his own stated allegiance to a tradition of black philosophical fiction makes clear. Writers from Frederick Douglass to W. E. B. Du Bois (as fiction writer), Richard Wright, and Ralph Ellison are examples of those whose work is frequently cited as philosophically significant. Johnson traces his own genealogy as a philosophical writer through Ralph Ellison, Richard Wright, and Jean Toomer. Toomer's *Essentials* (1931), a philosophical meditation on African American identity in the form of aphorisms, reflects his engagement with the ideas of the Russian mystic Georgei I. Gurdjieff. Richard Wright's career traces an evolving interest in three schools of philosophy that parallels in some respects Johnson's own evolution from Marxism to existentialist phenomenology to an interest in Eastern thought. A member of the Communist Party from 1934 to 1942, Wright became increasingly impatient with communism's failure to appreciate or to account for the importance of race, a dissatisfaction already prominent in *Uncle Tom's Children* (1938), more pronounced in *Native Son* (1940), and explicitly declared in "I Tried to Become a Communist" (1944). Wright's increasing contact with French existentialists after his expatriation in 1947 deepened his interest in existentialism, as is reflected in *The Outsider* (1953), a novel whose urban landscapes anticipate Johnson's treatment of the city in *Faith and the Good Thing*. Ellison's critique of "The Brotherhood" and development of the celebrated trope of "invisibility" in *Invisible Man* (1952) charts his own ambivalent relationship to Marxism and his engagement with existentialism. The fiction of Octavia Butler, Clarence Major, John Wideman, Toni Morrison, Colson Whitehead, and Percival Everett (who also studied philosophy formally), among others, continues a black literary tradition today that is deeply inflected by philosophical concerns.

But in spite of the transformative encounters with philosophy undertaken by blacks who studied it formally or who engaged it artistically in the early to mid-twentieth century, the generation of men and women who pursued graduate degrees in philosophy in the 1960s and 1970s constituted a very small group indeed—whether, like Outlaw, they studied at a historically black institution (Fisk) and, later, a Jesuit one (Boston College); or, like Cornel West, at the most elite of eastern universities (Harvard and Princeton); or, like Charles Johnson, at public universities (SIU and SUNY Stony Brook). Although by 1970 larger numbers of blacks were attending college than ever before in the nation's history, only 4.4 percent of African Americans had by that time completed four years of college (Farber and Bailey 346). Furthermore, among academic disciplines, philosophy was (and remains) among the slowest to incorporate ethnic diversity—institutionally or conceptually. According to a 1986 survey by the American Philosophical Association, as late as 1985 only 1 percent of the graduate degrees in philosophy were granted to African Americans—a figure that compares to 3.3 percent for Ph.D.s awarded generally.[17] As a philosophy student at SIU and SUNY Stony Brook, Johnson in fact became one of the fewer than *one hundred* black students across the United States who were studying philosophy in graduate programs (a number that includes Africans and West Indians). A 1974 report published in *Proceedings and Addresses of the American Philosophical Association* in the same year that Johnson left Southern Illinois to enter the Ph.D. program at Stony Brook found that only *thirty-five* blacks with the terminal degree in philosophy could be identified nationwide: "one black Ph.D. in philosophy for every million black citizens" (Jones, "Crisis" 119).

One difficulty in understanding Johnson's work in relation to this particular group of black intellectuals is that the history of late-twentieth- and early-twenty-first-century black philosophers has not yet been written. Such a project is complicated by the fact that up through the 1970s, and perhaps beyond, there was little agreement about the intellectual problems or canonical texts that could be said to make up the field of African American philosophy. In the late 1970s William R. Jones published an important article, "The Legitimacy and Necessity of Black Philosophy," in the first issue of *Philosophical Forum* devoted entirely to African American philosophy. There he

analyzed the disciplinary status of black philosophers in the academy, pointing out that African American philosophy was expected to "reply to questions not generally addressed" to other developments in the discipline: "Black
philosophy . . . must respond to the prior question of its legitimacy; it must
establish its right to exist as an appropriate philosophical position. . . .
Though we speak of German philosophy, Jewish philosophy and American
philosophy, many philosophers, both black and white, picture black philosophy as a bastard philosophy and semantic monstrosity" (149). If, on the
one hand, the unsettled nature of the field made African American philosophy an exciting venture for the small number of blacks who were entering
graduate programs or attempting to define it as an academic enterprise during the 1970s, on the other hand, a good portion of this group's intellectual
energy had to be expended in the task of legitimizing African American
issues, texts, and approaches to a generally hostile white philosophical establishment. As McGary points out, "when I first started out in philosophy
there was this whole issue about whether or not one could use the African-
American experience and African-American texts as sources of philosophical illumination" (Yancy, *African* 80–81).

But in spite of the difficulties that complicate the project of recovering the
history of this generation of black scholars, the groundwork for such a project has been laid. Jones's two analyses of the status of blacks in philosophy,
the 1978 *Philosophical Forum* piece and an earlier 1974 report published in
*Proceedings of the American Philosophical Association*, are important documents that help to clarify the position of blacks in the discipline in the early
part of this period. Since 1978, when *Philosophical Forum* published its issue
dedicated to African American philosophy, this field has received increasing
attention in a variety of scholarly publications. As mentioned earlier, in 1983
Harris published the first collection devoted to essays written by black
philosophers, including a piece by Slaughter. In 1992, fifteen years after its
first issue on the topic, *Philosophical Forum* published a special triple issue
dedicated to African American philosophy, which became the basis for
Pittman's collection *African-American Perspectives and Philosophical Traditions* (1997). That collection has been followed by important recovery work
by Yancy, whose *African American Philosophy: Seventeen Conversations*
(1998) is a collection of interviews with contemporary black philosophers
who reflect on their experience in philosophy departments across the nation.
The 1990s and early 2000s, especially, have seen an explosion in materials
related to the recovery, study, and canonization of African American philosophy.[18] Such documents help to contextualize Johnson's own experience as
a black student of philosophy and provide a field against which his philosophical fiction can be read. At the same time, Johnson's fiction provides a
rare and important window onto the particular problems faced by this

generation of black scholars (as my reading of Johnson's short story "Alēthia" later in this chapter demonstrates).

Although it might be argued that as a professor primarily of creative writing and literature Johnson should not be placed alongside a group of professional philosophers, there are good reasons for approaching his work from this particular historical, cultural, and disciplinary perspective. First, it is simply the case historically that Johnson was among the exceedingly small number of black students who studied philosophy in graduate programs during the 1960s and 1970s. His educational experience and the philosophical fiction that would grow out of that experience, therefore, are rightly a part of the history of this generation of black scholars. More important, Johnson's fiction helps to clarify—and makes its own powerful contribution to—this particular moment in the history of American philosophy. But there are other important reasons for considering Johnson's fiction in relation to this group as well. If historically the line between fiction and philosophy has often been blurred—as Plato's dialogues, Santayana's prose, and the twentieth-century proliferation of existentialist literature in a number of genres all attest—this is especially true in the case of African American philosophy, which by necessity in America has had its roots in nonacademic forms of writing. As Pittman points out, to define philosophy only in terms of a specialist discourse is to leave out "an entire world of intellectual life, and for traditionally excluded groups, any 'representation' at all" (xii).

Because of its unique history, African American philosophy tends to be pluralistic both in the sources it accepts as philosophically significant and in its methodologies. Mills makes a related point in *Blackness Visible*: he suggests that studies of African American philosophy are incomplete if they do not include as philosophically significant writings such as Frederick Douglass's investigations of the meaning of freedom or Ralph Ellison's conceptual work on "invisibility" in *Invisible Man*.[19] Others have pointed out that the critique of racism lends itself to "narrative analysis" in part because narrative recuperates a subjective perspective that has been systematically rendered invisible by traditional philosophical discourses (Cuomo and Hall 7; see also Yancy, *Philosophical*). In challenging traditional definitions of the proper limits of philosophical inquiry, then, African American philosophy has repeatedly demonstrated a willingness to consider literature a legitimate site for black philosophizing. The factors that have forged a relationship between philosophy and African American literature historically—the reliance by black thinkers on nonacademic forms of writing; the need to recuperate perspectives that have been habitually repressed; the continuing efforts of black philosophers to infuse abstract arguments with narratological, phenomenological, and social immediacy—provide important critical contexts for understanding Charles Johnson's fiction.

Moreover, it is clear that Johnson works to create philosophically significant fiction. As he unequivocally states, "I became a writer specifically to develop black (and thereby American) philosophical fiction" (Boccia 205). The
genesis of his philosophical fiction is often discussed in relation to the influence of John Gardner, Johnson's creative writing mentor. Since Johnson himself identifies Gardner as his "literary father," and has suggested that he
apprenticed himself to Gardner to learn literary technique ("I Call" 23), there
is good reason to see Johnson's relationship to Gardner as formative. Little
argues that Gardner had a "tremendous influence on the development of
Johnson's aesthetic" (*Charles* 61); Nash suggests that Gardner helped Johnson "to find a way to bring his ideal of resisting racial limitations to bear in
novels that expand understandings of black identity and black literature"
(*Charles* 25–26); and Gary Storhoff suggests that Johnson learned from
Gardner "the versatility of form in African American literature" (*Understanding* 4). While pointing out that Johnson eventually broke with Gardner's concept of moral fiction as too narrowly conceived an understanding of how
morality might function in literature, Little sums up well the features of Johnson's fiction that are commonly associated with Gardner, including the use
of an extensive variety of literary forms, the practice of genre crossing, a
focus on technical excellence, and an emphasis on narrative experimentation
(*Charles* 76).

As previously mentioned, Johnson's evolving relationship to the Black Arts
movement has also been widely discussed as an important influence on his
practice of philosophical fiction. Little identifies Johnson's attendance at a
reading by Amiri Baraka in the spring of 1969 as "one of the pivotal moments in Johnson's career" (*Charles* 20). Nash offers an especially detailed
description of that visit as it relates to the political climate on the SIU campus (*Charles* 17–29). Both discuss the reading as the event that inspired Johnson to create his first collection of cartoons, *Black Humor*, and they point to
the ambivalent attitude toward black cultural nationalism that is already detectable in those cartoons. Other critics have commented on how this ambivalence hardens over Johnson's career to a strong rejection of the separatist
tenets of black nationalism and the aesthetic creed of the BAM. Analyzing
*Oxherding Tale* specifically as a response to "cultural nationalist theories
and Black Power rhetorics of black social identity," Rushdy's complex analysis of the role that Black Power and BAM played in the development of the
neo-slave narrative genre aligns this turn in Johnson's career with the about-
face made by former radicals in the Second Thoughts group (*Neo-Slave*
169–80). In any case, it is clear that the Black Arts aesthetic provided a "negative" influence on Johnson by offering a position against which he could
refine his own aesthetic vision.

The definition, significance, and extension of the category of "black philosophical fiction" has itself also received critical discussion. Finding the category "well-defined," Rudolph Byrd suggests that the "tradition of adapting complex philosophical systems—Platonism, Eastern Philosophy, Continental Philosophy, Christianity, and psychoanalytic theory—to construct a coherent fictional universe seems to be, with the exception of selected novels by John Gardner and Rebecca Goldstein, the sole province of African American writers" (*Charles* 13; "Oxherding" 316). Alternatively, John Whalen-Bridge questions both "the utility of the concept" of black philosophical fiction and the claim that African American writers "delve into comparative philosophy more than European-American authors do" ("Whole" 256 "Waking" 511). He further warns that a "wish to identify a racially organized sub-tradition bespeaks a wish to racially separate rather than integrate authors" ("Waking" 511). In their collection of essays on Johnson, Marc Conner and Nash are more willing to take Johnson's own characterizations of the category as definitive, recognizing black philosophical fiction as a classification that "Johnson himself has largely defined, if not created" (*Charles* vii). In "Philosophy and Black Fiction," Johnson defines philosophical black fiction as "art that interrogates experience," and argues that "philosophical hermeneutics and the exploration of meaning are native to all literary production" (80, 84). Conner and Nash's introduction to *Charles Johnson: The Novelist as Philosopher* provides the most thoughtful overview to date of the various philosophical traditions, Western and Eastern, that energize Johnson's literary project.[20]

But the genesis of Johnson's philosophical fiction has not yet been historicized in relation to the practice of academic philosophy in the 1960s and 1970s. While critics often discuss Johnson's work in relation to specific philosophers, such as Merleau-Ponty or Lao-tzu, they rarely consider his fiction in relation to the disciplinary experience of black philosophers.[21] Similarly, while Johnson's aesthetic is often said to develop an alternative to Black Arts aesthetics, it is far less frequently discussed as constituting a considered response to the form of philosophy dominant in the postwar academy: analytic philosophy. But in fact the schools of philosophical thought with which Johnson's fiction is most frequently identified—phenomenology, Marxism, existentialism, Eastern philosophy, and pragmatism—all gained new (or, in the case of pragmatism, renewed) popularity in the postwar academy specifically as alternatives to the entrenched dominance of analytic philosophy. Moreover, those philosophical traditions proved of special importance to African American philosophy students and scholars. Johnson's fiction makes its own unique contribution to this critical moment in the history of American philosophy.

Johnson clearly traces the origins of his philosophical fiction to his work as a student of philosophy: "I began writing novels in earnest in 1970 with one specific goal in mind," he explains, "that of expanding the category we might call black philosophical fiction; i.e., opening up black literature to the same ethical, ontological, and epistemological questions—Western and Eastern—that I wrestled with as a student of philosophy. From the beginning, I've had no other aim as a literary artist" (Boccia 194). Originally Johnson planned to teach philosophy, not creative writing, and his model for the philosopher was shaped in part by black scholars whom he knew. In particular, at SIU Johnson was a student of Tom Slaughter Jr.—one of the philosophers listed by Outlaw as among the black scholars working to redefine the field. Slaughter was important to Johnson because, as Johnson emphasizes, he was "a role model for me. He was the first black philosopher I knew. . . . I wanted to *be* him."[22] Johnson saw in Slaughter, then, the possibility for his own future as a black philosopher. As an undergraduate and later as a graduate student in philosophy at SIU, Johnson talked with Slaughter "often and frequently" about philosophical, cultural, and political issues that concerned them both, and it was largely due to Slaughter's influence that in 1969 Johnson taught a discussion section of a course in black American history for the newly formed Black Studies Department at SIU. Their relationship was temporarily interrupted, however, when Slaughter left to take a position teaching Black Studies in New Jersey.

But in 1974 both Slaughter and Johnson entered the Ph.D. program in philosophy together at SUNY Stony Brook, two of approximately ten philosophy students admitted to the program that year. Eventually both men would complete dissertations under the phenomenologist Don Ihde, whom they had first met when he was teaching at SIU as a visiting instructor and who later was to became director of the philosophy program at Stony Brook.[23] Slaughter's dissertation was on Frantz Fanon, while Johnson's, a phenomenological analysis of African American fiction, would later be published in revised form as *Being and Race*. While they were studying at Stony Brook, the relationship between Slaughter and Johnson deepened as they took seminars together and met regularly for lunch to discuss, in Johnson's words, "the course material from a black perspective."[24] At times they were joined for these discussions by another black student at Stony Brook, Bob Bunch, who already held a doctorate in sociology but who was also working on a Ph.D. in philosophy. This group's informal discussions led over time to more formal deliberations when Johnson, along with fellow (white) graduate student Richard Hart, began a graduate student colloquium at Stony Brook. For the first event Slaughter presented a paper, "Epidermalizing the World," an earlier version of the essay that he would revise and publish in Harris's collection of essays on African American philosophy. At the colloquium Johnson responded to Slaughter's paper, and he would later continue that particular philosophical conversation in his fiction.[25]

Given Johnson's experiences as one of an exceedingly small number of black students studying philosophy, it is not surprising that his fiction resonates in meaningful ways with the attempts of other black intellectuals who studied it formally during the same period. Johnson's work shares several intellectual projects with these scholars, including the critique of the Western "subject" of philosophy, the furthering of what Mills has called "alternative epistemologies" more responsive to issues of social justice and to the lived experience of black people, and the prompting of reflection on the practice of philosophy itself, especially in regard to how unacknowledged assumptions about race have shaped the discipline's practices historically ("Alternative" 21). Furthermore, an understanding of the particular relationship of black philosophers to analytic philosophy during the period provides fresh insight into the genesis of Johnson's fiction. At the same time, appreciating Johnson as one among other young black students of philosophy in the sixties and seventies reveals the degree to which his fiction investigates—and sheds light on—the complex position of the black intellectuals who entered the discipline during this period.

## African Americans and the Crisis in American Philosophy, 1960–1980

In 1974, the year after Johnson completed his master's thesis in philosophy at SIU, William Jones presented a report by the recently formed Subcommittee on the Participation of Blacks in Philosophy to the American Philosophical Association. In that report, titled "The Crisis in Philosophy: The Black Presence," Jones argued that the small number of blacks in philosophy constituted a "crisis" in the discipline. Out of ten thousand members of the APA, the subcommittee was able to identify fewer than one hundred black members (including Africans and West Indians). As Jones pointed out, these figures meant that although blacks constituted approximately one out of every ten Americans, they accounted for only one out of a thousand members of the APA ("Crisis" 119). A few years earlier the APA had adopted a resolution promising to cooperate with the newly formed Subcommittee on Blacks "to seek causes and suggest remedies" for the lack of black representation. The deeply entrenched disciplinary factors that contributed to the low numbers—factors ranging from outright discrimination to more subtle forms of cultural bias to an ingrained institutional insularity—led Jones in 1974 to decry the "unimagined depth of the problem" (119). Indeed, after the subcommittee studied the question and considered the various economic, cultural, and disciplinary barriers that faced black students entering the field,

Jones was struck by the realization that "when one examined the situation dispassionately, one can only wonder why the few Blacks in the profession chose philosophy at all" (122).

The report's findings underscore the unique and challenging pressures faced by blacks undertaking work in philosophy at the time. First, material conditions made entry into philosophy difficult for a population that often could not afford the luxury of more speculative fields. Jones notes that blacks frequently adopted a "bread and butter" approach to education that led them to rank the desirability of disciplines according to how easily an undergraduate degree might lead to a job (121). The need to fund several years of graduate study for the Ph.D., combined with the relatively small economic rewards for those who persevered, ensured that until the post–World War II expansion of the university system and the advent of minority scholarships in the 1960s, only a small number of black students were willing to pursue the terminal degree in philosophy. As McGary reflects, in the 1970s philosophy did not appear to be "a subject that would be conducive to my making a living" (Yancy, *African* 76). Second, traditionally in African American communities those who were interested in philosophy studied for the ministry and then returned to the community to assume the respected position of church leader (who also might often be a prominent local political leader). Students who wanted to continue in the discipline of philosophy therefore frequently had to disappoint community and family expectations. Outlaw's mother, for example, was severely disappointed to learn that he had switched from preparing for the ministry to majoring in philosophy (*On Race* xviii). Although Charles Johnson did not face expectations that he study theology, he too recalls that "the members of my own family threw a fit when I telephoned them one evening to say that I was changing my major from journalism (a cash-value degree) to philosophy. . . . And who can blame them for the panic? I was the first person in my family to go to college. Six generations of Johnsons since slavery were counting on me to make good—that is, to make a good living" ('Where Philosophy" 92). Even though his lower-middle-class family contributed to his expenses, Johnson worked to help support himself throughout his undergraduate and master's degree programs until his last year at SIU, when he received a minority scholarship that enabled him to quit his newspaper job at the *Southern Illinoisan* and concentrate full-time on academics.

Blacks who entered philosophy programs in the 1960s and 1970s found their position further complicated by the fact that the discipline was traditionally organized around leading philosophers who expounded theories implicated in the articulation of racism or the rationalization of slavery, beginning with the Greeks. For example, Aristotle's hierarchy of Greek men, women, and slaves put forward in book 1 of the *Politics*, though not focused on people of African descent, was easily adaptable to later thinkers' elaboration of fixed categories of species, national character, or race. Johnson satirizes the Aristotelian rationale for slavery in one of his early short stories, "The Education of Mingo."[26] From Hume's claim in "Of National Characters" that "Negroes . . . are inferior to whites" (228n); to Kant's suggestions in *Observations on the Feelings of the Beautiful and the Sublime* that there is an inverse relationship between the blackness of one's skin and the level of one's reasoning ability (110–11); to Hegel's remarks in "An Introduction to the Philosophy of History" that "what we properly call Africa is unhistorical, underdeveloped Spirit, still involved in the conditions of pure nature" (95); to Locke's espousing of the natural rights of mankind even as he purchased shares in an African trading company; to the fundamental contradiction within the American tradition in philosophy that made race-based slavery a part of the attempt to build a nation based on the ideals of liberty, leading texts in Western philosophy confronted black students with an ingrained intellectual racism and the implicit argument that as African Americans, they were unsuited to the discipline.[27] The intellectual, psychological, and social difficulties faced by those entering a discipline whose most honored practitioners disparaged their natural fitness for such work led Mills to suggest that "all African American philosophy is 'political,' insofar as the insistence on one's black humanity in a racist world is itself a political act" (*Blackness* 17).

In addition to encountering the overtly discriminatory statements of Western philosophers on the subject of race, blacks entering graduate programs in philosophy faced other pressures generated by the "conceptual whiteness" of philosophy as it was practiced as a discipline. As Mills suggests in *Blackness Visible*, the modernist philosophical project defined the "subject" of philosophy in Cartesian terms as one that followed "laws" of Reason in order to establish "Truths" that were both "universal" and, because they could not be doubted, "necessary." In addition to generating a focus on abstract problems removed from social concerns—such as how a subject so defined could know with certainty that she or he existed—this conception of philosophy articulated a standard for consideration that tended to exclude difference as a matter of philosophical importance. From the lofty perspective of "universal" truth, issues of race appeared as the limited concern of a particular subgroup and, as such, beneath philosophical significance.[28] Much of the early energy of black philosophers went into demonstrating, therefore, that the universal truths of Western philosophy were often neither disinterested nor universal, but false claims that ignored the perspective of others while reflecting white Europeans' and European-Americans' own situated interests. Given the emphasis on a purified rationality and its attribution to certain kinds of people (Aristotle), nations (Hume), colors (Kant), or civilizations (Hegel), and given the failure to recognize difference or to grant it philosophical significance (including the failure to recognize African contributions to Western philosophy starting with the Greeks), blacks who entered graduate programs in the 1960s and 1970s bore the conceptual burden of what Gordon has aptly called "the structural collapse of universality into whiteness" (*Existentia* 89).[29]

The difficult position of African American students who undertook the study of philosophy in academic institutions was further complicated by organizational and disciplinary changes in American universities related to postwar expansion which had led to another perceived "crisis" in the academy. That expansion, initially brought about by World War II veterans returning from war, was sustained by a flourishing economy, the rising aspirations of the servicemen's "baby boom" children, and the nation's growing recognition that education had an important public role to play in the cold war against the Soviet Union. Government support for education grew considerably from 1940 to 1970: in 1930, spending on education amounted to 3.1 percent of the gross national product, but by 1970 that number had more than doubled to 7.5 percent (Farber and Bailey 345). As universities expanded and states developed extensive state college systems in the 1960s, philosophy programs became increasingly diversified, both demographically and conceptually. More students took philosophy courses, partly because more students were attending college, but also because, as Bruce Kuklick points out in *A History of Philosophy in America*, many students were "mandated" to take such courses as part of their general education requirements (239). Johnson, in fact, was first introduced to academic philosophy in a survey course that fulfilled the requirements for his undergraduate degree in journalism. As the number of colleges and universities offering advanced degrees in philosophy grew across the country, philosophy programs became more pluralistic, and analytic philosophy, which had previously dominated American departments, came under increasing attack for being narrowly focused and overly removed from social concerns.

At the end of the 1950s William Barrett galvanized the critique of analytic philosophy with the publication of *Irrational Man* (1958). Barrett's popular book sought to define for the American public the crisis in contemporary philosophy by focusing on the "professional status" of its practitioners in the modern university. "To profess," he argued, traditionally implied that one "acknowledges a calling to the world," akin to a religious "profession of faith" (4). But to profess philosophy in the contemporary world had come to mean working as a professor in a university system— fulfilling a "specialized social task—requiring expertness and know-how that one performs for pay" (4). Barrett believed that the philosopher's professional status created a troubling contradiction: the "degree to which one has become specialized and academic," he wrote, is the degree to which one's "importance beyond the university cloisters declined" (6). Diagnosing the crisis in academic philosophy as one of overspecialization, Barrett prescribed existentialism as the cure, and through *Irrational Man* he attempted to introduce existential thought to a broader American audience . (As we will see in chapter 2, in *Faith and the Good Thing* Johnson signifies upon Barrett's critique of academic philosophy by basing a character on his writings, with humorous results.)

The crisis in academic philosophy, defined primarily in terms of a conflict between analytic and more pluralistic approaches, had special implications for black students and faculty. Histories of American philosophy tend to include a discussion of figures like Barrett but to overlook the consequences of the circumstances that he describes for black students and scholars. In 1974, however, Jones argued that the dominance of analytic philosophy nationally was itself a primary factor in the discipline's inability to attract larger numbers of black students and faculty. Blacks do not resonate, he argued, "to the dominant and imperious voice of analytic philosophy and its occupation with meta-concerns that drown out other approaches and ways of philosophizing" ("Crisis" 121). The tendency for analytic philosophy to consider meaning only in terms of what can be conveyed in propositions or formal logic meant that the approach did not seem expansive enough to many black scholars for considering philosophical problems relating to the lived experience of black people, including questions of racial identity and social justice. Not surprisingly, many blacks in philosophy found themselves drawn to Marxism, existentialism, phenomenology, and pragmatism, philosophies whose insights seemed directly applicable to the economic, historical, and psychological status of marginalized groups. (Notably, these are philosophies of special importance to Johnson.) Universities, however, often preferred to hire those who worked in the analytic school. As Jones put it, "Admission into the philosophical community, especially its inner sanctum, appears to require the adoption of the particular philosophical orientation controlled by the white majority" ("Crisis" 121). Ten years later Cornel West would criticize analytic philosophy for making "a fetish of technical virtuosity and us[ing] it as a measure to regulate the intense careerism in the profession" ("Philosophy" 56). As late as 1993 he would argue that the popular image of the academic philosopher—as "an analytic philosopher who is clever, who is sharp, who is good at drawing distinctions, but who doesn't really relate it [philosophy] to history, struggle, engagement with suffering"—was still keeping blacks out of the discipline (Yancy, *African* 38).

In *Being and Race*, Johnson critiques the aesthetics of a form of fiction that he identifies specifically as the offspring of analytic philosophy: he writes of "positivists and analytic philosophers who, it's clear, have cornered the writer of fiction like a caged beast" (34). This aesthetic orientation is represented in Johnson's analysis by the fiction of William Gass (a writer who himself was formally trained in analytic philosophy). Significantly, Johnson faults such fiction for the same limitations that black philosophers attribute to analytic philosophy, arguing that it fails to open a "window in any way onto the world of real men, real women, or real events. It can reveal nothing but its own proliferating mechanisms" (34–35). Locked like logical positivism into "its own logical possibilities as a game," this mode of fiction suggests that the "proper model" for the writer is the "system builder or mathematician who, in a carefully wrought, coherent, internally consistent theorem, creates a beautiful architecture of meaning that may or may not have anything to do with the world of everyday experience" (34–35). By reducing art to a "linguistic location" that one appreciates as one would "the beauty of a logical proof," such literature seems to Johnson unequal to the task of black philosophical writers who work to produce "art that interrogates experience" ("Philosophy" 80). By rejecting the model of the writer represented by Gass, Johnson clearly extends the rejection of analytic philosophy into the literary realm.

In spite of the growing critique of analytic philosophy and the increasing conceptual pluralism among philosophy programs in the 1960s, the generation of students entering philosophy programs felt the conflict between the cloistered academy and outside world acutely owing to the pressing concerns of the civil rights movement and the expansion of the Vietnam War. For black students, the conflict between their academic aspirations and their social commitments was, understandably, especially intense. Outlaw has written perceptively about his own conflicting allegiances while studying philosophy at Fisk and Boston College. On the one hand, given the long-standing American tradition of educating blacks to stay in place, he writes about being inspired by philosophy teachers who expected him to think intensely, discuss engagingly, and write cogently about challenging ideas from the likes of "Sartre, Kierkegaard, Plato, C. P. Snow, Karl Marx, Joseph Conrad, Aristotle, Einstein, and Thomas Aquinas" (*On Race* xix). On the other hand, Outlaw points out that academic pursuits could seem frivolous in the face of the social and political upheavals of the 1960s, leading him to wonder, " With all those people moving in the streets, what was the point of my sitting at my desk and reading and trying to make sense of *Being and Nothingness?*" (xxvii). Joyce Mitchell Cook indicates that analytic philosophy at Yale felt especially removed from current events. "As a Black person," she recalls, "it felt odd to sit around asking such questions like 'How do you know when two non-existent objects are the same[?]' . . . There you are in the middle of the era of affirmative action, civil rights, women's movements, etc., and you're sitting around thinking about non-existent objects" (Yancy, *African* 168). At Harvard, Cornel West faced similar conflicts, crystallized for him in the competing values of one particular event. Unable to participate in the 1972 student protest and takeover of Massachusetts Hall because he had to complete two foreign language tests, West instead helped to organize outside support for the protesters (*Ethical* xviii).

Charles Johnson faced similar competing pressures at SIU. After a 1969 visit by Amiri Baraka to the SIU campus, during which Baraka urged students to "take talent back to the black community," Johnson cut classes to create *Black Humor*, a collection of political cartoons that would be his first book in print (Johnson, "Charles" 235–236). He also threw himself into his work as a discussion leader for the new Black Studies program at SIU: "I cut most of my classes that quarter because the discussion group that I led was so important to me" (Levasseur and Rabalais 264). If Johnson would later disavow the aesthetic and political positions that Baraka and the Black Arts movement which he helped to found represent, it is clear that during his undergraduate years he was to some extent influenced by those positions.[30] Johnson's work as a cartoonist became increasingly politicized during this period, as the cartoon in figure 1 suggests.

The cartoon, titled "Give the Pig an Apple," depicts a figure with clenched fists walking away from a representative of SIU who is lying on the ground, bound with rope. The figure, drawn as a pig, has a bomb with a lighted fuse in his mouth. Although Johnson would later become a practicing Buddhist and an advocate for nonviolence, and although in his novel *Dreamer* he presents Dr. Martin Luther King Jr.'s nonviolent approach to civil rights as superior to the more violent strategies that were sometimes embraced by Black

1. *Cartoon by Charles Johnson,*
*"Give the Pig an Apple."*

Courtesy Charles Johnson and the
*Daily Collegian*, Southern Illinois
University.

Power groups, this early cartoon seemingly endorses violent protest. Not surprisingly, around this time, Johnson recalls, the student newspaper at SIU (the Daily Egyptian) refused to print some of his cartoons as too incendiary ("I Call" 21).

For some black students, like Outlaw, West, and Johnson, the conflict between academic and political allegiances led ultimately to a decision to intensify their dedication to intellectual work. Outlaw suggests that he was able to "stabilize himself" in the 1960s by "renewing the commitment [he] had made at Fisk to prepare [him]self to contribute through teaching" (*On Race* xxvii). West dedicated himself to completing a Ph.D. in philosophy at Harvard. (A revision of his dissertation on Marx would later be published in 1991 as *The Ethical Dimensions of Western Marxism*.) After writing a master's thesis titled "Wilhelm Reich and the Creation of a Marxist Psychology" (1973), Johnson joined the Ph.D. program at SUNY Stony Brook. Significantly, at the end of his master's thesis, Johnson considers the possibilities for personal and social reformation centered on art and education. He speculates, "It may seem peculiar to think of art and scholarship as revolutionary, but what Marcuse calls the 'estrangement effect' of the former and the historical dedication to 'truth' of the latter, are, I think, essential conditions for an 'informed' public, the precondition of a democracy" (62). While these three black philosophy students certainly did not respond identically to the competing academic and social pressures of the 1960s and 1970s, all would nevertheless seem to agree on the value of what West calls "intense intellectual work" (*Breaking Bread* 144).[31]

## The Black Scholar in the White Academy: Charles Johnson's "Alēthia"

Johnson's own intellectual work demonstrates that he was sensitive to the social and disciplinary barriers that complicated the experience of blacks in U.S. academies, and in graduate programs in philosophy in particular. As Johnson explains in "Where Philosophy and Fiction Meet," the black philosopher "lives with the possibility of being badly misunderstood by blacks and whites both" (91). Moreover, Johnson's fiction repeatedly investigates the question posed by Barrett—"What does it mean to profess philosophy in the contemporary world?"—from the situated perspective of the black intellectual. In his short story "A Lion at Pendleton" (1998), for example, Johnson weighs Frederick Douglass's understanding of freedom against that of the whites in the abolitionist cause. In "Dr. King's Refrigerator" (2005), he treats King's philosophical ideal of the "beloved community" humorously, and in his novel *Dreamer* quite seriously. In "The Education of Mingo" (1977), Johnson satirizes Aristotelian views on slavery, and in

"Exchange Value," he signifies on Marx in order to racialize the concept of commodity fetishism. But if the question that defined for Barrett a post–World War II crisis in philosophy is one to which Johnson returns repeatedly in his fiction, an early short story, "Alēthia," is especially pertinent to any discussion of the embattled position of black philosophers in a predominantly white profession. The story deserves careful discussion here because it provides a rare contemporary window onto the disciplinary pressures faced by black philosophers.

In "Alēthia," Johnson uses the problematic relationship between a black professor and one of his undergraduate students to critique the state of academic philosophy in the period immediately before the story was published, to consider certain contradictions inherent in Western rationalism, and to enter into a philosophical disagreement between Kantian formalist and Schelerian nonformalist ethics—a disagreement that proves important to Johnson's own project of writing black philosophical fiction. Originally published in *Antaeus* in 1979 and included in Johnson's first collection of short stories, *The Sorcerer's Apprentice* (1986), "Alēthia" centers on the apparent seduction of a fifty-year-old black philosophy professor by a black undergraduate student from his Kant seminar.[32] Raised on books about "Negro uplift"—stories about "men who tried, in their own small way, to create lives that could be, if disciplined, the basis of universal law"—the professor at the outset of the tale has pursued a higher education and earned a faculty position in a primarily white university (102). Isolated in his office or "the three small rooms" that he rents near Northwestern's campus, the professor also represents the alienation of the black intellectual who has failed to remain what Cornel West, adapting Gramsci, has called "organically linked" to the black community ("Dilemma" 112). By threatening to accuse him of sexual harassment, the student, Wendy Barnes, blackmails the professor into going to a party on the South Side of Chicago, where he experiences a drug-induced vision of unity with the black world he left behind for the academy. The ambiguous conclusion takes place in Wendy's bedroom, as she takes off her clothes and lies down next to him. Has she saved the professor from a debilitating segregation in the white academy, or has she caused him to lose the last remnants of idealism and discipline that initially led him there? As a tale focused on the experiences of a black philosopher in the white academy (and as one that takes a philosophical concept as its title), the narrative explicitly alludes to the difficulties raised by attempts to revise Western philosophy to make it more responsive to the lived experience of black Americans.

The professor's association with Kant, the philosopher on whom he teaches his seminar, is important to Johnson's criticism of academic philosophy in several respects. Kant is generally considered to be the first professional philosopher, one whose university appointment is frequently contrasted

to the "philosophy of the marketplace" represented by a figure such as
Socrates. Moreover, Kant's learned critiques have come to define the sort of
technical analysis traditionally understood to merit the name of philosophical work. As the philosopher most clearly associated with the European
Enlightenment, Kant is also one whose work most clearly equates philosophical inquiry with the exercise of a rationality purified of personal inclination,
emotion, and desire. In *Anthropology from a Pragmatic Point of View* he
observes that "to be subject to emotions and passions is probably always an
illness of mind because both emotion and passion exclude the sovereignty of
reason" (73.155). Indeed, with his promulgation of practical reason as the
synthesizer of universal truths in epistemology, his claims to disinterested-
ness in aesthetics, and his evocation of formalism in ethics, Kant made
modern European philosophy practically synonymous with a purified rationality.[33] Kant is a signifier, then, for a specific path to philosophical enlightenment, one that is academic, highly technical, and decidedly rationalistic. This
is precisely the path that the bookish professor, who describes himself as
"living for knowledge," has chosen for himself at the outset of Johnson's tale
(103). Indeed, Kant functions in Johnson's narrative precisely as a literary
trope for the problems attending the professionalization of philosophy identified by Barrett. Before his encounter with Wendy Barnes, the professor's
own "monkish and contemplative" life recalls the bachelor Kant's ascetic
and circumspect existence, and the professor's medicine cabinet, stuffed with
remedies for a variety of complaints, brings to mind Kant's own reputation
as a notorious hypochondriac. In his work and in his life, then, the tale's
black philosopher-narrator is clearly linked to Kant, an association which
suggests that the modern professionalization of philosophy is partly responsible for the rarefied academic isolation the professor finds himself in at the
outset of Johnson's tale.

Although the professor's association with Kant is strong, however, it is
not complete. By describing himself as "stalking Kant," the professor suggests that the European philosopher in some sense eludes him, and his inability to complete his own book tells us that his relationship to the discipline is
problematic. More important, the ambivalence hinted at in the narrator's
identification with Kant permeates the narrator's conception of his own position in the university, which is clearly complicated in a way that Kant's was
not: by his blackness. The professor identifies not only with Kant but also
with "that towering sociologist W. E. B. Du Bois," whose classic statement on
double consciousness he applies explicitly to his own position as a professor
of philosophy. "A Negro professor is, although reappointed and tenured, a
kind of two-reel comedy" who no longer fits in the "bleak world of black
Chicago" he has left behind, or in the academy, where, "like a thief come to
the table, he hungrily grabs crumbs of thought from their genuine context,

reading Hume for his reasoning on the self, blinking that author's racial slurs" (99, 101–2). Attracted to higher education but also self-consciously aware of its traditions of racism, the professor understands that the position of black philosopher deviates from the discipline's historical norms.

With his personal insecurities reflecting the larger crises of legitimacy in the discipline that is analyzed by Jones, the professor complicates his position in the academy by contrasting his own reasons for entering philosophy as an idealistic "first-generation student" with the philosophical motivation of other teachers, who, "shaken by Wittgenstein," have "lost faith and were madly humping their teaching assistants" (102). Alluding to Wittgenstein's argument that a large number of philosophical questions should be dismissed as the simple result of confusion in the use of language, the professor's comment suggests that his white colleagues have become skeptical about the practice of philosophy at the precise moment when he has entered the discipline. Influenced by his reading in books for Negro uplift, the professor has claimed an education in order to demonstrate that blacks should be included in the formulation of universal Western norms, only to find that the academy itself is abandoning those norms. Furthermore, by describing himself as a "thief" (and possibly a stalker), the professor criminalizes his own presence in the academy, further betraying a sense of illegitimacy. It is clear that in spite of his tenure—and because of his blackness—the professor perceives his own position in the university as somehow precarious and temporary, as his rented rooms near Northwestern suggest.

The professor's troubled idealism contrasts sharply with the unabashed self-interest of his student Wendy, who attempts to blackmail the professor into giving her at least a B in the Kant seminar so she can remain in school. Wendy lays out her proposition in unmistakable terms. "If I don't ace this course," she tells the professor, "I'm gonna have to tell your chairman . . . that you been hounding me for trim" (105–6). In spite of their "philosophical differences," however, Wendy's determination not to be forced back into "factory" or "day work" corresponds to the narrator's own desires to escape the "ugly, lovely black life" he knew as a boy. The academically successful but culturally alienated professor and the academically marginal but culturally astute young woman represent two varieties of first-generation black college students, and the "rental library" books that Wendy carries signal—in addition to a lack of funds—that her own relationship to the academy is precarious too (100). The professor's attempt to hold contemporary black Chicago at bay—he reads "Hebrew, Greek, or Sanskrit" but never "tabloids or lurid newspapers" (102–3)—is broken when Wendy enters his office, reminding him of the "well-medicated blues singers backing up James Brown down at the Regal" (105). Opposing a blues tradition to the professor's readings in various classical traditions, Wendy embodies the black world that the

narrator perceives as making his position at the university problematic, and
her threats of sexual scandal serve to externalize his own inner doubts over
his position in the academy, described earlier through tropes of criminality.

Like one of Edgar Allan Poe's narrators whose fascination with a female
Other reveals the workings of his own conflicted psyche, the professor
through his changing relationship with Wendy exposes the inner confusion
beneath his own "outwar[d] calm" (100). Even as he complains of feeling
trapped by Wendy's "endless tricks" (106), the professor recognizes that to
some extent the "disaster was somehow all [his] own doing" (107). Arising
anima-like as if from his own repressions, Wendy visits his office on the very
day when he experiences a sudden new vision of her during his Kant seminar, a reevaluation that the professor attributes explicitly to his reading of
Max Scheler (1874–1928). A prolific German phenomenologist, Scheler developed a nonformalist ethics specifically as a response to Kantian formalism.
He grounded his own ethical system in love, which he understood to be an
intentional relationship prior to intellectual abstraction. Scheler writes, "Man
is, before he can think or will, *en amans*."[34] While Kant argues that moral behavior "wholly excludes the influence of inclinations" and secures his conception of duty in the universal laws synthesized by practical reason
(*Foundations* 51), Scheler argues in contrast that one encounters value
through acts of feeling. Scheler's ethics, then, privilege the very affectivity
that Kant seeks to repress. Upon reading a passage attributed to Scheler—
"contemplation of essence, the fundamental approach to Being peculiar to
metaphysical knowledge, demands an attitude of loving devotion"—the professor is stunned to realize that his method for reaching truth, a purified
Kantian rationalism, is suspect (100). For he has, as the professor tells himself, "misunderstood something that any salesgirl knew instinctively—that
living for knowledge, ignoring love, as I had, was wrong, because love—
transcendental love—*was* knowledge" (103). As someone who has been "*devoted* to books" and who has spent his life "*embracing*" ideas, the pedantic
professor realizes that his desire for truth has been misdirected (100, 102; emphasis added). The implication is that Scheler has enabled the narrator to
change his methods and to see Wendy anew, with the clarity of a phenomenological *epochē*—"the flash of clear vision . . . the gasp of recognition that
slaps you, suddenly, when a tree drawing in a child's book . . . recomposes
itself as a face" (101). The further implication is that the overly professionalized philosophical practice of the white academy would be reinvigorated
through the adoption of methods more responsive to black subjectivity.

Given Johnson's own interest in phenomenology, it is tempting to read
the professor's sudden change of heart at face value. But although the narrative endorses his reorientation, it also treats that new insight humorously by

dramatizing what might be called a seduction by phenomenological reduction. Johnson's short story is in fact structured around three separate moments of phenomenological insight: first, the professor's "fresh, new vision" of Wendy in the classroom (inspired by reading Scheler); second, the "new apprehension" he experiences at the party (at least partly induced by drugs); and third, the moment of phenomenological surrender in Wendy's bedroom. By no means an uncomplicated tribute to phenomenology, the story in fact is designed to probe the irony, humor, danger, and possibility in the professor's evolving epistemic positions. Such ironies are made clear by the professor's reaction immediately after his new apprehension of Wendy, when he dismisses his class and retreats to his office, chastising himself for an interest in his student that is by no means purely transcendental: "*O Shameful* to have hot flashes for a student" (101). In light of his own equation of his vision to "hot flashes," the professor's appeal to Scheler must be read in part as a philosophical rationalization, or sublimation, of an erotic desire for Wendy that has been present from the outset but repressed by the professor's Kantian discipline. Indeed, although he asserts earlier that he "seldom noticed" Wendy while lecturing, the details the professor does notice—her "sandalwood" perfume and "black leather boots"—are sexually suggestive, and the fact that he describes her as "sashaying seductively" into class and sitting with her "knees pressed together" reveals that he has been watching her rather more carefully than he admits (100, 99–100, 101). That Wendy Barnes comes to his office with her startling proposition on the very day when the professor experiences his new "vision" of her in class suggests further that Wendy comes to his office in part because she is aware of his attraction to her and intends to use his interest for her own purposes. In any case, Wendy's threat reduces the professor's prior idealistic projections about girls who "know about love" to an elaborate joke at his own expense. Such narrative ambivalence is maintained throughout much of Johnson's tale. Is the professor's idealism uplifting, naïve, or self-serving? Is Wendy's self-interest simply "vulgar" (as the professor initially finds her) and cynical (she suggests at one point that "civil rights is high comedy"), or is she a reliable guide for the professor out of the white academy to closer ties to the black community and a keener moral vision (105, 108)?

One thing is certain. Although the professor feels "trapped" by Wendy— he even describes her as having a face "like a trap door"—he is already ensnared at the tale's outset by his professional status as a philosopher and by his intellectual commitment to a restrictively formal rationalism (107, 106). From the outset his attempt to "get over" through education has been marked by mixed motives, propelled both by his idealistic boyhood dreams of living a life that could become, "if disciplined," a universal law and by the more practical desire to escape a neighborhood fate that seemed to lead inevitably to "(a) drugs, (b) a Post Office job, (c) Marion Prison, (d) Sunset Cemetery (all black), or (e) the ooga-booga of Christianity" (102, 101–2). In order to make his escape, the professor has buried himself in Padelford Hall, a building "as old . . . as a medieval fortress," and "barricaded [himself] in by books" (101, 103). But the release that Wendy—and Scheler—represent as an alternative to the rarefied world of the white academy is itself morally ambiguous. Wendy's threats to bring false claims of sexual harassment are clearly suspect, as is her inability to generalize norms of behavior more inclusive than those of her own personal self-interest, such as those of civil rights. Scheler's phenomenology—proposed as an answer to Kant for ignoring the importance of affectivity in the apprehension of value—represents a liberating alternative to the restrictive life of discipline to which the professor has committed himself. But as a model of the professional philosopher, Scheler also represents a significant danger: his notoriously undisciplined private life could not be more opposed to the circumspection attributed to the unmarried Kant. Twice divorced, Scheler pursued love affairs that led to the loss of more than one academic position.[35] The professor's growing sense that he is "damned if I seduce her. . . . damned if I didn't" is therefore perceptive (109). He will be damned if he seduces Wendy, because the principles on which he has based his life will be compromised (and because his faculty position will be put at risk), and he will be damned if he doesn't seduce her, because he will remain trapped in an academic, epistemic, and personal discipline no broader than the narrow confines of Padelford Hall.

Set in opposition to the restrictive milieu of the white academy is the rowdy environment of the area of black Chicago to which Wendy reintroduces the professor by taking him to a party in the "squalid Fifth Police District," an area referred to by the professor as a "sewer" (107). On the one hand, from the perspective of the professor's identification with a rationalist European philosophical tradition, black Chicago appears as an exoticized Other, which he consistently associates with matter, the body, and especially desire. Early in the tale the professor compares his attempt "to free himself from black Chicago" to the struggle of "Hegel's anxious Spirit . . . against matter" (101). His comparison alludes both to Hegel's description of the ascent of spirit and to the idealist philosopher's judgment that Africans as a people had not achieved "the category of universality" because Africa is "the unhistorical, Undeveloped spirit, still involved in the conditions of mere nature" (95). On the other hand, Wendy is the very embodiment of transgressive desire. For example, she drives the professor to the party at over 70 miles per hour, breaking the speed limit and "damned near blowing off both doors," while he sits tensely next to her, his "black hat crushed against the roof, hands gripped between [his] knees" (107).

But the suggestion that an unrestrained Wendy takes the reserved professor "for a ride" is complicated by his prior intimations of personal responsibility and his later admission at the party, "Even I was no longer sure what brought me" (110). Like Eliot's Prufrock at another gathering, he is clearly both attracted to and repelled by the pleasures the party affords, which provide the emotional release that, on one level, he so desperately seeks, while simultaneously threatening his carefully maintained self-control and the academic position that discipline has earned him. As the professor humorously—but perceptively—reflects, "Let me linger too long and I would never regain the university" (109). In his study of the categorical imperative, Roger Sullivan suggests that Kant *assumes* an internal conflict between reason and emotion (15). Feminist philosopher Robin May Schott argues further that by repressing emotion, Kantian epistemology practically guarantees the return of the repressed.[36] Through the professor's personal psychology and evolving relationship with Wendy, Johnson effectively dramatizes the internal conflict between reason and desire in Kantian epistemology, the repression of affectivity, and the consequent return of the repressed.

The two primary locales of the short story—university and party—themselves articulate a binary of mind/body, reason/desire, normativity/criminality. The party is designed to dramatize both the collapse of the professor's personal discipline and the artificiality of the categories established by his adherence to a rationalist epistemology that represses affectivity. When he enters the apartment the professor becomes disoriented, overcome by "the raw ugly scent of marijuana hashish congolene and the damp smell of an old cellar that [he] could taste as well as smell these violent odors as they coalesced . . . take hold of them in [his] hands like tissue" (109). Grouping the hair-straightening product congolene with the "raw ugly scent" of the old cellar and of hashish, the professor reacts to the party in a fashion that again associates the black community with impurity, materiality, and criminality. But his synesthesia—captured by the odors that he can "taste" and hold in his hands "like tissue"—also signals a blurring of his normal categories of discernment (an alteration that is reinforced at the sentence level by the lack of commas between elements). As the professor's confusion increases after he "unconsciously" swallows a pellet that someone presses into his hand, the party makes clear that his categories of interpretation are not a priori or universal but artificial and changeable.

The release of the affectivity he has previously repressed enables the professor to experience at the party a second vision of Wendy that is part LSD hallucination and part phenomenological insight. As he watches Wendy dance, "now fast, now slow," then lowers his eyelids to contemplate her afterimage, the professor achieves a new sense of unity with Wendy, the other partygoers, and indeed with the entire carnivalesque population of Chicago:

I suddenly saw Wendy—not as the girl who shotgunned me with blackmail back at Padelford Hall, who made me jump like a trained seal;
who stood outside me as another subject in a context of wills—but,
yes, as pure light, brilliance, fluid like the music, blending in a perfectly
balanced world with the players Muslims petty thieves blacks Jews
lumpenproles Daley machine politicians West Indians loungers Africans
the drug peddlers who, when it came to the crunch, were, it was plain,
pure light, too, the Whole in drag, and in that evanescent, drugged in-
stant, I did indeed desperately love her. (111)

Interpreting the professor's second vision as "an individual transcendence
that connects him with a larger appreciation of the whole," Little finds in this
insight an expression of Johnson's "own version of the Black Aesthetic," because rather than "fleeing blackness...the narrator learns to see within it the
particular and distinctive beauty it affords" (*Charles* 123). The professor's insight also recalls Franz Brentano's understanding of intentionality: Consciousness is always "consciousness *of something*" (124). From this perspective, the
subject and object are understood as giving rise to each other simultaneously
at the moment of perception. The professor realizes that his being is dependent on the black Others, then, just as their appearance before him depends
partially on him. Moreover, read from the perspective of Johnson's criticism
of the practice of academic philosophy, the professor's new appreciation of
Wendy can be seen as an argument against the historical failure of the
discipline to recognize that black experience participates in the universality
traditionally required for philosophical legitimacy. As Johnson argues in "Philosophy and Black Fiction," the "very particulars of Black life which see[m] so
at odds with universality" can "make the universal utterance possible" (81).

And yet there are elements of the professor's vision which indicate that his
intellectual emancipation from European rationalism at this point in the narrative may be incomplete. Indeed, the imagery of the second vision suggests,
ironically, that his identification with the black community may be predicated on the erasure of its particularity. For the second vision of Wendy—
realized after the professor turns inward and reflects on her afterimage—
replicates the generalizing tendencies of Kantian rationalism. At the moment
of his insight Wendy loses her particularity—both the specificity of her prior
actions (she is no longer "the girl who shotgunned me") and of her name, as
she becomes simply "the girl" (111). This process of abstraction continues
during the professor's revelation, as "the girl" is transfigured into "pure light,
brilliance . . . blending in a perfectly balanced world" (111). The professor's
qualification that he does "most desperately" love her "*at this moment*" (111;
emphasis added) suggests that he may love Wendy not as a particular woman
but only insofar as her particularity can be transcended.

Earlier in the narrative the professor, drawing on Scheler, defines Mind as an "opening that, if directed toward another, allowed him (or her) to appear . . . as both moral and beautiful" (103). The conclusion that he draws from this statement is that "Nature . . . needed man to clarify its meaning" (103–4). While the professor's conclusion expresses a new appreciation for an intimate relationship between mind and world, it also reveals a will to control, or at least a will to define. At the party Wendy occupies the position of Nature, while the professor, observing her, is in the position of Mind, whose purpose it becomes to clarify her meaning. He fulfills that purpose by transcending Wendy's concrete qualities in order to realize an idealized vision of "pure light." The fact that the professor strips Wendy of her distinctiveness—including her color—at the very moment when he "most desperately love[s] her" calls into question, at this point in the tale, both the precise nature of the professor's reintegration into the black community and the degree to which his insight frees him from an abstracting formalism.

If the professor's second vision is captured in the specular imagery often associated with the quest for purity characteristic of European rationality, the party also figures the professor's change in perception through a trope of homosexuality that is more inclusive of particularity and more responsive to the needs of affectivity. Of all his experiences at the party, the professor is most confused by "the flashy men in white mink jackets who favored women, the women who looked, in their pale, fulgurating light, like men" (109). Because he has organized his life in the academy around inflexible dualisms, it is precisely homosexuality's blurring of binary categories that most disturbs the professor's thinking. But the trope of homosexuality suggests that meaning (and subjectivity) may be better expressed through "masquerade" than through categorical purity. Thus the professor, through his identification with the other men at the party, is led to recognize those aspects of himself and the black community that he had earlier attempted to repress: "That man, the one in the Abo Po, lightly treading the measure, was me. And this one dressed like Walt (or Joe) Frazier was me. If I existed at all, it was in this kaleidoscope party, this pinwheel of color, the I just a function, a flickerflash creation of this black chaos, the chaos no more, or less than, the I" (110–11). A needed corrective to his earlier position of normative rigidity and epistemic superiority, the professor's identification with the men at the party suggests a path away from the false universalism of European rationalism, built on dualistic (and exclusionary) categories, into a more inclusive position that does not subsume the Other—as does perhaps his vision of Wendy—in categorical purity. For, as Johnson suggests in "Philosophy and Black Fiction," "the Black world *appears* in countless guises" (82).

Whether interpreted as a moment of transcendental insight, an attempt to transcend the particularities of black life, or a liberating expression of repressed need (or as some combination of all three), the second vision of Wendy does not conclude Johnson's narrative. Awaking in her bedroom the next morning, the professor discovers that a "stylized purity of line" has returned to his perception, and he reflects on the meaning of the previous night's events. Did he "dream the connectedness of Being the night before," or does he "drea[m] distinctions" now (111–12)? His intellectual quandary marks the return of the professor's dualistic patterns of thought and of his tendency to overintellectualize. Admonishing the professor for "still thinking like a fat boy" (112), Wendy takes off her clothes and joins him in bed. As he raises his arm so that she can "move closer" and at last lets his "mind sleep," Johnson's short story ends. Earlier in the tale the professor criticizes other faculty members for losing their faith in philosophy and "madly humping" their students: has he joined his disillusioned peers?

Given the specific character of Schelerian phenomenology, the narrative's extended trope of books, and Wendy's evolving role in the short story, it is likely that the professor's affair constitutes not a "fall" from transcendental heights but a further step away from Kantian formalism and toward Scheler's nonformalist ethics.[37] In describing philosophic practice, Kant, Husserl, and Scheler each advocate different methods. In "What Is Enlightenment?" Kant summarizes that period's intellectual motto as "Dare to trust your own reason," and he valorizes the individual's exercise of his or her own reason.[38] His formalist ethics require that reason be purified of personal inclination and desire in the service of universal truth. The proper philosophical path is, then, to follow the dictates of a reason so disciplined. Husserl, by contrast, urged philosophers to turn "back to the things themselves" in an attempt to ensure that inquiry did not limit itself to either the abstract conceptions of received theories or the sedimented accumulations of commonsense knowledge. Scheler, however, found Husserl's attempts to turn phenomenology into a rigorous science itself overly analytical and rationalistic, and he argued that the merely rational could not account for the richly existential, which is characterized by a phenomenological wealth that overflows the analytical or conceptual. The professor's relationship with Wendy Barnes dramatically evokes such abundance.

At the same time, the tale's ambivalence in regard to the practice of phenomenology suggests that Johnson is aware that the method can carry its own dangers. Before the professor's change of heart, for example, he is described as practicing some "perceptual tricks" he has learned from "Husserl's *Ideen*" (103). By characterizing Husserl's exercises as tricks, Johnson suggests that phenomenology — or at least Husserlian phenomenology — can run the risk of degenerating into mere mental operations or perceptual games. This is precisely the practice that Scheler hoped to avoid: to Scheler, as the philosopher John Staude summarizes, "phenomenology was not so much a method—in the sense of mental operations—as a special attitude," an orientation whereby "one could enter into a . . . relationship with things" (21). Against the Kantian philosophical subject who trusts the "sovereignty of his own reason," and unlike a Husserlian transcendent ego that analyzes its own acts of consciousness as they construct meaning, Scheler proposed, as Michael Barber emphasizes, that the "authentic phenomenologist turns toward being like a lover toward a friend" (143). This evolving philosophical disagreement in fact mirrors the movement of Johnson's narrative. If Kant believed that value is ascertained by acts of reason that require a mastery of affectivity (the professor's position at the outset of the tale), and if Husserl suggested that meaning is constructed through acts of intention that imply a certain mastery of an object (the professor's second position), Scheler argued that value is discovered through a loving surrender to the object or the Other. At the very moment when the professor lets his own "mind sleep" and allows Wendy to reveal herself to him, he comes closest, then, to realizing Scheler's nonformalist ethics. From this perspective, the professor's earlier vision of Wendy at the party can be read as a momentary "irrealization" that frees him from his preconceptions about her nature and prepares him, at the conclusion of the tale, to accept Wendy on her own terms.[39] "Alēthia" thus dramatizes almost precisely the process of phenomenological practice that Johnson describes in "Philosophy and Black Fiction."[40]

Johnson's critique of analytic formalism is intensified throughout the narrative by his skillful development of an extended trope of books, manuscripts, and papers. Certainly the tale abounds with allusions to books, from revered works of philosophy to children's coloring books, and from great works of literature to the professor's grade book. For the professor, books initially hold the promise—like Kant's formalist ethics—that abstract norms will provide effective models for life. Comparing the books he reads about "Negro uplift" to Plutarch's *Lives of the Noble Grecians* (102), the professor—from his boyhood reading through his classical training to his philosophical study of Kant—characteristically turns to books to discover patterns for thought and action (102). But in a way that recalls Ralph Waldo Emerson's contention that books, poorly used, can be the most dangerous of things, Johnson denigrates the professor's reliance on books by compounding images of the limitations that their forms can impose: from the "paint-by-numbers curriculum" the professor encounters in college, to the books that "barricad[e]" him in Padelford Hall, to the mental "tricks" the professor learns from Husserl's *Ideen*, to Wendy's judgment that his life amounts to nothing but "the Book—that dry ream of windy bullshit—you can't finish" (108). In other words, from the time he was a lonely little "fat boy" the professor has limited his "sources" about life, narrowing his search for meaning to preexisting paradigms. Significantly, his practice as a philosopher reveals the same secondhand methodology. When he lectures, he approaches Kant "by way of a playful verse attributed to Bishop Berkeley" (100), thereby interpreting the work of one philosopher through that of another. The practice of philosophy as ever more analysis of received tradition is precisely the model that phenomenology hoped to disrupt by turning the discipline to the "everyday" world of lived experience, a reorientation, Johnson's short story suggests, that would also better account for the lived experience of black Americans.

Significantly, Johnson's trope of the book also resonates with Scheler's belief that because of the propensity of concepts either to obscure or to displace the *qualities* of the object, a certain "de-symbolization of the world" is required if one is to perceive afresh.[41] This process of de-symbolization is dramatized at the party, where the book—representing rationality, abstract norms, and the white academy—is trumped by music, the agent of experience, desire, and the black community. As the professor recounts: "It played hob with my blood pressure. It was wild, sensual, clanging and languid by turns, loud and liquid, an intangible force, or—what shall I say?—spirit angling through the air, freed by cackling instruments that lifted me, a fat boy and student still, like a scrap of paper, then dropped me, head over heels" (109–10). In a reversal of the professor's earlier identification of spirit with the white academy and of materiality with the black community, music proves the more potent spiritual force, triumphing over the reified word, which is reduced to a mere "scrap of paper." The final paragraph of the story reinforces that potency: Wendy—who had earlier been reduced to an F student in the professor's grade book—sits with "one bare foot on [the professor's] briefcase," an image suggestive of the triumph of unembellished life over abstract thought (112).

Representing the aspects of phenomenological experience that do not fit into the professor's formalist preconceptions, Wendy Barnes plays several important roles in the narrative. Certainly Johnson is interested in more than simply a realistic development of her character. That becomes clear when Wendy—her hair "crack[ling] with electricity"—assumes a prophetic voice, pronouncing on the condition of philosophy, the professor, and contemporary society in language that far outstrips her usual vocabulary (108). As a result, the professor remarks, "If I'd known she was this smart, I'd have given her an A the first week of the term" (109). Wendy, as indicated earlier, represents the return of the repressed, both as an agent of the black world the professor has abandoned for the white academy and as the embodiment of the personal desire that he has repressed as part of the discipline of Kantian rationality. Wendy's unbridled commitment to her own personal interests is precisely what Kantian ethics attempts to suppress in order to achieve its formalism. But Wendy also claims to represent a certain kind of knowledge: as she tells the professor, "I know how this place works" (105). Over the course of the short story, the roles of teacher and student in fact become reversed. When Wendy first enters his office the professor says to her, paternalistically, "There now. . . tell me about it" (105); but by the end of the tale it is Wendy who corrects the professor, chiding him as "you poor fool" (112). Just as the professor's original commitment to received norms created a need to control—both his own inclinations and the "criminality" he associates with the black community, his second vision at the party, while providing a needed corrective to his preconceptions about the black community, nevertheless demonstrates that his commitment to abstraction fails to account for the phenomenological richness of the Other. As Wendy disrobes and reveals herself to him in all her embodied particularity at the end of the tale, the professor gives up control and allows himself to be taught by the Other.

The final role that Wendy plays in the story, then, is as the embodiment of *alethia* itself, understood in specifically Schelerian terms as "a guide away from symbolizing thought" to the "self-given phenomenon."[42] In performing the role of guide for the professor's journey out of Kantian rationalism, Wendy signifies upon the role of Diotima in the *Symposium*.[43] In Plato's famous dialogue, Diotima instructs Socrates and the other men at Agathon's drinking party on the proper path to truth, which she describes as an ascent from the sensuous love of the beloved's body to the rarefied love of ideal forms. By leading the professor out of his study, back to the black community, and ultimately to her own bed, Wendy comically reverses the philosophical journey that Diotima describes, as she educates the professor in the phenomenological abundance that overflows rationalist forms.

The alienated professor's reintroduction to the black world in "Alēthia" invites comparison to James Baldwin's renowned story "Sonny's Blues," in which an educated man who has also distanced himself from the black community comes to a new understanding of his younger brother Sonny's motivations, his family's history, and his community's resilience. Like the estranged professor of Johnson's tale who initially disdains the "braying" and "crackling" music that he hears at Wendy's party, only later to experience its power, Sonny's older brother initially dismisses jazz and the blues as merely "good time" music, which he associates with the forces (such as drugs) that threaten the black community. Through the power of Sonny's playing, however, he is led to a new appreciation for the blues, his brother, and the black community. Although both of these stories chart the return of an educated but alienated black man to his community, there are important differences between them in theme and narrative technique. As a powerful piece of realistic fiction, Baldwin's narrative is characterized by unified character development and a carefully maintained tone appropriate to its serious elaboration of the historical, familiar, and communal ties that bind the black community.

In contrast, the professor and student in Johnson's tale are not so realistically drawn, and the tale's tone is markedly mixed, as is its genre, which draws on elements of the seduction tale, the horror story, and the romance. As is often the case in his fiction, Johnson's characters resemble the emblematic characters one finds in a fable or allegory; and like allegory, the tale is designed to be read on several levels: as a satire of a problematic sexual encounter that raises certain ethical questions (such as whether the professor is seduced or seducer), as an exploration of certain contradictions within reason itself as historically realized in European philosophy, and as a critique of the practice of academic philosophy in the period immediately before the tale was written—especially to the extent that the practice of philosophy fails to accommodate the lived experience of black people. Both Baldwin's and Johnson's approaches to the short story, as illustrated by these two narratives, offer certain opportunities and limitations. Baldwin's realism buys him immense emotional power, while the satiric distance often required by Johnson's critique can have the effect of distancing readers from his characters even as it creates opportunities for multiple readings, humor, and philosophical complexity.

An excellent example of Johnson's practice of philosophical fiction, "Alēthia" also resonates powerfully with Barrett's identification of a crisis in philosophy in terms of a conflict between formal and more pluralistic methodologies and with Jones's 1974 identification of a crisis in the discipline with regard to black representation—a crisis that Jones relates explicitly to the professionalism that Barrett decries. By figuring Kant as a trope for professionalization and Wendy Barnes as the representative of philosophical pluralism, Johnson is able, in a few short pages, to anatomize the embattled position of black philosophers in the post–World War II academy in relation to white philosophers, to the discipline's historical and conceptual norms, and to the black community. By doing so, Johnson's short story provides a rare firsthand (if fictionalized) commentary on the concrete disciplinary context out of which his philosophical fiction emerged.

## Black Philosophical Fiction: A World of Possibility

> This decadence is inessential; it is that of a certain type of
> philosopher. . . . Philosophy will find help in poetry, art, etc.;
> in a closer relationship with them, it will be reborn.
>
> *Maurice Merleau-Ponty*, Notes de cours

In 1976 Johnson accepted the offer of an acting assistant professorship from the University of Washington in Seattle. At the time he was a struggling student with a wife and a new son, Malik, who was born in 1975. Although Johnson's decision to leave the Ph.D. program in philosophy to accept the faculty position in creative writing was partially motivated by increasing family responsibilities and decreasing financial resources, a faculty appointment with an institution as outstanding as the University of Washington was obviously attractive on its own merits. Autobiographical details in "Alēthia" suggest, however, that disciplinary factors may also have played a role in Johnson's decision to leave academic philosophy and commit himself to the practice of philosophical fiction.

A number of autobiographical allusions in "Alēthia" link the professor's situation to Johnson's own experience as an academic.[44] Most obviously, the professor lives close to Northwestern, near the area where Johnson grew up, and he has an office in Padelford Hall, Johnson's own university home at the time the story was written. But other details also lead readers to connect the professor's conflicted relationship with the academy to Johnson's own. For example, Wendy threatens to report the professor to his "chairman, Dick Dunn, and to Dean David MacCracken" (106). At the time Johnson wrote "Alēthia," Dunn was in fact his chairman, and McCracken, who worked in the dean's office, had an office directly across from Johnson's in Padelford Hall. If the professor's troubled relationship to academic philosophy serves as a comment on the pressures encountered by black scholars in the discipline in general, details such as these suggest that the professor's experiences may also comment on Johnson's relationship to academic philosophy in particular.

In fact the professor's apparent decision—and perhaps Johnson's—to leave the profession of philosophy follows a historical trend among black students of philosophy. The tendency among black scholars to study philosophy but to practice in another field, even within the academy, is well documented. One of the most famous philosophical defectors was W. E. B. Du Bois, who reports being driven by "James with his pragmatism and Albert Bushnell Hart with his research method" to abandon "the lovely but sterile hand of philosophic speculation."[45] Jones accounted for this phenomenon in the early postwar years partly by pointing out that no historically black colleges offered a philosophy major; instead, philosophy courses were more likely to be offered by departments of religion ("Crisis" 122). To this day Cornel West, probably the nation's most widely recognized African American philosopher, has never held a position in a department of philosophy. As Leonard Harris argues in an impassioned 1995 article in the *Proceedings of the American Philosophical Association*: "The most noted Black philosophers are relegated to the status of kitchen help on the plantation: Cornel West, at Harvard, holds a joint appointment in African American Studies and the Harvard Divinity School; [Kwame] Anthony Appiah, also at Harvard, holds a full time faculty line in African American Studies. Neither costs philosophy any money" (133). Although West and Appiah have both moved since Harris wrote his article (and although it is extremely problematic to equate appointments at Harvard with the kind of kitchen work performed by Johnson's grandmother for the white sorority at Northwestern), Harris's polemical comparison drives home what he sees as the woeful progress made in black representation in academic philosophy by the end of the twentieth century. Indeed, by marshalling demographic evidence, such as the fact that in 1995 there were still "no Blacks on the faculty in the Philosophy Department at any of the eight Ivy League universities and no Blacks on the faculty in the Philosophy Department at nine of the eleven Big Ten universities," Harris brings Jones's 1974 identification of the crisis in black representation in the discipline up to the first decade of the twenty-first century (133).

Charles Johnson is not alone among the black students of philosophy in the 1960s and 1970s who did not pursue a permanent position as an academic philosopher, as the persistence of a crisis in the discipline of philosophy in terms of black representation might suggest. Interestingly, both Barrett's identification of a crisis in philosophy and his personal example of leaving the academy only to return eighteen years later may have influenced Naomi Zack's decision to leave the academy and to return some twenty years later herself. Zack, a mixed-race philosopher, studied with Barrett, and when she later left academic philosophy, she explains, she would "think of Barrett, well, if Barrett did it, maybe I can do it if I ever want to come back" (Yancy, *African* 233). Anita Allen, who moved from philosophy to law, suggests that some black scholars leave the discipline because philosophy as it is practiced does not make it the best intellectual site for realizing one's scholarly, personal, and social aspirations. As Allen says, speaking of black women scholars in particular, "a black woman who has the smarts to do philosophy could do law, medicine and politics with greater self-esteem, greater financial reward, greater visibility, and greater influence" (Yancy, *African* 172). As discussed in chapter 3, Jan Willis, who studied philosophy at Cornell in the late sixties, became a named professor in religion at Wesleyan University (and, like Johnson, a practicing Buddhist). Moreover, the historical trend for black scholars to study philosophy but to practice it outside of philosophy departments still holds true if, as Gordon has claimed, blacks who do philosophy today are still likely to do it elsewhere than in philosophy departments: "A place where you'd find most Black people who do philosophy, but are not listed as philosophers, will be in religion. . . . Black Studies, American Studies, and political theory . . . are next. Philosophy departments are near, if not at, the bottom of the list" (Yancy, *African* 111).

In "Where Philosophy and Fiction Meet," Johnson explains that when he was faced with criticism from family and friends for switching his major from journalism to philosophy, he found support for what he calls his "need" for philosophy in "the finest works of Afro-American literature" (92). To those who regretted his decision, he spoke about the philosophical background of other black writers, and he pointed to the example of Du Bois's "great hopes" to "develop a philosophical method for the interpretation of race relations" (92). Moreover, Johnson discovered in African American literature itself a philosophical tradition, a "tradition of broaching fundamental questions of being and race, culture and consciousness" (92). The explosion of interest over the past few decades in marking out a black philosophical tradition that incorporates a number of works of African American literature suggests that others agree with Johnson's estimation. In any case, it is clear that African American letters provided Johnson with both cultural validation for his passion for philosophy and a creative venue through which that passion could be expressed. Speculating in 1988 that "the vitality of philosophical discourse has passed in the latter half of this century from the small province of academic seminars to the pages of our finest stories," Johnson echoes the critique of academic philosophy and the dissatisfaction with traditional philosophical discourse found in "Alēthia" (92–93). He concludes that the novelist might reach "a broader audience than his counterpart does in stuffy journals" (92). If in his short story Johnson describes Wendy as having a face like a "trap door," by the end of the tale she comes to embody the sort of "unpredictable possibility" that Johnson also attributes to the artistic use of language: a trap door, after all, signifies not simply the presence of a trap but also a way out of that trap. If conventional language has the power to calcify perception, language also has the power, Johnson is convinced, to break down established habits of interpretation: "It's like a trap door, [it] drops you down to this whole other level of seeing" (O'Connell 29). Despite his criticism of the power of sedimented language to cover over and conceal, Johnson strongly endorses a belief in the defamiliarizing power of art. As his identification with the professor in "Alēthia" and his comments in "Where Philosophy and Fiction Meet" imply, philosophical fiction became Johnson's chosen means to intervene in the disciplinary constraints of academic philosophy. By unabashedly claiming the literary as a powerful site for black philosophical agency, Johnson locates the genesis of his fiction precisely in the attempt to open wide the halls of academic philosophy to a new world of artistic and intellectual possibility.

Johnson's practice of philosophical fiction is usually read from the standpoint of literary tradition as an attempt to infuse literature with philosophical import, and certainly this is one effect of his creative practice.[46] But as the examination here of the disciplinary context out of which that aesthetic project emerged suggests, his philosophical fiction can also be read as an attempt to infuse the calcified discourse of academic philosophy with phenomenological, narratological, and artistic force. In "Philosophy and Black Fiction," an article published only a year after "Alēthia" first appeared and one that reflects Johnson's thinking about the relationship of philosophy to black fiction at the same time the short story was composed, Johnson speaks explicitly about the "area where fiction and philosophy overlap" (80). His analysis of this discursive territory demonstrates that he does not recognize the bifurcation of reason and desire that rationalism presupposes; for there is, Johnson asserts, an "analytic dimension native to literary art," and, further, "feelings" themselves are "shamelessly analytic" (79, 83). Since he understands conception to be shaped by the emotions that inform intentionality, Johnson's phenomenological orientation leads him to reject the possibility of a reason purified of emotion. As he explains, "We aim perceptually at something and, through the emotions of anger or love, cause it to *appear* before us as it could not otherwise" (83). The belief that thought and inclination never arise separately provides Johnson with an epistemological rationale for practicing philosophically engaged fiction (as he will argue in more detail in *Being and Race*). By working with philosophy in a literary mode, in other words, Johnson seeks a phenomenological intensity that academic forms of philosophical writing lack — or, as is suggested by his short story "Alēthia," that they systematically repress. In a 2004 interview Johnson remarked: "Ideas do not begin in some abstract realm floating high above human experience. Rather, they originate in the historical muck and mud of our daily experience, cloaked in the immediate particulars of this world, and only later do we abstract them for the purpose of study and reflection. What a philosophical novelist does — what I do — is simply return those ideas to the palpable world of experience from which they first sprang. That way, I hope, readers *experience* the ideas viscerally, with flesh put back on their abstract bones" (Ghosh 374).

Moreover, Johnson's claim to write "philosophical fiction" should not be understood simply to imply that some works of literature — his among them — have philosophical significance. Rather, his creative practice should be appreciated as constituting a critique of academic philosophy's traditional rationale for distinguishing among literary and critical classes of language in the first place. In 1979, the same year that Johnson's "Alēthia" first appeared, Richard Rorty argued in *Philosophy and the Mirror of Nature* that analytic philosophy's epistemological foundation was being eroded by poststructuralism's emphasis on textuality and neopragmatism's insistence on the social character of meaning. Furthermore, Rorty suggested, analytic philosophy was undermining its own foundation through the work of philosophers such as Willard Van Orman Quine, Wilfrid Sellars, and Nelson Goodman.[47] From the perspective of such criticism it is not the category of "philosophical fiction" that needs to be explained or justified but rather the categorical distinctions traditionally drawn between various forms of reason (such as analytic and synthetic) or those between philosophy and other forms of writing. As Pierre Machery argues in *The Object of Literature* (1995), "There is no more a pure literary discourse than there is a pure philosophical discourse" (5). Or as Johnson claims in *Being and Race*, "Philosophy and fiction—both disciplines of language—are about, at bottom, the same business" (32). In other words, Johnson's project of writing philosophical fiction should also be understood as a challenge to the neo-Kantian epistemological grounds for academic philosophy's claim to enjoy a privileged relationship to truth—the rationale on which modern academic disciplines in general, and analytic philosophy's ascendancy in particular, were founded.

Like those of other black students in philosophy programs in the United States during this period, Johnson's early experiences in the discipline of philosophy reveal both a deeply felt passion for intellectual pursuits and a self-conscious awareness of the unique status of minorities in relation to philosophy's historical and conceptual norms. Against a narrowly conceived philosophical tradition, Johnson discovered in alternative epistemologies such as phenomenology, Marxism, and pragmatism a method for exploring the repressed subject position of African Americans and a justification for practicing black philosophical fiction. Within a philosophical discipline characterized by an ongoing crisis in black representation, Johnson found in the example of African American letters a site where African American philosophical agency had persisted under difficult circumstances. The factors that forged a relationship between philosophy and African American literature historically—the reliance by black thinkers on nonacademic forms of writing; the need to recuperate perspectives that have been habitually repressed; the continuing efforts of black philosophers to infuse abstract arguments with narratological, social, and phenomenological immediacy—provide important contexts for understanding Johnson's creative practice. In addition, because Johnson is one among a handful of African Americans who studied philosophy in the 1960s and 1970s, his fiction offers a rare window onto the situated experience of a generation of black scholars whose history, to this point, has not been written. In his study of American existentialism, George Cotkin emphasizes the important role that literary texts played in the dissemination of that philosophy in the United States during the early to mid-twentieth century and the canonical status that literary texts received when the discourse of existentialism was codified nationally in the 1950s. In the canonization of late-twentieth-century African American philosophy that is currently under way, Charles Johnson's philosophical fiction has a similarly important role to play.

As I have argued in this chapter, Charles Johnson's philosophical fiction emerged from a concrete historical and disciplinary context. In 1974 Jones predicted that a stronger African American presence in the discipline of philosophy would necessarily "raise inescapable questions about every facet of the philosophical discipline," including what was accepted as "the 'proper' approach to philosophizing." Or, as he advised the American Philosophical Association, blacks would of necessity "rearrange the philosophical furniture" ("Crisis" 124). The dominance of analytic philosophy had special ramifications for black students and faculty as they moved into philosophy departments across the nation because it seemed to articulate a standard that defined the philosophical concerns of African American thinkers as beneath disciplinary consideration. In the process of legitimating black philosophical interests and approaches in the 1960s and 1970s, black scholars raised new questions and investigated from a uniquely situated perspective traditional philosophical questions such as those relating to the definition of the subject of philosophy, the nature of enlightenment, and the relation of the universal to the particular, as they simultaneously undertook to reform the practice of philosophy itself. Johnson's philosophical fiction is an important part of this larger revisionary project.

# 2

---

# From Marx to Marcuse in
# *Faith and the Good Thing*

> Black intellectuals must pass through it [Marxism],
> come to terms with it, and creatively respond to it if
> black intellectual activity is to reach any recognizable
> level of sophistication and refinement.
>
> *Cornel West, "The Dilemma of the Black*
> *Intellectual"*

CHARLES JOHNSON'S FIRST PUBLISHED NOVEL, *Faith and the Good Thing* (1974), begins with the strange and remarkable death of Faith's mother, Lavidia. Compulsively and somewhat mysteriously, Lavidia makes a count of each inhalation she takes, convinced that when she draws her four hundred–millionth breath, she will die. And precisely after taking that breath, Lavidia does die, setting Johnson's narrative in motion with her final, cryptic words of advice to her daughter: "Girl, you get yourself a good thing" (4). Lavidia's injunction raises several philosophical questions for readers of Johnson's fiction — questions, most obviously, about precisely what a "good thing" might be, but alternatively (and just as important) questions about what it might mean to "get" or to "possess" that good thing. A consideration of Johnson's novel from the perspective offered by his master's thesis on Wilhelm Reich, Freud, and Marx indicates that the answer to the second question — one that requires an understanding of Marx's analysis of desire and creative appropriation — proves essential to answering the first. Indeed, Johnson's engagement with Marxist ideas early in his career would have vital and lasting consequences for the practice of his fiction — and accounting for Marx's economy of desire proves particularly essential to answering many of the questions posed by Johnson's first novel.

---

In the period leading up to and overlapping with Johnson's undergraduate and graduate student years at SIU, Marxism was being influenced by several important developments, including the emergence of the New Left; the growth of national liberation movements in Africa, South America, and third world countries; and the efforts of civil rights and black liberation movements.[1] The 1956 Soviet invasion of Hungary had directed interest away from Eastern models of Marxism toward the Marxisms developed in western Europe by Lukács, Gramsci, and Korsch in the 1920s and by the Frankfurt School in the 1930s and 1940s, while the growth of national liberation movements was providing new revolutionary models. Writers associated with the oppression of colonial peoples, such as Frantz Fanon, C. L. R. James, and the West Indian radicals George Padmore and Walter Rodney, drew increasing attention. At the same time, various civil rights and black liberation groups drew on Marxist critique in organizing to fight racial oppression. Socialist expectations in general were high, having been fueled by the fall of repressive regimes across the globe and by the rise of international protest movements by workers, students, and ethnic minorities.

Johnson thus began his study of Marx at a time when Marxist critique was an energizing presence in American universities and when its principles were increasingly providing conceptual frameworks for black and student social protest in the United States. In the 1960s and 1970s Marxist social analysis was important to several black liberation organizations, although the degree of engagement with Marxist thought by various groups differed widely. On the one hand, some Black Panthers like Huey Newton charged those with more Pan-Africanist leanings (such as Stokely Carmichael) with failing to understand that the root cause of racism was economic and that the African nations supporting Pan-Africanism were often allies of U.S. imperialism (Dawson, "Black Visions 12).[2] On the other hand, some nationalist and cultural nationalist organizations accused groups sympathetic to class analysis of having been co-opted by whites (a charge leveled by Maulana Karenga against the Black Panthers). Positions within organizations changed over time as well: for example, the cultural-nationalist Congress of African Peoples (CAPS), established by Amiri Baraka, became progressively more Marxist in its orientation. Furthermore, differences in the degree of agreement with Marxism were apparent even within groups, as between the Oakland chapter of the Black Panthers, which drew heavily on class analysis, and other chapters of the Panthers, sometimes more nationalist in orientation. The mixtures of nationalism, Pan-Africanism, and Marxism that characterized black liberation efforts during the period were varied, underscoring on an organizational level multiple applications of Marxist thought.[3]

The generation of black intellectuals who were studying philosophy found in Marxism a fascinating, important, but imperfect tool for understanding their own marginalized position. In chapter 1 I discussed the first collection of essays published by African American philosophers, *Philosophy Born of Struggle* (1983). Many of the essays in that collection draw significantly on Marxist thought. One, "Unfinished Lecture on Liberation—II" by Angela Davis, uses Marxist analysis to explain Frederick Douglass's development of a "theology of liberation." Maulana Karenga seizes on Marx's analysis of alienation as helpful to understanding the position of African Americans ("Society" 217). "Liberation Strategies in Black Theology: Mao, Martin, or Malcolm?" by senior scholar William R. Jones—whose advocacy on behalf of blacks in philosophy is detailed in chapter 1—compares the "transformational models" of Mao Tse-tung, Martin Luther King, and Malcolm X. In "Philosophy, Politics, and Power," Cornel West draws on Marx to argue that the practice of academic philosophy is "inextricably linked to politics and to power" (51). And in "Epidermalizing the World," Tom Slaughter (the black philosophy professor to whom Johnson was close at SIU and who would become his fellow graduate student at SUNY Stony Brook) employs both Marx and Fanon to analyze the phenomenological experience of black people.

Significantly, an important feature of the dissemination of Marxist thought during the 1960s and 1970 was a development that Manning Marable has described as the "merger of black intellectual thought as embodied by programs at black institutions such as Howard, Fisk, and Atlanta University with the implicitly racist, bourgeois structure of white education" (44). Demographic shifts that resulted in increasing numbers of black students attending primarily white institutions combined with the influence of black liberation movements on higher education to contribute to the establishment of Black Studies programs at several U.S. universities. In 1968 SIU formally recognized the Black American Studies Program, one of the earliest programs in the nation to be established at a predominantly white institution. Johnson's interest in a materialist social critique was intensified in 1970 by the time he spent as a discussion leader for a history course in the program. When Johnson was only a freshman (in 1966), the Free School at SIU was already offering courses in "Working Class History," "Race Economics," "Revolution," and "Education for Anarchy" (Keith 13). At the same time, Slaughter, Johnson's teacher and friend, was writing about Marxism for local alternative papers, the *Southern Free Press* and the more radical *Big Muddy Gazette*, to which Johnson contributed political cartoon. Speakers appearing on SIU's campus ranged from Jesse Jackson (who reportedly spoke from a "Marxist viewpoint"), Le Roi Jones, Howard Fuller, and Fred Hampton (Keith 29). Bill Moffet, a black member of the Young Socialist Alliance, was a leading campus activist. In the philosophy department, Doug Allen (later to lose his position for his protest activities) and Garth Gillan (Johnson's master's thesis adviser) would eventually offer courses on Marxism. From visiting speakers, to a Black Panther presence on campus, to the increasing radical-ization of the local Students for a Democratic Society, to the newly formed Black American Studies program, to philosophy courses in Marxism, SIU provided a surprisingly varied exposure to Marxist thought for what one might mistakenly assume to be a sleepy midwestern campus (Keith 90).[4]

By Johnson's own account, Marxism was his "passion and political orien-tation throughout graduate school" at SIU ("I Call" 23). He first encoun-tered Marxism in the late sixties through "black nationalist and cultural nationalist books." His intellectual interest in Marxism was intensified by his own economic situation during the period: as Johnson recalls, "I found myself broke and I wanted to know why; in other words, my interest in eco-nomics and its relationship to Everything became personal."[5] During this period Johnson immersed himself privately in Marxist thought, including, as he recounts, "every text by Marx and Engels" that he could find.[6] Later, as a graduate student, he sat in on the first day of Garth Gillan's course in Marxism but stopped going when he heard the professor say that there was "no separate black culture" and that "black culture was simply derived from American culture in general," which, Johnson says, "struck me as wrong."[7] Johnson was also exposed in college to forms of black activism that relied to some degree on Marxist analysis. In the spring of 1969 he attended a read-ing by Amiri Baraka (then LeRoi Jones) ("I Call" 19). Inspired by Baraka, Johnson cut class to complete his first book of cartoons, *Black Humor* (1970), focused on African American history and culture (see figure 2). By the spring of 1970, after the U.S. action in Cambodia, the cartoons he regularly contributed to the *Daily Egyptian*, Southern Illinois's student newspaper, had become, Johnson asserts, "so archly political in their call for revolution" that the editor of the newspaper canceled a series of his panels ("I Call" 21). As a graduate student at SIU Johnson would eventually become interested in the various applications of Marxist thought to contemporary culture which had been formulated by the Frankfurt School in general and by Herbert Marcuse in particular—against the objections of his writing mentor, John Gardner. In 1972 he completed an independent studies course on the subject. The Frankfurt School provided Johnson with an important philosophical transition from Marxism to phenomenology, a transition anticipated, I sug-gest later in chapter 1, by the conclusion to *Faith*.

After he left Southern Illinois for Stony Brook in 1973 for a teaching assistantship in the Ph.D. program in philosophy, Johnson also taught Marx-ism—"everything from *The 1844 Manuscripts* to Mao"—in his own course, "Radical Thought" (Boccia 201). (Rather ironically, one of Johnson's stu-dents in that class was Richard Gelfond, who would become a wealthy New York lawyer, Stony Brook trustee, and co-owner of Imax, the big-screen company.) In 1975 he would name his son Malik, partly after El-Hajj Malik

El-Shabazz (Malcolm X). If after 1974 the trajectory of Johnson's philosophical interests would move away from Marxist philosophy toward phenomenology—and toward a deepening engagement with Buddhism—Johnson's early immersion in Marxism would have a significant impact on his fiction. Given Johnson's interest in Marxist philosophy at the time he was composing *Faith*—he completed his master's degree the year before the novel first appeared—it is surprising that his thesis has not attracted more critical attention and that his first novel has not yet been the subject of sustained analysis from the perspective of his engagement with Marxism.[8]

At the same time, it is important to remember that black students like Johnson who encountered Marx for the first time in the 1960s–1970s constitute only one part of a larger history of the dissemination of Marxist theory in the twentieth century and, in particular, of a broader effort to deepen Marxism's engagement with issues of ethnicity and race. From the beginning of the century, black reformers drew on Marx to provide social analysis and organizational structures that could be marshaled against the oppression of black Americans. From churchmen like the Reverend George Washington Woodbey and Bishop Reverdy Ransom (whose Christian Socialism anticipated in some ways Cornel West's position today), to the

2. *Cartoon by Charles Johnson, "There'll Never Be Another Minister of Defense Like Malik."*
From *Half-Past Nation Time*. Courtesy Charles Johnson.

class-inflected black nationalism of Hubert G. Harrison (whom Marable identifies as a forerunner to Malcolm X and Stokely Carmichael), to Cyril V. Briggs (who established the African Blood Brotherhood in 1917 and became the first important black leader in the Communist Party USA), to A. Philip Randolph (founder of the Brotherhood of Sleeping Car Porters in 1925 and co-editor, with Chandler Owen, of the socialist magazine *The Messenger*), black reformers were influenced by, responded to, and adapted Marxist thought in their efforts to analyze the social conditions of minorities and to devise strategies for combating oppression. In 1933 W. E. B. Du Bois taught at Atlanta University the first course on Marxism to be offered in an American university, "Marxism and the Negro." In March of the same year he issued a call for work applying the insights of Marx to the situation of black Americans in an editorial in *The Crisis*, "Karl Marx and the Negro." There he maintained, "It was a great loss to American Negroes that the great mind of Marx and his extraordinary insight into industrial conditions could not have been brought to bear at first hand upon the history of the American Negro" (399).

Du Bois's work was joined by that of other black scholars and writers, notably sociologist Oliver Cromwell Cox, whose *Caste, Class, and Race* appeared in 1948, and Caribbean author C. L. R. James, whose *Black Jacobins* (1938) would initiate the Marxist-inspired examination of the plight of colonized peoples that continued through the 1960s.[9] By mid-century several black writers were engaging Marxism in a different way, by dramatizing their own or their fictional counterparts' disenchantment with Marxism and the Communist Party. During a cold war period that led many people, black and white, to reassess the promise that Marxism seemed to offer for black liberation, writers such as Chester Himes in *The Lonely Crusade* (1947), Ralph Ellison in *Invisible Man* (1952), and lapsed Communist Party USA (CPUSA) member Richard Wright in *The Outsider* (1953) described a party that seemed more committed to using minorities as tools for furthering its own agendas than to advancing racial justice. Recently, work based on newly available archival material has challenged this cold war account of manipulation.[10]

Today Cornel West is widely recognized as the nation's leading black philosopher. Like other black intellectuals of his generation, including Johnson, he studied Marxism before developing his own philosophical positions. Although West criticizes Marx's "monocausal, unilinear philosophy of history," he argues that "Marxist theory as a methodological orientation remains indispensable—though ultimately inadequate—in grasping the distinct features of Black American oppression" ("Race" 258). In his landmark essay "The Dilemma of the Black Intellectual," West furthermore suggests that Marxism is a "brook of fire" that all black intellectuals must past through if their thought is to reach any level of complexity (119). In his master's thesis in philosophy and his novel *Faith and the Good Thing*, Johnson crosses that brook of fire, offering his own intellectual and creative responses to Marxist thought.

## Charles Johnson and Marxist Critique in the Late 1960s and 1970s

"We have a galaxy of different Marxisms," Paul Thomas has argued, "within which the place of Marx is ambiguous" (26). To bring order to the variety of schools of analysis influenced by Marx in the twentieth century, Marxist critique is sometimes divided into three broad categories: the classical school, the critical school, and the school of critical classicism (or antihumanism).[11] Although this classification simplifies the complex history of Marxism's diversification over the course of the twentieth century, it is useful in helping to situate Johnson's engagement with Marx in the years immediately preceding the publication of *Faith*. The term "classical" (or "orthodox" or "scientific") Marxism is commonly used to refer to a form of Marxism that originated in the nineteenth century. Positivist in approach, classical Marxism tends to emphasize the "laws" of historical materialism and a rigid model of economic determinism. In his master's thesis Johnson cites George V. Plekhanov—disapprovingly—as a leading representative of this school. As its name implies, critical Marxism—the branch of Marxism to which Johnson was most clearly aligned as a college student—was critical of the classical or orthodox school's positivist emphasis and uninflected models of economic causality, and attempted to develop a more flexible and complicated account of the relationship among economics, culture, and subjectivity than the one it found in the classical school. In France, another form of Marxism originated in the late 1960s and early 1970s—critical classicism—that critiqued the critical Marxist school itself for a perceived lack of scientific rigor. The leading figure of critical classicism, Louis Althusser, would advocate a "return" to a more scientific Marx.[12] In the late twentieth century, many critical classicists would follow Althusser's lead in abandoning the "problematic of the subject" and developing an "antihumanist" Marxist critique. But in 1966 it was critical Marxism that was widely taught in American departments of philosophy, and it is to critical Marxism that Johnson developed an early philosophical allegiance.

A popular collection of essays published in 1972, *The Unknown Dimension*, offers an illustration of the characteristic concerns of critical Marxism at the time when Johnson was reading Marx and drafting *Faith*. The title of the collection positions the analysis contained within as revealing a "hidden dimension" or "underground tradition" in Marxism—a tradition that orthodox scholars, with their emphasis on economic determinism, had allegedly obscured. In particular, this "underground tradition" rejects a classical Marxism that identifies Marx with "broadly sweeping and 'inevitable'" laws and is only "peripherally interested in culture, ethnic diversity, [and] spiritual life" (Dick and Klare 6–7). Finally, the collection identifies two goals of the critical tradition: first, to restore "human consciousness, human subjectivity to the heart of Marxism," and second, to use the concepts of "totality" and "concrete universal" to uncover the meanings revealed in each "concrete aspect of daily life about the nature of the social system as a whole" (7, 8, 9). As examples of social criticism important to critical Marxism, the collection cites Georg Lukács's work on reification, Wilhelm Reich's critique of sexuality, Antonio Gramsci's analysis of Italian social history, the cultural criticism of the Frankfurt School, Henri Lefebvre's analysis of urban and rural life, and work by Herbert Marcuse on "one-dimensionality" (6).

While the breadth of approaches included in this list suggests that the identification of a "hidden tradition" in Marx studies should be taken loosely, it is nevertheless the case that these approaches to Marxism were popular on American campuses at the time when Johnson was beginning to study Marx, and, more important, that they are reflected in Johnson's own rejection of more positivist, scientific readings of Marx in favor of critical Marxism's interest in "culture, ethnic diversity, and spiritual life." In his master's thesis, "Wilhelm Reich and the Creation of a Marxist Psychology," Johnson would distance himself from thinkers in the "more traditional Marxist circles," whom he thinks mistakenly believe that "the economic base is the first and final cause of ideology" (55). Instead, Johnson finds in Marx's own writings a more complicated analysis of the relationship between economic forces, ideology, and cultural production than that articulated by the classical Marxists. Citing Marx's claim from *The German Ideology* that "consciousness is a social product," Johnson argues that by this Marx meant not the "naïve realism of Lenin" but "the belief that men, through the ensemble of social practices which they find themselves in or create, receive both the form and content of their conscious life" ("Wilhelm Reich" 6, 7). Johnson's rejection of classical Marxism for subscribing to a rigid version of economic determinism informs his later criticisms of black nationalism, which he would similarly charge with holding one-dimensional attitudes toward race. Nevertheless, Johnson was fascinated by the possibility of using Marxist philosophy to investigate the economic and psychological circumstances of black Americans, as he demonstrates in works such as "Exchange Value," *Faith*, and *Middle Passage*, in which racial commodification and reification play important roles. Not surprisingly, his interest in a critical Marxist approach to subjectivity is both literally and figuratively at the center of his master's thesis, approximately one-fourth of which is devoted to what Johnson calls Marx's "theory of consciousness" ("Wilhelm Reich" 31).

## Johnson on Marx, Reich, and Freud: Desire as "Metabolic Interchange"

Like the critical Marxists who sought to "return subjectivity . . . to the heart of Marxism," Johnson brought to Marx an early—and what would prove to be an abiding—interest in "the relationship between mental processes and the world" ("Wilhelm Reich" 7). That interest clearly informs his thesis, which devotes separate chapters to psychoanalysis, to Marx's theory of consciousness, and to Reich's model of libidinal repression, all in an effort to evaluate Reich's attempt to combine insights from Marx and Freud in order to create a "Marxist psychology." Johnson's interest in Reich's project reveals that the young writer—like many other twentieth-century thinkers—was himself fascinated by the possibility of bringing together in a single comprehensive theory Marx's materialist analysis of the social and economic forces that shape subjectivity and Freud's psychological description of the inner drives that motivate the self. Of the three thinkers he considers in his thesis—Freud, Marx, and Reich—Johnson is clearly most sympathetic to Marx. Indeed, in the philosopher's description of subjectivity as emerging from an intimate "metabolic" interchange between subjects and the objects they desire, Johnson would first be introduced to an account of the self as dynamic, social, and potentially creative. Furthermore, Marx's account of metabolic desire is especially important because it provides the central trope for the development of subjectivity in *Faith*.

In a Marxist economy of desire, individuals are understood to have powers and needs that can be developed and satisfied only through their relationship to objects or others outside themselves. This orientation to the world and to others gives to Marx's account of subjectivity, as Johnson perceived, a certain dynamism and a nascent antiessentialism. Like other critical Marxists who also valorized Marx's early writings, Johnson suggests that Marx's "most thorough discussion of the relationship between mental processes and the world occurs in his so-called 'young' or 'early' period: *The 1844 Manuscripts*, the Feuerbach section of *The German Ideology*, and in portions of the *Poverty of Philosophy*" ("Wilhelm Reich" 7).[13] In *The 1844 Manuscripts*, Marx seeks to distinguish Hegel's analysis of the relation of self-consciousness to its objects from his own. Although he agrees with Hegel that subjects objectify or "express" themselves by appropriating objects and adapting them to fit their needs and desires, Marx criticizes the idealist philosopher for implying that human life is "equivalent to *self-consciousness*" (179). Instead,

Marx stresses that his own analysis focuses on the relation between "embodied, living, real" beings and their "essential objects" (182, 181). In his description of subjectivity as emerging from the dialectical and historically situated relationship between men and women and the objects of their desire, Marx offers, Johnson realized, a dynamic rather than static account of subjectivity, one in which, as Johnson points out, "some portion of what is human reality is an ongoing project fashioned by human activity itself" ("Wilhelm Reich" 34). Marx's account also points toward an antiessentialist understanding of the subject: if people appropriate objects through their labor, simultaneously fulfilling their needs and "express[ing] their being" (*1844* 182), then "human nature" is not an unchanging essence but a historical product, the result of specific relationships between conditioned beings and the world. In Marx's description of creative appropriation Johnson therefore found early in his philosophical studies an account of subjectivity as dialectical, changing, and self-creative.

Johnson also found in Marx the outlines of an alternative to philosophical dualism. While Marx frequently seems to adopt dualistic language in speaking of subjects and objects, he also clearly attempts to define each in terms of an unfolding relationship to the other. In order to capture the intimacy of this relationship, Marx sometimes describes subjects and their objects as sharing a single, living body: "To say that man *lives* from nature means that nature is his *body* with which he must remain in a continuous interchange in order not to die" (*1844* 101). The subject's appropriation of the object is therefore considered by Marx to be a life activity as natural as breathing: the action of "real corporeal man, inhaling and exhaling all the powers of nature" (181). In *Capital* Marx further describes the individual and nature as sharing a single "metabolism," and he defines labor as "a process through which, man . . . mediates and regulates . . . the metabolism between him and nature" (*CW* 1:283–84). It is precisely from this intimate and "continuous" interchange, Johnson suggests, that Marx understands subjectivity to emerge: "Marx, like Sartre and Whitehead, is opposed to viewing human nature as static; rather, labor alters the material conditions, thus changing both subject (man) and the object (nature). The contours of human consciousness emerge from this dynamic interchange through the available external materials to satisfy human needs, and labor" ("Wilhelm Reich" 34)

Contrary to the strict economic determinism that he criticizes in classical Marxism, then, Johnson found in Marx's own writings a description of an interchange between subjects and objects that appears neither uncomplicated nor one-dimensional. While Marx understands labor as a real, objective activity that results in products that have a real, objective existence outside the minds of those who produce them, Johnson understood that this dialectical account includes a subjective dimension: intentions and needs are expressed through labor; labor itself plays a part in reshaping subjectivity; and, finally, individuals are self-conscious and therefore able to reflect on their creative activity. In this "dialectically conceived relationship," Johnson argues, "the relationship between man and nature" is in fact not one-directional but "reciprocal" ("Wilhelm Reich" 55).

Marx's emphasis on subjects as sensual beings potentially related to their objects in a "manifold," *aesthetic* manner was also attractive to Johnson. Marx understands appropriation not simply as an alienation of consciousness (the view he attributes to Hegel) but as a natural life activity. He therefore argues that subjects are affirmed or expressed in their objects not only through their self-consciousness or intelligence but—an important point— through all their senses: "Man appropriates his manifold being in an all-inclusive way, and thus as a whole man. All his *human* relations to the world—seeing, hearing, smelling, tasting, touching, thinking, observing, feeling, desiring, acting, loving—in short all the organs of his individuality . . . are . . . the appropriation of this object, the appropriation of human reality" (*1844* 131). Opposed to one-dimensional accounts of subjectivity, Johnson found in Marx a description of an aesthetic subjectivity that was potentially capable of appropriating its "manifold being" in an "all-inclusive way." In the *Manuscripts* Marx famously contrasts this subject to the individual under capitalism, who relates to his or her objects in a "one-sided" manner and in whom "*all* the physical and intellectual senses have been replaced by the simple alienation of *all* these senses; the sense of *having*" (132). By describing the transformation of a rich, multifaceted desire into the narrow articulations of capital, Marx's account of the crippling transformations to which subjectivity is liable provided Johnson with a powerful tool for social critique and fueled his evolving interest in the relationship between "being and having."[14]

By suggesting that subjects are related to their objects aesthetically, Marx's analysis also provided Johnson with an early rationale for a belief in the potential for an "aesthetic education" of the self.[15] As natural beings, Marx argues, subjects have desires and certain powers to fulfill them, but these needs and powers become truly "human" only by being transformed through a process of education. As people adapt nature to desires, they change nature, creating "human objects" and a "humanized nature" that have been altered by human activity. Simultaneously, as they "exercise" themselves through their activity, subjects develop truly "human" powers. In other words, Marx argues, human reality, in the sense of being adequate to all the *potential* "wealth of the human and natural being", is not simply given but must be achieved: "It is only through the objectively deployed wealth of the human being that the wealth of subjective *human* sensibility (a musical ear, an eye which is sensitive to the beauty of form, in short, senses which are capable of human satisfaction and which confirm themselves as human faculties) is

cultivated or created" (134). This process of cultivating the subject's sensibil-
ities and desires is not one that is guaranteed developmentally; it must be
produced historically through labor and education.[16] Marx's understanding
of the importance of an aesthetic education, of its social character, and of
the effort required to master cultural forms had a lasting influence on Johnson's thinking, one that is reflected in his statement that cultural inheritance
is never simply a "given" but must be earned ("Second" 182).

An intersubjective understanding of the self is one of the most characteristic elements of Johnson's fiction, one important to the positions he takes
against both philosophical essentialism and cultural nationalism. Critics tend
to ground Johnson's interest in intersubjectivity in his study of phenomenology. But in fact it was Johnson's early encounter with Marx that first provided the young writer with a systematic model of a social understanding of
the self. To Marx, it is not just the material conditions necessary for life that
are produced socially but the particular determinations of subjectivity itself:
"Man is a *zoon politikon* in the most literal sense: he is not only a social
animal, but an animal which can isolate himself only within a society" ("Economic Manuscripts, 1857–8," in *CW* 28:18). Johnson quotes Marx's somewhat paradoxical position that the subject can "individualize himself only
within a society" ("Wilhelm Reich" 40). Elsewhere Marx identifies production as an activity akin to language use that can only develop socially: "Production by an isolated individual outside of society . . . is just as preposterous
as the development of language without individuals who live *together* and
speak to one another" ("Economic Manuscripts, 1857–8," in *CW* 28:18).
Like Marx, Johnson finds in language a potent argument for a social understanding of the self, and the trope he turns to most commonly in order to
illustrate the bonds of intersubjectivity is the production of a single page of
text—a page that, as Johnson elaborates, can be written by "an American,"
but is "made of paper invented by the Chinese and printed with ink evolved
out of India and from type developed by Germans using Roman symbols
modified by the Greeks who got their letter concepts from Phoenicians who
had adapted them partly from Egyptian hieroglyphs" ("Whole" 19).[17]

In the Marxist economy of desire, then, Johnson found a compelling and
systematic account of a social subject who is dynamically related to her objects, energized by a rich, multifaceted desire, and capable of increasing her
powers and satisfactions through the aesthetic education that results from
her own historically situated labor. Significantly, Marx's description of the
material and social cultivation of subjectivity provided Johnson in the late
1960s and early 1970s with an account of personal change not reducible
either to a Hegelian progression of stages in self-consciousness or to the
classical Marxist's unproblematic march of economic determinism. If, on the
one hand, Marx argues that "it is not consciousness that determines social

existence but social existence that determines consciousness," on the other hand Marx's dialectical analysis of creative labor suggests that, as Johnson summarizes, "some portion of what is human reality is an ongoing project fashioned by human activity itself" ("Wilhelm Reich" 34). As subjects appropriate objects and create products, their subjectivities are also produced through their own activity and the existing material, social, and economic conditions in which they labor. As they alter those conditions, subjects are also changed materially, intellectually, and spiritually. Or as Johnson notes in his master's thesis: "Society, for Marx, is the accomplishment of the union of man and nature. It is also this: the creator of human character" (40).

## Character Analysis: Charles Johnson and Wilhelm Reich

In Marx, Johnson found a description of subjectivity as both producer and produced, and much of his early fiction, notably *Faith*, explores the various opportunities and complications for human agency that the dialectical production of subjectivity creates. The attractions that Marx's economy of desire held for Johnson become even more apparent when Marx's analysis of the productive interchange between subjects and their objects is contrasted to Wilhelm Reich's libidinal economy of desire. Building on Marx's suggestion that subjects and objects participate in a "metabolic interchange," Reich takes as his task an analysis of the specific mechanisms that might regulate such a process. He concludes that subjectivity—or in his own terms "character structure"—is created out of the psychic and social regulation of specifically *libidinal* energy.

A psychiatrist who worked with Freud from 1922 to 1929 in the Psychological Dispensary in Vienna and an avowed Marxist from 1927 through the early thirties, Wilhelm Reich attempted to create a Marxist psychology.[18] This effort led to the formulation of his theory of "sex economy" or "sexual politics," based on the assumption that all neuroses can ultimately be traced to the damming up of libidinal energy by repressive social forces. Reich's activism in sexual politics led to his expulsion from the Communist Party in 1933 and to his exclusion from the International Psychological Association in 1934. In 1939 Reich immigrated to the United States, where his publications on sexuality and his promotion of eccentric "orgone" therapies and products led in the mid-1950s to his being investigated for racketeering and fraud. Although Reich died in Lewisburg Federal Penitentiary in 1957, his theory of sex economy was revived during the late 1960s and early 1970s; and more recently, his analysis of desire has become important to theorists through the dissemination of the work of Gilles Deleuze and Félix Guattari.

In his master's thesis Johnson reads Reich against both Marx and Freud. From Marx, Johnson suggests, Reich took the idea that there is an intimate relationship between subjects and their social and material conditions. During his early years in clinical practice, Johnson points out, Reich was struck by the fact that patients were seldom asked about their social conditions, even though these were sometimes quite desperate. As Reich reflects: "That there were poverty and need, one knew; but somehow that did not seem to be relevant. In the clinic, however, one was constantly confronted by these factors. Often enough, social help was the first thing necessary" (quoted in "Wilhelm Reich" 5).[19] Reich's frustration at the lack of concern for such facts in the traditional clinical setting and at the failure of psychoanalysis to achieve a cure in many of his patients led him to consider the role that social conditions might play in their illnesses. In particular, he sought to create a Marxist psychology capable of describing "the means and mechanisms by way of which social experience is transformed into psychic structure, and with that, into ideology" (quoted in "Wilhelm Reich" 9).

From Freud, Johnson suggests, Reich took — and later expanded on — the idea that sexual excitement is the result of a quantifiable neurophysiological energy. Johnson points out that Freud's later model of id, ego, and superego had its antecedent in the physiological concept of the "neurone," understood by Freud to be a structure that could be empty, or filled with a quantifiable amount of energy to be "cathected," or discharged ("Wilhelm Reich" 12). Building on Freud's idea that there is a quantifiable amount of energy in what he frequently refers to as the "biosystem," Reich attempts to account for subjectivity by analyzing the economy — or the regulation and release — of libidinal energy. In what may have been a bizarre development of Freud's concept of the neurone, Reich would later come to believe that he had identified the physical source of libidinal energy in the "orgone," related to respiration: "In each of the cells the living organism is composed of, it contains orgone energy, and through breathing, increasingly recharges itself, orgonotically, from the atmosphere" (*Function* 328–31). In his "orgasm formula," Reich sought to summarize the mechanisms for the regulation of libidinal energy in the life rhythm of tension, charge, discharge, and relaxation. If built-up energy is not discharged through orgasm, Reich argues, that energy is available to power neuroses. In a Reichean economy of desire, therefore, healthy respiration and orgasmic potency contribute to the development of character.

Like Marx, Reich attempts to specify an interchange between subjects and the objects of their desire. In Reich's case, however, character is understood to be formed primarily through sexual repression. When libidinal needs are frustrated by the outer world, Reich reasons, individuals erect a sort of armor to protect the ego from further disappointments and pain. As subjects attempt to negotiate what Reich calls the basic "struggle" between need and world (*Character* 159), specific personalities or "characters" develop. Reich describes this process as the "armoring" of the ego, and he conceives of it as involving—in addition to a psychic component—a physical rigidity in the body (due in part to orgone buildup) that can be detected in such physical signs as a characteristic stance or facial expression. In other words, Reich believed that repressed libidinal energy reshapes the body as well as fueling neuroses, or in other words, that there is a somatic as well as a psychic element to neuroses. As I will suggest, Reich's analysis of the physical effects of repression would in fact shape Johnson's description of certain characters in *Faith*, including Arnold T. Tippis, Isaac Maxwell, and Faith Cross herself.

Because character structure is understood by Reich to evolve out of an exchange between need and outer world; and since others serve both as objects of libidinal desire and as agents for its repression, Reich, like Marx, understands subjectivity as *social* in nature. But both Reich and Freud, Johnson ultimately concludes, posit determinisms so narrowly conceived that they leave little space for productive subjectivity. Although Reich at times escapes the biological determinism that Johnson detects in Freud—for example, Johnson notes that Reich conceives of the Oedipal complex in historical terms as a configuration based on the patriarchal family rather than in Freudian terms as a universal structure—he criticizes Reich for arguing (along Freudian lines) that basic human drives have been determined by their evolution from lower organic and even inorganic stages. Johnson further argues that Reich's strange analysis of the physical nature of cosmic orgone energy binds him to a functionalist understanding of desire and to a mechanistic theory of its regulation. Johnson concludes that Reich's account of subjectivity and desire is *more* deterministic than either Freud's or Marx's.

Significantly, Johnson's thesis also considers Marxist and Reichian descriptions of subjectivity in relation to questions of social practice. In spite of his judgment that Reich fails in his attempt to create a Marxist psychology, Johnson finds Reich's commitment to social praxis attractive, and he contrasts it favorably to Freud's program of individual psychoanalysis. Johnson is not in agreement, however, with the specific form that Reich's social activism takes. For Reich, the patriarchal family is the primary means through which repressive ideology is enforced. Social praxis thus takes the form of sexual politics; for example, Reich advocates for the abolition of marriage as a requirement for the development of genital primacy. Arguing that Reich's theory of genital primacy itself should be historicized, Johnson suggests instead that social reform may require the reshaping—but not the abandonment—of the family. Drawing on Marx's warning to nineteenth-century workers not to destroy the machines in factories but instead to appropriate them to their own needs, Johnson suggests that "the family, with its patriarchal emphasis eliminated, might also be a desirable social unit, in contrast to either commune or collective" ("Wilhelm Reich" 60). Although he is critical of the family in its present form and even willing to entertain the possibility that "the essential structure of the family is related to social oppression"—just as the structure of some machines embodies "their ideological or economic purpose" (as in cases of planned obsolescence)—Johnson concludes that the "so-called 'bourgeois' family structure, comparatively, is still the best for child rearing" (59). Johnson's early defense of the family over the collective or commune anticipates Andrew Hawkins's upholding of "householder" values in *Oxherding Tale*, Rutherford Calhoun's "submission" to marriage at the end of *Middle Passage*, and Matthew Bishop's marriage as a sign of personal and political maturity at the end of *Dreamer*.

But if Johnson questions Reich's agenda for the family, he is also critical of the type of social reform advocated by Marx: class struggle. Here Johnson's criticism largely follows Marcusean lines: first, he suggests, Marx's analysis of class no longer reflects the state of current economic and social relations because changes in the relationship of management and labor during the postwar period have led to a weakening in the revolutionary potential of the working class; second, Johnson argues, in contemporary society the technologies of social engineering have grown to such an extent that they alter the very nature of repressive forces and complicate the opportunities for effective resistance. As Johnson asserts, "Technology offers the possibility of the manipulation of consciousness such that 'class struggle' becomes an archaic term" ("Wilhelm Reich" 57). Thus if Johnson would say in 1996 that he "still believes the Marxist critique of capital" although he "no longer much believe[s] in Marxist solutions to social and economic problems" (Boccia 201), his master's thesis makes clear just how many years earlier he was already suspicious of class struggle as an effective means of social reform.

Johnson's thesis concludes with a brief (and rather hasty) consideration of the possibilities for personal and social reformation centered on art and education.[20] Johnson speculates, "It may seem peculiar to think of art and scholarship as revolutionary, but what Marcuse calls the 'estrangement effect' of the former and the historical dedication to 'truth' of the latter, are, I think, essential conditions for an 'informed' public, the precondition of a democracy" (62). Although Johnson raises this point only in conclusion and does not develop it methodically, his analysis points to the path that he would follow in his doctoral dissertation in philosophy (revised and published as *Being and Race* in 1988), which considers in more detail the possibility that art may provide an estrangement effect capable of facilitating a critical perspective on the status quo, and in his fiction, which frequently explores the possibility that the practice of art may provide an aesthetic education capable of cultivating a creative subjectivity—just as storytelling does for Big Todd in *Faith*, carving develops for Reb in *Oxherding Tale*, writing accomplishes for Rutherford Calhoun in *Middle Passage*, and painting achieves for Chaym

Smith in *Dreamer*. Johnson's analysis of the three thinkers and the conclusion of his thesis together suggest that the young writer and thinker was partially motivated by his own desire to find a systematic account of subjectivity that would provide him with a philosophical rationale for a personal commitment to art and to higher education.

Significantly, Johnson's criticisms of Freud, Reich, and classical Marxism often center specifically on what he judges to be their reductive theories of artistic creation. For example, he criticizes Freud for attempting to reduce all "psychic phenomena"—even the art of Michelangelo—to an expression of biological determinism ("Wilhelm Reich" 56). Similarly, he condemns classical Marxism for adopting an economic reductionism so complete that it must maintain that "such things as decorative art, the origins of poetry and even Descartes' phenomenology are reducible . . . to technological causes" (55). Finding this view "unacceptable," Johnson returns to Marx to salvage a space for a productive subjectivity that is not precluded by the hyperdeterminism he finds characteristic of the other accounts: as he argues, "considerable research indicates that, as Marx emphasized, the relationship between consciousness and nature is reciprocal" (56). In Marx's dialectical analysis of desire, then, Johnson found a conception of subjectivity that seemed to account for the social and material determination of the self, while reserving a space for productive agency, the aesthetic education of individuals, and, finally, the potentially liberating function of art.

"Wilhelm Reich and the Creation of a Marxist Psychology" is important to critics of Johnson's fiction, then, for several reasons. First, it helps to situate Johnson's early study of Marx in the discourse of critical Marxism that was disseminated in American universities in the late 1960s and early 1970s. Indeed, Johnson's analysis suggests that the young student and apprentice writer never appreciated Marx as the classical Marxists did: as the major proponent of economic materialism. Instead he was drawn to Marx primarily (if not exclusively) as the leading theorist of a productive subjectivity. Johnson's thesis thus helps to identify the specific nature of the ambivalence that some critics have detected in the young writer's attitudes toward Marx. That ambivalence is explained by the fact that Johnson simultaneously rejects certain tenets of *classical* Marxism while he endorses *critical* Marxism. Second, Johnson's study of Marx, Freud, and Reich sheds light on the origins of several important features of the writer's philosophical orientation, for in Marx's dialectical account of the dynamic interchange between subjects and the objects of their desire, Johnson was first introduced to a systematic understanding of subjectivity as dynamic, social, and potentially creative. Third, in Marx's analysis of the "manifold," aesthetic manner in which subjects appropriate the objects of their desire, Johnson found a philosophical rationale for a belief in the development of a rich, multifaceted subjectivity that stands against a narrow one-dimensionality. Fourth, Johnson's thesis deepens critical understanding of the development of several of Johnson's political positions. In particular, Johnson's criticism of classical Marxism (for promoting an uncomplicated version of social causality) informs his similar criticisms of black nationalism, and his early questioning of Reichean sexual politics and Marxist class struggle as effective means of social remediation are important precursors to his turn to a more idealistic form of social reform in *Dreamer*. Fifth, Johnson's thesis provides an indispensable philosophical framework for his first novel, *Faith*, for there a Marxist economy of desire proves crucial to understanding Lavidia's mysterious breathing condition and, ultimately, the nature of the good thing that Faith seeks.

## *Diagnosing Lavidia: Metabolic Desire in* Faith and the Good Thing

*Faith and the Good Thing* narrates the story of Faith Cross, who, after the deaths of her parents, sets out north from Hatten County, Georgia, to fulfill her dying mother, Lavidia's, directive that she find herself "a good thing." Because it retraces the trajectory of nineteenth-century escaped slaves who followed the North Star in search of freedom and that of early-twentieth-century southern laborers who poured into northern cities in search of new opportunities during the Great Migration, Faith's journey resonates with the historical weight of the aspirations and, all too often, the disappointments of the actual black men and women who traveled north in search of their own "good things."[21] Faith's journey also follows the path of Johnson's maternal ancestors, who set out from rural Georgia to settle in Chicago. Drawing primarily on Marx, but also on Reich, Freud, Marcuse, and a host of other thinkers who haunt this philosophical and highly allegorical tale, Johnson uses Faith's search for the good thing to critique a capitalist economy of desire in which the sensual, aesthetic, and ethical possibilities of life have become distorted through the complex articulations of commodity relations. By appropriating elements from the *Bildungsroman* and the Western philosophical tradition, and by fusing both with African American literary forms — the folktale, slave narrative, and urban gothic novel — Johnson creates in *Faith* his own distinctively syncretic "portrait of the artist" and tribute to the subversive power of fiction.

Johnson's narrative begins with the worsening of Lavidia's mysterious breathing condition twelve years after the tragic death of Faith's father, Big Todd, at the hands of southern racists. Lavidia's careful policing of her own respiration and her fearful warnings to her daughter that "you'll live longer if you hold your breath" stand in direct contrast to Marx's description of vigorous subjects "inhaling and exhaling all the powers of nature" as they actively shape the world to fit their needs in a "metabolic exchange." Lavidia's breathing difficulties are in fact symptomatic of her failing personal health and of a larger social disorder. Drawing on Marx's metabolic figure for a healthy economy of desire and on Reich's identification of troubled respiration as the primary symptom of a disordered psyche, Johnson employs the dominant narrative trope of repressed respiration throughout his novel to signal a systematic disturbance in the healthy relationship between desiring subjects and their world.

The specific etiology of Lavidia's breathing problems underscores the cultural significance of her condition. Two events in the first part of the novel are especially important in shaping her unusual respiratory habits: Lavidia's attendance at a revival meeting with Faith shortly after Big Todd's death and her meeting approximately six months afterwards with a local physician, Dr. Lynch. These two meetings not only help to identify the onset and significance of Lavidia's breathing troubles but also expose Lavidia and her daughter to two very different "philosophies"—one Christian and idealist, the other scientific and materialist. Both philosophies contribute to the formation of Lavidia's strange respiratory troubles by leading her to reject what Marx perceives as an organic, qualitative unity of desire in favor of a principle of rationalization based solely on what is and can be calculated.

Lavidia is first stricken at a revival meeting she is urged to attend by her minister, Reverend Brown, shortly after the lynching of Faith's father. A strange mix of African American religious traditions, Puritan homiletics, and philosophical reflections on the nature of evil, the revival is led by the Reverend Alexander Magnus. Named after Albertus Magnus, the famous medieval philosopher, churchman, alchemist, and purported magician, Magnus is described as a "spirit man" with fingers "like claws," whose sermons cause people to "catch their breaths and hold them for what seemed like an hour" (9). Magnus's sermon, which is designed to convince his audience that earthly life is contemptible, is structured as a quasi-philosophical catalogue of the classes of evil in the world: natural evil, "the fury of storms, floods, droughts"; moral evil, "poisoned food, senseless slaughter"; civil evil, "revolutions"; and the form of evil most philosophically challenging to the belief that the world that is fundamentally good, the suffering of innocents ("witness crib death and the diseases of childhood" [10]). The thrust of Magnus's sermon—that one should hate life and love God—is in fact a warning about the danger of desire, summarized by his admonition to the congregation, "Woe unto you who would dare to love this world" (11).

Although in his fourth novel, *Dreamer*, Johnson would treat African American religious traditions and practices positively, he is clearly critical of the effects of Magnus's brand of religion on his congregation. Under Magnus's influence, the parishioners are disturbingly transformed. Faith's

unusually named future lover, Alpha Omega Holmes, is altered until he is
"almost unrecognizable" (9). The description of others is equally disquieting,
from the "cripple" who plays on an "off-key accordion" to the old woman
who begins to dance a "mad" cakewalk, "the way a snake writhed or maybe
like something dead but newly risen — like something that had no business
dancing at all" (9, 10). Not surprisingly, when Reverend Brown urges Faith
to participate in the service, she finds herself unable to speak or even to
"inhale" because the air around her seems "swirling, thick and weighted with
invisible things" (11). With the very air swarming with the illusory creatures
that Magnus's sermon has conjured up, both Lavidia and Faith find that their
breathing is compromised.

The revival's imagery of repressed respiration recalls Johnson's analysis
of Reich, who argues that because respiration is the primary means of charging the body with energy, "the inhibiting of inspiration [is] the physiological
mechanism of the suppression of emotion, and consequently, the basic mechanism of neurosis in general" (*Function* 308–9). Repressing the healthy
breathing of his congregation, Magnus seeks to inhibit their desire by defining it as sin. He tells the congregation: "You are damned for delighting in this
world. Your tongues savor fatback and burgoo, your flesh hungers for other
flesh. . . . Worms will be your supper soon" (9). By defining desiring subjects
and their relation to the world as evil, Magnus, in opposition to Marx, promotes a vision of the good that is based on the cultivation of ascetic subjects
and their relation to an immaterial object. Furthermore, by arguing that "all
that is given to man . . . is stolen from God" (10), Magnus inverts Marx's argument that the more power man attributes to God, the less he has left in
himself. Drawing on both Marx's and Reich's respiratory tropes, Johnson
uses the breathing problems experienced by the congregation as a sign of the
estrangement of their desire. Ironically, the revival service functions as a
ritual of alienation rather than one of communion.

And it is doubt rather than belief that the revival fosters in Faith, disturbing both her sense of self and her cherished memories of her relationship
with her father. In particular, the revival augments other attempts to explain
away the horror of Big Todd's death by placing it within a Christian economy of sin and retribution. Some six months earlier the loss of her father at
the hands of white racists had been made even more traumatic when Faith
came upon his body hanging from a pine tree. Because of the terrifying
manner in which he died and because her own loving memories of her father
are in conflict with the opinions she hears voiced by others, Todd's death
assumes the status of a painful mystery for Faith. Others are quick to blame
Todd himself for being lynched at the hands of three white men. Even
Lavidia tells Faith that Todd had "sneezed his soul away" and that his death
was "just" (8). At the moment Faith finally joins in the revival meeting, she

too assents to an interpretation of Todd's death in terms of an economy of sin and punishment, now understanding "her father's swinging feet as retribution for his terrible pride and passions" (11). Magnus's sermon thus provides Faith with an interpretation of history that unsettles the sense of self she developed through her personal interactions with her father until she can "no longer be certain of the images of herself that shone in her father's eyes" (12).

Lavidia's breathing, incapacitated at the revival, grows worse after her subsequent meeting with the town physician, Dr. Lynch. A "man of science" rather than a man of the cloth, he diagnoses her problems in strictly materialist terms (33). Thus when Lavidia asks the doctor how "she *really* was," he takes the question as an opportunity to lecture her about evolutionary origins, beginning with the big bang, moving through the organization of inorganic matter, and leading to the creation of organic life—the creation not of man but of "*slime*" (35, 37). When Lavidia questions him further—"Why do you live?"—Lynch clarifies his philosophical position: "To function. To keep breathing when you know your breaths are numbered, and that the circuit will break to return you to stone" (39).

Through Lynch's functionalism, Johnson critiques the biological determinism he detects in positions like those of both Freud and Reich, wherein subjectivity and psychology are, as Johnson puts it, ultimately "governed by chemico-physical laws" ("Wilhelm Reich" 11). In his master's thesis Johnson considers Freud's argument that there is an inorganic, evolutionary origin to life and his promotion of "a death instinct arising from the possible inability of organic life to maintain itself for long durations of time" (15–16). Similarly, in Lynch's evolutionary scheme, inorganic matter comes together to create organic life, but it cannot sustain that life indefinitely: the "weakening of the syncopated cells" and the "death of the organism" inevitably follow (*Faith* 37). Lynch also echoes Reich, and his long lecture to Lavidia on the importance of respiration in providing energy to the body recalls Reich's belief in the importance of respiration in giving the body the energy it needs to keep functioning. Most important, Lynch reduces the subject to a Reichean economy based on the rhythms of tension and discharge: "That's what you *are*, no more than a complicated plexus of cells through which energy travels like an electrical current. . . . Tension and release, Mrs. Cross, nothing—absolutely nothing beyond that can be called real" (39). Dr. Lynch's model of tension and release becomes a narrative trope for a mechanistic understanding of the subject, an understanding that leads Lynch to locate the good in physiological release: "Discharge was what was good. Release" (40). Lynch's prescription for the good life therefore substitutes mechanics for ethics. He concludes, "The best I can do is keep living, unloading my day's energy, *élan vital*, essential juices, the best I can" (39).

Although Lynch advises Lavidia on the importance of respiration, it is clear that his own health is compromised. Lynch smokes a pipe from which he takes "painfully controlled breaths" (36), and the physician's own ill health—as Lynch admits, "I can't heal myself"—casts doubt on his ability to heal Lavidia (39). As with Magnus's narrative of sin and retribution, Lynch's diagnosis of Lavidia's condition provides Faith with an interpretative heuristic through which she rereads the terrifying circumstances of her father's death. Under the sway of Lynch's materialist diagnosis, Faith comes to a new understanding of his demise: "Todd was dead; that was that. Dead, slain by the hands of three men, each of whom probably unloaded a large quantity of his tension, his vital juices in Todd's execution. Dead. Returned to stone or slime" (46). If in Magnus's Christian economy the wealth of the subject is rejected in favor of an asceticism believed to lead to future joy, in Lynch's materialist and functionalist economy that wealth is reduced by physical processes to mere "stone or slime."

The ideologies of both Magnus and Lynch, Johnson suggests, impede a healthy economy of desire. This disruption is perhaps more apparent with Magnus, who advocates an ascetic rather than an aesthetic subjectivity and whose economy of sin and retribution explicitly defines the things of the world as evil. But Lynch's libidinal economy should also be seen as a rejection of the aesthetic subject. Marx's analysis stresses the potentially "manifold" way in which subjects appropriate their objects. In Lynch's libidinal economy, however, subjects have a one-sided relationship to the object. In the final analysis they are understood to function merely as a conduit for electrical energy: "That's what you *are*, no more than that complicated plexus of cells through which energy travels like an electrical current" (39). Within Lynch's (and Reich's) economy of tension and release, spiritual strivings and artistic accomplishments alike lose their specificity as they come to be valued only as *means* for unloading tension: "The pitiful struggle of Jesus with his flesh—what was that but tension and release? Michelangelo's *Pieta*, van Gogh's *Starry Night*, Bach's *Sinfonia to Cantata No. 29*, or Dante's *Divine Comedy*? Nothing but novel ways to unload tension. . . . That's your meaning of life—bigger and better means to detumescence" (39).

Through Lynch, Johnson critiques the view that creative activity can be understood solely in terms of physiological processes. Lynch's attitudes toward art reflect those of Freud that Johnson criticizes in his master's thesis and signify, perhaps, on Freud's "Three Essays on Sexuality," wherein Freud maintains, "There is to my mind no doubt that the concept of 'beautiful' has its roots in sexual excitation and that its original meaning was 'sexually stimulating'" (7:156). Lynch's theory of libidinal economy attenuates the erotic relationship between desiring subject and desired object by reducing both the variety of associations and the range of senses that lead to satisfaction.

Thus the polymorphous sensuality of Marx's "rich human being" is replaced by a narrow focus on the genital gratification of the mechanical subject. Not surprisingly, Dr. Lynch's exegesis is not even satisfying to himself, and his admission that "the truth isn't beautiful, and it doesn't make me feel good" (39) serves as a final indictment of a theory that leaves little room for aesthetic satisfactions.

Lavidia's encounters with Magnus and Lynch explain both the onset and the culmination of her unusual respiratory condition. From Lynch she takes "the reference to breathing," which Lavidia fuses with Magnus's analysis of God's omnipotence to create her own unusual brand of theo-physiological determinism: "I've almost took four hundred million breaths; it's God's will. Everybody's got a certain number to draw 'fore they die. That's His way" (40). Accepting portions of both Magnus's and Lynch's discourses on desire and spending the final portion of her life's energies in the self-absorbed, quantitative process of counting her own inhalations, Lavidia expires upon taking her four hundred–millionth breath, just as she herself has predicted, the apparent victim of her own rejection of a qualitative economy of desire in favor of a quantitative rationalization based on what is and can be calculated.

## *"The Good Thing": Desire and Aesthetic Education*

The philosophies of both Magnus and Lynch disrupt the qualitative relationship between subjects and world—the relationship that Marx identifies as the source of value. They are not successful in repressing Faith's own desire permanently, however, for the young girl soon finds herself visited by a "hunger unsatisfied by further prayer meetings" (12). Drawing on Marx's figure of a shared metabolism, the narrative dramatizes a more expansive understanding of desire than that found in the philosophies of either Magnus or Lynch, as Faith becomes aware of the need for a more "complete freedom" that takes in "breaths beneath her own, move[s] with her limbs. Demand[s] its rights" (12). This alternative understanding of desire is further articulated in the first section of the novel through Faith's relationships to nature, to Alpha Omega Homes, and—especially—to her father, Big Todd.

Unlike Magnus's ascetic subject, Faith as a young girl delights in the sensual pleasures offered by the world, luxuriating, for example, in the "sudden rush of rippling warmth through her skin whenever she st[ands] on the highest hillslopes of Hatten County" (40). By figuring a natural world that "languishe[s]" when she herself is "sad," Faith grasps her relationship to nature in terms of a shared metabolism (41). Unlike Lynch, she posits a correspondence between her capacity for appreciation and the qualities the world has to offer—a correspondence that is one condition for gratification. These moments of girlish intimacy with nature inform Faith's later awakenings of desire, which come to her like "a lover or a lecher," but are figured in terms of nature's sensual attractions: "stealing through her bedroom window like the scent of night-blooming flowers or the whispering rustle of wind in the trees" (12). If Lynch and Magnus fail to convert Faith to their "philosophies" as they do Lavidia, that failure is in part attributable to the fact that Faith's intimations of what the good thing might be are conditioned by the pleasure she has received through her polymorphous sensual enjoyment of the external world.

The pleasure Faith experiences in her relationship with nature also anticipates and informs those she enjoys during her early relationship with her first love, Alpha Omega Holmes. In contrast to the troubled breathing of the congregation at the revival and to Lavidia's self-absorbed respiration, Faith's rhythmic breathing during the "afternoons she spent spooning" with Alpha signals a healthy exchange between the two lovers and nature: they "lie in the tall grass, holding each other until their in and out breaths coincided, breathing as a single body" (13). By experiencing Alpha and nature "as a single body," Faith seems to undergo a transcendence of self, as she is "carried through the world as though she had wings" (13). Significantly, however, this feeling of transcendence does not carry Faith "toward Glory, never toward Glory," but only back to "earth, deep within its strange fabric" (13). Transcendental or ecstatic moments like this one are important to the design of several of Johnson's narratives. For example, in *Oxherding Tale*, Andrew experiences an unanticipated liberation through his previously dreaded confrontation with Soulcatcher, and in *Middle Passage*, Rutherford Calhoun achieves a heightened moment of awareness through his meeting with the mysterious Allmuseri god imprisoned in the slave ship's hold. It is therefore significant that in his first novel Johnson figures transcendence as something achieved not through a renunciation of pleasure (as these later works suggest) but through the subject's passionate relationship with an Other. In *Faith*, transcendence is understood not as an escape *from* the world but as an immersion in the world, as a living *beyond* oneself, ecstatically.

Opposed to those who attempt to convert Faith to an ascetic subjectivity, Big Todd is one of the novel's most persevering proponents of pleasure, and he explicitly attempts to provide his daughter with an aesthetic education. That Todd and Lavidia have sharp differences about what constitutes the good life is clear from the beginning of their relationship, when Todd, a down-and-out former circus rowdy, wanders into a "backwoods Baptist church" to see Lavidia singing in the choir (45). Attracted to Lavidia because she looks "exactly like his opposite," Todd pursues her, and finally persuades her to marry him by lying about being a wealthy "liniment salesman" who will take her north (45). While Lavidia enters their marriage dreaming of "butlers and ballets" and other perquisites of the well-to-do, Todd is convinced that more immediate pleasures will suffice: they will simply "eat well . . . their stomachs full. Their hearts full too" (46). Lavidia's meager life as a sharecropper's wife, however, leaves her embittered and vindictive—unable to enjoy the pleasures of life and unwilling to see others do so, either. Consequently, Faith is raised in a divided household. Her parents' differences over desire and gratification are made clear at mealtimes, when Todd offers Faith "fruits and sweetmeats . . . and encourag[es] discussions," while Lavidia eats "sliced beets and potatoes" and suggests that mealtime is not "appropriate for talking" (41).

The conflicting attitudes toward sensual pleasure and intimacy implied by her parents' attitudes toward food and conversation are encapsulated after Todd and Lavidia's deaths by the epitaphs carved on their respective headstones, which reiterate two opposed interpretations of desire. On Lavidia's is written, "She Was Given 400,000,000/Breaths and Took Them All" (32); on Todd's, "*Carpe diem, quam minimum credula postero*," or "Seize the day with little thought about the future" (40). Lavidia's headstone reflects a quantitative understanding of appropriation, as her focus in life had been on how *many* breaths she had been allotted. Big Todd's, by contrast, emphasizes sensual enjoyment over abstract accounting. His inscription stresses the qualitative experiences of the moment. Unlike George Hawkins in *Oxherding Tale*, Big Todd is not suspicious of pleasure; his epitaph acts as a directive to those still living to embrace the pleasures life has to offer.

Because they enable a nurturing intersubjectivity, develop an expansive conception of desire, and offer a model of productive agency, the "metaphysical yarns" Big Todd shares with his daughter serve several important purposes in the narrative. First, through the time he spends creating fabulous tales for his daughter, Todd nurtures her deeply. Among Faith's chief pleasures as a child is taking long walks with Big Todd, during which she urges him to "tell me another mile" (43).[22] The pleasure Todd takes in spinning his yarns and the pleasure Faith takes in listening to them create a shared intimacy.[23] After his death, Faith finds in remembering those stories a vitality missing in her relationships with other adults, including Lavidia, who doesn't approve of discussions at mealtime; Lynch, who "doesn't like to be interrupted when he's speaking"; and Magnus, whose sermons have the effect of robbing listeners of their very breath. In times of duress, Faith uses her father's stories as she would a protective talisman, recalling them when she walks through a woods alone at night or, more significantly, to answer the disagreeable philosophies to which she is subjected. When Reverend Brown warns Faith that the world is simply a "shadowy cave full of crazy sounds if you've got nothing to light it up," Faith remembers her father's "stunning fictions and well-meant lies" and concludes, "I've heard different" (14). Against the judgment that the world is contemptible, then, Todd's tales stand as an endorsement of creation.

In contrast to Lavidia's renunciation of pleasure and Lynch's reduction of gratification to the libidinal, Todd's tales also develop an expansive conception of desire that is made especially clear in his treatment of sexuality. Extending her ascetic renunciation to the conjugal bed, Lavidia feigns sleep or illness to avoid sex. She also attempts to influence Faith's attitudes toward sexuality: "Love is perfect till somebody pulls back the bedcovers on you," she tells her daughter (42). Todd's anger at Lavidia's comment conveys his fear that she will pervert Faith's ability to take pleasure in her sexuality. To make his own views clear, he adapts a tale from Plato about the origin of the sexes: "Time was, he said, when all animals had no sex. Unsex, he called it, because they all had the same male and female equipment." Later, after a god split people into two sexes, they found that "living half-lives like that wasn't pleasant at all. Everything on earth — birds, beasts, grubworms, and especially men — were and still are incredibly lonesome, and suffer a lot until their lost halves are found" (42). Like Marx's metaphor of metabolic exchange, Todd's appropriation of Aristophanes' speech from the *Symposium* figures the intimacy of one's relationship to the Other through the metaphor of a shared body. Although Plato's myth has been criticized for embodying a nostalgic yearning for a fictitious lost holism, in the context of Johnson's novel the emphasis is more on future satisfactions — on finding one's other half or on the potential of life to provide for the fulfillment of human needs. In Lynch's libidinal economy, desire serves mechanical processes, and the Other serves merely as a *means* to physiological release; the doctor's theory thus is literally conservative, since sex serves to relieve tension and to reinstate stasis. Alternatively, Big Todd places libidinal desire in the service of an intimacy with the Other that satisfies a dynamic need for self-realization.

Somewhat surprisingly, Todd's storytelling also serves to exemplify the satisfactions of productive labor. According to Marx, it is through labor that subjects transform nature and develop their own potentialities, simultaneously creating a truly human subject and a humane object. Given his devil-may-care attitude, his unusual work history, and his emphasis on the pleasures of the moment, Big Todd may seem an unlikely exemplar of labor's transformative power. Indeed, before he and Lavidia marry, Todd's own account of his aspirations reflects his negative attitude toward work: he does not want "to be a salesman, or own butlers, or do anything other than amble around his farmyard each afternoon and feel loose dirt and green grass between his bare brown toes" (45). Nevertheless, by drawing on the African American folk tradition to create new stories for Faith, Big Todd also works on the world he has inherited and attempts to humanize it; he even, as Faith points out, gives names to "pots and pans" (16). While his position as a share-cropper means that his opportunities for a productive agency are limited, through his storytelling Big Todd assumes a creative relationship to the world; he feels "godlike when spinning metaphysical yarns" (42). Significantly, Todd links that feeling of empowerment to a similar one he experienced before becoming a sharecropper, when he ran away from home to work at the circus. Representing a space relatively free of the overdetermined relations of capital that shape the economy of sharecropping, the circus provides Big Todd with the opportunity to experience labor as a form of self-realization. While working there he begins to feel that "he *could* cleave waves and fell giants if he tried hard enough" (42). By comparing storytelling to work at the circus, then, Todd identifies it as a form of productive activity through which he experiences a pleasurable expansion of his own capabilities.

Moreover, by offering Big Todd's storytelling as an imperfect but important model for productive subjectivity, the narrative suggests that pleasure is a critical component of self-realization and that the denial of freedom robs the subject of his pleasure as assuredly as it robs him of the fruits of his labor. For subjects whose "own realization exists as an inner necessity, as need," as Marx suggests, working under a system of coerced labor denies individuals the satisfactions of recognizing themselves in the world they create (*1844* 137). For slaves, work is robbed of its pleasure and becomes entirely a burden. In chapter 10 of his *Narrative*, Frederick Douglass describes his own degradation from a "man" into a "brute" through the brutalizing work of plantation labor. Similarly, in *Up from Slavery*, Booker T. Washington regards servitude within the "machinery of slavery . . . so constructed as to cause labor, as a rule, to be looked upon as a badge of degradation, or inferiority" (10). Under such abject conditions, black laborers historically turned to the production of slave tales, music, and religion to ensure their own psychic survival and to reserve for themselves a taste of the satisfactions of productive self-realization. Within the context of sharecropping, then, Big Todd's storytelling can be understood in part as a subversive attempt to claim the pleasures of productive creativity.

After Big Todd's death, Lavidia works to undermine the aesthetic education he has provided for his daughter and to reassert Magnus's ascetic indoctrination by spoiling her daughter's burgeoning sexual relationship with Alpha Omega Holmes. Lavidia's efforts to transform Faith's sexual ardor into religious fervor eventually drive Alpha out of the county. Faith's doubts about the quality of the relationship she and Alpha share are deepened by her mother's claims to have paid Alpha to court her daughter. More significant, however, is Lavidia's attempt to undermine the aesthetic basis for Faith's belief in shared intimacy. Her question to Faith, "Just *how* did you know he loved you?" (16), prompts the young woman to reevaluate the very grounds for their relationship: "Concerning his feelings, Alpha's face told her nothing. . . . Love was a myth born in imagination, pieced together from the inferred softness of a stare, deduced, probably from false premises or undistributed middle terms, from his smile: it could have been deceit" (16). Because an Aristotelian syllogism answers to different standards of validity than the "softness of a stare," Lavidia's requirements for abstract certainty cannot be met by Faith's memories of Alpha's face. Accordingly, as Faith adopts an increasingly analytical perspective, she loses the ability to appreciate the quality of their relationship. With Big Todd and with Alpha, Johnson suggests, Faith had "known" what it was to love and to be loved. But with Todd's death and Alpha's loss, Faith is severed from the relationships that had given her world value.

After Lavidia's death, a similar transformation of value is figured through the subtle alterations in the farmhouse Faith had shared with her mother since her father's death. As the African American philosopher Lewis Gordon has pointed out, "desire plays a central role in what objects mean" (26). Although Lavidia espouses a philosophy that attempts to restrict desire, the transformation of her farmhouse after her death reveals the degree to which its contents had in fact been animated by her own agency. After her mother passes away, Faith observes that "the kitchen had changed. . . . Though old, dissipated, sometimes evil, [Lavidia] had been the focus of the farmhouse since her husband's death, its most crucial node, surely its mistress. Without her the kitchen, the house, the world beyond fell apart" (5). Through the transformation of the house after Lavidia's death, Johnson suggests that value is not simply a material attribute of objects but a contingent feature of their relationship to human aspiration.

Bereft after her mother's death, Faith attempts to regain a sense of belonging by focusing on those aspects of the farmhouse with a special connection to her own childhood. She contemplates the wall against which her mother had measured her height for eighteen years, as well as the kitchen door where—inspired by Todd's storytelling—she had imagined faces in the wood grain (6). But the world as enlivened by her father's imagination or as shaped by her mother's will remains inaccessible to Faith: the kitchen remains "beyond her: *out there*. Inaccessible to love, to need" (6). Faith's perception of the objects in the kitchen as unavailable to her contrasts with her earlier feelings of identity with nature and her delight in her father's giving personal names to simple kitchen utensils, signaling her heightened perception of a breach between subject and object. Estranged from others and from her own body, Faith loses the sense of self she formed through her concrete relationships with others and with nature: "No longer was she Faith, only child of Todd and Lavidia Cross, no longer was she what she believed herself to be;

only a self-conscious pressure drifting about the empty, changing, charged-with-otherness kitchen" (6).

As its title suggests, *Faith* is in part a fictional exploration of what constitutes the good. But as its title also suggests, the novel investigates what constitutes faith. In the first section of the work, Big Todd introduces his daughter to a form of faith that differs from those advocated by Magnus, Lynch, and Lavidia. Magnus's faith in God is rooted in his conviction of the subject's unworthiness, while Lynch espouses a faith in the ability of science to account for life. Traditionally, faith has been defined as the ability to maintain Magnus's belief in God in the face of Lynch's scientific explanations. This is the seemingly contradictory (and ultimately fatal) position of the "theo-physiological determinism" that Lavidia adopts. Big Todd, however, espouses another form of faith: trust in the potential of life to provide the subject with satisfactions, and a corresponding faith in the subject's ability to enter into a productive relationship with the world. The first section of the novel ends with Faith in a state of profound doubt, separated by death or distance from those she loves and moving through a world in which things seem to have "only a tenuous connection" (6). She therefore sets out north, to Chicago, in the hope that she will be able to find the good thing.

## *Chicago: Value and the Estrangement of Desire*

In the Georgia sections of Johnson's narrative, Faith's relationships with nature, Alpha Omega Holmes, and her father together figure the possibility of a many-sided sensuous existence that provides scope for the development of satisfactions and the growth of individual powers. At the same time, Magnus's asceticism, Dr. Lynch's materialism, and Lavidia's sexual repression work against the education of the senses that Big Todd seeks to provide. In the Chicago section of *Faith*, Johnson draws upon Marx to investigate the effects of a *systematic* breakdown in the metabolic relationship between subjects and the objects they desire. While Faith's movement north recalls that of classic nineteenth-century slave narratives, Johnson also blends philosophy, fantasy, realism, and the African American storytelling tradition to reinterpret that movement in twentieth-century terms: as the flight to an urban landscape that is the very spectacle of capital—a complex cash nexus through which desire is distorted by the disfiguring power of money that becomes, in Marx's terms, "the universal value of all things."

Under the capitalist mode of production, Marx argues, the manifold "wealth of human and natural being" is increasingly articulated as monetary gain. Marx's analysis of this process provided Johnson with a penetrating analysis of a destructive form of social sorcery. In his master's thesis

Johnson summarizes the results of this transformation in the well-known tri-partite analysis of alienation under capitalism through which the subject becomes alienated from himself, from his product, and from other men.[24] According to Marx, subjects become alienated from their products because workers no longer satisfy their own needs in producing them but instead serve the ends of others. They therefore no longer see themselves in their products but perceive them as "alien objects" that stand against them as a "hostile force" (*1844* 95). As the multidimensional relations of subjects to their objects become narrowed and limited to the production of commodities for the market, Marx suggests, "being" takes the form of "having." Social relations then increasingly take on instrumental forms, since relations that are directed toward noneconomic ends are discouraged or coerced into the service of the market. Under the spell of commodity relations, desire therefore becomes materially, aesthetically, intellectually, and socially impoverished.

Marx's critique of the disfigurement of desire by commodity relations informs the Chicago section of Johnson's novel. Upon her arrival in Chicago—a city whose unhealthy metabolism is signaled by the smoke that belches from mechanical engines and countless cigarettes—Faith is confronted by a stranger who steals her money and the laundry bag she is using for a suitcase. Coming to her apparent rescue is Arnold T. Tippis. Alone and hungry in a strange city, Faith agrees to go with him when he offers to take her to get something to eat. Leading her to a smoke-filled all-night tavern, Tippis explains to Faith his personal conception of the good thing while buying her several drinks. Once Faith is intoxicated and vulnerable, he then leads her to a cheap hotel, where he rapes her. After the attack, Tippis leaves twenty dollars on the bed, having effectively initiated Faith into the profession of prostitution and into a mode of urban life firmly under the spell of capital.

Johnson signifies through Tippis on Lynch's scientific speculations and the psychoanalytic theories that depend on them. Indeed, the rapist's personal pathology is designed specifically to satirize the subjectivity constructed by psychoanalytic theory and practice. Having been told by his analyst that his problems are "fifty per cent in [his] head and fifty per cent in the world" (57), Tippis has adopted the position that "subject-object antagonism" is inevitable (58); accordingly, he tries to persuade Faith to abandon her search for the good thing and to follow his own path of "self-analysis" instead. While plying her with drinks, Tippis espouses a psychoanalytic interpretation of desire, explaining that "everything you want is an object for the satisfaction of drives developed in childhood" (57). To make his point clear, he draws diagrams on a napkin that are strikingly similar to the diagrams Johnson included in his master's thesis on Reich, Freud, and Marx.[25] Those diagrams illustrate for Faith the process through which drives are thwarted by the world and libidinal energy is directed back upon itself, so that "the libidinal energy of the instinct itself feeds the neurosis" (60). Advising Faith that "you're in serious trouble if you have a drive for which there's no object," Tippis equates gratification with tension and release, with the satisfaction of crude physiological needs like "scratching, sneezing, or the pleasurable feeling when the valve to your full bladder opens" (58).

Through the novel's darkly comic account of the childhood origin of Tippis's problems, Johnson draws on his master's thesis to critique both Freudian and Reichean analyses of the repression of desire. Revealing his own disordered metabolism as he alternates between drawing on his cigarette and "blowing smoke from the side of his mouth" (55), Tippis recounts to Faith the details of his childhood, including his life with the aunt and uncle who raised him following the death of his parents: "'I called him Uncle Bud, and he played a banjo like nobody's business—he taught me chords and transitions, the whole works. Naturally, I wanted to be a traveling musician, he being my ego-ideal and all. But my aunt wouldn't hear of it. . . . She used to beat my fingers with a poker whenever she caught me playing Uncle Bud's banjos after he died. . . . She broke those two once. They never did come back exactly right. But she had my best interests at heart—I know that now'" (60). The extreme measures taken by Tippis's aunt to repress his passion for music leave Tippis with two broken fingers and a crippled hand. Too self-conscious to date girls and unable to play the banjo after his injury, Tippis represses his musical aspirations, his sexual drive, and his anger at his aunt until a psychiatrist persuades him to let his feelings out. Admitting that "all my life there've been things I've wanted to scream at, to strike out of my path, or trample under my heel" (56), Tippis finds the "object [he] need[s]" for his repressed rage in his rape victims (60). Tippis's Freudian conception of desire—that "everything you want is an object for the satisfaction of a need developed in childhood"—functions as a convenient excuse for his actions, since it implies a psychological determinism that exempts Tippis from personal responsibility: "you can't escape history," he rationalizes, "or the needs and neuroses you've picked up like layers and layers of tartar on your teeth" (58). Through Tippis's childhood trauma and his subsequent use of psychoanalysis to avoid blame for his actions, Johnson thus satirizes psychoanalytic theories of desire that define subjects in terms of deterministic drives, also a target of critique in his master's thesis.

Just as important, Johnson uses Tippis to introduce an analysis of estranged labor to the urban section of his novel. When Tippis first meets Faith, he is a frustrated musician who has become a dentist, and then a porter. Tippis subsequently appears in the narrative as a dictionary salesman, a waiter, an usher in a theater, and finally a nurse. Tippis's failure to become a musician emphasizes the polymorphous crippling that results when the individual is severed from the activity of productive labor. Whereas Marx argues that productive activity is a dialectical process through which subjects fulfill their needs and express their powers, Tippis perceives work as alien: when he reads the want ads, he complains, "Nobody wants me—they want accountants, salesmen, movie ushers, and male nurses, but not *me*!" (83). His series of unsatisfying jobs signals Tippis's separation from creative labor, an estrangement Marx describes as a self-estrangement—a condition in which labor "mortifies [the] body and ruins [the] mind" (*1844* 275, 274). His hand crippled and his mind troubled by "voices," Tippis represents the estranged subject in danger, as Faith notices, of "flying apart." Condemned to searching for his "good thing" outside the potentially enriching activity of creative labor, Tippis degenerates into a creature of crude need. When satisfaction is reduced to a simple matter of tension and release, Johnson suggests, the Other becomes simply a means to an end. Rape then becomes the model of desire.

Johnson deepens his analysis of work, desire, and productive subjectivity in the narrative through an examination of the labor of other characters, including Faith's work as both prostitute and housewife, Isaac Maxwell's work as a reporter for the *Chicago Sentry*, and Alpha Omega Holmes's career as an artist. Through the labor of each, Johnson charts the difference between the rich gratifications of a multifaceted desire and the attenuated forms of commodity relations. Faith's actions make the points most clearly. During her rape, Faith calls on a dualistic perspective to convince herself that some part of her remains beyond Tippis's grasp: "This was not happening to her, only to another, to a shadow of herself. To a thing apart, *out there* (62). She thus attempts to ensure that some part of her remains inviolate and "well protected" (61), able to transcend the ugly reality of her victimization and any susceptibility to "circumstance and chance" (62). But Johnson presents Faith's attempts to disassociate herself from her body and from her tragic encounter with Tippis in terms of Sartrean bad faith, as even she seems to recognize: "This is *bad*, Faith. Bad . . . Faith" (62). According to Sartre, in bad faith, "I deny my body as mine through convincing myself that my 'real perspective' is my perspective beyond the body" (*Anti-Semite* 151). In an attempt to flee her personal objectification, then, Faith falsely posits herself as pure consciousness, denying the embodiment that is both the condition for gratification and the basis for an aesthetic education of the self.

Influenced by Tippis's appeal to the causal effects of childhood trauma, Faith remembers after her rape an incident from her own childhood that she had apparently earlier repressed. As a young girl on her first trip to town with Todd, Faith found that she needed to use the bathroom. But when Big Todd asked the attendant at a gas station where she might relieve herself, the attendant, merely a boy, told Todd that Faith could relieve herself "in the bushes . . . behind the station" (64). As she recalls the incident, Faith first remembers her father raging at the white boy in response to this insult to his daughter, but she quickly revises that memory, picturing Todd "grinning sheepishly" and "lowering his eyes" to the attendant before leading her past the "clean women's room" to "set her down in the bushes" (63, 64). Because Faith's memories have been shaded by her rape and by her encounter with Tippis, the accuracy of the events she "remembers" is unclear (as were her earlier rereadings of her father's history immediately after her previous encounters with Magnus and Lynch); in any case, she now reevaluates both the significance of Big Todd's actions during his life and the meaning of his death. Judging any resistance on Todd's part to be an exception to his usual servile behavior, Faith reads Big Todd's lynching not as the result of a brave refusal to give in to the white men's demands but as a sad capitulation to necessity. Significantly, Faith also revises the meaning of Todd's storytelling, reading it now as nothing but a desperate means of releasing tension: "His world of pots and pans with proper names was not created by an act of freedom, but by necessity—an escape it was. A valve" (64). If during her rape Faith imagines that some part of her remains untouched, afterwards she envisions all history under its coloration. She now interprets her relationship with her father as emblematic of a black past that constitutes an inescapable necessity—"final" and "irreversible" (65).

When Tippis leaves after the rape, Faith looks at her reflection in the mirror and judges herself as object, echoing an appraisal that he had made of her in the bar: "Nice-looking. . . . Cute" (67). Having had her marketability forcefully impressed upon her, she picks up the twenty dollars that Tippis left on the bed and begins a career as a prostitute. Plagued by headaches symptomatic of a newly disordered metabolism, Faith increasingly perceives herself as the passive object of circumstance or as the creation of another's will. Her desperate circumstances lead Faith to forget her father's faith in the wealth of the human and natural worlds: having failed to find the good thing "outside" in creation, Faith also denies that it can be found "inside," for the simple reason that, as she despairingly concludes, "there's nothing inside, and there's nothing outside" either (79). Under the weight of her "bondage" as a prostitute and the burden of the tragic history of the black past, Faith's girlish intimations of rich, sensuous interchange are eventually transformed into a cynical perception of human relations that she expresses in Hobbesian terms as an "incessant war of billions of wills" (69).

That war of wills plays out in the form of sexual politics in the bedroom of a new love interest, Isaac Maxwell. Having noticed that women "less nice-looking, less cute than she" lived far more comfortable lives as wives, Faith decides to manipulate Maxwell into proposing to her (81). For his part, Maxwell, who has no idea that Faith is a prostitute and who believes himself "crippled" by asthma and therefore undesirable, wants at first simply to increase his social cachet by being seen in the company of a beautiful woman. Soon, however, he presses Faith sexually, attempting to "possess more and more of her" even as she attempts to coerce him into marrying her (109). Playing to Maxwell's sexual insecurities and to his need to feel dominant in their relationship, Faith employs "an elaborate act of submissiveness" that ironically prompts him to make his first advance. Eventually she discovers that although he is "incredibly slow," Maxwell can be "cajoled into anything she willed through an elaborate process of innuendo and suggestion that left her fatigued and frustrated, but always victorious" (104). Seeing the success with which she can manipulate Maxwell, Faith concludes that Dr. Lynch was right: "Everything was stimulus and response" (104).

Based on an instrumental view of the Other, Faith's relationship with Maxwell is nothing more than a sanitized version of the prostitution she practices with her customers: "They . . . work[ed] out a comfortable agreement, an unwritten contract involving, on his side, food, furniture, comfort, and security somewhere in the surrounding crime-free suburbs, and on her side, the provision of children . . . [and] the obligatory sacrifice of sex" (114). With his own faulty metabolism signaled by a breathing disorder and skin the color of "urine from enflamed kidneys," Maxwell is the embodiment of Reichean emotional armoring (99). Faith realizes that he may be "like a suit of armor, empty inside," but she decides to go ahead with the marriage because even a "suit of armor, after all, would shield her from the cold" (112). Casting Maxwell as an instrument or tool, Faith fails to see him in more than mechanistic terms, and she imagines that in answer to her provocations she can hear the "click click click" of his automatic response (106). Although Faith finally provokes Maxwell into proposing by asking him to "be [her] good thing" (124), he is in fact never truly the object of Faith's desire. Maxwell is never loved or desired for his own qualities but is valued only in the quantitative terms of exchange: as Faith admits, "he could be replaced easily, as an object you love could not; he could be Isaac Maxwell, Tom Maxwell, Dick Maxwell, or Harry Maxwell—and she wouldn't give a tinker's damn" (123).

If Faith's estrangement is reflected in her philosophical vacillations between idealism and nihilism, Maxwell's disaffection takes the form of nearly schizophrenic oscillations between an abject inferiority and a smug superiority. At times Maxwell belittles himself—"I'm nobody—I'm a *cripple!*" (105)—but at other times he asserts his innate superiority in Nietzschean fashion: "Some people are naturally weak and, to tell it like it is, deserve to be flunkies, others—like myself—are strong . . . way down deep" (100). An important character in the novel, Maxwell exposes many of the positions Johnson wishes to critique. Through him Johnson satirizes philosophies of willpower from their more theoretical manifestations in Nietzsche to their simplistic proliferation in the self-help manuals of popular American culture and their banal expression in the spectacle of American sport.[26] Furthermore, because his opinions are often misappropriations of Marx, Maxwell also serves to remind readers of specific aspects of Marxist analysis (and especially of Marx's analysis of "The Power of Money" from *The 1844 Manuscripts*). More important, Johnson uses Maxwell's work as an assistant editor at a Chicago newspaper, the *Sentry*, to racialize his analysis of estranged labor by considering in more detail the unique circumstances of the black worker.

When Maxwell explains to Faith that "what's good is what makes a man feel more powerful" (99), he echoes Nietzsche's famous response to the question "What is good?": "Everything that enhances people's feeling of power, will to power, power itself" (*Anti-Christ*, 4). The evolution of Maxwell's fascination with willpower can be traced from his high school commencement speech on the "Power of Will," to his recent newspaper editorial on "The Contest of Wills," to what he pompously explains to Faith as his whole "theory of Will Power" (116). According to Maxwell, that "theory" came to him one day "like a revelation" as he was watching the Rose Bowl game: "All those men in conflict and one of them carrying the ball across the field through dint of pure Will. Beautiful! . . . Will Power can overcome anything, you see?" (116). Connecting philosophies of will to the American dream of economic success and to a superficial philosophical idealism, Maxwell fills his library with such volumes as *The Power of Will* and *Will for Success*, in addition to other books by Horatio Alger and Norman Vincent Peale and "one slim one about a sea gull" (116). Maxwell embraces the American dream of economic advancement through individual effort, and he believes that he can make "fifty thousand a year if [his] Will Power's strong enough" (103). Endorsing an instrumental view of the subjects' relation to nature that privileges egocentric manipulation, Maxwell not surprisingly embraces an understanding of the larger society as the inevitable clash of wills. As he explains to Faith: "Society's composed of individuals, and every one of 'em's got an individual will. Society *thrives* on the clash of those wills" (99). Finally, Maxwell twists Marx's famous claim that previous philosophers had only "*interpreted* the world in various ways, the point is to change it" (see "Theses on Feuerbach," in *CW* 5:5), as he condemns those who identify power with social reform: "The weak ones go out to demonstrate, march, boycott, strike and picket—they try to change the world, you understand? The point is to use it" (100).

Maxwell's pointed misappropriation of one of Marx's most famous dictums underscores his definition of power in purely economic terms. As he explains to Faith, "*real* power," or "what's really good," is "cash money" (100). Maxwell's analysis of money relies heavily on Marx's critique of the power of money in his *1844 Manuscripts*, and the newspaperman's own fortunes later provide a compelling racialized example of the transformation of value that Marx describes. Marx argues that money becomes the "supreme good" by replacing labor as the "truly creative power" (*1844*, in CW 3:324). As money attains the social power to convert human wishes from their "imagined or desired existence to their *sensuous, actual* existence . . . the quantitative value of money becomes the 'universal value of all things,'" robbing both "the world of men and of nature—of its specific value" ("Jewish Question," in CW 3:172). In such a society, Marx suggests, what individuals are capable of is determined by the quantitative value of exchange: "The extent of the power of money is the extent of my power. Money's properties are my—the possessor's—properties and essential powers. Thus, what I *am* and *am capable of* is by no means determined by my individuality. I *am* ugly, but I can buy for myself the *most beautiful* of women. . . . Money is the supreme good, therefore its possessor is good" (*1844*, in CW 3:324). Because money does not reflect the actual talents of real men and women, money has the power to deform the subject. The person with money need not develop his own abilities, because—as Maxwell paraphrases—"Why, you can be as ugly as a witch, you can be evil and selfish and wicked, but cash money can make you beautiful, right? . . . If you haven't got talent, you can buy folks who do" (100).

But Maxwell's "analysis" of the social power of money is on a collision course with his optimistic belief in his own ability to climb the corporate ladder through individual willpower, as the narrative clarifies through his position as an assistant editor at *The Sentry*. Finding his job of editing, rewriting, and sitting through morning news conferences quite "a cross to bear" (101), Maxwell dreams of getting the big break that will enable him to prove his abilities. Confident that his boss, Ragsdale, "doesn't have anything *I* don't have, except that he's white" (103), Maxwell tells Faith, "Someday I'm gonna run that newspaper" (103). Maxwell's big break comes in the form of a six-feature series on day-to-day life in the prison in Joliet. Although Maxwell demonstrates his lack of sympathy for the prisoners by remarking that "those characters belong right where they are," he submits a proposal for managing the series in hopes of moving up "a couple of notches" (106). When his proposal is chosen over others', Maxwell is convinced that his worth has been recognized by the powers that be: "They're finally giving me some responsibility. . . . They *trust* me" (113).

Two episodes, however, reveal that Maxwell is perceived by his higher-ups not as a talented worker but as an undifferentiated member of the black "race" whose value to the newspaper lies in his being a hot commodity in the marketplace. The first incident occurs at the annual Christmas party. When a drunken Ragsdale approaches Faith to inquire about Maxwell's career interests, he asks her whether she prefers being referred to as "black, colored, or Negro." Faith replies pointedly, "For myself . . . Mrs. Maxwell" (136). Ragsdale's question reveals that he perceives Faith in terms of racial categories, while Faith's response emphasizes the respect she expects to be offered as an individual. Oblivious to her reproach, Ragsdale makes a point of telling her about their last black reporter: "*He* ran off from us to the *Times*, and the other people we had of your, eh, persuasion, took choice government jobs. It's damned hard to keep a black newsman with competition like that!" (136). Ragsdale's comment makes it clear that Maxwell's worth at the newspaper is defined by his value as a scarce commodity rather than by his abilities as a writer. By expecting Maxwell to cover the heavily black South Side of Chicago and by giving him the series on prison life, Ragsdale is effectively assigning Maxwell to his proper "place" in the organization. While Maxwell believes that his appointment as editor of the series attests to the boss's recognition of his superior abilities, the assignment in fact simply fulfills Ragsdale's assessment of the work appropriate for a *black* reporter.

A second incident at the paper underscores the degree to which Maxwell's status is determined by racialized expectations. One morning Maxwell arrives at work to discover a uniformed police officer waiting at his desk. Someone has filed a complaint charging that he has stolen a company car. When Maxwell confronts Ragsdale, the editor explains apologetically that "the parking-lot attendant says he saw you take the car yesterday. . . . I'm sorry, Isaac" (138). But at the precise moment when Maxwell is being led away by the policeman, a young black employee walks in with the keys to the missing car. The case of mistaken identity emphasizes Maxwell's identity as an interchangeable member of a category of workers subject to suspicion at the slightest provocation, whether Ragsdale labels that group "black, colored, or Negro." Although Maxwell keeps his job, his belief that his abilities will be recognized and that his relationships with white management might be founded on "trust" are proven stunningly incorrect.

In *The 1844 Manuscripts*, Marx suggests that "Prostitution is only a specific expression of the general prostitution of the laborer" (CW 3:295). Because Maxwell's experiences at work are increasingly understood to replicate Faith's experiences as a prostitute, the structure of the Chicago section of Johnson's novel provides a dramatic elaboration on Marx's insight. Johnson underscores Marx's point by bringing together at the Christmas party the narrative strands that develop Maxwell's experiences at work and Faith's experiences at home. Immediately before they leave for the get-together, Faith shocks Maxwell by telling him the truth about her past as a prostitute. Maxwell's disillusionment and anger play themselves out at the party, where he gets drunk and approaches Faith with a scandalous proposition. Telling her that Lowell, the senior copyeditor, has "his nose open" for her, Maxwell hands Faith the keys to the car and tells her that he will take a cab home (136). As a senior editor, the repellent Lowell is one of the three men who approved Maxwell's proposal for the series on prison life. To Faith's confused reaction to his pandering her to Lowell, Maxwell explains, "You're going to carry the ball for once" (136). Maxwell thus exposes his earlier appeals to willpower as the ideological counterpart of the performance principle imposed by capitalism, whereby all human action is expected to take forms that increase capital.

The metamorphosis of value that results becomes clear afterwards when Maxwell's supervisors express enthusiasm about his writing. As Maxwell tells Faith: "I figure that it was mainly you, and what you did for me with Lowell, that turned the trick. He was raving about [the] column all morning long, and I know it's not *that* good!" (162). With his column reduced to a commodity in a proliferating system of exchange that includes his wife's body, Maxwell is uncertain about the role his own talents play in the success of his labor. The importance of his work, as well as the satisfaction Maxwell finds in his labor, are therefore diminished. The result is that Maxwell, like Faith, constricts his understanding of the good thing to commodities that fail to satisfy. He tells Faith: "As long as you carry the ball there's nothing we can't do together. In a year, maybe two, we'll have every damn thing we want" (162).

Although Maxwell is described as "a writer, a worker with words" (182), the manner in which he practices his craft contrasts with that of the other "workers with words" in the novel—Big Todd, Alpha Omega, the Swamp Woman, and Faith herself. Maxwell's work at the *Sentry* provides a compelling example of the transformation that occurs when writing is commodified. Marx contends that the first freedom of the press consists in its not being a business. According to Marx, making money should not be the end of writing, or else the means and ends of art—the Alpha and the Omega—become confused. Marx writes, "A writer must of course earn a living to exist and to be able to write, but he must in no sense exist and write so as to earn a living" ("Debates," in *CW* 1:174). Rather than serving as a laborer bent energetically on his work, the subject who is dominated by the power of money comes to see little value in his own production. This is precisely what happens to Maxwell, who ultimately identifies his relationship to his column as that of a mere scribe, admitting to Faith, "I just wrote down what your home boy said" (161). Johnson adeptly uses Maxwell's experiences at the *Sentry* to anatomize a specific transformation of value—the process whereby money deforms labor and appropriates its talents. Read symptomatically, Maxwell's earlier schizophrenic self-appraisals—as both superman and cripple—thus signal the contradictions inherent in a society in which *being* increasingly takes the form of *having*.

For the role she plays with Lowell, Maxwell "pays" Faith with a new car, which symbolizes the transformation of value explored in the Chicago section of the narrative. Although she knows that the vehicle is "merely metal," Faith nevertheless senses a mysterious power in the car. Designed with doors that are "cleverly concealed to give its surface the effect of . . . an imporous surface like the robe of Christ, of power hidden beneath the hood," the car is endowed with a quasi-religious value that surpasses its sensible qualities (162). The car's worth is in fact created by the spell of commodity fetishism and resides in the quantitative value it has as a rare product in a complex system of exchange: it is one "of a limited line" and "expensive" (162). Faith's attraction to the vehicle reflects a process of social engineering designed to produce subjects with mass rather than multidimensional needs. Deeply inflected by Johnson's early engagement with Marx, this section of the novel figures a destructive form of social sorcery through which objects like cars take on power, life, and efficacy, while subjects like Faith and Maxwell become increasingly one-dimensional.

## Desire and the Artist

With a voice that sounds like Georgia and a penchant for storytelling like Big Todd's, Alpha Omega Holmes, when he reappears in the narrative, reawakens specific memories of the pleasures of Faith's girlhood. After Lavidia chases him away from her daughter, Alpha travels north to Chicago, where his several attempts to find work fail. Preferring stealing to going on relief or begging, he begins a life of petty crime and is eventually imprisoned. After three years of incarceration, Alpha is granted an early parole—for agreeing to serve as the subject of Maxwell's column. Faith's reaction when she discovers the true identity of Maxwell's prisoner demonstrates that Alpha arouses desires in her that differ qualitatively from the needs articulated by commodity fetishism: when Alpha walks through the door, Faith feels herself sinking through the apartment's thick carpet all the way to the "white-hot center of the world" (139).

Faith's childhood experiences of a rich, multifaceted desire—from the sensual pleasures she and Alpha enjoy as children to the burgeoning adolescent love that motivates Lavidia's maternal intervention—both anticipate and inform the love affair the two begin in the second section of the novel. To Tippis, Faith had been "unreal," merely "a thing in which to violently unload . . . energy" (153), while Maxwell had wanted "passively to receive that energy, to be acted upon like soft clay" (153–54). Both the sadism practiced by Tippis and the masochism favored by Maxwell leave Faith suspicious of the pleasures that sex might offer. She reflects: "It had never worked out before. It had to be an exchange, give and take" (153). In her affair with Alpha,

Faith realizes "the desired exchange" (154) as she experiences sex in which "the energy [i]s released, displaced, and sent shuddering back and forth" (154). The intimacy she shares with Alpha momentarily regulates Faith's disordered metabolism and orders her respiration. As her "pulse" and "breaths" take on a rhythm ordered by Alpha's own, Faith rediscovers "a bit of the enchantment of her childhood in being a woman" (154). The pleasure Faith finds in Alpha is sexual and genital, but her enjoyment is also associated with the polymorphous sensuality she experienced as a child, mingled as it is with images of a "frieze of a frost-sprinkled earth" (154). Earlier Lavidia attempted to alienate Faith's affections from Alpha by posing the question, "Just *how* did you know he loved you?" (16). As Faith embraces Alpha after his return and listens to his heart, she silently answers her mother's question: "She was certain. That was all" (148).

The same interchange proves crucial to understanding the nature of Alpha's art. When Faith visits Alpha's room in a section of town so run-down that it "made her nauseous" (147), she is surprised to discover that his dingy space, decorated only by a naked light bulb and some of Alpha's charcoal sketches, has "a presence and warmth that glowed behind Holmes's poverty" and offers to her "a sort of voluntary retreat from the world, similar to the atmosphere of a tree house or a cave where children hide" (149). By comparison, Faith recognizes, the expensive apartment she shares with Marxwell is nothing but a "spiritual slum" (149). As a painter living on the fringes of society, Alpha serves as a model of artistic production that is analogous to Big Todd's storytelling: a form of creative productivity outside the performance requirements of capital. Confined by sharecropping, Big Todd has little room to exercise his creative subjectivity except in the telling of tales; in the confines of prison, Alpha paints because "durin' the day hit was the *only* time I was in control of my life. . . . Hit was the only time in my whole life that I had something to say about what went into, or was taken out of, my world" (158). For both men, the narrative suggests, art provides a limited but vital sphere for the creation of a "human object" and the development of a "humane subject."

At one point Alpha summarizes for Faith his own attempts to understand the value of art: "One guy told me hit was supposed to show life as hit *is*, another said hit wasn't no good unless hit made him forget alla his problems. . . . A teacher in the joint said *what* I painted wasn't as important as *how* I did hit. A Muslim said my work was worthless unless hit was instrumental to his cause, and another guy—a damned fool!—said all that mattered was my puttin' alla my feelings in hit, like kids do, and forgettin' form" (158–59). Rejecting all of these alternative theories as inadequate interpretations of the value of his art, Alpha defines art as a pleasurable activity tied explicitly to self-actualization: "All I know is that doin' hit makes me feel good, the way goin' to Sunday Meeting with Reverend Brown never could (159)." The productive interchange Alpha describes is, then, both Alpha and Omega—a dialectical interplay wherein desire leads to satisfaction and the development of new capacities, which in turn produce new needs and desires. Alpha Omega's unusual name therefore raises the possibility that in his work as an artist he may have found the proper relationship between the means and ends of art.[27]

Like Marx's analysis, the description of Alpha also figures the intimacy of the relation between desiring subject and his object through the trope of a shared metabolism. As Alpha paints, Faith notices that he unconsciously licks the paint while he is working, "swallow[s] it, and sen[ds] it streaming through his system. He was that close to this thing" (159). While watching him paint, Faith realizes that the canvas is Alpha's "object," and that it is "through his object, not in spite of it, [that] he seemed to find release: the Good Thing" (158). Furthermore, when he paints, Alpha seems to fuse with his artwork, "his broad shoulders framed by the square canvas and his movements strangely ritualistic, merged, so to speak, with the canvas itself" (157). Providing an image of the artist who is not estranged from the process or the product of his labor, then, Alpha's painting offers a model of artistic production that contrasts sharply with Maxwell's work as a writer for the *Sentry*.

As the narrative progresses, however, Alpha's art itself becomes increasingly enmeshed in the system of commodity relations. Ironically, it is Faith who urges Alpha to sell his paintings in an attempt to "make a living out of this thing" (164). Her advice is understandable, perhaps, in light of the fact that she has begun to support him as his "resources r[un] thin" (164). But when Alpha learns that Faith is pregnant, he begins to offer a number of rationalizations to explain why he cannot assume fatherly responsibility for the child. His "eyes narrowing," Alpha first appeals to a form of biological determinism, rationalizing that he cannot take on the responsibilities of parenthood because he has been physiologically programmed to be an artist: "Honey, I'm different—I can't settle down, or raise kids, or nothin' like that. I'm . . . an *artist*. . . . [N]ature did somethin' strange to me—gave me a screwed-up nervous system so I see things different from most people" (165). Next Alpha evokes a romantic stereotype in order to argue that his life's pathway is already laid out; being an artist, he explains, "means I'm going to suffer, hit means I'm going to be frustrated, and die inside, and wake up in gutters or in hotels with strange women" (165). Finally, Alpha adopts an idealistic position—quite the opposite of the determinism with which he began—in order to explain that as an artist he is nothing but "a hypothesis. That's right, a theme. And I can't let nothin' tie me down until I see how far the damn theme goes" (165). Alpha's vacillations expose his arguments as self-serving, and the fact that his breathing "become[s] an ordeal, a painful thing to both their ears" (165), indicates that his metabolism is becoming disordered.

Thus, like Faith's work as a housewife and Maxwell's work for the *Sentry*, Alpha's avocation as an artist also eventually submits to capitalistic rationalization. Seemingly reconciling himself to Faith's pregnancy, Alpha promises Faith that he will explain their situation to Maxwell. But what Alpha actually explains is quite different. As Maxwell reveals, "He said he was leaving town to take a goddamn job as a goddamn illustrator for a god-damn ad firm in New York City" (171). By selling his services to an adver-tising firm (an industry that reshapes desire in order to sell commodities), Alpha Omega confuses what Marx calls the alpha and the omega of art. After he leaves, Faith returns to Mrs. Beasley's boardinghouse, hoping to begin a new life focused completely on her child and reassuring herself that "the child, in an odd way, was the answer—it was all history focused on a single point" (168). But Faith's identification with a romantic discourse of feminine creative superiority parallels Alpha's artistic rationalization. The narrative qualification that follows her assertion about the child—"or so she believed"—confirms that her attempt to found her existence on the in-fant is another form of bad faith. Faith's fantasies of identity with a univer-sal creative power are tragically ended when a fire sweeps through her apartment, killing her infant daughter and burning Faith so badly that she is unrecognizable. Abandoned by Alpha, rejected by Maxwell, stripped of her child, and fatally injured: Faith's search for the good thing seems drawn to a tragic close.

The hospital scene that follows vividly dramatizes the final fate of desire in the Chicago section of the novel. Having lost her right eye, nose, ears, and much of her skin to the fire, Faith inhabits a body effectively robbed of its or-gans of aesthetic satisfaction. Suffering from a "collapsed lung" and burned beyond recognition, she is reduced, like Lavidia, to a quantitative existence, which Faith spends listening to time "mechanically clicking away in the wall clock near the door" (181). In the face of her tragedy, Maxwell can offer only laughably inappropriate advice about the efficacy of willpower and the economic consolation of a twenty-dollar bill he drops on the foot of Faith's bed as he leaves the room, in case, as he tells her, "you need anything tonight" (183). Not only does Maxwell's gesture recapitulate Tippis's payment to Faith on her first night in Chicago, but also his final words demonstrate that his understanding of her needs is tragically limited. Indeed, Faith's condition is the reductio ad absurdum of the process begun when she first arrived in Chicago, whereby the rich human subject who is distinguished by a wealth of capabilities is increasingly subjected to the disfiguring logic of economic value. Maintained by an artificial respirator and trapped inside a body that doesn't "respond to her will," Faith is emblematic of the subject deprived of her dynamic relationship to the world (181).

## Conjuring Desire: The Conclusion of Faith

Through Lavidia's policed breathing, Magnus's breath-stealing sermon, Lynch's mechanical theory of respiration, Tippis's incessant cigarette smoking, Maxwell's asthma, Alpha's emerging breathing difficulties, and Faith's ultimate dependence on a mechanical respirator for her very life, Johnson's dominant narrative trope of troubled breathing progressively figures the crippling of desire under a social system that robs subjects of the intimate interchange that would develop their potentialities and satisfy their desires. Georg Lukács suggests that the principle at work in capitalism is "the principle of rationalization based on what is and *can be calculated*," a standard that entails "a break with the organic, irrational, qualitatively determined unity of production" (88). When Faith is cut off from the mechanical respirator that sustains her and she dies, her subjection to this principle seems complete.

If the novel ended here, with Faith's death and with Alpha's seemingly irremediable acquiescence to the performance principle of capitalism, Johnson's narrative would trace an economic determinism as intractable as those his master's thesis criticizes in Freud, Reich, and Soviet Marxism. But the realistically narrated Chicago section of the novel, which seems to conclude with Faith's demise, suddenly gives way to a fantastical account wherein Faith rises from her hospital bed and returns to the Georgia bogs to confront the Swamp Woman about the identity of the good thing. Through that encounter Faith regains a belief in the world's possibilities and ultimately assumes the Swamp Woman's role as conjure woman. As the novel closes, two young children approach the shanty in the bog and Faith makes plans to entertain them with tales about "Aristotle's Illusion" and "Stackalee's great battle with Lucifer in West Hell" (196). Combining elements from the Western philosophical tradition with African American folklore, Faith's practice as Swamp Woman reflects both the form of Johnson's syncretic fiction in general and the major narrative strands of *Faith* in particular. Faith's assumption of the Swamp Woman's role can thus be read as Johnson's fictional announcement of his own artistic intentions. The narrative concludes as Faith reclaims an aesthetic orientation to the world that parallels the author's own faith in fiction, defined in this novel as an exuberant refusal to accept the restrictions placed on desire by either the burdens of history or the contemporary requirements of the performance principle.

Faith's return to the bog in fact constitutes a resurrection of desire, a narrative overflowing of the seemingly inevitable first conclusion to the novel,

wherein various characters capitulate to the organizing tendencies of capitalism. Through Faith's final encounter with the Swamp Woman, the narrative
attempts to reconstitute desire in plenitude rather than in lack. Simultaneously, the narrative voice becomes increasingly self-conscious as Faith's life
history is clearly identified as a fiction—one version of a story that could be
told in any number of different ways. As an increasingly intrusive storytelling
narrator remarks: "People never tire of hearing Faith Cross's tale. An old
farmer sitting before the kitchen stove, petting his rooter-dog, may make it
an odyssey involving the fate of the world; harlequin-faced grandmothers
will grin, giggle, and tell it as a gallyflopper spiced with the morals they want
you to hear" (184). Replacing the hyperdeterminism of the Chicago section
of the novel with an evocation of a seemingly inexhaustible narrative productivity, the reflexivity of the conclusion serves to focus readers' attention
specifically on the relationship of storytelling to desire.

A storyteller and a philosopher, the Swamp Woman represents both
broadly historical and more narrowly personal forms of desire. In part she
represents the historical desire for freedom and social justice. She first becomes a werewitch after her people are taken captive aboard a slave trader.
Preferring death to slavery, the Swamp Woman jumps overboard, dedicating
herself to an afterlife spent "torment[ing] her people's captors forever from
the dank swamps" (17). In her reincarnation as the conjure woman for a
rural community in the American South, she works her magic on the personal desires brought to her doorstep by individuals in search of their own
"good things": love potions, youth, and in one case a quick death. Moreover, because she understands the strange and unpredictable ends to which
human longing may lead, the Swamp Woman practices her craft with a well-
developed sense of irony. Her conjuration on behalf of Old Massa Ferguson
is a case in point. Old Massa comes to the Swamp Woman one day asking
to be made young again. The next morning he awakes to discover that her
spell has indeed made him young—but it has also changed him from white
to black. Old Massa has been mysteriously transported into the body of his
slave, Jug, and he can only look on as Jug, now inhabiting the master's former body, puts a "protective arm" around his wife. The next day the "new"
master sells the Old Massa, frees the slaves, and "thr[ows] a party in the
Massa's Big House every weekend for thirty years until he die[s]" (18). Drawing on plantation trickster tales, Old Massa's comeuppance identifies the
Swamp Woman's power with the subversive African American folktale tradition, whose very existence testifies to the failure of repressive social structures to reshape desire completely, even within the brutal confines of
plantation slavery. Sanctioning a rich, multifaceted desire, the Swamp
Woman also serves as an alternative mother figure to Lavidia. Finally, by
combining the authority of the conjurer in the African American tradition

with an extensive knowledge of Western philosophy, she assumes the role of a spiritual guide who instructs Faith in the nature of desire, both recalling and revising the role played by Diotima in Plato's *Symposium*.[28]

The specific form of desire that the Swamp Woman endorses is suggested by her association with Imani, a character in a tale she recounts to explain to Faith how the good thing was lost to humankind. Signifying on the Faust legend, Descartes's *Meditations*, and Plato's *Symposium*, the Swamp Woman uses the tale of the two lovers, Imani and Kujichagulia, to instruct Faith in the nature of desire and its relation to the good. In the beginning, the Swamp Woman explains, Kujichagulia lived in the presence of the good thing, but soon after his birth he began to ask questions such as "Who *am* I?," "*What* am I?," and "What can I *know?*" (28). Deciding that the good thing must reside "in the mountains where the gods were" (29), Kujichagulia set out to seize it, successfully overcoming all the obstacles the gods threw in his path, except for one—a beautiful young girl named Imani. Deflected from his quest by love, Kujichagulia settled down, temporarily forgot his search for the good thing, and fathered several children with Imani. But at the age of sixty-three he resumed his quest again, despite Imani's attempts to persuade him "to stay, to love and work" (30). When Kujichagulia succeeded in reaching the top of the mountain and beheld the good thing, the sight killed him. In response to his presumption, the Swamp Woman suggests, the gods decided to hide the good thing from humankind in order to "torment all men with the curse of restlessness and questioning" (30). After Kujichagulia's death, Imani raised their children alone, and then set out to climb the mountain herself in order to die beside her husband. Her fate differed from Kujichagulia's, however: when Imani reached the mountaintop, the gods decided not to punish her because she had "never once questioned the good things like Kujichagulia" (191). Instead, the gods gave Imani a gift—the gift of conjuring.

The tale of Imani and Kujichagulia is specifically designed to contrast two forms of desire. Kujichagulia, whose name means "self-determination" in Swahili, represents a doubting, Cartesian self-consciousness in search of certainty; Imani, whose name means "faith," represents a belief in the world's ability to provide a plenitude of "good things." While Kujichagulia embodies the Enlightenment project of understanding the world rationally, Imani figures a more capacious relation to world. Kujichagulia's desire is one-dimensional, narrowly intellectual rather than broadly aesthetic: even his longing takes the form of "thoughts" that "burn his brain" (29). More important, because he conceives of the good thing as a supranatural, immutable object, his commitment to that disembodied ideal leads him to undervalue, and eventually to turn away from, the things of the world. In short, Kujichagulia's journey to the mountaintop figures desire as a form of transcendence that leads away from Imani, the community, and the world.

Imani, by contrast, chooses another way to go beyond the given, the path of "love and work." Involving an aesthetic, qualitative relationship to the world, Imani's path connects her to earthly abundance. Kujichagulia, representing a form of desire grounded in *lack*, seeks the one ultimate object that will satisfy all desire and put an end to all his searching; Imani, figuring desire as an orientation to *plenitude*, implies that the good can be known only through concrete, particular satisfactions. Johnson's point is that the good is irreducibly qualitative and experienced in the concrete moment of life. The gift of conjuring with which the gods reward Imani is a clear endorsement of desire understood as an orientation to plenitude, and it is precisely as the representative of this productive understanding of desire that Imani formally takes up her role as Swamp Woman.

If the Swamp Woman is identified with Imani, Faith's quest for the good thing clearly associates her with Kujichagulia. Like him, Faith initially searches for the one thing that would put an end to her searching, as is revealed when Faith changes her mother's dying injunction, "Girl, you get yourself a good thing," into a search for "the *one* Good Thing—the one thing all those [good] things have in common" (24). Faith's "belief in certainty," as the Swamp Woman explains, leads the young woman to distance herself from the "joys of the earth" (193). As she instructs Faith in the ways of desire, the Swamp Woman offers her own interpretations of how the young woman lost the "good thing." She explains Faith's fall into a limited, dualistic rationality as the inevitable result of the growth of self-consciousness that comes with maturation: "Ya broke your bonds with the world when ya got smart. . . . Object-ivity: standin' back away from the world to check it out." At other times the Swamp Woman attributes Faith's failure to maintain her childhood belief to historical forces, explaining that the girl was born "in the winter of the Age of Reason—an ugly age . . . filled with disillusion, rife with conflictin' theories that bend and fold and mutilate men like a computer card" (192). The Swamp Woman thus ties the Marxist critique of capital that holds sway in Chicago to a more general critique of the Enlightenment project.

But Faith's name also signals her kinship to Imani, and through the Swamp Woman's tutelage she is finally led to abandon her quest for the "*one* good thing," to accept the Swamp Woman's philosophy of a more capacious desire, and to assume her role as conjure woman. Faith's transformation takes place at the moment when—pushed to exasperation by the young woman's continuing questions about the identity of the good thing—the Swamp woman finally instructs Faith to "Just look outside" (193). Becoming attentive to the world outside the Swamp Woman's shanty, Faith is struck by "the sustained orchestration of songbirds: hooting, cooing, chirping, squawking, and crying on the unseen undercurrent of the wind" (193). As

Faith once again adopts an erotic orientation toward the world and re-discovers her girlhood pleasure in what William Desmond has called the "aesthetic show of being" (9), the Swamp Woman tells her to "Systematize *that*!" (194). The conjure woman's ironic instruction points to a plenitude that is irreducible to rationalization, and her instruction to "Just look outside!" is in fact suggestive of the outward thrust of desire. The aesthetic show of being is thus offered as something more original than either an empiricist's impression of sense or an idealist's object of consciousness: as an encounter that reminds Faith of her original orientation to alterity.

Understanding desire in terms of creative appropriation, Marx argues that individuals must productively alter the given situation in order to meet their needs and develop their powers. Going beyond the given for Marx does not mean the transcendence of a pure rationality, however, but refers to a practical surpassing. Because such transcendence is material, it must be "suffered" or experienced aesthetically. Significantly, it is through this practical process that value is born. The Swamp Woman echoes Marx's point when she explains, "To be human *is* to suffer, child—to feel, to be sentient" (189). Because sentience entails an aesthetic orientation to the world, suffering is a part of existence, transcendence to a realm of absolutes is contrary to the human condition, and the good thing is to be realized only in relation to particular goods: as the Swamp Woman explains, the Good Thing is "*absolutely* nothing, but *particularly*, it's everything" (193). Fundamentally qualitative rather than quantitative, value is realized in each concrete moment of life.

At the end of the novel Faith replaces the Swamp Woman as conjure woman and becomes the novel's final figure of desire. Her own aesthetic practice is captured through two tropes—"taking a path" and "conjuring"—to which Johnson will return frequently in his fiction. The discussion of "taking a path" draws from Marx's analysis of sensuous practice while anticipating Johnson's growing interest in Eastern thought, to which he turns in a systematic fashion in his next novel, *Oxherding Tale*, a novel more deeply influenced by a Buddhist conception of desire. In the words of the Swamp Woman: "Ya take every path: the oracle's, teacher's, the artist's, and even the path of the common fool, and ya learn a li'l bit from each one. That's life, girlie" (187). In light of Johnson's later immersion in Eastern thought, the Swamp Woman's emphasis on a multiplicity of paths could be read as an endorsement of reincarnation, but in the context of his first novel, that proliferation serves more as a trope for the orientation of desire to plenitude—as the recognition that there are "a thousand 'n one ways to look for what's good in life" (187). Unlike Kujichagulia's quest—which has a predetermined end—the idea of taking a path is open-ended and dialectical; it retains some of the productive force of Marx's analysis of creative labor.

## From Marx to Marcuse

The nature of the good thing as it is developed in Johnson's first novel is related to the difficult question of the author's understanding of concrete universals at the time when he was writing the novel. Johnson has frequently noted that he believes in universals, but, as he is also quick to qualify, "*concrete* universals." Those who criticize Johnson for his "universalism" often fail to account for the complex nature of the universal in his writing. The genealogy of the term as used by Johnson can be traced from Hegel's use of the phrase in his criticism of the Kantian abstract, through Marx's critique of Hegel, to Marcuse's revision of Kant, Hegel, and Marx in his own thinking about substantive universals. Marx understands abstractions not as preexisting categories of mind that help one to organize the flux of the world (like Kant) or as unfolding ideals (like Hegel) but as real, historical instances of abstraction performed by men and women. Real abstractions differ from idealistic understandings of universals in that they are the product of historical, social, and human forces: historical, since they are conditioned by "all previous ages"; social, since abstractions arise within and are confined by particular social formations; and human, because individuals practically demonstrate a "power of abstraction" in going beyond the given to reshape the world so that it more perfectly answers to their needs. In one well-known passage Marx clarifies his point by contrasting the labor of animals, which create merely out of instinct, to the work of people, who create "universally": "What distinguishes the worst architect from the best of bees is that the architect raises his structure in imagination before he erects it in reality" ("Process," in CW 1:187). For Marx, human production entails a *power* of abstraction and imaginative projection, an insight important to Johnson.

In *Faith*, Johnson sets out to dramatize both the potential—and the potential danger—of such powers of abstraction. On the one hand, the ability to abstract enables subjects to go beyond the given, to envision a better, more satisfying world. On the other hand, abstractions can come to serve as disembodied Ideals that rule over individuals. Johnson's narrative figures both the possibilities and the dangers inherent in the power of abstraction through the parable of Kujichagulia and through the character of Richard Barrett, the out-of-work philosopher who steals Faith's purse when she first arrives in Chicago. Barrett later reappears to make amends and to explain to Faith his history as a university professor who left his job and family in order to search for the good thing. Here Johnson almost certainly evokes William Barrett, the author of *Irrational Man*. By critiquing the manner in which philosophy had become excessively professionalized and by leaving the academy himself, the historical Barrett anticipates the career of the fictional Barrett. Moreover, William Barrett's analysis of the manner in which philosophical abstraction increasingly threatens an "authentic" existence provides a key for understanding the fictional Barrett's character.

Although Barrett and Faith come to see each other as fellow travelers in their quests for "absolute certainty" (93), Barrett dies on a park bench shortly after they discuss their aspirations. He leaves to Faith his "Doomsday Book," in which he has recorded everything he has learned during his search for the good thing. Upon opening the book after Barrett's death, Faith discovers it to be "empty"; the blank pages reveal "words and phrases" only when she "conjures them there" (94). Barrett's legacy is therefore ambiguous: on the one hand, the book's blank pages stand as a dumb indictment of his search for certainty, a mute testament to his failure to pass on anything of significance; on the other hand, those pages represent the possibilities for Faith's own creative productivity. Barrett's ambiguous bequest implies that the meaning Faith finds in life will be the meaning that she herself actualizes.

Like his "Doomsday Book," Barrett's character is also disarmingly ambiguous. After his death Barrett functions as ghostly conscience in the form of an ethereal apparition that haunts Faith when she limits her desire in ways that fall short of her life's promise. For example, on the evening when Faith agrees to marry Maxwell, Barrett appears in her mirror as a reminder that life has more to offer than the loveless arrangement she has contracted. By continuing to haunt Faith, Barrett dramatizes the manner in which ghostly abstractions can empower subjects to go beyond the given by helping them envision a world that more perfectly satisfies desire. But Barrett's own life history underscores the dangers of abstractions when they come to serve as ideals that rule over people. When Barrett argues that everyone needs "a guiding principle" that must "first, in every instance, be wholly removed from us and exist in some absolute, unsullied, perfect form" (91), the "foolosopher" sounds disturbingly like Kujichagulia. To be what "we desire," Barrett falsely suggests, the good "must seem completely other, greater than we are" (91). Barrett's commitment to a supranatural good means that although he can perceive his wife's beauty—"such *haecceitas* you've never seen"—he is unable to take pleasure in her attractions, for he cannot "look at a rose" without longing "for roseness" (93). Barrett's reason undermines his aesthetic relationship to alterity: even when he is "drunk ...with joy, or in the middle of sex," he wonders, "Is this *really* the greatest good," and his questions cause him to "sober up immediately" or to "lose [his] erection" (90). Barrett's way of conceiving of universals as "wholly removed from us" robs the world of its particular pleasures.

Marcuse develops Marx's understanding of "real abstractions" in a direction that is very close to Johnson's use of "concrete universals" at the time he was writing *Faith*. Johnson developed a strong interest in the Frankfurt School, and in Marcuse in particular, while working on his master's degree in philosophy. He reports reading "everything then in print" by Marcuse and writing more than one seminar paper on his thought.[29] Beyond the image of Marcuse as the "guru" of the counterculture, Johnson may have been attracted to Marcuse because of the philosopher's widely admired work on Marx. Johnson was no doubt also attracted to Marcuse for the same reason that he was drawn to Reich, for both attempt to combine the insights of Marx and Freud into a single theory of desire. In any case, Marcuse's influence can be detected throughout *Faith*, from the text's insistence that the denial of pleasure is an important feature of domination to the Chicago section's development of "carrying the ball" as a variation on the performance principle of capitalism. But it is in the alternative conclusion's unblinking endorsement of the potentially subversive power of art that Johnson's interest in Marcuse is most striking.

Marcuse discusses the power of abstraction in the context of arguing against both the "one-dimensional mode of thought" that he finds characteristic of analytic philosophy and the equally mistaken elevation of "Logos over Eros" that characterizes classical philosophy (*One-Dimensional* 147). Just as the Swamp Woman criticizes positivistic attempts to reduce the subject to information that can be recorded on computer cards, Marcuse criticizes those who attempt to define away abstractions such as "Mind, Consciousness, Will, Soul, and Self" (203) by reducing them to analytic statements. Such concepts as mind and self—vague and "ghostly" as they may be—are not successfully exorcised by analytic philosophers, Marcuse argues, because "the ghost continues to haunt" (203). Such apparitions have important roles to play in thought and perception. In developing his analysis, Marcuse argues that universals are constituted through particular tensions—tensions between the historical and the suprahistorical, the concrete and the abstract, the personal and the social, the immanent and the transcendental. These tensions deserve discussion here because they capture what Johnson means by the phrase "concrete universals," because they bear directly on the nature of the "good thing," and because they shed light on certain characteristic tensions in Johnson's thought.

At a basic level, Marcuse argues, "no mode of thought can dispense with universals" (111). As he summarizes, "Nobody really thinks who does not abstract from that which is given, who does not relate the facts to the factors which have made them, who does not—in his mind—undo the facts" (134). As a way of "undoing the facts," abstraction constitutes for Marcuse a means to go beyond the given. But Marcuse also wants to avoid a mistake he detects in classical thinkers who elevate Logos over Eros to the point where "ideas become ideals" and the "concrete, critical content" of the universal "evaporates" (148). Arguing that universals are concrete rather than ideal, Marcuse suggests that they both arise from and are in some sense constrained by the particulars that they "overshoot" (xi).

Understanding substantive universals as both concrete and abstract, Marcuse also argues that they are simultaneously historical and trans-historical. Building on Marx's analysis of "real abstractions," Marcuse argues that "abstraction is a historical event in an historical continuum . . . and it remains related to the very basis from which it moves away: the established societal universe" (134). Unlike the merely formal universals of Aristotelian logic, substantive universals are "constituted" in the "inter-relationship between (thinking and acting) subjects and their world" (139). Here Marcuse anticipates Johnson's presentation of the good, which is also actualized through the relation of subjects and world. In other words, for both Marcuse and Johnson universals have an *aesthetic dimension*: they are not simply "logical" but "primary elements of experience or 'qualities' of the world" with which one is "daily confronted" (211). Beauty is known not abstractly but aesthetically or sensibly, because it is experienced: "seen, heard, smelled, touched, felt, comprehended" (210). Universals, however, are never simply personal, since they are constituted from a position *within* a social formation and "historical continuum" (134). In other words, concrete universals reveal tensions precisely because they are *not*, as Barrett suggests, wholly removed from us in some "absolute, unsullied, and perfect form."

Finally, Marcuse argues that substantive universals are both immanent, as the claim that they are encountered in the world suggests, yet in some sense transcendent, since through them individuals synthesize experiential contents into new ideas (125). Marcuse uses the term "transcendence" in what he terms an "empirical" and "critical" sense (xi). Substantive universals reveal a tension between "what is and what is not" or "what is and what could be." They offer, as Marcuse titles one of the chapters of his *Eros and Civilization*, "The Chance of the Alternatives"—not a fully realized alternative but the possibility of one. Just as Barrett's ghostly image haunts Faith, reminding her of the limitations of her existence, universals for Marcuse have the ability to "haunt the established society as subversive tendencies and forces" (12). Marcuse's thinking was an early and important influence on Johnson's belief in the defamiliarizing power of art. In *Faith*, Johnson offers the folktale tradition as a historical example of the subversive power that Marcuse attributes to concrete universals, the positing of a "could be." After Faith recounts to one of her customers a tale about her father's humorous escape from a "show down" with Jim Slaughter, for example, the customer laments, "It's a shame the world isn't really like that, isn't it?" Faith's tale has reminded him of the way the world *could* be. For Johnson, the critical function of folk and slave tales is thus to provide an important historical warrant for the efficacy of the estrangement effect of literature.

Because they are identified with narrative productivity and a multifaceted desire, the Swamp Woman's conjurations demonstrate an analogous power, as can be seen in her conjuring in the case of the bereaved Casey Fudd. Despondent, Fudd decides to take his own life in a manner that he believes is guaranteed to succeed. He purposely builds redundancy into his suicide plan: he intends to kill himself by rowing a boat under a low-hanging branch, tying a rope to the branch, putting the noose at the other end of the rope around his neck—and then dousing himself with kerosene, swallowing poison, and raising a pistol to his head. But Fudd's carefully laid plans go awry when he kicks the boat out from underneath himself and pulls the trigger, because the "bullet br[eaks] the rope, the river douse[s] the fire and, [after] he g[ets] a lungful of water, he gag[s] up every drop of that rat poison" (185–86). Because Fudd's death instinct is humorously trumped by the Swamp Woman's agency, the tale implies that there is "a chance for an alternative" even in a situation as seemingly overdetermined as Fudd's suicide. The practice of conjuring thus functions as a counter-spell to a narrow instrumentality that is effectively satirized through Fudd's elaborate preparations for death. In *Faith*, Johnson fuses his philosophical studies with the historical function of the slave tale in order to validate the subversive power of fiction.

## Desire as Counter-Spell

Because Faith's final confrontation with the Swamp Woman is far removed from the material conditions analyzed in the Chicago section of the novel, the aesthetic awakening Faith undergoes in the alternative conclusion runs the risk of suggesting that emancipation is simply—or primarily—a matter of seeing the world from a new perspective. As a cure for the systemic economic and social ills dramatized earlier, Faith's personal awakening can seem woefully inadequate, and her return to the Swamp Woman's fanciful home in the bog may appear little more than a retreat to a utopian "nowhere." Those suspicious of the subversive possibilities of utopian thinking and art—including the Soviet Marxists—frequently reject fantasy as a flight from reality that constitutes an escape from, rather than a clarification of, social relations. From this perspective, Faith's return to the bog may appear as nothing more than mere wish fulfillment—an imaginary projection of the young woman's dying desire to escape her tragic racial history and repressive social reality. Critical of utopian movements, Marx argued repeatedly that the social problems caused by relations of capital could not simply be overcome by seeing the world from a new perspective. Yet Marx also argued that some philosophical problems are solved by abandoning the false view that generates them. Faith's mistaken quest for the *one* good thing can be read as such a distortion: by abandoning her search for the one, supranatural thing that all good things must have in common, Faith is freed to seek the good through creative appropriation — through conjuring.

Johnson has stated that Marcuse's work provided a "transition" between his early interest in Marxism and his later interest in phenomenology.[30] This transition was an important alteration in Johnson's thinking that took place at precisely the time he was drafting *Faith*. If the Chicago section of Johnson's narrative presents a more characteristically Marxist analysis of material relations under capitalism, the scenes that take place in the Swamp Woman's bog move the novel's social critique closer to a Marcusean revision of Marx — especially in regard to the subversive potential of art. Marcuse was certainly aware of the susceptibility of all areas of social existence, including art, to the rationalization of capital. Nevertheless, somewhat like Ernst Bloch, he interpreted the utopian element of fantasy to be a "not yet" rather than a "nowhere." Linking the critical function of art to future possibilities, Marcuse located it in fantasy's "refusal to accept as final the limitation imposed on freedom and happiness by the reality principle," or the "refusal to forget *what can be*" (*Eros* 131). In this refusal Johnson found a rejoinder to the hyperdeterminism that he decried in his master's thesis and that he dramatizes in the Chicago section of his narrative. It is possible that a faith in the subversive power of fiction may also have contributed to Johnson's eventual decision to leave academic philosophy for a career in creative writing. Certainly Johnson has maintained that faith: writing in a period when claims for the liberating effects of creative art have come under attack by postmodernism and popular-culture critique, Johnson unabashedly asserts that fiction — at its best — has the "capacity to change our lives forever" ("Elusive" 39).

In his account of the subversive potential of fantasy in film, Hector Rodriquez analyzes Charlie Chaplin's film *The Pawnshop* in order to dramatize how fantasy can constitute a critical response to repressive social conditions. He concentrates on a scene in which Chaplin responds to repetitive labor by transforming his tools into elements of play: taking his broom and sweeping pieces of string into a straight line, Chaplin pretends to balance on them as though they were a tightrope. Chaplin's playful pantomime subverts the stultifying conditions of the workplace and offers a paradigm of "discernment that runs counter to dominant forms of representation." Rodriquez concludes, "The behavior of the tramp passes a moral judgment on a social practice" (271). In a similar fashion, the alternative conclusion to Johnson's novel offers a self-conscious evocation of fantasy meant to be read *against* the narrative's earlier analysis of capital. As a counter-spell to an overrationalized society, the more fantastical elements of Johnson's narrative pass a moral judgment on — and offer a counter form of discernment to — a repressive social system that distorts desire. Not presented as an immediate solution to entrenched relations of capital, the fantastical conclusion to Johnson's novel nevertheless expresses a hope — or faith — in the possibility of an alternative. Against a world deprived of all enchantment, Johnson's first novel offers an unapologetic assertion of the potentially subversive pleasures of fiction, captured in the work's final, exuberant address to the reader: "Was it Good? Was it Beautiful? All right!" (196).

# 3

## The Emergence of Black Dharma
## and *Oxherding Tale*

"If it's about liberation, black people will come."

*Wayne Shorter (black Nichiren Buddhist,*
*composer, and sax player)*

IN THE MID-1990S ROSA PARKS WAS ASKED TO CHOOSE THE SINGLE photograph that best epitomized her life for inclusion in a book titled *Talking Pictures*. The editors of the volume solicited photos from people they considered to be "the most interesting people of our era," and they urged contributors to choose the single photo that "mattered most" to them (Heiferman and Kismaric 10). Surprisingly, Parks—whose December 1, 1955, protest against racial segregation on city buses in Montgomery, Alabama, is widely considered to be a defining moment in the civil rights movement—chose a picture not of her activities in Montgomery but of her 1993 meeting with Daisaku Ikeda, the president of Soka Gakkai, an international Buddhist organization (see figure 3).[1] It is clear from her explanation of why she chose the photo of her meeting with Ikeda that Parks understood their encounter to be a most important event: "This photograph is about the future, and I can't think of a more important moment in my life. It shows an unprecedented private meeting I had in 1993 with Daisaku Ikeda, and it reminds us how people of very varied opinions and unique personalities from two different cultures have an opportunity to work together on a mission of world peace.... Our meeting can serve as a model for anyone. So the photograph of our first meeting is very important because it is history in the making" (198). Bringing together two groups not commonly identified with each other, blacks and Buddhists, the picture of Parks and Ikeda reflects in iconic fashion the international exchange of ideas about human rights that is one result of globalization. Offered both as an example of "history in the

*3. Rosa Parks and President Daisaku Ikeda of the
Soka Gakki International Buddhist Organization, 1993.*
Photo by Seikyo Shimbun. Courtesy Soka Gakki International.

making" and as "about the future," the photo is positioned by Parks to point toward a future direction in human rights advocacy that she understands to resonate with her past work for civil rights reform.

The photograph also hints at another form of history in the making: the emergence of what *Turning Wheel: The Journal of Engaged Buddhism* calls "Black Dharma"—or the increasing number of black Americans who have been drawn to Buddhist practice in the post–civil rights era. Like the disciplinary history of blacks who entered philosophy programs in the 1960s and 1970s, the history of black Buddhists in the United States has not yet been written. Nevertheless, the emergence of Black Dharma provides an important cultural and critical context for understanding Charles Johnson's fiction and constitutes a significant cultural development in its own right.[2] While several critics have analyzed the importance of Buddhist ideas in Johnson's fiction and as his chosen personal religious and ethical practice, this study derives its critical apparatus from a consideration of the emergence of black Buddhism as a cultural phenomenon—from its early roots in the nineteenth century to the growing interest in black Buddhism as reflected in Buddhist publications, the increasing number of Web-based list serves or "cyber-sanghas" available to Buddhists of color, and to the number of recent books published by black Buddhists, including those by bell hooks, Jan Willis, and Charles Johnson.

Although Johnson has been interested in Eastern thought since he was fourteen, when he discovered one of his mother's yoga books and experimented with meditation for the first time, he has become more outspoken about his Buddhism since the 1990s, contributing a number of essays to leading Buddhist journals, speaking freely about his Buddhist practice in interviews, and publishing in 2003 *Turning the Wheel*, a collection that includes seven essays on Buddhism. While Buddhism is not the only Eastern religion or philosophy important to Johnson, and while critics often comment on the complex fusion of *multiple* Eastern influences in his fiction, Buddhism is undoubtedly the most important in his life and in his art. Johnson's increasingly public stance on Buddhism is partly due to his deepening personal commitment to Buddhist practice—a commitment that led him on November 14, 2007, to take formal Buddhist vows—and partly a response to increased calls for blacks to speak out about their Buddhist practice. This chapter draws on the writings of black Buddhists to recover the history of Black Dharma and derives from that history a critical apparatus for understanding the evolution of Johnson's fiction. His four major novels reveal a changing understanding of the relationship between personal enlightenment and civic action as Johnson moves from a Buddhism more aligned with traditional (Mahayana) Buddhist readings of the nature of suffering, enlightenment, and engagement to a black Buddhist position that reads Buddhism through a civil rights heuristic.[3] The tension between private enlightenment and civic engagement in Johnson's fiction is therefore most pronounced in *Oxherding Tale*, Johnson's second novel and the one in which he first turns from a neo-Marxist economy of productive subjectivity to a Mahayana Buddhist conception of enlightenment that posits civic engagement largely in altruistic rather than activist terms.

## The Beginnings of Black Dharma in the United States

At the opening ceremonies of the 1893 World's Parliament of Religion—part of the historic World's Columbian Exposition in Chicago—a small number of Buddhists and blacks joined four thousand other attendees to inaugurate what historian Richard Hughes Seager calls "a first of its kind event in the history of the world" (*Dawn* 8). Although black Americans may have first encountered Buddhism on American soil on other, less dramatic occasions—such as in working alongside Chinese immigrants on the building of the Transcontinental Railroad—the 1893 parliament provides what may be the first well-documented gathering of black people and Buddhists in the United States.[4] African American representatives included Frederick

Douglass, Bishop Benjamin William Arnett and Bishop D. A. Payne (from the African Methodist Episcopal Church), and Fannie Barrier Williams (a Unitarian laywoman). Buddhist representatives included Angarika Dharmapala from Ceylon and Japanese Buddhists Zenshiro Negachi, H. Reverend Zitsuzen, Horen Toki, and Zen Master Soyen Shaku. Held on September 11, a day that over a century later would become infamous for a tragedy that seemed to epitomize the kind of religious antagonism that the World's Parliament of Religions—taken at its best—sought to surmount, the opening ceremony began as the Columbian Liberty Bell was rung ten times and as delegates from the "world's ten great religions" entered the Hall of Columbus arm in arm.[5]

Designed to commemorate the four-hundredth anniversary of Columbus's "discovery" of the Americas, the Parliament of Religions holds a special, if problematic, place in the history of religious pluralism. The Columbian Exposition itself was in part a grand display of national, cultural, and racial supremacy. In order to protest its treatment of African Americans, Ida B. Wells published *The Reason Why the Colored American Is Not in the World's Columbian Exposition* (1893), a work that documented the fair's denial of good-paying jobs to black workers and the racist showcasing of "primitive" African peoples. At the Parliament of Religion the great majority of speeches were by white Christians, whereas other religious traditions and racial and ethnic groups were more meagerly represented: Native Americans were represented in part by a white woman ("Miss Alice C. Fletcher of Cambridge, Massachusetts"), African Americans by a disturbingly small delegation, and Africans and South Americans largely by scientists with an anthropological perspective (Barrows 2:812). Somewhat ironically, several white Christians used the parliament explicitly to speak out against religious pluralism and against the call by some speakers—notably the popular Swami Vivekananda—for the development of a universal religion. Representing Vedantic Hinduism, Vivekananda argued that "every religion is only ... evolving a God out of the material man; and the same God is the inspirer of all of them" (2:977). White Christian William Wilkerson, however, argued against religious pluralism and asserted that the attitude of Christianity toward other religions must be one of "universal, absolute, eternal, unappeasable hostility" (2:1249). Although the parliament is often pointed to as a landmark event in the history of Christian ecumenicalism, religious pluralism, and the development of comparative religious studies, its relation to all of these movements obviously is culturally and racially complex.

But however problematic a place the 1893 World's Parliament of Religions holds in the history of religious pluralism, the event's importance to the establishment of Buddhism in the West is undeniable. As Seager observes, the parliament marks the beginning of "full-scale Asian missions to the

Western nations" (*Dawn* 10). Significantly, one of the Asian delegates to the parliament was the first Buddhist Zen master to visit the United States, Soyen Shaku, who was asked by Paul Carus, publisher of *Open Court* (and editor of *The Monist*), to stay in America in order to translate books on Asian religion.[6] Although Shaku declined, one of his students, D. T. Suzuki (1870–1966), came to the United States in 1897 to work with Carus on a translation of the *Tao Te Ching* (Verhoeven 217). Thus began the career of perhaps the twentieth century's leading Buddhist scholar in the West. As a result of the World's Parliament, other Asian religious groups also sent representatives to begin missions in the United States—a consequence that the parliament's planners had probably not anticipated.[7]

While other Asian Buddhists were also important to the dissemination of Buddhism in the West, Suzuki's influence on Western Buddhism over the course of the twentieth century as a translator, writer, teacher, spiritual leader, and lecturer is especially significant. He was important to both the growth of Beat Buddhism in the 1950s and to what is commonly referred to as the "Buddhist Boom" in the 1960s and 1970s.[8] Suzuki's knowledge of several languages, his extensive travels across Europe and the United States, and his influence as the leading scholar on Zen Buddhism during his lifetime were critical to the Western dissemination of Buddhism. More important for this study, however, is that Suzuki influenced other mid-century thinkers directly tied to the critique of analytic philosophy that would become so influential to the generation of philosophy students that included Charles Johnson (discussed in chapter 1). William Barrett, whose critique of the professionalization of the academy would resonate with those black philosophers who attempted to reinvigorate the discipline of philosophy in the last third of the twentieth century, put out an edited collection of Suzuki's writings, *Zen Buddhism* (1956), two years before he published his immensely popular *Irrational Man* (1958). While writing his dissertation, Johnson used the translation of Marx's *1844 Manuscripts* by Erich Fromm, who studied with Suzuki at Columbia in the 1950s. Fromm's own work comparing Freudianism and Buddhism, *Buddhism and Psychoanalysis*, was published in 1970. As an adherent to the Buddhist understanding of "interbeing," or the recognition of the dependent co-origination of all beings, Johnson would probably be pleased to reflect on the numerous ties that connect him to 1893 World's Parliament of Religions, which include his use of the thought of delegate Vivekananda to explain the practice of "mindfulness" in his 2003 collection of essays, *Turning the Wheel* (36)—and the fact that delegate Shoyen Shaku, by sending his student D. T. Suzuki to the United States, established there the form of Buddhism (Zen) to which Johnson would dedicate himself approximately one hundred years after the World's Parliament ended.[9]

*Out of the Shadows: Recent Developments in Black Dharma*

"The time has come," bell hooks declared in a 1994 issue of the Buddhist journal *Tricycle*, "for more people of color in the United States to move out of the shadows of silence and speak about the nature of their spiritual practice" ("Waking Up" 44). From the 1990s to the early 2000s, the visibility of black Buddhists in fact increased dramatically as a number of Buddhists of color began to speak out more publicly about their religious affiliation in Buddhist publications such as *Shambhala Sun, Tricycle: The Buddhist Review*, and *Turning Wheel: The Journal of Socially Engaged Buddhism*.[10] In 1993 Tina Turner's film *What's Love Got to Do with It* dramatized her own conversion to Nichiren Buddhism at movie theaters across the country. By 2003 interest in black practitioners had grown to the point where *Turning Wheel* published a special issue titled "Black Dharma," which included pieces by Alice Walker, Jan Willis, and Johnson, among others. In the pages of Buddhist journals, in collections such as *Dharma, Color, and Culture* (2004), edited by Hilda Gutiérrez Baldoquín (which includes an essay by Johnson), and in books such as Johnson's *Turning the Wheel*, Willis's *Dreaming Me: An African American Woman's Spiritual Journey* (2001), Angel Kyodo Williams's *Being Black: Zen and the Art of Living with Fearlessness and Grace* (2000), and Faith Adiele's *Meeting Faith: The Forest Journals of a Black Buddhist Nun* (2004), the work of black Buddhists provides new perspectives on and contexts for understanding the character of American Buddhism. From the late 1990s on, scholarly studies of American Buddhism have also demonstrated a greater awareness of the need to account for an African American presence in Western Buddhism, as is reflected in Christopher S. Queen's *Engaged Buddhism in the West* (2000) and *Action Dharma: New Studies in Engaged Buddhism* (2003), edited by Queen and others, as well as in articles in scholarly journals such as the *Journal of the International Association of Buddhist Studies* and the *Journal of Buddhist Ethics*. More recently still, black Buddhist bloggers have begun debating the dharma on sites such as "Blogging While Black" and "Zen under the Skin: Reflections of an African-American Practitioner."[11]

Like the black philosophers discussed in chapter 1 who faced unique disciplinary pressures when they entered the largely white field of philosophy, black Buddhists encounter a distinctive set of social pressures as their participation in American Buddhism becomes more visible. In particular, they are frequently put in the position of having to defend either their Buddhism or their "blackness." Many black Buddhists write about the covert disapproval or overt antagonism they receive from both whites and blacks who learn about their Buddhist observance. hooks has felt "singled out" for her interest in Buddhism when white people ask her insinuatingly, "Why are you interested in Zen?" ("Waking Up" 42). In "Moving toward an End to Suffering," Marlene Jones, an African American woman who practices in the Theravada Buddhist tradition, describes being asked by white Buddhists: "What would a black person be doing at a meditation center? I thought that you liked Baptist churches and dancing" (43). As the black Japanese practitioner Ramon Calhoun suggests, being both black and Buddhist "confounds people's expectations"—such as that Asian Buddhists are "serene, contemplative, deliberate" while blacks are "outspoken, expressive, emotional" (Calhoun 39). Such preconceptions can easily degenerate, as the experiences of many black Buddhists would seem to suggest, into forms of racist and Orientalist essentialism.

Black Buddhists also face criticism from African American Christians who worry that the practice of Buddhism constitutes an abandonment of black people's traditional religious heritage in America. Concerns range from religious anxieties that individual Buddhists may be putting their immortal souls in danger to the more culturally based criticism that a conversion to Buddhism simply continues the cultural devastation of black Americans wrought by Western slavery and its aftermath. In a 2000 article in the *Cleveland Plain Dealer*, Buddhist La Vora Perry writes of being told by another African American woman with whom she had been having a friendly chat in the waiting room of a maternity ward, "Your father didn't raise you right, that's your problem" ("Religion" 3). Ironically, Perry identifies the religious training she received from her father—a Baptist minister—as important preparation for her later conversion to Buddhism. To those who suggest that she is a cultural sellout for not being a Protestant Christian, Perry responds, "Like many Blacks, I believe that Jesus probably had African ancestry, but most folks also believe he lived in the Middle East, and that area's not known for having much American-style, 'it's-a-Black-thing' flavor" (2). bell hooks may name the cultural anxiety that lies at the heart of such objections when she suggests that converting to Buddhism, for many black people, is "synonymous with choosing Whiteness" ("Waking Up" 42). Given the majority white membership in most convert Buddhist organizations, some black Buddhists argue that such fears are legitimate, and they point to the difficulties that blacks have experienced in incorporating black cultural practices into various Buddhist communities as evidence that American Buddhism should adapt to the needs of black Americans. As Choyin Rangdröl explains, "To African Americans this can appear to be a destructive cultural process that goes against the grain of their historicity, their heritage, and their legacy in America as survivors of cultricide" (Rangdröl 23).

The response of black Buddhists to racial, cultural, and religious criticism of their practice is of necessity emotionally and intellectually complex.

Against the accusation that they are not being "black enough" in choosing Buddhism, some black Buddhists point out that Christianity served the oppressor's interests until black people adapted it for their own spiritual, social, and political needs. Their point resonates with the analysis offered by Lawrence Levine in his classic study of slave culture, *Black Culture and Black Consciousness* (1977), in which he argues that enslaved people were not "passive receptors" of Christianity but rather they "selectively" chose those parts of the religion that spoke to their oppressed situation—and by doing so, turned the oppressor's religion into an "instrument of life, of sanity, of health, and of self-respect" (70). Or, as Carol Cooper succinctly suggests in an interview with bell hooks, "we tend to transform the things we embrace" ("Black Folks" 1). In a 2005 article, "Buddhism and the Body Problem," African American Buddhist scholar and sympathizer Lori Pierce points out that in spite of the predominance of Protestantism among African Americans, some "members of the black community have made other religious choices" during their history in America (such as the choice to become a Black Muslim). These choices, she asserts, also reveal "deliberate attempts to create a new, empowering ethnic and religious identity that validated and explained the African American experience" (21, 22). Black Buddhists demonstrate that they understand their practice as part of a similar process of transformation—one that may require, as Alice Walker suggests, that they give themselves "permission to posit a different way from that in which [they were] raised" ("This Was Not" 195).

While some black Buddhists simply claim as a basic human right the freedom to choose the religious affiliation that they find best satisfies their spiritual needs, others argue that one need not give up Christianity to become a practicing Buddhist. Willis, for example, has called herself a "Baptist Buddhist" ("Dharma" 221). Since Buddhism has sometimes been classified as more of a philosophy or a mental and spiritual discipline than as a religion in the usual Western sense of the word—at the World's Parliament of Religions, Dharmapala called it a "philosophical religion" rather than a "theology" (quoted in Barrows 2:863)—it is probably not surprising that many practitioners do not see a conflict between their Buddhist practice and the religious beliefs they maintain from other traditions. As bell hooks explains in a 1995 feature in *Shambhala Sun*: "In the morning I sit zazen [Zen meditation], but then I always take time to say my Christian prayers at the same time. It's like those two traditions have walked with me through my life and I haven't been able to just choose one as the right one for me. I still feel like the sweetness of both of them enhances my life" ("bell hooks" 8). Like many other black Buddhists, hooks frequently cites the writings of the Vietnamese Buddhist monk Thich Nhat Hanh (who was nominated by Dr. Martin Luther King Jr. for the 1967 Nobel Peace Prize) as further support for blending Christian and Buddhist traditions. In *Living Buddha, Living Christ* (1997), Hanh emphasizes the similarities between Buddhism and Christianity; and in *Going Home: Jesus and Buddha as Brothers* (2000), he suggests that Buddhists who have felt anxious about leaving their Christianity behind can reclaim that religion while still participating in Buddhist practice. Other black practitioners argue further that Buddhist practice can enhance their Christianity: as Jan Willis explains, "I can use *Buddhist* methods to practice *Baptist* ideals" ("Dharma" 221).

In his humorous but powerful early short story "China" (1983), Charles Johnson investigates the sorts of cultural and religious tensions that can arise from black Americans' practice of Buddhism by dramatizing the conflict that develops between a married couple when the husband acquires a sudden passion for the martial arts and Eastern philosophy. At the beginning of the narrative the husband, Rudolph, and his wife, Evelyn, share a marital intimacy that seems to be grounded in a mutual resignation to the disappointments of life. Rudolph, an out-of-shape middle-aged man plagued with heart trouble and impotence, is resigned to an early death, while Evelyn maintains that "everything failed; it was some kind of law" (78). The crisis in their marriage occurs when they attend a low-budget kung fu movie and Rudolph is mesmerized by the seemingly impossible leaps the actors make high into the air. As Evelyn is quick to point out, the leaps are in fact impossible: the actors are supported by wires that are visible on screen. The movie nevertheless inspires in Rudolph a sudden zeal for the martial arts, which, over the course of the short story, leads him to reclaim his health, to develop an interest in Eastern thought, and to acquire a new set of diverse friends (some of whom Evelyn suspects of being gay).

To Evelyn, Rudolph's newfound interests directly challenge both African American culture in general and their marital intimacy in particular. Rudolph starts to spout Eastern views that "no Negro preacher worth his name would speak" and to reject her "heavy soul food dishes" for "vegetables, seaweed, nuts, and fruit" (87, 79). Because Evelyn had originally fallen in love with Rudolph in the Mount Zion Baptist church, where he first attracted her as a "Christian soldie[r], . . . the cream of black manhood," his actions appear especially suspect (67). She tells Rudolph: "You grew up in Hodges, South Carolina, same as me, in a right and proper colored church. If you'd *been* to China, maybe I'd understand" (90). An idealistic youth who hoped to attend Moody Bible Institute, Rudolph has found his adult life to be one disillusionment after another. Turned down by Moody's, forced to work at unfulfilling jobs, Rudolph has lost all sense of control over his life. Through the martial arts, however, he reshapes his body, reclaims his lost sense of agency, and rediscovers his idealism, while Evelyn battles with herself to accept the changes that she fears will lead him away from her.

Although most of Johnson's narrative concentrates on Evelyn's disapproving, fearful, yet humorous (and sometimes quite understandable) reactions to Rudolph's sudden obsession, Evelyn herself experiences a radical transformation in the narrative's conclusion. She attends a martial arts exhibition to watch her husband compete and sees Rudolph leap high into the air, "twenty feet off the ground in a perfect flying kick" (95). Evelyn's vision of her revitalized husband, who previously had to "rest and run cold water on his wrists after walking from the front stairs to the fence to pick up a copy of the *Seattle Times*," shatters her conventional patterns of thinking and enables her to give her heart's assent to her husband's transformation, even if it means he may leave her or that she may die first (94). Significantly, because Evelyn achieves her spiritual insight in an exhibition hall that Johnson figures in language drawn explicitly from the African American spiritual tradition, one in which the voices of the audience affect her "like the pitch and roll of voices during service," the conclusion suggests that their marriage may be able to accommodate the changes in Rudolph—and that African American culture may also be able to incorporate "Baptist" and "Buddhist" ideals (Willis, "Dharma" 94).[12]

In addition to encountering accusations that they are not being black enough, African American practitioners also find themselves charged by white Buddhists with being *too* ethnocentric. Because Buddhists are trained to recognize the ways in which reified categories—what Johnson calls "calcified, prefabricated thinking" in "Reading the Eightfold Path"—may limit understanding, one's national, ethnic, and racial practices can sometimes be interpreted from a Buddhist perspective as limiting forms, something to overcome rather than to celebrate (138). In "Black Buddha: Bringing the Tradition Home," however, Rangdröl argues that culture can serve as a path to enlightenment and that blacks should insist on the legitimacy of both their cultural practice and their Buddhism: "African Americans can use their own culture, too. No one questions Tibetan, Japanese, or Chinese culture in Buddhism, but the moment African Americans say, 'this is my culture and I am Buddhist,' people say we are being ethnocentric" (24). Rangdröl's position seems in keeping with the teaching of dependent co-origination, which argues that because everything arises from a complex set of causes in a specific situation, its appearance is necessarily contingent. Or as Lewis Wood, the editor of the "Black Dharma" issue of *Turning Wheel*, insists, "*all* Buddhism is culturally hyphenated Buddhism" (2).

Although black Buddhists encounter negative reactions to their practice that range from the mildly inquisitive to the forcefully disrespectful, they also find that Buddhism resonates deeply with their situated experience as black Americans. In particular, practitioners of African descent write eloquently about their powerful responses to Buddhism's emphasis on suffering and liberation, about the efficacy of their Buddhist belief in providing concrete practices for realizing spiritual goals (especially for combating the debilitating psychological effects of racism), and about their attraction to Buddhism's radically egalitarian values, particularly as those values are realized in what has been termed "engaged Buddhism."

Several black Buddhist practitioners assert that the history of black oppression in America led them to respond powerfully to the First Noble Truth expounded by Buddha, "There is suffering." As Johnson writes, "The black experience in America, like the teachings of Shakyamuni Buddha, begins with suffering" ("Sangha" 46). Willis suggests further that black people's history of oppression may enable them to grasp the discussions of suffering in Buddhist thought more quickly than those from other backgrounds: "People of color, because of our experience of the great and wrenching historical dramas of slavery, colonization, and segregation, understand suffering in a way that our white brothers and sisters do not, and . . . this understanding is closer to what is meant by the Buddhist injunction [to understand suffering]" ("Dharma" 220). Thus the oppression of black people both serves as a compelling motivation for some African Americans' initial attraction to Buddhism and provides them, as Willis asserts, with a sort of "head start" in comprehending Buddhist philosophy (217).

It is not only the historical experience of oppression that enables black practitioners to respond to the Buddhist emphasis on suffering but also, as several black Buddhists insist, the depth of black people's present psychological, spiritual, and social suffering. Black Americans, as Alice Walker observes, are "being consumed" by suffering ("This Was Not" 191). In a 2001 interview bell hooks ties her decision to become more open about her Buddhist practice specifically to a concern for such distress: "That's why I've been coming out of the closet myself about spirituality period. Because I don't think we can afford to stay in the closet, our circumstance is too dire. . . . I came out of the whole, 'my spiritual practice is private bag' because I just thought, hey, our people are suffering" (Cooper, "About" 3). hooks stresses that the extent of black people's suffering goes largely unrecognized in American society. As she indicates in *Rock My Soul* (2003): "Throughout our history in this nation, black people as a whole have wanted to minimize the reality of trauma in black life. It has been easier for everyone to focus on issues of material deprivation . . . than to place the issue of trauma and recovery on our agendas" (23). For some black people, the Buddhist emphasis on the truth of human suffering seems to validate both their historical and their contemporary experience, providing Buddhism with the power, as Rangdröl explains, to "reverberate down to the core of the hurt so many of us carry" (23).

It is important to note that while black Buddhists may understand their suffering as a manifestation of the universal validity of the First Noble Truth, they nonetheless insist on the distinctive historical and cultural character of that suffering. As Ralph Steele explains in an interview with William Poy Lee, "Being a black person in a particular land or culture leads to a particular kind of suffering" (2). Steele, born on Pawley's Island in a Gullah Gee Chee community, experienced racism both in the United States and in Japan, where he moved with his military family as a youth. He credits Buddhist practice with enabling him to overcome the traumas of racism and his war service. Other black practitioners also testify to the power of Buddhism in enabling them to overcome the traumatic effects of racism, from more subtle forms of "mental colonization" to the debilitating effects of psychic trauma caused by terroristic acts. Growing up near Birmingham, Alabama, Willis participated in the Birmingham campaign led by Martin Luther King Jr. in 1963. Afterwards the Ku Klux Klan burned a cross in her family's yard in response to a newspaper account that she had won a scholarship to Cornell. Buddhism, she contends, enables her to transform her rage so that it is not self-destructive ("You're Already" 32). For many black practitioners Buddhism seems to provide, as Johnson asserts, a "the richest of refuges from a predominantly white, very Eurocentric and culturally provincial society almost completely blind to the dignity and deeds, well-being and needs, of people of color" ("Reading" 127). Or, as Johnson summarizes—Buddhism offers "an exquisite manual for survival" ("Reading" 128).

Westerners often tend to understand meditation and chanting as contemplative activities with few practical consequences. While insisting on the cultural specificity of their suffering, however, black Buddhists such as Steele, Willis, Sara Steinbach, and Johnson emphasize that Buddhism provides them with a practical means for transforming suffering. For Merle Kyoto Boyd, Zen practice offered a "new way of defining suffering and a new way to end it" (102). In particular, black adherents write of the personal empowerment and increased sense of agency they discover through Buddhist practice, and they frequently refer to Buddhism as something they "do" rather than something they "believe." It is not uncommon for practitioners to compare the rigors of Buddhist training, especially as it is taught in the meditative traditions, to physical training in the martial arts. Indeed, Steele, Williams, and Johnson all practiced the martial arts before becoming Buddhists. Johnson also co-directed the Twin Tigers kung fu studio where Martin Hughes, future *babot* of the Diago-ji temple in Osaka, trained when he was living in Seattle. In Johnson's short story "China," Rudolph first discovers Eastern thought through kung fu films. Only afterward does he learn that "*gung-fu* means 'hard work' in Chinese" and apply that lesson to his mental and spiritual discipline as well as to his physical conditioning (76). Many black Buddhists argue that just as physical exercise is a practical way to transform the body, so mental and spiritual exercise offers an effective way to reshape one's attitudes, thinking, and habits. Willis elaborates on the practical character of meditative practice when she explains just how she uses "Buddhist methods to practice Baptist ideals." When she found that she was having difficulty abiding by the Christian injunction to "love your enemy," Willis practiced a series of meditations specifically designed to develop loving kindness by progressively leading from the cultivation of compassion for oneself, to the practice of compassion for loved ones and friends, to—finally—the practice of compassion toward those from whom one has experienced hostility ("Dharma" 221). Moreover, a belief in the practical benefits of meditative practice has also led some black Buddhists, such as Willis and Rangdröl, to create new meditations specifically aimed at changing racist attitudes.

Significantly, in addition to attesting to Buddhism as a practical tool for personal transformation, a large number of black Buddhist practitioners advocate for what Thich Nhat Hanh has labeled "engaged Buddhism," or the practice of Buddhism as a tool for social reform.[13] In his study of engaged Buddhism, "Responding to the Cries of the World," David Rothberg points out that the phenomenon includes "a broad range of approaches, unified by the notion that Buddhist teachings and practices can be directly applied to participation in the social, political, economic, and ecological affairs of the nonmonastic world" (268). By leaving the monastery to work among the war-stricken populace during the Vietnam War, Hanh provided an exemplary illustration of such practice: as he explains in support of engagement, "Once there is seeing, there must be acting" (*Peace* 91). Engaged Buddhists undertake various kinds of social reform, ranging from grass-roots activism (such as working in local shelters and providing AIDS volunteerism) to participating in poverty, peace, reform, health, and civil rights movements worldwide. Willis is active in prison outreach programs in the United States, a growing Buddhist service.[14] At the same time, Buddhist organizations like Soka Gakkai, an official nongovernmental organization of the United Nations, are active in various international civil rights, relief, and peace movements (Hurst 94). By contrast, Laurence Ellis practices engaged Buddhism through his regular employment, which he understands as an application of the Buddhist concept of "right livelihood." A graduate of the University of North Carolina and a former Rhodes Scholar, Ellis serves as an organizational consultant for Amnesty International, health organizations, and several large corporations, where he applies "values-based strategies" to make organizations more "just" (Lee, "Black" 2). According to Ellis, Buddhism offers "concrete tools" that can be used to transform "institutions that perpetuate systematic suffering, domination, and violence" (3).

While their published writings suggest that a majority of African American adherents are drawn to some form of engaged Buddhist practice, since the 1980s scholars of Western Buddhism have demonstrated a growing interest in evaluating the "legitimacy" of engaged Buddhism in relation to traditional Buddhism. One important controversy is the degree to which a socially activist practice may conflict with fundamental Buddhist teachings on liberation, suffering, and the nature of the self. Obviously, such a conflict would be of concern to all engaged Buddhists, but especially so to those who are members of oppressed minorities. Bardwell L. Smith identifies one potential conflict in his discussion of whether certain twentieth-century "reinterpretations" of Buddhist teachings on liberation run the risk of confusing "what is primary" in Buddhism with what is not: "The primary goal of Buddhism is not a stable order or a just society but the discovery of genuine freedom (or awakening) by each person. . . . For Buddhists to lose this distinction is to transform their tradition into something discontinuous with its original and historic essence" (106). In an article titled "Engaged Buddhist Ethics," James Deitrick argues in a similar fashion that engaged Buddhism misinterprets key Buddhist teachings on suffering by confusing social and material suffering with a "more profound" spiritual suffering (265). Elsewhere, Derek S. Jeffreys also seems to undermine the grounds for an engaged Buddhist practice by arguing that the adoption of human rights discourse by engaged Buddhists is "philosophically problematic." Such rights are historically and logically grounded, he argues, in a Western conception of the individual as a "stable agent who possesses rights"—a conception obviously in conflict with the Buddhist teaching of "no self," the view that a belief in the existence of an unchanging, substantive self is merely an illusion (271). By raising questions about the degree to which engaged Buddhists may be altering central Buddhist teachings and by pointing to possible philosophical inconsistencies in engaged Buddhists' espousal of human rights, these scholars question the degree to which Buddhists' practice of "engagement" coheres with traditional Buddhist teachings on "enlightenment."

To articulate a response to such criticisms and to explain their own practice, engaged Buddhists draw on several textual, historical, and philosophical justifications for their practice. The description of Buddhism as a passive religion concerned only, or even primarily, with inner cultivation is countered as a mischaracterization of traditional Eastern Buddhism—one that is fueled, perhaps, by an unconscious Orientalism.[15] More precisely, to rebut the assertion that historical Buddhism advocates ascetic quietism, scholars cite textual and historical antecedents for twentieth-century engaged practice. In addition, engaged Buddhists offer careful interpretations of Buddhist teachings on "suffering," "no self," and "dependent coorigination" in order to demonstrate that the tradition either provides room for, encourages, or in fact *requires* engaged practice.

For example, the claim that the Buddhist conception of "no self" undermines the grounds for supporting human rights is countered by arguments which suggest that the concept has been mistakenly interpreted in the West in nihilistic terms, when it should be interpreted to mean something closer to the claim that there is no "permanent, essential self." Such an understanding of the self requires not that one give up an appreciation of personal dignity, defenders of engaged Buddhism argue, but rather that one give up a Western understanding of the source from which that dignity arises. Understanding the self as necessarily impermanent, for example, can imply a respect for others that is grounded in their very capacity to change: a person cannot logically be dismissed as *being* a liar or a thief if one does not believe in a permanent self, since there is always an expectation that the person can change.[16] Similarly, Thich Nhat Hanh finds the grounds for compassion and a respect for others in "emptiness," which he translates not in terms of nothingness but through the neologism "inter-being." Rather than an essentialized state of nothingness, he understands "emptiness" to mean empty of individual essences. In "Reading the Eightfold Path," Johnson explicitly discusses Hanh's claim that "there is no such thing as an individual" (132). There he contends that this claim entails not nihilism but rather an understanding of reality as a "*We*-relation" (132). Understanding reality as a We-relation obviously does not pose the same philosophical problems for justifying compassion for others as does an understanding of human reality as composed of atomistic individuals, although it may well raise other philosophical problems of its own, such as those involving individuation.

To justify their activist practice, socially engaged Buddhists also point to specific textual and historical antecedents, beginning with the Buddha himself. Viveka Chen, a member of the Western Buddhist order, an engaged Buddhist order whose Web site announces the somewhat paradoxical intent "to create new Buddhist traditions relevant to the 21st century," calls Buddha "a freedom fighter who launched a spiritual movement empowering people to end mental, physical, and spiritual enslavement" (111). While the designation "freedom fighter" smacks of anachronistic hyperbole, the Buddha did admit people of different castes, classes, nationalities, and genders into his religious community, an action considered by some scholars to be a radical one for the period.[17] Significantly, many engaged Buddhists find particularly important antecedents for their practice in Mahayana Buddhism, which is believed to have emerged in the first century CE in reaction to Theravada Buddhism's emphasis on the necessity of monastic practice for achieving enlightenment. In Sanskrit, *yana* means "cart" or method of conveyance: different "yanas" thus signify different methods of conveying—practicing or disseminating— Buddhism. The Theravada method is primarily that of the ascetic, who separates from the world in order to achieve enlightenment through rigorous monastic training. The Mahayana method, by contrast, emphasizes the path of laypeople who seek enlightenment while engaged *in* the world. Because it understood itself to be opening the path of enlightenment to all, Mahayana Buddhism disparaged Theravada Buddhism as "Hinayana," the "smaller" vehicle, while naming itself the "greater" ("Maha"). In addition to articulating a Buddhist economy of enlightenment in a way that emphasizes immersion in the world, Mahayana Buddhism stresses the ideal of the bodhisattva, a figure frequently evoked as providing a precedent for engaged Buddhism. As Johnson emphasizes, the bodhisattva is a person of great spiritual achievement who, "due to his compassion, renounc[es] full immersion in nirvana in order to work indefatigably for the salvation of all sentient beings" ("Reading" 136).

In "Reading the Eightfold Path," Johnson explains the bodhisattva ideal by comparing it to the figure of the Oxherder in Zen master K'uo-an Shih-yuan's twelfth-century *Oxherding Pictures*. Designed to illustrate the stages of Zen enlightenment through progressive pictures of an oxherder's search for his lost ox, Shih-yuan's illustrations follow the Oxherder from his tracking of the ox to his finding, taming, and returning with the ox.[18] As Johnson points out, different picture series of the Oxherder by other artists offer only five or eight drawings in the series, and they end with a picture of an empty circle, which suggests that the final stage of enlightenment is an ascetic state in which both ox and self have been forgotten. In Shih-yuan's series of paintings, however, there are ten pictures, and the last one depicts the Oxherder ending his successful search by, according to the title, "Entering the Marketplace with Helping Hands." Shih-yuan's series thus suggests that enlightenment is realized most profoundly in compassionate service to others. For Johnson, the different series of paintings suggest the different economies of enlightenment found in Theravada and Mahayana Buddhism, with Mahayana Buddhism and the figure of the bodhisattva ideal providing conceptual and historical Buddhist precedents for engaged Buddhism, or a Buddhism that "enters the marketplace with helping hands."

Significantly, in addition to offering conceptual arguments and historical or textual precedents for engaged Buddhist practice, Western Buddhists—especially but not exclusively Buddhists of color—discuss their practice through comparisons to the U.S. civil rights movement. While such a validation may seem both historically and culturally confused, by reading Buddhism though the history of civil rights (and by reading the history of civil rights through their Buddhism), Buddhists of color enact a type of heuristic that is characteristic of the dissemination of religious thought. In describing the religious world of enslaved black people, Levine emphasizes that slaves appropriated Christianity selectively by focusing on those passages of biblical texts that had special resonance with their own condition, such as the exodus of the Israelites out of Egypt or Daniel's escape from the lion's den. In effect, slaves brought an existential hermeneutics to sacred text, one that functioned to foreground certain meanings available in holy writ while de-emphasizing others. Black Buddhists writing in the post–civil rights decades also adopt an interpretive heuristic in their appeal to the history of the civil rights movement to illuminate their practice. By so doing they translate ancient Buddhist teachings into a contemporary American and African American cultural language while selectively emphasizing certain meanings available in both the history of the civil rights movement and in Buddhism. By reading Buddhism from a post–civil rights location, then, black Buddhists, including Charles Johnson, participate in the kind of global conversations that Queen finds characteristic of twentieth-century engaged Buddhist practice as they create an innovative, hybrid form of Western Buddhism.

Most important, Western Buddhists find intellectual and historical support for their engaged Buddhist practice in the civil rights philosophy and practices of Martin Luther King Jr., whose association with Eastern religious and moral philosophies provides a (very limited) historical warrant for such an identification. King's relationship to Eastern thought deepened over his lifetime through an increasingly sophisticated engagement with Gandhi's writings; through his work with a number of self-avowed "Gandhians" who had adopted the Indian reformer's methods for social transformation (notably former Communist Party member Bayard Rustin and the Reverend Glenn Smiley); through his contact with Gandhians from India who were sent to the United States to support civil rights workers; through his trip to India in 1959 (as a guest of the Gandhian Peace Foundation); and through his increasing familiarity with the ideas of Thich Nhat Hanh, one of the factors that contributed to King's taking a public stance against the Vietnam War. King formally announced his opposition to the war while sitting next to Hanh at a press conference in 1967. Although historical associations such as these tie King more to Eastern thought in general than to Buddhism in particular, King's willingness to combine insights from the social gospel tradition with those of Eastern religious thought, and his forging out of that combination the nonviolent protest method of "direct action," provide engaged Buddhists with a powerful example of a social reform movement regulated by a religious or moral ideal. As King described his civil rights practice, "Nonviolent resistance . . . emerged as the technique of the movement, while love stood as the regulating ideal" (quoted by hooks, "Surrendered" 52).

In April 2003 the San Francisco Zen Center offered a retreat on "The Dharma of Martin Luther King." Just how such a dharma (a Buddhist teaching or way) might be understood by black Buddhists is suggested in the Winter 2005 issue of *Shambhala Sun*, which features a close-up of King on its cover and a special section inside titled "The King We Need Now More Than Ever." Both hooks and Johnson contributed articles to the issue (which also includes an interview by John Whalen-Bridge with Maxine Hong

Kingston about how her Buddhism affects her work).[19] In their essays, hooks and Johnson foreground King's commitment to nonviolence, both as the basis for social action and as "a Way, a daily praxis people must strive to translate into each and every one of their deeds" (Johnson, "The King We Need" 48). hooks's analysis centers on two important conversions that she believes King's practice demanded: a personal conversion to nonviolence and a collective conversion of values ("Surrendered" 52). Johnson also emphasizes King's moral commitment to nonviolence, which the civil rights leader illustrated in dramatic fashion on the night of January 30, 1956, when King responded to the bombing of his house in Montgomery by calming an angry crowd of black people, some of them armed, who had gathered to defend (and possibly to avenge) him and his family ("The King We Need" 48). To document the commitment to nonviolence that guided civil rights workers in Montgomery, Johnson reprints in full the "commitment blank" signed by members of the Southern Christian Leadership Conference, which begins, "I hereby pledge myself—my person and my body—to the nonviolent movement" (48). Elsewhere, in "Reading the Eight-Fold Path," Johnson specifically ties that document to Buddhist ethical principles by inviting readers to compare the "ten commandments" in the commitment blank to the "Eight-fold Path," the primary dharma of the Buddha's teachings. Both hooks and Johnson find in King's example the implication that a radical revolution in values is needed to regulate social reform efforts if those efforts are to be both effective and just. By representing Buddhism in dialogue with King, then, black Buddhists draw on King's moral authority to buttress their own practice of nonviolence, while they simultaneously cite the early successes of the civil rights movement as a historical warrant for the efficacy of nonviolent reform movements.

In addition to linking King to the Buddhist ethic of nonviolence and the dharma of the "Eight-Fold Path," black Buddhists also evoke the civil rights movement (perhaps more surprisingly) to explain specific Buddhist teachings on matters such as the character of the *sangha* (religious community), suffering, "no self," and inter-being. Boyd, for example, draws on Rosa Parks and the 1955–56 Montgomery bus boycott to explain the Buddhist distinction between "pain" and "suffering." While Buddhism teaches that all sentient beings are subject to pain, suffering itself is understood as a particular relation to that pain, a distinction Boyd illustrates in her description of the hardships faced by boycotters who gave up their transportation to work during the boycott. She writes, "People in Montgomery walking miles back and forth to work, were probably in pain, but they were not necessarily suffering" ("Child" 105). Willis makes a similar point when she describes her experience marching in the 1963 Children's Campaign in Birmingham as a fifteen-year-old. Although she marveled to learn that "water could *burn* so," she nonetheless also discovered that "because we knew we were morally and spiritually right, we were physically energized" (*Dreaming* 60).

Having read extensively in King's writings, having made the famous civil rights leader "the subject of [his] meditation for five years," having written a hagiographical novel about King's northern campaigns (*Dreamer*), and having co-produced a photo-biography of King, Johnson not surprisingly also alludes frequently to the civil rights leader in his nonfiction essays to illustrate Buddhist ideas. In particular, Johnson draws on King to illustrate the Buddhist understanding of "inter-being," in support of which he often quotes a particular passage from King's "Letter from Birmingham Jail": "It really boils down to this: that all life is interrelated. We are caught in an inescapable network of mutuality, tied in a single garment of destiny. Whatever affects one directly, affects all indirectly." Offered by King specifically in response to the charge that he was an "outside agitator" in Birmingham, this comment is interpreted by Johnson largely in phenomenological and Buddhist terms as demonstrating that "King understood that our lives are *already* tissued, ontologically, with the presence of others in a we-relation" ("The King We Need" 49).

Johnson's reading of King is better represented, perhaps, by another passage that he frequently cites from "The World House," an essay based on King's 1964 acceptance speech for the Nobel Peace Prize and one to which King gave prominence by including it as the final chapter to *Where Do We Go from Here: Chaos or Community?* (1967):

> All men are interdependent. Every nation is an heir of a vast treasury of ideas and labor to which both the living and the dead of all nations have contributed.... When we arise in the morning, we go into the bathroom where we reach for a sponge which is provided for us by a Pacific Islander. We reach for soap that is created for us by a European. Then at the table we drink coffee which is provided for us by a South American, or tea by a Chinese or cocoa by a West African. Before we leave for our jobs we are already beholden to more than half of the world. In a real sense, all life is interrelated.... Whatever affects one directly affects all indirectly. (181)

For Johnson, King's speech resonates so powerfully with the Buddhist conception of "inter-being" that he fictionalizes the essay's moment of composition in his 2005 short story "Dr. King's Refrigerator." In Johnson's homage-paying tale, the originary moment of King's trope is fictionalized as an insight that King has late one evening when, frustrated by his inability to complete a sermon, he peers into his refrigerator, searching for a midnight snack. Discovering the refrigerator brimming with groceries that Mrs. King has purchased for a meeting the next day of the Ladies Prayer Circle, King is struck by a sudden revelation as he furiously begins to unpack food from the refrigerator. As the following passage suggests, Johnson's description of King's epiphany freely weaves elements from King's "Letter from Birmingham Jail" and "The World's House" speech with the Buddhist understanding of inter-being:

> There were bricks of cheese and wine from French vineyards, coffee from Brazil, and from China and India black and green teas. . . . All of human culture, history, and civilization lay unscrolled at his feet, and he had only to step into his kitchen to discover it. No one people or tribe, living in one place on this planet, could produce the endless riches for the palate that he'd just pulled from his refrigerator. He looked around the disheveled room, and he saw in each succulent fruit, each slice of bread, and each grain of rice a fragile, inescapable network of mutuality in which all earth's creatures were codependent, integrated, and tied in a single garment of destiny. (27)

Elsewhere Johnson relates King's conception of *agape* to the respect for others that develops out of a Buddhist understanding of impermanence by defining it as the "ability to love unconditionally something not for what it currently is (for at a particular moment it might be quite unlovable, like segregationist George Wallace was in the sixties) but instead for what it might become . . . a love that recognizes everything as process . . . and sees beneath the surface to a thing's potential for positive change" ("The King We Need" 49). Finally, in a stunningly bold appropriation of King's legacy in *Turning the Wheel*, Johnson places Buddhism squarely in King's lineage, declaring it the "logical extension of King's dream of a 'beloved community'" (xvi).

Johnson, like Willis, hooks, and Walker, belongs to a generation of black Americans who matured as King's nonviolent approach to reform was becoming increasingly disparaged within the black community as "Uncle Tomism." hooks describes herself as "mesmerized" by the militant stance of Black Power activists in her youth: "If we had to choose between Malcolm and Martin, my vote was definitely going to be for Malcolm" ("Surrendered" 53). When she became politically active in college, however, hooks found herself turning to King's writings for "inspiration and wise counsel" (53). Her effort to unlearn the lessons of militarism, she suggests, were not completely achieved until she returned to King's ideals twenty years later, when she found in his message "a vision not unlike that taught during the Vietnam War by beloved Monk Thich Nhat Hanh" (53). Like hooks, Johnson testifies to being drawn to a Black Power stance as a college student. In "The King We Left Behind" (1996), he describes himself as viewing "non-violence as unmanly" and listening with "greater interest to the speeches of Malcolm X" (197). When his son was born in 1975, Johnson named the boy Malik in honor of Malcolm X, who had changed his name to El Hajj Malik El-Shabazz. Tying his own experience to that of a generation of Americans who "left King behind," Johnson ends his essay with a call for a return to the values that King represents.

If such accounts demonstrate how difficult it can be to determine whether it is King's vigorous moral vision that provides a pathway for some black people to Buddhism or whether it is Buddhism that provides a pathway for their rediscovery of King, such comments nevertheless speak to the compelling moral resonance that some African Americans detect between the two traditions. David Chappell suggests that one of the main factors attracting blacks to Soka Gakkai is that organization's commitment to human rights in general and to President Daisaku Ikeda's reputation in particular for supporting civil rights efforts worldwide (195). By choosing a picture of herself with Ikeda to represent her life in *Talking Pictures*, Rosa Parks suggested that she, too, felt a resonance between engaged Buddhist practice and her own efforts in support of civil rights reform.

In his important study of the neo-slave narrative genre, Ashraf Rushdy argues that Johnson turned in his thinking from a Black Power position to one reminiscent of the Marxist radical turned conservative commentator David Horowitz. While Rushdy is correct to see a change in Johnson's thought that includes a rejection of Black Power and black nationalist stances, the comparison of Johnson to Horowitz and his Second Thoughts group of former radicals is, as even Rushdy suspects, politically and intellectually inexact.[20] Johnson was never so radical as was Horowitz in the 1970s, nor is he nearly so conservative as Horowitz subsequently became. (As I argue in chapter 2, Johnson's interest in Marx's conception of productive subjectivity never led him to endorse class warfare.) Rather, the turn in Johnson's thinking is best understood in relation to the group of black Buddhists described here, people who are in the process of constructing a unique form of Western Buddhism from a post–civil rights location. Whether or not one interprets the tendency of black Buddhists to read Buddhism through a civil rights heuristic as a legitimate appropriation of King's thought or as something akin to the stance of those conservatives who appropriate King in order to argue against affirmative action — an argument with which, in fact, neither Willis, Johnson, hooks, nor Walker would agree — the emergence of Black Dharma in the post–civil rights era is a historical, intellectual, and cultural phenomenon in its own right.

In addition to providing an important cultural and critical context for interpreting the creative productions of such practitioners and fellow travelers as bell hooks, Jan Willis, Alice Walker, Trey Ellis, and Charles Johnson, taking black Buddhism into account will necessarily change the outlines of the history of Buddhism in the United States. For example, World's Parliament of Religion representative Anagarika Dharmapala's work as a social reformer in Sri Lanka and India is commonly discussed in Buddhist scholarship in relation to Colonel Henry Steele Olcott.[21] Dharmapala's contact with Booker T. Washington and his visit to the Tuskegee Institute in June 1903 are not mentioned by the standard studies of engaged Buddhism. Two letters from Dharmapala to Washington, however, can be found in *The Booker T. Washington Papers*, one written before his visit to Tuskegee in June 1903 and another written afterwards. As Dharmapala writes in his second letter, "I have gained from my visit to Tuskegee an experience that I shall never forget" (Dharmapala, letter of December 23, 1903, 508). The purpose of his trip is named in his first letter to Washington, in which Dharmapala describes his intention to "stay two days with you studying the methods" (Dharmapala, letter of June 20, 1903). Since Dharmapala's own system for reform combined a reformed Buddhist practice with the practical methods of self-reliance and industrial education, his visit to observe "the methods" of industrial education as they were developed at Tuskegee may well have influenced his own work.[22] In any case, such a meeting of two famous social reformers illustrates the kinds of encounters that taking account of the relationship between blacks and Buddhists can illuminate.

Buddhist scholars often comment on the remarkable adaptability to new cultures that Buddhism has exhibited during its long history of dissemination over two millennia and six continents. As a world religion that originated in northern India in the sixth century BCE and spread to numerous Eastern countries before its migration to the West, as the fourth-largest religion in existence today (counting over 360 million people as members), and, perhaps most important, as a philosophical religion that encourages the intellectual critique of inherited dogma, it is perhaps not surprising that Buddhism has been judged to embody a "tradition of originality" (Thurman 8). The black Buddhists discussed here represent the latest chapter in that history of innovation, as they transform Buddhist practice from their particular location as black American minority practitioners. Deeply influenced both by the globalization of values that is one characteristic of the postmodern period and by their personal experience of racism, black American Buddhists articulate a new Buddhist practice through a civil rights heuristic. In taking up Buddhist practice, black Buddhists encounter unique cultural tensions as they attempt to fuse an ancient Eastern philosophical and religious practice with contemporary African American religious and cultural traditions. At the same time, the multiple commitments of engaged black Buddhists work to foreground the important question of precisely how a Buddhist understanding of enlightenment relates to engaged social practice, a question that is at the center of Johnson's second novel, *Oxherding Tale*.

## Personal Enlightenment and Civic Engagement
### *in* Oxherding Tale

Animated by the vigorous processes of cultural assimilation that Buddhist scholars identify as characteristic of the dissemination of Buddhism and by the attendant dislocations that occur when venerable teachings are adapted to new conditions, *Oxherding Tale* is a work that encodes a particular tension between Buddhist and more traditional African American conceptions of civic engagement.[23] Deeply informed by Johnson's developing Buddhist practice, *Oxherding Tale* is the first novel by Johnson to develop a Buddhist economy of liberation in a consistent fashion. The novel was composed from 1975 to 1982, the period after Johnson's philosophical interests had shifted from Marx through Marcuse to phenomenology, after he had left the discipline of philosophy to accept a faculty position in creative writing at the University of Washington, and during the period when his commitment to Buddhism deepened. Partly because of the transitions he was undergoing in his personal, spiritual and intellectual life, *Oxherding Tale* encodes a dramatic conflict between altruistic and activist forms of engagement. Johnson's selection of the neo-slave narrative genre to express his changing intellectual and spiritual positions intensifies this conflict. That is, as *Oxherding Tale* inventively *assimilates* a wide variety of disparate Eastern and Western cultural forms, it also *displaces* a more collective economy of liberation, one characteristic of the slave narrative genre. Written at a time when Johnson was turning more seriously to Eastern thought but before he immersed himself in the writings of King, before he made the civil rights leader the subject of his daily meditation for five years (a striking example of the fusion of Buddhism and the African American tradition in an individual's private devotion), and before he began to interpret Buddhism more consistently through a civil rights heuristic, *Oxherding Tale* is the novel in which the dramatic tension between a personal and a collective understanding of suffering, enlightenment, and engagement is most palpable.

Because there is a distinction between older practices of Buddhist engagement and newer forms characteristic of the twentieth century, the development of engaged Buddhism provides an important critical framework for interpreting *Oxherding Tale*. As we have seen, while Theravada Buddhism emphasizes rigorous monastic practice and the personal cultivation of virtue, Mahayana Buddhism subsumes these forms of practice and emphasizes instead the lay-based practice of altruistic service to others. But although Mahayana Buddhism is itself an adaptation of the dharma, contemporary forms of engaged Buddhism move in a new direction. On the one hand, as Queen emphasizes in the account of engaged Buddhism that he develops within the introductions to his three edited collections, "engaged Buddhism is radically different from the Mahayana path of altruism because it is directed to the creation of new social institutions and relationships" (*Engaged* 17). On the other hand, he notes, the social practice of Mahayana Buddhism largely consists of altruistic actions such as "nursing the sick, leading the blind, helping the downtrodden, feeding those who are hungry, and providing lodging for those who are needy" (14). While such actions are certainly focused on helping others, they are different in character from today's engaged practices, which include "direct challenges to official policy and state powers" (*Action* 20). The shift from the typical form of engagement practiced by Mahayana Buddhism to those characteristic of current engaged practice is so substantial, Queen argues, that twentieth-century Buddhism is in process of creating a "new yana"—a fourth vehicle for Buddhist transmission. This distinction is extremely helpful in interpreting the progress of Johnson's novels: while *Oxherding Tale* presents a position more in consonance with the traditional Mahayana position, Johnson's final novel, *Dreamer*, is more representative of a modernized, activist Western form.

From the perspective of the development of twentieth-century engaged Buddhism, and especially from the post–civil rights perspective of Black Dharma, the Mahayana practice of altruistic service differs from forms of engagement that are committed to influencing public policy and establishing new cultural forms. These changes reflect a contemporary modification in the understanding of Buddhist economy of liberation away from a more traditional Buddhist understanding in which suffering, enlightenment, and engagement are defined largely in personal terms. Traditionally, suffering itself is understood as a state of dis-ease that arises from an individual's experience of the radical contingency of consciousness. More specifically, anxieties over impermanence lead people to cling to objects or conceptualizations in an attempt to achieve a permanent identity. Enlightenment enables one to let go of such grasping desires and to help others achieve the same liberation. Suffering, enlightenment, and engagement are thus defined primarily in personal, psychological, and epistemological terms.

Although Mahayana Buddhism extends the Theravada understanding of suffering to include a variety of social ills and expands the understanding of service to others, it still tends to trace the origins of suffering to personal dis-ease rather than to social causes. Its forms of engagement consequently tend to focus on individual acts of altruism rather than on institutional reform. Twentieth-century engaged Buddhism, by contrast, demonstrates a new appreciation for the collective features of suffering, enlightenment, and engagement. At the time he was writing *Oxherding Tale*, Johnson was presenting an economy of liberation understood primarily in Mahayana terms, as an individual's relation to his or her suffering that is overcome by personal enlightenment and expressed through altruistic service to others. As I argue in this chapter, because Johnson chooses the slave genre as the one through which to transmit this particular Buddhist soteriology, his text is marked by a series of striking narrative disruptions.

In his introduction to *Oxherding Tale*, Johnson calls the novel his "platform" book, a term meant to announce a new direction in his artistic and intellectual development, and indeed the novel constitutes a decisive turn from Marxist critique to Buddhist reflection. Johnson uses the term "platform," as he emphasizes, as a "reference to the zen 'Platform Sutra of the Sixth Patriarch,' meaning that everything else [he] attempted to do would be based up and refer to it" (xvii). The novel's association with the sutra of Hui-neng (638–713 CE) also indicates that the narrative is deeply implicated in the processes of cultural transmission and dissemination that the *sutra* itself enacts.[24] The Platform Sutra itself was an innovative teaching designed to help spread the ancient Buddhist doctrine in its adopted country of China. The "platform" in the title refers to a small platform raised above the ground from which the sutra is spoken, or transmitted, by the patriarch to his listeners. The Platform Sutra, moreover, is not only the record of a specific act of transmission of Buddhist doctrine—a record of the Sixth Patriarch's words as taken down by one of his listeners—but also a text that is profoundly *about* the processes of transmission and dissemination. Beginning with a passage that recounts the history of the First Patriarch to carry the dharma to China, the sutra continues through a retelling of the history of each of the succeeding patriarchs, and ends as the Sixth Patriarch commissions his own listeners to disseminate his teaching—the Platform Sutra itself. This particular frame invites readers to understand texts as a single moment in an evolving process of assimilation and dissemination that looks both backward and forward in time. Similarly, Johnson's novel, set in nineteenth-century America, plays anachronistically with past and future, also looking backward and forward in time. Situating his novel in relation to the Platform Sutra, Johnson identifies the transmission and innovation of literary tradition with the tradition of the Buddhist teacher who assumes the platform to offers a new instruction in ancient teachings. Like the Platform Sutra, Johnson's novel self-consciously sets out to innovate established conventions by translating ancient Buddhist teachings for their dissemination in a new country.

*Oxherding Tale* leads its protagonist, Andrew, on a journey from suffering to enlightenment as it charts his attempt to escape slavery and, in dramatic terms, to escape as well the ominous character called the Soulcatcher, Horace Bannon, who pursues him from the time he first leaves his plantation birthplace. Scholars of Johnson's fiction commonly celebrate *Oxherding Tale* as the novel that best illustrates Johnson's "integrationist aesthetic." Jonathan Little suggests that the novel is "the perfect embodiment of Johnson's additive and integrationist aesthetic, in which all is contained, and nothing is lost" (*Charles* 82). Elsewhere, Rudolph Byrd uses the concept of the palimpsest to capture the integrationist, multilayered texture of Johnson's fiction.[25] But as John Whalen-Bridge has pointed out in another context, the palimpsest is not simply a textual space on which something is inscribed; it is also one from which something else has been erased ("Whole" 225). The rest of this chapter focuses on what is "erased" or "covered over" in Johnson's novel by analyzing the narrative disruptions that are created by Johnson's particular approach to his materials. As Johnson emphasizes, he does not write "historical novels" but instead uses "history as metaphor" ("Philosopher" 59). In order to encode a Mahayana soteriology, *Oxherding Tale* enacts a complex series of metaphoric displacements and substitutions. Primary among these is the metaphoric displacement of the slave's body and of the nation's bloody Civil War.

## *Disease and Dis-ease in* Oxherding Tale

*Oxherding Tale* does not ignore the suffering endemic to slavery; rather, the narrative consistently thematizes that suffering as Buddhist dis-ease through metaphoric substitution. In the novel's climactic chapter Andrew and the Soulcatcher, Horace Bannon, meet in a much anticipated final showdown. As Andrew gazes in horror at Bannon's face, he reads there a catalogue of the "countless victims" that have fallen to slavery's force: "women and children murdered with pistols knives tramped by his warhorse strangled whipped suffocated lynched beheaded burned to death starved stoned bombed thrown from heights pushed into machinery drowned clubbed impaled killed by flame tortured" (169). But at the same time that Andrew reads in Bannon's features a litany of terror that recalls the one recorded in chapter 4 of Frederick Douglass's famous *Narrative*, the novel translates the institutional causes of the slave's suffering into personal and phenomenological forms of Buddhist dis-ease. Indeed, because others cannot see the horrors that Andrew detects, he recognizes that they are in fact a projection of his own mental state: "Paranoia come to stay. Unpacking its bag, propping its feet on your table: the slayer of souls in a balandranas and kneeboots. The Negro's private flask of hemlock" (169). Underscoring Johnson's metaphorical approach to historical materials, Bannon becomes a figure for Andrew's internal state of paranoia, the "slayer of souls," externalized and decked out in "balandranas and kneeboots." As Bannon figures parts of Andrew's own psyche, the body of suffering in *Oxherding Tale* is repeatedly thematized to represent a dis-ease whose etiology is ultimately located in personal rather than political sources, as the nineteenth-century slave catcher, enforcer for the institution of slavery, becomes translated into a symbol for the destructive paranoia of the twentieth-century black man.

Johnson's narrative is littered with diseased and deformed bodies, but special attention is paid to the illnesses of the slaves at Flo Hatfield's plantation; of George, Andrew's enslaved father; and—in particular—of Andrew's first love, the slave girl Minty. In its description of each, the narrative design operates to replace material sources of illness with spiritual and psychological pathologies.[26] As the bodies of slaves pile up at the plantation, the veterinarian who treats them, Hiram Groll, suggests that the bondsmen are dying because they lack "Life-Assurance," arguing, "There's no medical explanation, as far as I know . . . when bodies pile up like cords of wood in the barn. . . . The cause of death for these black men was, strictly speaking, not physical at all, not a material failure in the usual sense, though their affliction is perhaps the oldest disease in the world, . . . the belief in personal identity" (57–58). We may be tempted to read the vet's diagnosis in the same vein as those offered by nineteenth-century physicians like Dr. Samuel Cartwright, who argued that slaves ran away because they had succumbed to the illness of "draptomania." In "Diseases and Peculiarities of the Negro Race" (1851), Cartwright suggests that "the cause in the most of cases, that induces the Negro to run away from service, is as much a disease of the mind as any other species of mental alienation." Johnson's novel, however, seems to endorse the Groll's diagnosis by assigning the bondsmen's death, in essence, to a failure to grasp the Buddhist teaching of *annatta*, or "no self." In his introduction to the novel, Johnson identifies a similar affliction as the one that enables the Soulcatcher to capture escaped slaves. Bannon is effective, Johnson suggests, because he operates by using "black fears—and a rigid, essentialist notion of the self—to trap his prey" (xvii). In other words, the enslaved body in *Oxherding Tale* suffers from an illness understood primarily in epistemological and ontological rather than institutional and material terms.

Such a metaphorical displacement of institutional meanings also appears in the discussion of the illness that plagues Andrew's father, George. A privileged house servant who is banished to the field after a drunken evening in which he and Master Polkinghorne end up exchanging beds (and wives), George afterwards attempts to purify himself "of all things European" and adopts an increasingly oppositional position to whites, telling his son, "If they say *hup*, Hawk, it's gotta be *down*" (24). As several critics have pointed out, over the course of the narrative George's character is identified with the racial essentialism that Johnson finds characteristic of a black nationalist understanding of black identity.[27] White people, according to George, are "devils or, worse, derived in some way he couldn't explain from Africans, who were a practical, down-to-earth people" (24). As George is both plantation slave and figure for black nationalism, the slave's body seems to oscillate between time frames, inhabiting at some points the terrain of slavery and at others the landscape of twentieth-century America. Although he eventually leads an uprising on the plantation and escapes, George is later hunted down by Bannon and killed. In explaining to Andrew why his father was easy to overcome, Bannon attributes his success to George's being diseased: "He was carryin' fifty-'leven pockets of death in him anyways, li'l pools of corruption that kept him so miserable he *begged* me, when Ah caught up with him in Calhoun Falls, to blow out his lights" (174). That George's illness should be read metaphorically is supported not only by Johnson's comments in the introduction about his methodology but also by Andrew's earlier diagnosis of his father as suffering from an illness, "the *need* to be an Untouchable. . . . My father kept the pain alive. He *needed* to rekindle racial horrors, revive old pains, review disappointments like a sick man fingering his sores" (142). Thus the imaginative task that Johnson undertakes in *Oxherding Tale*—that of assimilating widely divergent philosophical, religious, and literary traditions—enacts a metaphorical substitution for the slave's body by using it as a vehicle to communicate the tenor, or meaning, of a Buddhist understanding of disease.

Johnson's metaphorical narrative method, however, may create in the reader his or her own sense of dis-ease. The metaphorical substitution of the spiritual or psychological suffering of contemporary black Americans for the physical suffering of enslaved people can be jarring to readers, who naturally sympathize with the slave's condition and may feel that there is something disproportional about using the bodily suffering of slaves as a figure for other forms of human misery, no matter how debilitating. Johnson insists, however, on the contemporary artist's creative freedom to find new meanings in old genres, and his use of history suggests a similar creative freedom in his appropriation of the black past. As Andrew says at one point in *Oxherding Tale*, "Memory, as the metaphysicians say, is imagination" (109). Certainly one way to understand the reader's dis-ease, then, is as the intended result of artistic defamiliarization.[28] Johnson shocks his audience in order to unsettle their generic expectations, to transform their ordinary habits of interpretation, and to enable them to reconceptualize contemporary black identity. In *Being and Race* Johnson implicitly defends the metaphoric narrative method adopted in *Oxherding Tale* by criticizing naturalistic modes of African American literature. Such forms, he argues, ignore the power of simile and metaphor, which he calls "those inherently existential strategies that allow a writer . . . to illuminate one object by reference to another" (6). Rejecting "metaphoric power," naturalists hold "the imagination close to the ground by creating the camera-like illusion of objectivity" (6). In discussing defamiliarizing strategies in *Theory of Prose*, the Russian formalist Viktor Shklovsky uses the example of *Tristram Shandy*—a novel that *Oxherding Tale* purposely evokes both through direct allusion and through the adoption of the textual strategies of authorial intrusion and parody—in order to argue enthusiastically that the defamiliarizing capacity of art is liberating.[29] Yet Fredric Jameson has argued in *The Prison-House of Language* that the defamiliarizing strategies of art can also serve as the primary strategy through which literature attempts to establish its "literariness"—and perhaps attempts to define itself *out* of the world of engaged concern. The metaphoric displacements enacted by *Oxherding Tale* create shifting problems of interpretation as the text brings these two understandings of defamiliarization into tension by striking readers at times as disturbingly ahistorical and at other times as refreshingly original.

Such displacement is perhaps most pronounced in the narrative's representation of the diseased body of Minty, the slave girl with whom Andrew falls in love at Cripplegate Plantation. Living a life of relative comfort as Master Polkinghorne's privileged servant Andrew as a youth never experiences the worst of slavery, even after he is banished by his white mother, Anna, to George and Mattie's cabin. It is his love for Minty that first awakens Andrew's desire for freedom and leads him to ask Master Polkinghorne for permission to leave the plantation in order to earn the money needed to purchase her freedom and that of his family. Polkinghorne instead sends Andrew to Flo Hatfield's plantation, where he serves as her sex slave. Although he later escapes, events and Andrew's own self-centeredness conspire to keep him from returning to Cripplegate to free Minty. Instead, he experiences a series of adventures that take him ever farther from the plantation and lead eventually to his passing as a white schoolteacher, William Harris, in Spartanburg, South Carolina. There Andrew falls in love with a white woman, Peggy Undercliff, and marries her. At just this point in the novel, when Andrew seems to have forgotten Minty, she reappears as a narrative symptom of Andrew's own repressed slave past. Stumbling upon a secret slave auction being held one evening in a saloon, Andrew sees Minty on a makeshift platform being offered for sale.

On one level, Minty's diseased body effectively represents the black woman's suffering under the institution of slavery. In the slave auction scene, however, she undergoes a rapid series of metaphoric displacements from enslaved woman, to burlesque performer, to beauty pageant contestant, to human oddity, as she also becomes a figure for contemporary society's devaluation of the black body. As he enters the saloon, Andrew observes white men exiting who look as if they are leaving a "burlesque hall" (150). Later the auctioneer appears as a "theatrical agent" who tells Minty that she'll have "no more pancake and greasepaint" (156). Her body so disfigured and weakened that no one wants to buy her at any price, she is described as the

"token black girl at [a] beauty contest" (154). The auctioneer, barking at
Minty, is compared to "P. T. Barnum on a slow day, giving the Crocodile
Woman her severance pay" (154). The metaphoric displacement of the body
marked by slavery to that of beauty contest participant, burlesque actress,
and human oddity creates disruptions that may strike readers as insensitive
to the slave girl's actual plight. What the figures have in common is that each
positions her body as *spectacle*.

The abused condition of Minty's body is described in minute detail at
several places in the text. The earliest descriptions tend to foreground the
institutional causes of her disfigurement. Minty has been "badly used" by
slavery, her body reduced to "work-scorched stretches of skin and a lattice-
work of whip marks" (154). She has been treated like a "farm tool squeezed,
with no thought of preservation in the seigniorial South, for every ounce of
surplus value" (155). Johnson's comparison of Minty to a tool recalls his
critique of slavery in the short story "The Education of Mingo," in which he
dismantles Aristotle's definition of the slave as a tool by revealing its logical
and existential inconsistencies. Similarly, his evocation of "surplus value"
brings to mind his use of Marxist theoretics in *Faith and the Good Thing* and
in the short story "Exchange Value" to analyze contemporary African Americans' economic and psychological condition.[30] In *Oxherding Tale*, however,
Johnson moves in a different direction. The institutional abuse that is apparent in the description of Minty's body is eventually elided by her own diagnosis: "People with what I got—pellagra—just rot away, unless they get
treatment. I've had it a *year*. Colonel Woofter didn't care. And no one knows
what causes it. It's like something you do to yourself, make a space for it inside, like a year ago, when they sold me to Colonel Woofter and I couldn't
stand how he touched me, what he made me do, I stopped caring. I hated
being alive that much. It's like the way you *feel* turns into something solid
and grows and kills you" (158). Given her history at the hands of a series of
masters who are "like principals in a gang rape," the attribution of the cause
of her disease to one that "no one knows" or "something you do to yourself"
is particularly striking (158).

While Andrew's reunion with Minty could provide the motivation for him
to take a stance against the institution of slavery, or perhaps to declare his
mixed-race identity in a show of solidarity, instead it becomes a catalyst for
Andrew's personal cultivation, as his attitude toward her changes from one
of "passion" to "compassion" (155). By purchasing Minty at the slave auction, Andrew fulfills the vow he made to Master Polkinghorne, but he does
so not as the heroic ex-slave who has proven himself in the world and returned to liberate a bondswoman, but as a white man who stumbles upon an
abused black woman at a slave auction and buys her. Although the scene

forces Andrew to confront the institution he has been fleeing, he does so as *spectator* (of slave auction, beauty pageant, vaudeville act, and circus exhibit) and even as an unwilling participant. In addition, although he purchases Minty in order to set her free, that transaction does nothing to strike a blow at slavery as an institution; rather it provides the occasion for Andrew and Peggy to practice altruism in the domestic sphere by caring for Minty in their home during her illness. In other words, by taking Minty in, Andrew and Peggy practice the form of engagement recommended by Mahayana Buddhism and summarized by Queen: "nursing the sick, leading the blind, helping the downtrodden, feeding those who are hungry, and providing lodging for those who are needy" (*Engaged* 14).

## *The Civil War as Domestic Engagement in* Oxherding Tale

With a narrative action that begins in 1841 and ends in 1865, *Oxherding Tale* could be considered Johnson's Civil War novel, one that establishes as its backdrop the outbreak, conduct, and conclusion of the nation's bloodiest military engagement. Indeed, references to the Civil War appear throughout the narrative from the first page, on which Andrew's conception is dated to "an unrecorded accident before the Civil War," to the last, on which readers learn that Dr. Undercliff "took leave of this life on the eve of Grant's capture of Fort Henry" (3, 176). But as the bodily suffering of the slave is displaced in Johnson's narrative to a thematics of Buddhist dis-ease, so the epic landscapes of the Civil War are collapsed into the domestic spaces of the householder and the ontological landscapes of the divided self.[31] At one point in the novel Andrew hears rumors of a coming civil war and comments: "Sir, we were *already* in the midst of a Civil War. Blacks and whites. Blacks and blacks. Women and men—I was in the thick of diversity, awash in the world's rich density" (50). Andrew's remark reveals his characteristic tendency to displace national conflict either to the more intimate spaces of intersubjective relationships or to the ontological ground of the "world's rich density." Similarly, the novel's horizon of interpretation characteristically presents national occasions as markers of personal events, as Grant's taking of Fort Henry is used to date Dr. Undercliff's death. Occurring on February 5, 1862, Grant's victory there established him as a rising national hero ("Unconditional Surrender Grant") and opened the Tennessee and Cumberland rivers to the movement of U.S. troops and materials, giving the North an important strategic advantage in the war. But the military battles and stratagems of the violent internecine conflict that would claim the lives of over 600,000 Americans and lead to the elimination of the institution of chattel slavery are not the sorts of engagements that Johnson's narrative is designed

to foreground. Instead, the narrative characteristically translates the cata-
clysmic conflict of national warfare into forms of domestic discord that are
best resolved by the ripple effects of altruistic action over time.

An important illustration of how the novel's horizon of interpretation operates both to recall *and* to displace nationalist understandings of engagement occurs when Andrew and the slave Reb have been banished to work in
Flo Hatfield's mines. On the way there Andrew conceives of a plan to escape
by passing for a white man traveling with his manservant, Reb. Andrew's
plan is tested when they encounter an armed toll road guard, a young boy of
fifteen, who has already been alerted that runaways are in the area. In a scene
that brings to mind both the African American trickster tradition and the
various stratagems that Huck Finn adopts to avoid detection in Mark
Twain's own picaresque revision of the slave narrative, Andrew eludes
capture by inventing a false biography: he boldly informs the guard that he
doesn't have any identity papers because they were stolen by two escaped
slaves (who are, of course, Reb and Andrew himself). Duped by Andrew's
fabrication, the boy responds with a racist outburst, revealing that he considers "all Negroes" to be nothing more than "two-faced liars and thieves"
(110). Strangely, Andrew responds to the boy's obvious racism by commenting, "I'm hardly being fair to this fellow; he was not a bad sort, considering
the day" (110). At this point in the text a footnote is inserted to supply the
toll guard's future history. In two years the boy will be wounded while fighting with Major Robert Anderson at Fort Sumter. Nursed by a black woman
afterwards, he will choose "love over bigotry" and marry her (110). In the
twentieth century, their great-granddaughter Ellen will become an early
NAACP worker, "integrate a lunch counter on April 23, 1935," and eventually die "on the Northeast Side of Carbondale, surrounded by admirers,
white and black" (110).

Remarkable as the only footnote included in the novel, this passage both
recalls and displaces to its textual apparatus the Confederate attack on Fort
Sumter on April 12, 1861. Rather than focusing on the national significance
of this military engagement as the first battle of the Civil War, the footnote
presents that confrontation as evidence of the guard's personal potential for
moral growth. Moreover, the footnote works to define the conflict between
blacks and whites as one between competing personal emotions of "love"
and "bigotry." Defined in personal terms, the conflict is represented as one
that is potentially ameliorated not through a military victory (in fact the
Union lost the battle at Fort Sumter) but through a domestic triumph, the
union of the guard and his nurse—a marriage that anticipates Peggy and
Andrew's own union later in the novel. The guard, then, has a positive impact on the larger society primarily through the ripple effects of his marriage
over time—specifically, through the actions of his great-granddaughter.

Displacing the guard's military service to a footnote, the passage also relocates social engagement to a future time and to a future form of nonviolent resistance. In the twentieth century, the great-granddaughter's own deeds work to resolve the conflict between blacks and whites in two different but related ways: first, by her mounting a direct, but nonviolent, challenge to the segregation of public space, and second, through that action's ripple effect over time, which earns her respect and leads to the further integration of whites and blacks at her funeral. By foregrounding the individual's potential for moral cultivation and by tracing the ripple effects of a personal choice of "love over bigotry" through several generations, the footnote thus provides an evolutionary history of social engagement that replaces violent forms of military action with nonviolent resistance and stresses a Mahayana Buddhist understanding of the positive outcomes of personal ethical choice over time.

The relationship of the footnote to the text proper also serves as an analogue for the narrative's larger design, which operates to displace the epic spaces of national warfare to the domestic terrain of sexual warfare. Although the encounter with the toll guard takes place "on the road," in typical picaresque fashion, the narrative more commonly traces Andrew's episodic journey from slavery to freedom by his movement through a series of different households: from Master Polkinghorne's richly upholstered plantation home, to George and Mattie's frugal cabin, to Flo Hatfield's ostentatiously adorned boudoir, to Reb's spare room, to Dr. Undercliff's richly decorated house, and finally to the small, dilapidated cabin that Andrew and Peggy work together to rebuild. By locating its primary action in domestic space, the narrative translates the conflict between blacks and whites into the question of the proper integration and functioning of households. Moreover, the form of warfare contested in the narrative's domestic spaces is most commonly that of "sexual warfare" (28). Indeed, Andrew's conception, the "unrecorded accident" that occurs before the Civil War, itself instigates battles in both "house and field." In the plantation house, the marriage of Jonathan and Anna Polkinghorne, which had previously experienced only "minor flare-ups, easily fixed by flowers or Anna's favorite chocolates," breaks out in open skirmishes that eventually lead to Anna's arming herself with Master Polkinghorne's "flintlock" and barricading herself in her bedroom in an uneasy "truce" (8). George and Mattie's cabin also becomes a battlefield on which the couple fight over everything from his meals to his manners to his friends. "George Hawkins and Jonathan Polkinghorne differed in ways doubtlessly important to them," remarks Andrew, "but in my father's cabin, in the family house I saw the same ancient war—or, more precisely, the same crisis in the male spirit" (28). Andrew's comment tends to erase the racial and class differences between house and field in order to focus on a problem common to both locales: the question of masculinity. "In this

*age of sexual warfare,*" Andrew confesses, he is most perplexed by the difficulty of "creating some meaning for what it meant to be male" (28; emphasis added).[32] Gender battles are also central to other relationships in the
narrative, such as the marriage of Minty's mother and father, also characterized as a battleground. Finally, even Andrew's service to Flo Hatfield as her
sex slave—the encounter that provides the most in-depth analysis of the
master-slave relationship in the novel—positions that relationship primarily
in terms of sexual warfare. The novel's horizon of interpretation thus operates to transform the "Civil War era" into, in Andrew's words, the "age of
sexual warfare" (28).

By translating the conflict between the races into the domestic battles of
the war between the sexes, the unfolding dramatic logic of the narrative suggests that the conflict introduced through the earlier pairings can be resolved
by having Andrew and Peggy establish at the end of the novel the proper domestic relationship. As Andrew points out when he is first married, "I
brought no images of prior success into my marriage to Peggy; I felt during
the first few weeks off-center, my footing unsure, and without a map of this
new territory" (144). Significantly, the new territory that Andrew discovers
is not the heroic space of conquest or battle but the intimate dimensions of
the intersubjective space to which he is introduced through marriage. His
marriage to Peggy succeeds because they focus "not on each other but on a
spot between and just ahead of us both. Not, in other words, on what she
wanted, or I. But on what we built in the interstices. Which was both of us"
(145). Although Andrew had seen before "no evidence that cohabitation
didn't end in conflict," the battlegrounds of the earlier relationships are replaced by the new territory that Andrew and Peggy discover and by their
growing appreciation of the space "between"—a nascent perception of the
Buddhist understanding of "inter-being." The dramatic logic of the narrative
thus works to displace the national engagements of the battlefield with the
skirmishes of sexual warfare, and then to resolve those conflicts with the
"domestic tranquillity" established by Andrew and Peggy. As national space
is displaced to domestic space, the form of civic action privileged by the narrative is not one of epic engagements but those of the everyday "common
tasks" that Peggy and Andrew carry out, such as the refurbishing of their
cabin (145).

It is in fact Andrew's rejection of heroic space and military forms of engagement that wins Dr. Undercliff's approval of his marriage to Peggy in the
first place. As part of the invented biography that Andrew uses to pass for
white when he first arrives in Spartanburg, he tells Dr. Undercliff that his
grandfather Edwin Harris was a hero in the Revolutionary War. Later Dr.
Undercliff warns Andrew, "There's a war coming . . . a greater war than anything seen in this country, and all on account of the Negro" (132). And he

inquires of Andrew, "Have you . . . dusted off Edwin Harris' flintlock?" To the question whether he will fight in the upcoming war, Andrew responds, "I am not, like my Grandpa, a fighting man" (133). Rather than earning him Dr. Undercliff's disapproval, however, Andrew's response in fact raises his standing in Dr. Undercliff's estimation. "If he had not rejected his grandfather's bloody history," says the doctor, "I would have shown him to the door" (133). It is significant that Andrew thus proves his worthiness to assume family responsibilities by rejecting the violent engagements of the battlefield.

The narrative's privileging of domestic over national forms of engagement is also dramatized through an important exchange between Andrew and Peggy that takes place shortly after their marriage. While the two of them spend a quiet evening at home, Peggy reads a newspaper story reporting that Alabama may secede if Lincoln is elected, a possibility that leads her to raise questions about the potential collapse of the nation. At the same time, Andrew is occupied by looking up the proper spelling of the word "tranquillity" in the dictionary, as he grades student papers. The scene is specifically designed to juxtapose the threat of civil war with the domestic tranquillity the pair have achieved in their household:

> "It says here that the Alabama legislature's formally resolved to secede if Lincoln is elected. Can they do that? Secede, I mean? William? . . . What happens to *us* if the country breaks down?'
>
> I look up. *Tranquillity?*
>
> "Wife, you're thinking *essences* again. Giving nouns the value of existence. People endure. Not names. There are no 'Negroes.' Or 'women.' There are no 'nations.' We tear down one shop sign *America*, we put up another, *Atlantis*. And we blunder along as usual. Patching up the house." (146)

To reassure Peggy, Andrew *domesticates* the threat of war by comparing the potential breakdown of the nation to the disrepair of their cabin, a problem that will only require that they "blunder along like usual," engaging in common, everyday tasks. By replacing the troubled national landscape of "America" with the fictive land of "Atlantis," Andrew again reveals his tendency to dissolve national space into other terrains.

In one respect Andrew's comment reflects a Buddhist skepticism toward language, based on the view that words construct conventional ways of thinking that are largely illusionary. This skepticism includes a suspicion of the process of nominalization itself, which Buddhists believe covers over experience with concepts that mistakenly grant substance to abstract ideas. On the one hand, such an analysis suggests that Andrew's answer to Peggy's question could be read as a critique of nationalistic fervor, understood as the allegiance to an illusory ideal. On the other hand, Andrew's response seems

itself to translate national unrest into abstract terms, by theorizing the growing threat of the nation's rupture as a kind of discursive or epistemological
error. Indeed, Andrew's comment tends to erase the contingent, historical
cause for the war that Dr. Undercliff clearly identifies, as being "on account
of the Negro" (132). Andrew's answer to Peggy replaces such causal analysis with a philosophical critique of the process of nominalization itself—or
the assertion that "there are no 'Negroes'" (146). But Andrew's critique of
essences runs the risk of equating history with utopian fiction—of replacing
"America" with "Atlantis." The exchange ends when Peggy comes over to
give Andrew a loving squeeze at the very moment when he thinks again of
the word "tranquillity." The couple's own intimacy is thus offered as an
existential definition of the term that Andrew has been looking up in the
dictionary. By suggesting that nations are but fictive nominalizations, while
Andrew and Peggy's relationship is tranquillity realized, the scene implies
that interpersonal relations, or the spaces "between," are the only terrain in
which "domestic tranquillity" may realistically be achieved.

Moreover, the process through which Andrew and Peggy achieve tranquillity evokes a Buddhist understanding of dis-ease and health in several respects. Buddhism commonly teaches that dis-ease is caused by three poisons:
greed (or grasping), hatred, and illusion. By avoiding these poisons, one may
attain a state of health, defined specifically in Buddhist terms as the achievement of "tranquillity," or a state of mind characterized by serenity and com-
posure. Similarly, one of the reasons why Andrew and Peggy succeed in their
marriage where others have failed to establish domestic harmony, the narrative suggests, is that they are able to avoid certain "poison[s]" (145). Shortly
after their marriage, Andrew begins to raise questions about their relationship: "Had I married a loser? Had she?" (145). Wisely, however, the couple
does not give in to such unhealthy speculations. "Suspecting these questions
were poison—perhaps not even *real* questions—we did not give them
voice," says Andrew (145). Instead, the two concentrate on the small tasks
they share in rebuilding the cabin, which enables them to avoid dis-ease and
in fact to become the healthy embodiment of tranquillity itself. In his response to Peggy's question about the breakdown of the nation, Andrew suggests that her concerns, like those he raises about the nature of his marriage,
are also not "real questions." The question of how their personal efforts to
achieve domestic tranquillity relate to larger problems of how broken institutions at the national level might be healed is therefore one that goes unanswered, except in terms of the ripple effects of altruistic action over time.
In *Dreamer*, however, Johnson will propose a more complex and more compelling answer to this question.

As Minty's diseased body reappears in the text in part as a narrative symptom of Andrew's repressed slave past, so Minty's integration into Andrew

and Peggy's household functions as a test of the quality of the couple's domestic harmony. Andrew explains to Peggy when he returns home from the slave auction with Minty: "I am *indebted* to her. . . . There are duties I must discharge, if I am ever to be free. . . . We are born, even slaves, into such richness, and if I cannot somehow repay them, my predecessors and that girl outside, then I am unworthy of any happiness whatsoever, here with you, or anywhere" (161). His comments tie his altruistic service to Minty to his becoming worthy of freedom, and worthy of his life with Peggy. For her part, Peggy does not seem to pick up on Andrew's implied confession that he is passing for white—and in fact his language is ambiguous. She is more interested in knowing whether Minty was once his lover. She asks him, "Did you make love to her?" (161). Peggy's question is in keeping with Andrew's earlier description of their marriage as one in which the "only act forbidden me was infidelity" (144). By focusing on Andrew's physical relationship with Minty, Peggy's comment locates the field of ethical action squarely in the arena of sexual warfare. Conflict does not break out in their household as it did in Master Polkinghorne's and George's, because Peggy's "fear of sharing love [is] tested, then transcended" (164). Moreover, because Peggy does not reject Andrew and agrees to help him care for Minty, he realizes that not "everyone in the White World" is "out to get" him (162). This knowledge seems to free Andrew in a way that enables him to care for Minty: "With no self-induced racial paranoia as an excuse for being irresponsible, I turned—and Wife turned—to the business of Minty's recovery" (162).[33]

Isolated from the larger world, Minty, Andrew, and Peggy are able to maintain domestic tranquillity in spite of Minty's illness, her slave past, Peggy's whiteness, and the presence of a love triangle in the cabin. When Peggy falls silent upon learning that he and Minty had indeed been lovers, Andrew points out that in some works of literature such a silence "would have been the lull before a cheap emotional outburst, an embarrassing scene: the horror-stricken belle pulls out her tresses like chicken feathers, she throws her husband, the beast, out on his behind. But Peggy Undercliff was no character in a novel" (161). Critics often read Andrew's comment as drawing a distinction between Peggy's response and those of the heroines of more sentimental fiction. But this metafictional moment in the text actually serves to bring attention to, rather than to deflect notice of, the fact that Peggy is indeed a character in a novel. While Johnson's self-conscious deployment of the sentimental distances itself from certain excesses of that tradition, several features of this section of the novel recall elements of sentimental fiction. Both Peggy, in the role of "Wife," and Minty, as former lover, bring to mind the characters of romance. Peggy, for example, practices good Victorian self-renunciation when she tells Andrew, "If you decide, later, that you prefer her [Minty], and that she can make you happy[,] . . . I want what you want, even if your pleasure means I experience pain" (162). Minty's role, moreover, is especially romanticized. In spite of her past abuse at the hands of white men, the fact that her ex-lover is now married to a white woman, and her debilitating illness, she willingly takes over "Wife's education." She teaches Peggy how to clean the cabin properly, how to fix the meals Andrew likes (dishes like the "Salt Fish Cakes," for which he developed a taste for on the plantation), and "how to landscape [the] postage-stamp sized property" (163). Minty even tells Andrew that she approves of his marriage to Peggy. As Minty comes to function in a way analogous to the more experienced woman in American domestic fiction who instructs the new wife in home management, her presence in the cabin thus serves to enhance rather than to unsettle domestic harmony. At the same time, such domestic tranquillity is maintained in part by the failure to recognize the severity of both Minty's desperate condition and that of the nation at large.

In *Oxherding Tale* Johnson adopts the sentimental novel's domestic settings, emotional valence, and characteristic foregrounding of moral issues because they lend themselves to his narrative project of conveying a Mahayana Buddhist understanding of dis-ease and altruistic engagement. As in many works of sentimental fiction, the novel includes a dramatic deathbed scene, which achieves its emotional charge by juxtaposing Peggy's and Andrew's unrealistic hopes for Minty's recovery to her rapidly degenerating condition. As Dr. Undercliff examines Minty in the cabin, Peggy and Andrew wait outside, where Peggy is suddenly "struck by a thought": "She could write her Aunt Olivia in Boston. There, Minty could find work. Make her way as a freewoman" (166). Completely taken with an idea that is utterly unrealistic, Andrew picks Peggy up and "twirl[s] her dizzily until [they] both dro[p], lips locked, in the high dry grass." As Andrew remarks, "Everything . . . was winged" (166). The image of husband and wife twirling around outside the cabin in which Minty lies dying recalls similar improbable scenes in the sentimental tradition. Afterwards, Andrew is called into the cabin, where Minty dies at precisely the moment when he tells her about their plan to travel to Boston that very night. At this point sober reality intrudes. "A gush of black vomit bubbled from her mouth onto my hand," Andrew recounts. "The Devil came and sat on Minty, his weight pressing open the valve to her bladder and bowels" (167). In Johnson's revision of the sentimental novel, the deathbed becomes the final stage on which the black woman's body appears as spectacle.

## Class, Masculinity, and Domestic Discord

The translation of the "Era of the Civil War" to the "Age of Sexual Warfare" in *Oxherding Tale* also works to redefine class conflict in terms of domestic discord, as is illustrated especially through the fate of Ezekiel William Sykes-Withers, Andrew's tutor. As the resident intellectual at Andrew's plantation home, Ezekiel and his eclectic interests combine several Eastern and Western philosophical traditions: he is an Idealist (a "member of George Ripley's Transcendental Club" [10]); a student of Eastern philosophy ("the only man in North America who truly understands the *Mahàbhárata*" [9]); and a devotee of Marx (the owner of the only surviving copy of the *Deutsch-Französische Jahrbücher*, a newspaper for which Marx worked as editor [29]). As Andrew points out, Ezekiel's cabin is "an extension of [his] tutor's mind—namely, a catastrophe of books" drawn from all over the world (29). Ezekiel's intellect is in fact a confused jumble of disparate intellectual systems, as is the program he establishes for Andrew's "perfect moral education," a curriculum that draws from the plan for John Stuart Mill's education and the rules proposed for the training of Buddhist monks (12). Ironically, many of Ezekiel's intellectual interests correspond to Johnson's own, but his character is in fact designed to represent the dangers of a certain kind of philosophical practice in which a commitment to abstract ideals alienates people from the phenomenological richness of life. Like the professor in Johnson's short story "Alēthia" (discussed in chapter 1) and Barrett in *Faith and the Good Thing* (discussed in chapter 2), Ezekiel represents the intellectual who cannot "live without certainty" (29). A lonely "recluse" who is "awkward with people," he functions in the novel as an example of failed domestic engagement (83).

Furthermore, by detailing Ezekiel's family history, his encounter with Karl Marx at Master Polkinghorne's plantation, and his tragic demise, *Oxherding Tale* translates class conflict into forms of dis-ease and personal pathology, rewriting the social critique found in the Chicago sections of *Faith*. When Ezekiel first tells Andrew about his family, his background reads like a selection from one of Marx's treatises on economic exploitation: "My father spent twelve, maybe fifteen hours a day in a brass foundry, where I was employed for a time when I was fifteen, and for a pitiful wage. If all he could expect was poverty—if, I say, Andrew, all he could see ahead was sixty years of bad news, the breakdown of his family, debts and disappointments, without hope of change, without consolation, wasn't it better to be done once and for all with the person feeling, eh? It is not easy to be a full-grown man, Andrew" (30). The class elements of Ezekiel's family history clearly identify exploitation in the workplace as a primary cause of domestic suffering. But just as Andrew had earlier translated sectional conflict into the battle between the sexes, Ezekiel also shifts the focus from the class critique apparent in his family history to that of "creating some meaning for what it meant to be male." Ezekiel continues: "We are not like women. . . . Perhaps all philosophy boils down to the simple fear that the universe has no need for us—men, I mean,

because women are, in a strange sense, more essential to Being than we are"
(30). Like Andrew, Ezekiel translates the social conflict in his family history
into philosophical speculations about sexual difference.

Ezekiel's encounter with Marx is introduced into the narrative through a
flashback that occurs at a point when Andrew and Reb are being driven to
work in Flo Hatfield's mines by her coachman, Sam Plunkett. Although little critical attention has been given to the scene, the incident proceeding
Marx's arrival in fact provides an important context for interpreting the
socialist's surprising appearance in the narrative. As they are traveling to the
Yellow Dog Mine, Plunkett tells the men that if they had "come this way
just ten years earlier . . . you wouldn't'a seen nothin'. Sprawlin' wilderness.
Forests fulla deer" (79–80). Over the past ten years, however, the wilderness
has been transformed into the site of the mine, an enterprise that employs a
constant stream of black slaves and poor whites as "shovelers and wheelers,
borers and slave teams" who are needed to "replace those who peris[h] from
consumption" (79). Plunkett's account of the wilderness's transformation
into a mine clearly represents national space as shaped primarily by economic relationships and class conflict. Worker's bodies, moreover, are
wracked by illnesses that are caused by their labor. The social landscape that
Plunkett describes and the social history that he recounts together introduce
a Marxist analysis into the text even before the fictional Marx arrives in
Spartanburg.

Plunkett's character, however, is designed to call certain Marxist claims
into question. Claiming to be a "Socialist," he tells Andrew and Reb, "I'm
on your side!" (80), continuing: "I *hate* slavery! Nobody's free, 'specially a
workin' man like myself. We're brothers. . . . Don't let nobody tell you Sam
Plunkett ain't for Revolution" (81). The solidarity that Plunkett espouses is
undermined, however, when he comments: "You men should pull together. I
mean, *we* oughta pull together" (80). Plunkett's slip confirms that he does not
actually believe that the captives' interests and his own are identical, in spite
of his stated allegiances. His protestations, moreover, fall on deaf ears, since
Reb, a saltwater African who had "never heard of Socialism," is intuitively
(and wisely) suspicious of Plunkett throughout the trip (81). Advocating
worker solidarity even as he drives the others to what he believes to be certain death in the mines, Plunkett subverts the very views to which he gives
voice, while at the same time, his willing participation in the exploitation of
the other men poses a textual challenge to the socialist argument that the
working class, as the "subject of history," will provide the enlightened point
of view that is needed to fuel an effective social revolution.

Plunkett's comments about the economic transformation of national
space, worker solidarity, and revolution are in fact designed to evoke an understanding of social causation that Marx's visit to Cripplegate will surpris-

ingly overturn. In its place, the fictional Marx espouses a form of social causation that radiates *outward* from the domestic to the social spheres. Indeed, Marx's arrival at Cripplegate functions like other features in the text to displace social relations to domestic relations and to replace economic causality with the ripple effects of altruistic action over time. Ezekiel's comic preparations for the visit of his intellectual hero leave him near collapse "from nervous exhaustion" by the time of Marx's arrival, but he soon discovers that Marx is not interested in talking about the subjects near to Ezekiel's heart, "social evil and deep-ploughing philosophy" (84). As Andrew comments, "Marx did not, like Ezekiel, live for ideas, political or otherwise; he was, in the old sense—the Sanskrit sense—a householder. The Marx of Ezekiel's fancy, the humorless student radical of the 1830s, was— you cannot guess—a *citizen* devoted first, and foremost, to his family: a droll, Dickensian husband who . . . [was] going fat" (84). Andrew's comment anticipates his own later realization that his own "dharma, such as it was, was that of the householder" (147).

By identifying Marx with the figure of the householder in Eastern philosophy, Andrew's comment also locates the ground for "citizenship" in the domestic terrain.[34] He describes the householder as someone who places "children and wife, colleagues and acquaintances in a widening circle that soon envelop[s] the entire community" (92). The suggestion is that the actions of the householder radiate outward from domestic space in a "widening circle" to affect the social sphere. The ideal of the householder thus *reverses* the historical Marx's emphasis on the mode of production as the determining factor in social causality. Indeed, the Marx who visits the plantation endorses this view. As he instructs Ezekiel: "Vhen two subjects come together, they realize in their reciprocal intersubjective life a common vorld. . . . The universal name for this final, ontological achievement, this liberation—Occidental or Oriental—in vhich each subject finds another essential is *love*" (86). The "common vorld" that Marx describes is not that of economic necessity but that of intimate reciprocity. As A. T. Spaulding suggests, Johnson converts Marx "into a phenomenologist" (16). As the narrative logic is designed to displace the epic landscapes of the Civil War onto the domestic terrain of sexual warfare, so Marx's visit to Cripplegate Plantation functions to translate the country's economic landscape described at the beginning of the chapter to the intimate territory of a "common vorld" (86). The economic analysis so primary in the Chicago sections of *Faith* is therefore itself emphatically displaced in *Oxherding Tale*.

The dramatic logic of Marx's visit also works to displace the causality for social ills to personal dis-ease. Before Marx arrives at the plantation, Andrew introduces the issue of diseased and healthy bodies through a passage that extends to Marx's own health. Andrew explains: "As of late, political affairs affected Marx physically. When he felt a headcold coming on, a toothache, he looked immediately for its social cause. A new tax law had cost Marx a molar. Nearby at a button factory a strike that failed brought on an attack of asthma. These things were dialectical. As the political world declined so did Marx's health" (82). Through a reductio ad absurdum Andrew satirizes the idea that one's personal health can be adequately explained in terms of economic causality. Afterwards, when Marx arrives at Cripplegate, he also works to relocate the causes of suffering by diagnosing the origin of Ezekiel's misery. Ezekiel believes that he is troubled because suffering is legitimated by social conditions. He is "prepared for suffering" by the truth as he sees it: "Was not the spirit enslaved everywhere? The planet raped? The government in the hands of criminals? War prophesied?" (88). Ironically, Marx detects a different etiology for Ezekiel's illness. He asks Ezekiel, "Do you haf a lover?" (86).

In a comic scene that presents him as more a philosophical psychotherapist than an economic determinist, Marx poses several questions that lead him to locate the source of Ezekiel's illness in personal rather than social pathology. As he asks Andrew: "You *chose* to be miserable. Why?" (85). When Ezekiel begins to read to Marx a paper he has written on ontology and the nature of Truth, Marx stops Ezekiel to correct him, explaining, "Truth is some*one*" (85). From one perspective Marx's comments can be read as a critique of Ezekiel's latent Hegelianism, an intellectual position signaled earlier in the text by the tutor's membership in the Transcendental Club. According to Marx, Ezekiel's idealistic philosophy, like Hegel's, may invert the relationship of truth to life: truth is not a disembodied ideal but a material someone. But the fictional Marx's comments also provide a new definition of socialism to replace Plunkett's insincere platitudes, a definition that itself privileges the intimate territory of intersubjective relationships. Marx elaborates, "Everything I've vritten has been for a voman — is *one* vay to view Socialism, no?" (87). The appearance of Marx as a character in *Oxherding Tale* thus serves as a textual proclamation that Johnson has turned from the Marxist critique he developed in *Faith* to a Mahayana Buddhist understanding of social causality and engagement. Johnson will modify this position in his later novels: an analysis of the economic forces of slavery will play a more important role in his next novel, *Middle Passage*, and Johnson will present a fully integrated analysis of the relation of both personal and material causes of social inequity in his powerful tribute to Martin Luther King Jr., *Dreamer*.

Ezekiel's fortunes after his encounter with Marx illustrate the tragic fate of those who fail to achieve domestic tranquillity. Ironically, when Ezekiel decides to act on Marx's advice, the impractical tutor pursues a relationship with an imaginary rather than a real woman. Plagued by self-doubt and heart trouble after Marx's visit, Ezekiel attempts to drown his problems at a local saloon. There he meets Shem Moses, who introduces himself to Ezekiel as a hired man from Greenwood Farm. Moses, a coarse alcoholic, shows Ezekiel a picture of his fifteen-year-old daughter, Althea, and confides to Ezekiel that she suffers from a rare neurological illness, "transverse myelitis" (89). To convince Ezekiel that the tale about his daughter is true, Moses pulls a smudged daguerreotype of the girl out of his pocket (much as Jay Gatsby provides props for his invented biography in *The Great Gatsby*). The illness, Moses laments, has left Althea paralyzed below the waist, while providing for her care has consumed all of his financial resources. Although Ezekiel instantly sizes Moses up as a "parasite" and realizes that the picture could be of "Zachary Taylor's sister" for all he knows, he gives Moses an entire month's salary for the girl's support (90). Afterwards, he and the hired man continue to meet, and Ezekiel continues to provide support for Althea, until one day Moses shows up with a letter from Althea and a proposition for Ezekiel: as he tells the tutor, "She's for sale" (92). Outraged at Moses but eager to rescue Althea from his sphere of influence, Ezekiel agrees to buy the girl for four hundred dollars, convincing himself that he will be freeing her from bondage. After he borrows the money to pay Moses, he drives to Greenwood Farm to collect Althea, only to find that the farm has not been occupied for years. Unlike the professor in Johnson's short story "Alethia," Ezekiel discovers no living woman to lead him out of his reclusive intellectualism. His hopes of achieving domestic tranquillity destroyed, Andrew walks through the farmhouse from room to room, his steps resounding on the old wooden floor "like the crack of a coffin shrinking," until he succumbs to an apparent heart attack (94).

Ezekiel's personal history incorporates into the narrative a study in faulty enlightenment, failed domesticity, and flawed altruistic practice. As Mahayana Buddhism stresses, it is not enough simply to meditate and to cultivate *feelings* of compassion; instead one must actually *help* people. Since individuation and socialization are understood to be correlated processes, it is through the actual practice of compassion that one's own character is cultivated. Ezekiel's altruism, by contrast, consists of nothing but good intentions. In terms of the novel's dramatic logic, he attempts, but fails, to be effectively engaged because his efforts are foolishly one-sided. Ezekiel never discovers the "new territory" that Andrew and Peggy enter and that Marx describes as "a common vorld" of reciprocity. That Ezekiel's altruistic intentions fail to cultivate his character is seen partly through his unchangingly hostile attitude toward Moses. Like Plunkett, Moses functions in the narrative to call notions of worker solidarity into question. For his part, Ezekiel disdains Moses, both because he recognizes him to be a "swindler and whore-chaser" and because of Ezekiel's own class pretensions. These are revealed by his comments to Marx about "certain lower, less polished classes of people" and by his fantasies of rescuing Althea from her lower-class background. As Ezekiel admits, he finds Althea "all the more beautiful for her bondage to Shem Moses" (93). Ezekiel's reasons for practicing altruism are in fact decidedly mixed. In part he hopes to end his own inner confusion, signaled earlier by his jumbled intellectual interests. His plans to buy Althea lead him to develop a "vague feeling of purpose. And order" (93). But as Ezekiel fixes "his mind on the girl, who was the radix for this revolution in his life," he discovers that his "hatred for the hired man increased" (93). Ironically, Ezekiel's efforts to practice altruism lead not to the cultivation of compassion but to his increasing susceptibility to one of the three primary poisons identified by Buddhism as a source of dis-ease.

Althea's alleged illness can be read as a symptom of Ezekiel's own inner pathology, the outer representation of an ineffectual idealism and, perhaps, of a deeper disorder. The daguerreotype that Moses offers is nothing more than the reflection of Ezekiel's latest intellectual fantasy, a fetish that he imbues with special powers as the "luminary, the object of his new hope" (93). Such fantasies, furthermore, may be a sublimation of other, less savory features of Ezekiel's character, features that help to explain why the imaginary girl exerts such a compelling attraction on the tutor.[35] Certainly there are sexual overtones to the bargain that he makes with Moses. When Ezekiel first meets Moses and asks if he can keep Althea's picture for a day or two, Moses responds, "You ain't with the law are you?" (90). Moses's furtive demeanor is more suggestive of a pimp or a pornographer than a concerned father. Later, in presenting his "proposition" to Ezekiel, Moses suggestively remarks: "You might's well do for her *directly*. Without me in the way" (92). While Moses's suspicious behavior might be explained simply as the result of his engaging in what amounts to a blackmail scheme, there are other warnings that the picture appeals to disquieting elements of Ezekiel's own character. When he first arrives at Cripplegate, Ezekiel carries letters of reference (from Bronson Alcott, among others) that state, "This candidate knows as much about metaphysics as any man alive, and has traveled in India, but you must never leave him alone for long in a room with a little girl" (9). Althea, one remembers, is fifteen. Furthermore, although the letter "from Althea" emphasizes that she loves him as her benefactor and "like a father," Ezekiel's own preparations for their meeting correspond more closely to those of a lover. Ezekiel raises money from friends to buy Althea by explaining that he was "engaged, soon to be married" (93). In the days leading up to their meeting his sobs can be heard throughout the plantation, from his cabin to the slave quarters, the "broken song of a lonely man desperately in love" (93). Finally, when Ezekiel leaves to pick up Althea at Greenwood Farm, he goes dressed as a suitor, "painted and powdered," wearing "his highhat, his tight, square-toed shoes," and carrying a "bouquet of flowers" (93–94). Ezekiel's attempt to achieve domestic tranquillity is flawed from the outset by his desire for the young girl, his altruism at least partly inspired by pathological rather than philanthropic motives.

Moreover, the narrative suggests that Ezekiel's disordered condition stems in part from a family history of instability. Indeed, family genealogies in *Oxherding Tale* imply that the primary threat to domestic tranquillity may be a masculine propensity for violence that leads to destructive consequences over time, consequences that flow counter to the positive effects of altruistic action and domestic tranquillity. As Ezekiel recounts, one night his father broke down and killed nearly his entire family: "He shot my mother and sister, and would have blown me to Kingdom Come, too, I assure you, had I not been away that evening. When I arrived home, they were all dead, over their *apéritif*, at the dinner table" (11). While Andrew's shifting accounts of his family history tend to call some elements of his biography into question—for example, the image of a poor worker's family enjoying "apéritifs" at the dinner table—his father's actions offer an extreme example of violent male behavior in the household and provide an additional explanation for Ezekiel's own inability to establish domestic harmony.

Other families in the narrative are also threatened by masculine violence, as illustrated especially by the home life of Minty's father, Nate McKay. "He'd whale Addie," Andrew recounts, "pound her with both fists, and squeeze her throat until she clawed at his eyes or kneed his testicles. His son Jerome (sixteen), daughters Ann (twelve) and Minty (six) would join in, swinging, trying to unlock his fingers from Addie's hair—the whole family spilled like a creature with ten legs into Nate McKay's yard. It was not a pleasant household, those nights" (104). A blacksmith who espouses black solidarity while preferring "more polished" ladies to those from the quarters, Nate reputedly has fathered over twenty-five children, "sprinkled on farms throughout South Carolina" (103). When Andrew's father, George, attempts to chastise Nate for his treatment of his family by quoting to him from the Bible, Nate rejects George's moral instruction by arguing that because the Bible was given to them by the white man, its morality doesn't apply to black men: "We been treated different, so we gotta have different rules" (105). Nate's contempt for black women and the brutal treatment of his family are designed to suggest, however, that the black solidarity he professes is actually a rationalization for his philandering lifestyle, and his failure to achieve domestic harmony is presented as a consequence of poor personal ethical choice rather than social inequalities.

The most striking representation of male pathology in the novel is provided by the personal history of the Soulcatcher, Bannon. Historically, slave catchers performed a policing function for the institution of slavery, their violence both necessitated and authorized by a brutal economic system.

Bannon's personal history, however, traces the origin of his contemptible practice to his upbringing:

> "You know what happens when you grow hup in a house like that?" He paused again, bleakly. "If there's a stain on yo mattress in the mawnin', you might's well walk right to the woodshed, drop yo drawers, wait for the old man to wake hup, then hand him the strop. Me, Ah couldn't afford to have no stained mattress. Whenever gism started buildin' in my groin, Ah'd get me a candle, sneak out to the henhouse, and strangle a chicken. During my teens we lost fifty chickens. . . . Pretty soon, Ah *enjoyed* killin' more'n pullin' my pud." (112)

Recalling the psychological profiles of twentieth-century mass murderers (and to some extent Reich's theories regarding sexual repression discussed in chapter 2), Bannon's violent tendencies are attributed to an overly strict upbringing. Also reminiscent of such profiles, Bannon begins his life of violence with the mistreatment of animals and later graduates to crimes against people. His position as slave catcher is thus presented as the logical outcome of his upbringing, and his biography works like other features of the text to replace political causality with domestic pathology. As Bannon argues, "Ah knows mah nature" (111). Like Andrew's father, Bannon eventually murders his own family, deciding on the very night when he "poleax[es]" them that "Gawd didn't *want* me to be a peaceful man" (112). Claiming to have found a higher meaning in his violent behavior, Bannon contends, "Ah, too, performs a service to Gawd" (111). Identifying Bannon as Shiva's agent, Andrew seems to endorse the view that he serves as God's scourge.[36] As the narrative works to displace the national space of civil conflict onto the intimate spaces of domestic reciprocity or to the plane of ontological diversity, so Bannon's biography translates social causality into the terms of personal pathology or ontological necessity.

## The Body Mosaic: Enlightenment in Oxherding Tale

The final chapter of *Oxherding Tale*, entitled "Moksha," is framed by two elaborate descriptions of the Soulcatcher's body. The chapter opens with Andrew's remarkable vision of the catalogue of terror reflected on Bannon's face, which, as we have seen, is represented as an externalization of Andrew's own inner paranoia. The chapter closes as Andrew, in his final showdown with the Soulcatcher, once again gazes at Bannon's body, watching in wonder as the elaborate tattoos covering his skin seem to come alive and shift shape:

> Not tattooes at all, I saw, but forms sardined in his contour, creatures Bannon had killed since childhood: spineless insects, flies he'd dewinged;

yet even the tiniest of these thrashing within the body mosaic was, clearly, a society as complex as the higher forms, a concrescence of molecules cells atoms in concert, for nothing in the necropolis he'd filled stood alone, wished to stand alone, had to stand alone, and the commonwealth of the dead shape-shifted on his chest, his full belly, his fat shoulders, traded hand for claw, feet for hooves legs for wings, their metamorphosis having no purpose beyond the delight the universe took in diversity for its own sake, the proliferation of beauty, and yet all were conserved in this process of doubling, nothing was lost in the masquerade. (175)

Specifically designed as a revision of the earlier reading of Bannon's figure, the description of the "body mosaic" transmutes the earlier examples of the slave's suffering into moments in a cosmic process of metamorphosis and diversification. The personal history of the Soulcatcher becomes part of a vast evolutionary process through which life is continually regenerated. At the same time, Andrew's personal history with his father is also transformed, as he encounters his father's face in every fantastic figure he sees. Andrew thus experiences his father's love, of which he has been doubtful, given back to him in a thousand different forms. Because the Soulcatcher had copied aspects of Andrew himself during the chase, Andrew is brought to tears when he sees his father's face reflected back to him in his own form. In a sudden appreciation of the innumerable ways in which he is connected to his father in the larger scheme, Andrew recognizes that he is his "father's father," while his father is his "child" (176).

In his introduction to *Oxherding Tale*, Johnson points out that Andrew is "the first protagonist in African American literature to achieve classically defined Moksha (enlightenment)" (xvi). Significantly, although all Buddhist sutras teach a Way to enlightenment, the doctrines within them differ considerably. In their introduction to the English translation of the Platform Sutra, the Buddhist Text Society emphasizes that the sutra is "a special kind of moral and psychological work, aimed at a particular *personal* transformation" (*Sixth Patriarch* xii; emphasis added). The personal transformation taught by the sutra, which is in the Mahayana tradition, is that of the "Teaching of Sudden Enlightenment": the view that enlightenment can be achieved by a sudden personal illumination rather than by exhaustive monastic practice or through the earning of merit through good actions (91). As the suggestive words of the sutra itself propose, "Although the sea of suffering is inexhaustible, a turning of the head is the other shore" (86). By describing *Oxherding Tale* as his own Platform Sutra, then, Johnson suggests a specific interpretative framework for Andrew's enlightenment, connecting it to the Way taught by the Sixth Patriarch. Faced with the difficulty of making Buddhism available in its adopted country of China and eager to widen the path to enlightenment to those other than monks, the Sixth Patriarch taught that enlightenment could be achieved through a sudden illumination that would enable one to overcome the poisons that cause dis-ease, adopt a new relation toward one's suffering, and achieve intellectual and spiritual health. Andrew's renewed vision of Bannon's body is similarly presented as profoundly therapeutic—and as offering a resolution to the trope of dis-ease developed throughout the novel.

That he does not simply kill Andrew is certainly partly due to Bannon's earlier encounter with Reb.[37] After Andrew breaks his promise to journey with him to freedom, Reb sets off north, a lone black man without the protection provided by Andrew's assumed white identity. Andrew's fear that Bannon has murdered Reb seems confirmed when he gives Andrew Reb's ring as a "gift." But in their final confrontation Bannon reveals that he did not kill Reb and, furthermore, that he has actually arranged for this last meeting in order to inform Andrew that he is no longer catching slaves. Earlier Bannon had bragged about his method of slave catching, vowing, "If Ah ever meet a Negro Ah can't catch, Ah'll quit" (116). Because Reb was a slave who could not be caught, Bannon has abandoned his profession. As he explains, "You got to have somethin' dead or static already inside you—an image of yoself—fo' a real slave catcher to latch onto" (174). In other words, because Reb has no inner pockets of dis-ease, both he and Andrew are able to escape Bannon's designs.

Earlier in the novel Andrew's answers to Peggy's questions implied that nations are but fictive nominalizations. Andrew's enlightenment at the end of the novel, moreover, suggests that he will pledge his allegiance not to the civic state but to the "state" of inter-being. Of that country Reb is the novel's uncontested leader. Although he inhabits the United States, Reb is not really *of* the nation; even his shed, unlike Ezekiel's cabin, reveals no evidence of his presence. With a name that signifies on rebel and rebellion, Reb functions, like the bridge guard, both to recall and to displace activist forms of civic engagement, with the intent to valorize an inner, rather than an outer, revolution. At one point in the novel Andrew explicitly compares Reb's form of subversion to more militant kinds of engagement, contrasting it with both Ezekiel's "saber-rattling style" of activism (75) and with the violent abolitionists' attack at Harper's Ferry. Reb practices "a much softer and more devastating Old World" subversion that makes "Harper's Ferry look foolish" (75), says Andrew. From the New World to the Old World, from the African village of Reb's birth located "between Cape Lopez and the Congo River" (48) to his membership in the fictional tribe of Allmuseri, from serving as a figure for a fictional African past to his becoming a figure for the Eastern religious concept of "no-self," the multiple metaphoric displacements of the slave's character are designed like other elements in the narrative to shift readers' attention from the domain of civic conflict to the dominion of inner tranquillity. Reb's final action in the novel, building "his finest coffin" for Abraham Lincoln, demonstrates that the endangered slave outlasts both southern rebel and northern soldier alike, his spiritual leadership enduring after the passing of the great Civil War president himself. In *Dreamer*, a novel in which Johnson will develop a different understanding of the complex relationship of the spiritual to the political, Martin Luther King combines elements of both Reb and President Lincoln as the ethical and political leader of the nation's great battle for civil rights.

One cannot say that by the end of the novel Andrew has earned his enlightenment: he has not completed rigorous monastic practice, achieved a state of "no self" (like Reb), or accumulated merit (enough) through good actions. Indeed, as he rides out with the Soulcatcher for their final showdown, Andrew is struck by the feeling that he "had betrayed all the bondsmen [he]'d ever known: [his] father, by passing; Patrick, by not risking Flo Hatfield's displeasure; Minty, who'd trusted [him]; and Reb, by failing to leave Spartanburg" (171). Andrew seems correct in his assessment. Johnson's narrative repeatedly resists the temptation to position Andrew as heroic (sometimes, perhaps, to the consternation of his reader). Revising the Western historical novel's attempts to establish the characteristics of the heroic individual, Johnson purposely seeks to unsettle those qualifications and the notion of the imperial subject that they imply. Instead, because Andrew's enlightenment is not earned but is nevertheless achieved, his liberation at the end of *Oxherding Tale* has the quality of an unexpected grace. Andrew's final vision of Bannon therefore powerfully captures a faith that contemporary black people, who labor yet under the burden of the slave past, may set that burden down—may overcome despair, paranoia, the loss of "life assurance," and a whole host of other intellectual and spiritual poisons—and achieve a healing liberation.

Although *Oxherding Tale* seems at times to risk replicating white racist discourse about the pathology of the black body, one way to understand the novel's thematization of suffering as Buddhist dis-ease is specifically as an attempt to provide an *alternative* to white discourse about black embodiment. In "The Phenomenology of the Black Body" Johnson analyzes the status of the black body as a figure of contamination, one that is reduced by whites to a "myth of stain, evil, and physicality." The article, a revision of a paper that Johnson wrote as an assignment for the Ph.D. program in philosophy in 1975, draws on existential phenomenology in general and Frantz Fanon in particular to argue that "in a situation structured by a color-caste system, a black's consciousness and his lived world . . . are frequently epidermalized" (608). In a postscript to the article Johnson attributes the usage of the term "epidermalize" to an unpublished paper by his early mentor and friend, the black philosopher Thomas T. Slaughter. Slaughter's paper, "Epidermalizing the World: A Basic Mode of Being Black," was presented at the first meeting of the graduate student colloquium series that Johnson helped to establish while he and Slaughter were in the Ph.D. program together.[38] Both essays demonstrate the potential that the two students detected in phenomenological existentialism as a tool for analyzing questions of vital importance to blacks in philosophy. What is important here, however, is that both essays work to define a debilitating condition for which Johnson in *Oxherding Tale* offers a Buddhist conception of dis-ease as a cure.

At one point in the novel Andrew contends that the worst thing about slavery is "the fact that men had epidermalized Being" (52). In "The Phenomenology of the Black Body" Johnson provides several examples designed to illustrate how such epidermalization is experienced by contemporary black people. In one example he describes a black man who is thinking about mathematics at the moment when he enters a bar occupied by whites. But when he is caught by their objectifying glances, Johnson suggests, it is "Good bye, Boolean expansions" (115). Reduced by whites to a physical presence, the black man finds that his "world is epidermalized, collapsed like a house of cards into the stained casement of [his] skin" (115). In "The Epidermalization of Being" Slaughter investigates a similar dynamic through which blacks could be said to "pigmentize" their "total environment" (285). Slaughter identifies two complementary processes in the colonization of consciousness, which he analyzes not only in terms of an *interiorization* of inferiority, but also in terms of a process of *exteriorization* whereby blacks "epidermalize the world" or the totality of their relationships (284). What is at stake in epidermalization is not simply a matter of how whites perceive blacks but how blacks *live* their bodies and their world.

In "The Phenomenology of the Black Body" Johnson observes that black people adopt several responses to the epidermalization of their world. One is to "police" themselves so that they give no support to the "myth of contamination" that whites project onto them (116). Such an effort serves ironically only to reinforce the fact that black people live relative to the racist projections of the white majority. As Bannon remarks in *Oxherding Tale*, the easiest way to find an escaped slave is to "look for the man who's policin' hisself, tryin' his level best to be *average*. That's yo Negro" (115). Another response is to invert the terms of white racism by insisting on the purity or superiority of blackness, a strategy that Johnson believes is characteristic of black nationalist thought and one that is adopted in *Oxherding Tale* by George, who "invert[s] Big House values at every turn" (24). According to Johnson, such responses are compromised because the terms of their signification still issue from a white Other. That is to say, even when the terms are inverted, blackness still fails to signify except from *within* the critical space of white discourse.

While the shifting metaphorical displacements in *Oxherding Tale* seem at times to invite an identification of blackness with pathology in a manner that simply reiterates the terms of racist discourse, the narrative's representation of Buddhist dis-ease can be read specifically as an attempt to account for the polluting effects of racist discourse *without* positing that discourse itself as the very condition for meaning. By proposing a different etiology for illness and a distinctive therapeutic cure, the thematization of suffering as dis-ease attempts to displace the terms of racist discourse that characterize the black body as polluted by *nature*. By suggesting that pathology is "something one does to oneself," the novel's representation of Buddhist dis-ease relocates the source of illness to the adoption of false views of one's condition—such as the false "myth of biological stain, evil, and physicality" about the black body that is promulgated by racist discourse. In his essay Johnson suggests that whites identify black people so strongly with the body that blacks appear to them as mere "physicality" ("Phenomenology" 115). By emphasizing the conceptual, psychological, and spiritual aspects of suffering, therefore, the Buddhist conception of dis-ease can be seen to foreground the very aspects of black personhood that white discourse attempts to erase. Finally, by suggesting that pathology is neither essential nor unchangeable, Buddhism implies that dis-ease is something that can be "cured"—something from which sufferers may find release and, more important, something over which they may exercise agency. The novel's thematization of suffering as Buddhist dis-ease can therefore be read as Johnson's attempt to account for the debilitating effects of racism without making American racist discourse itself the ground for African American identity.

In 1974, while he was in the midst of gathering materials for the composition of *Oxherding Tale*, Johnson wrote in a letter that he hoped he could convince his readers that "certain aspects of the Zen Buddhist vision are social."[39] Johnson's comment reveals that he was not blind to charges that Buddhism leads to quietism and, furthermore, that the social consequences of Buddhism were of some importance to him. And yet a piece is still missing from the "body mosaic" represented on Bannon's form and, to a significant extent, from Johnson's narrative itself. While Andrew sees a "society" on the Soulcatcher's figure, it is not a commonwealth of civic engagement but a "necropolis," a "commonwealth of the dead" (175). As suffering and death become understood as moments in a larger process, the national sphere of internecine conflict is diffused across vast spans of time and the far expanses of the cosmos. The solidarity that Andrew discovers at last—with his father and indeed with all creation—takes the form of an appreciation of inter-being, of the co-dependent origin of life. Citizenship is thus defined in terms of membership in a grand cosmic process of diversification rather than in national terms. Johnson's dramatic turn from the representation of a Marxist economy of productive subjectivity in his first novel to the depiction of a Mahayana soteriology of enlightenment in his second thus leads to a displacement of the national sphere itself.

The social vision dramatized in *Oxherding Tale* reveals that when he composed his second published novel, Johnson understood the social effects of Buddhism primarily in traditional Mahayana terms, as those that result from the ripple effects of altruistic action over time. Animated by the vigorous processes of cultural assimilation that Buddhist scholars identify as characteristic of the dissemination of Buddhism *and* by the attendant dislocations that occur when venerable teachings are adapted to new conditions, *Oxherding Tale* enacts a series of metaphoric displacements: the physical suffering of the slave is displaced onto forms of Buddhist dis-ease, the nation's bloody civil war is translated to the battlefields of domestic discord, and social causality is concentrated in personal histories or diffused across vast cosmic operations. As its narrative logic operates both to recall and to displace more collective and more institutional understandings of suffering and engagement with those of a Mahayana soteriology, *Oxherding Tale* dramatizes a series of narrative disruptions that can be both disturbing and exhilarating. Unmatched among his other novels for sheer inventive vigor, *Oxherding Tale* is Johnson's first attempt to work out an understanding of the social effects of engaged Buddhism in dramatic form, an understanding that would mature with his increased participation in an emergent form of engaged Western Buddhism.

# 4

The Rise of the New Black
Intellectual and the Varieties
of Cosmopolitanism in
*Middle Passage*

The bourgeoisie has through its exploitation of
the world market given a cosmopolitan character to
production and consumption in every country.

*Karl Marx*

In a single town, there is no wisdom.

*Asante Proverb*

I speak as a citizen of the world.

*Dr. Martin Luther King Jr.*

CHARLES JOHNSON'S *Middle Passage* (1990) ENTERED THE LITERARY
marketplace at the precise moment when several scholars who were proph-
esying the demise of the American public intellectual were in the process of
being proved stunningly incorrect. In 1987 Russell Jacoby argued in his well-
known book *The Last Intellectuals: American Culture in the Age of Academe* that American public intellectuals were in decline. The independent
scholars of an earlier generation who wrote for a broad readership were
being replaced by university professors who wrote only for other special-
ists: "Where the Lewis Mumfords or Walter Lippmanns wrote for a public,
their successors 'theorize' about it at academic conferences" (xv). Credited
with putting the term "public intellectual" back into contemporary circulation, Jacoby ironically provided the phrase that appeared in an avalanche

of scholarly studies and popular commentary over the next two decades on the very phenomenon he had pronounced in decline: the American public intellectual.[1] As he has since admitted, Jacoby had been too tied "to an obsolete model of intellectual life, privileging the old white guys and gals from the past," to recognize the emergence of other important models of intellectual practice, in particular the unanticipated explosion of "new black public intellectuals" on the national scene in the 1990s (xv). He confesses, "in no way did my book anticipate their appearance" (xix).

While the visibility of black intellectuals was increasing in mainstream media and academic outlets at the end of the twentieth century—a group often referred to as the *new* black intellectuals, to distinguish their generation from the long tradition of black intellectuals who preceded them in American life—Charles Johnson was becoming increasingly visible as a national literary figure. Certainly the 1990s were propitious years for Johnson: in addition to publishing two novels, *Middle Passage* (1990) and *Dreamer* (1998), he received the National Book Award at the beginning of the decade (in 1990) and a MacArthur Award near its end (in 1998). With a Ph.D. in philosophy, a chair at a leading American university (the S. Wilson and Grace M. Pollock Professorship at the University of Washington), and Guggenheim, MacArthur, and American Academy of Arts and Letters awards, Johnson is undeniably among the nation's academic elite. Over the course of the 1990s he also became increasingly identified as a public intellectual himself. Johnson was included, for example, in *American Literary History*'s 1998 forum on public intellectuals, "Thinking in Public" (other participants included such figures as Richard Rorty, Charles Bernstein, Todd Gitlin, and Martha Nussbaum). Given the breadth of his written work, Johnson also fulfills the qualification for the designation "public intellectual" suggested by Steven Mailloux, who, while granting that the university is itself a distinctive type of public forum, argues that the term should be "reserved for those thinkers who directly engage with or are engaged by nonacademic publics" (144). Johnson's fiction and prose essays do engage such audiences, as do his screenplays (including *Booker*), his growing contributions to Buddhist publications, and his essays for outlets such as the *American Scholar, Common Quest,* the *New York Times,* the *Wall Street Journal,* and *Crisis* (the late-twentieth-century reincarnation of the magazine established in 1910 by the NAACP). In addition, since 1977 Johnson has published over fifty reviews for well-known national and international outlets such as the *Los Angeles Times,* the *Washington Post,* the *New York Times,* the *Times Literary Supplement,* and the *Times* of London. Although Johnson himself finds the term "intellectual" suspect for reasons that will be examined shortly, by the 1990s he himself was widely recognized as having achieved that status.

The social phenomenon of the new black intellectual illuminates several features of Johnson's career and fiction. Johnson himself has long been interested in investigating the complicated position of black intellectuals through fictional re-creations of historical figures from the African American intellectual tradition (such as the Reverend Richard Allen, Absalom Jones, Phillis Wheatley, Frederick Douglass, and Martin Luther King Jr.); through the creation of characters who occupy the social positions of black intellectuals (university professors, ministers, lawyers); and through an analysis of the status of contemporary black intellectuals in his essays. Three of his four novels have as their protagonists exceptionally well educated black men: *Oxherding Tale*, *Middle Passage*, and *Dreamer*.[2] In addition, several of Johnson's essays consider more directly the contemporary situation of black intellectuals, including "The King We Left Behind," "Second Front," "Shall We Overcome?," "Thinking in Public," and, notably, "The Role of the Black Intellectual at the Beginning of the Twenty-first Century." Because Johnson matured with a particular generation of black intellectuals, because he consistently writes about black intellectuals in his fiction and nonfiction, and because he has attained the status of public intellectual himself, his writing not surprisingly resonates with a number of critical issues that have attended the social emergence of the new black intellectuals. His winning the National Book Award in 1990 is, moreover, a moment of some significance in that history. Finally, the rise of the new black intellectual offers an important context for understanding Johnson's award-winning *Middle Passage*, a novel that contributes to the effort by some contemporary intellectuals to redefine the conceptual boundaries of cosmopolitan thought.

## A New Generation of Black Intellectuals

In March 1995, the cover of the *Atlantic Monthly* featured a provocative illustration of a black fist raised in defiance. Interestingly, that fist was holding a pen. The text accompanying the illustration announced, "The New Intellectuals . . . Suddenly They're Back. And They're Black" (see figure 4).

While black intellectuals had in fact never been gone, the emergence of a new generation of black intellectuals in the final decades of the twentieth century was nevertheless a significant phenomenon. As Early observed, "For the first time in African-American history there is a powerful, thoroughly credentialed and completely professionalized black intellectual class, something wished for since March 5, 1897" (the date when Alexander Crummell, W. E. B. Du Bois, and A. H. Grimke established the American Negro Academy in Washington, D.C.) ("Black" 7). The publication of Ewart Guinier's obituary in the *New York Times* on February 7, 1990, seemed to mark both the passing of an individual and a generational shift occurring across the

A POLITICAL PORTRAIT OF PHIL GRAMM / FICTION BY JOHN BARTH

# The Atlantic Monthly

MARCH 1995

## THE NEW INTELLECTUALS

Sophisticated, political, morally aware, at times

fiercely contentious— the breed known as "public intellectuals" has seemed close to extinction. Suddenly they're back. And they're black.

BY ROBERT S. BOYNTON

4. Atlantic Monthly *cover from March 1995*
*on the new black public intellectuals.*
Courtesy *Atlantic Monthly.*

nation with the increased visibility of younger scholars such as Henry Louis Gates Jr. Following Guinier as head of Black Studies at Harvard, Gates was lauded by the *Times* as "Black Studies' New Star" and portrayed as a youthful phenomenon who was working hard to boost the status of a marginalized discipline (Begley 24). If Black Studies programs—institutionalized in the U.S. university system since 1968—were hardly new by the 1990s, they were in fact newly controversial, in part owing to the coverage given by national newspapers such as the *Times* to racially charged (anti-Semitic) comments by Leonard Jeffries at City College. The ideological division and controversy that attended the increasing visibility of new black intellectuals are reflected in the title of a July 20, 1992, column that Gates wrote for the *Times* in response to Jeffries, "Black Demagogues and Pseudo-Scholars." With a growing number of people of color obtaining the status of public intellectuals across a wide spectrum of fields, debates about the history, opportunities, and responsibilities of black intellectuals increasingly appeared in the pages of mainstream national outlets such as the *New York Times*, the *New Yorker*, the *New Republic*, the *Los Angeles Times*, the *Atlantic Monthly*, the *Village Voice*, and the *Boston Review*, as well as in more specialized academic journals such as *Critical Inquiry*, *Social Text*, the *Journal of Negro Education*, and the *Journal of African American History*.[3] In addition, a number of book-length studies published in the 1990s focused explicitly on the history and current status of the black intellectual, including bell hooks and Cornel West's *Breaking Bread: Resurgent Black Intellectual Life* (1991), William Banks's *Black Intellectuals: Race and Responsibility in American Life* (1996), Joy James's *Transcending the Talented Tenth: Black Leaders and American Intellectuals* (1996), Ross Posnock's *Color and Culture: Black Writers and the Making of the Modern Intellectual* (1998), Wilson Moses's *Afrotopia* (1998), and Hazel Carby's *Race Men* (1998). In the following decade this trend would continue with the appearance of Anthony Bogues's *Black Heretics, Black Prophets: Radical Political Intellectuals* (2003), Clarence Taylor's *Black Religious Intellectuals* (2002), Grant Farred's *What's My Name? Black Vernacular Intellectuals* (2003), David Troutt's *After the Storm: Black Intellectuals Explore the Meaning of Hurricane Katrina* (2006), and Houston Baker's *Betrayal: How Black Intellectuals Have Abandoned the Ideals of the Civil Rights Era* (2008). The turn of the millennium was therefore a period in which both the academy and the nation at large seemed to be developing, as Early suggested, a "romance with the black mind" ("Black" 7).

As critics and commentators scrambled to explain, celebrate, or critique the new black intellectuals, adjectives proliferated to modify the term "intellectual." Adapting Gramsci, Cornel West had earlier called in "The Dilemma of the Black Intellectual" (1985) for the development of "organic" black intellectuals, or intellectuals who overcame their alienation in white universities by remaining organically linked to the black community. In 2000 John Michael responded to West with a chapter in *Anxious Intellects* that analyzed new black intellectuals as "*in*organic representatives," or as intellectuals necessarily in an "inorganic relationship to those for and to whom he or she speaks" (24). In a 1998 study of the history of black intellectuals, Ross Posnock focused attention on a historical tradition of "black cosmopolitan intellectuals," or black intellectuals who adopt a cosmopolitan position on universal human rights in order to oppose racism. Pointing out that discussions of black intellectualism often leave out women's achievements, Thulani Davis, bell hooks, and Hazel Carby refocused attention on the "black woman intellectual."[4] In *Transcending the Talented Tenth*, Joy James argued that by concentrating on academic intellectuals, scholars ignored important contributions by "radical-worker intellectuals." (In 2003, James published another book titled *Imprisoned Intellectuals*.) During the same period the phrase "black public intellectual" was itself deconstructed. Some black intellectuals objected to the phrase "public" as a deprecating invention of the right (West), others preferred that the modifier "black" be dropped, and still others suggested that the term "intellectual" might itself be derogatory (Johnson). Critics debated what the proper extension of the term "intellectual" might be and considered whether "hip-hop intellectuals" (such as Tupac Shakur) and "black vernacular intellectuals" (such as Muhammad Ali and Jamaican musician Bob Marley) deserved the designation.[5] In 2001 Robert Reid-Pharr seemed to sum up the difficulty of accounting for the complicated genealogies that contributed to black intellectualism in the United States by coining the term "Cosmopolitan Afrocentric Mulatto Intellectual."[6]

The somewhat playful proliferation of terms reflected here, however, does not diminish the significance of the phenomenon that they attempt to describe or the importance of the critical task of characterizing the distinctive features and social circumstances of this new generation of black intellectuals. Hortense Spillers argues that "the implications of the paradigm shift" for black intellectuals has been "fairly massive since 1967," when Harold Cruse published his influential study *The Crisis of the Negro Intellectual* (91). As we have seen in the introduction to this book, various factors contributed to the dramatic demographic change in the number of black students who entered U.S. institutions of higher learning in the late 1960s and 1970s, factors that include the post–World War II baby boom, expansion of the American university and college systems, civil rights successes in the 1950s and 1960s, and advocacy by Black Studies programs for curricular and admissions changes. As a result, by the end of the twentieth century a new generation of college-educated black scholars were achieving distinction in a number of fields across the nation.

At the same time, black Americans had capitalized on their increased access to other areas of the nation's public sphere. As Michael Bérubé points out, the new black intellectuals came of age during an "extraordinary cultural moment," when the nation was experiencing an "explosion in Black popular culture from Hollywood to hip hop" (74). They also matured at a time when the divide between middle- and lower-class black people appeared to be widening, and when the community resources that had sustained a separate black intellectual culture for earlier generations seemed at risk. As Adolph Reed observes, "The demise of *Black World* and atrophy of *The Black Scholar* both fuel and reflect the shriveling of an autonomous domain for black debate" (34). Finally, changes in the technologies and structure of the public sphere at the end of the century meant that new black intellectuals who wanted to reach a broad public had to undertake a difficult negotiation between the academy and new forms of media culture, such as the celebrity culture. The changing conditions for black intellectualism led several commentators to criticize the latest generation of black intellectuals as constituting an intellectual class that is especially alienated from the black community, especially concerned with celebrity, and—most important for a consideration of Johnson's participation in the rise of new black intellectualism—especially committed to a controversial, hybrid cosmopolitanism.

The charge that new black intellectuals are likely to be isolated in white universities reflects several features of the contemporary public sphere. Critics like Jacoby and Robert Boynton suggest that contemporary public intellectuals—both white and black—have lost the independence enjoyed by earlier groups, such as the New York intellectuals. Other critics, however, approach the incorporation of new black intellectuals in white universities from a different perspective, contrasting them not with the primarily white (and Jewish) New York intellectuals but with the black intellectuals of earlier generations, who were more likely to be situated at historically black institutions and to be active in black social and political organizations. Michael Hanchard, for example, argues that the current generation of black intellectuals, unlike their predecessors, have "no specific constituency or constellation of organizations to answer to, which would place their actions in a political context that speaks to both local and global communities" ("Intellectual" 23). At the same time, the increased specialization of academic discourse—for instance, the advent of deconstructive discourses in the humanities—renders it increasingly difficult for black intellectuals to share their work with a wider public. University tenure systems also discourage the broad dissemination of scholarship by rewarding publication in specialized journals while discouraging generalist work.[7] Somewhat ironically, then, the very success that new black intellectuals achieve at integrating into mainstream universities, corporations, and governmental positions runs the risk of distancing them from other black Americans.

Exacerbating the alienation that can result from the black intellectual's incorporation into primarily white institutions are changing economic and social conditions that seem to be widening class divisions among black Americans in the nation at large. At the same time that greater numbers of black people are entering college, several factors are eroding the economic base of the black working class. The Fordist economic policies of the early twentieth century, built on a manufacturing economy, are being replaced by a post-Fordist service economy, with calamitous ramifications for the black laborers who depend on relatively high-paying factory jobs to support their families. Labor unions have been weakened, and new competition from abroad is sending jobs and capital overseas. The result is that more black people are completing college and entering the middle class at the same time that the traditional economic supports for the black working class are eroding. In addition, as an increasing number of black people move to the suburbs, the withdrawal of middle-class blacks and their institutions from urban centers have also contributed to a class divide.[8] (As we saw in chapter 1, in his short story "Alēthia" Johnson investigates both the alienated position of the black intellectual in the white academy and this widening class divide.)

In addition to charges that new black intellectuals are more isolated from other black Americans than previous generations of black scholars, critics also suggest that because of changes in the media industries, today's public intellectuals are more likely to be "public" in the sense of being celebrities than were previous generations. Johnson remarks in "The Role of the Black Intellectual in the Twenty-first Century" that "the black 'public intellectual' . . . enjoys in America a celebrity hitherto unknown to predecessors like sociologist E. Frazer Franklin and Charles S. Johnson" (86). Some black intellectuals enthusiastically embrace new media, celebrity, and performance culture as a way to reach nonacademic audiences. For example, Mark Anthony Neal, a professor at Duke University, has invented the alter ego "thugniggerintellectual."[9] He writes: "I wanted to use this idea of this intellectual persona to do some real kind of 'gangster' scholarship, if you will. . . . When I'm not trying to be the collegial colleague. When I'm not trying to sell books. When I'm not trying to get students into my classes. When I'm not trying to be politically correct. This is this other persona. I wanted to really do a book project that spoke to raising these kinds of questions, ultimately, within this guise that, in some ways, identity is all performance" ("Hip-Hop"). Unabashedly listing his occupation as "public intellectual" on his

Internet blog, Neal clearly embraces both the newer technologies and the more performative aspects of black intellectualism.

Many other critics and black intellectuals, however, are suspicious of the celebrity status of new black intellectuals and are worried about its consequences for scholarship. Partly because he believes that the term "intellectual" is trivialized by its association with celebrity, Johnson prefers the word "scholar."[10] He explains: "When one's reputation is founded not so much on a ground breaking work of scholarship but rather being well-known, it follows that one must strive mightily to stay newsworthy, no matter how shallow, hastily executed, or ephemeral one's work becomes. The painstaking, slow work of scholarship becomes replaced by media appearances, often shameless self-promotion, and even the dubious distinction of being 'controversial' buys one a headline in the press and Andy Warhol's fifteen minutes of fame on the Oprah Winfrey show" ("Role" 87). Spillers also expresses serious reservations about the performative conditions that obtain in the new public sphere for black intellectuals. She argues that "public discourse has been immeasurably diminished since the late sixties and the explosion of image industries" (104). Criticizing Cornel West's decision to leave Harvard for Princeton (after his confrontation with then–Harvard president Lawrence Summers), Thulani Davis notes that the new black scholar's increasing celebrity can lead to "power plays" driven by a desire "to enhance . . . already cushy careers" ("Spinning"). In short, with the growth of blogs, talk shows, twenty-four-hour news cycles, sound bites, and what Spillers calls the increasing "theatricalization of culture," many critics and public intellectuals—including Johnson—are concerned that the public sphere now privileges the fleeting cameo appearance over the sustained scholarly project (105).

Related to the celebrity status enjoyed by many new black intellectuals is a concern that the roles intellectuals are asked to perform are becoming increasingly reductive. Discussing the social function of intellectuals, Early points out that black intellectuals are "bankable" to the degree that they can "speak for one public while being able to speak to the other" ("Partisanship"). While the cultural position of black public intellectuals would seem to enable them to serve a valuable role as cultural translators in an increasingly heterogeneous society, the danger is that the position of cultural translator is often reduced to the single function of interpreting black culture for the interest—or simple curiosity—of whites. Even so gifted a cultural translator as Martin Luther King Jr., for example, had to work to keep his white interviewers focused on questions of civil rights, because they often attempted to shift the conversation to more titillating subjects, such as whether the movement would lead to increased "intermarriage" between whites and blacks.[11] A growing celebrity culture is believed to increase the danger of white co-optation. In a blistering 1995 critique published in the *Village Voice*, "The Current Crisis of Black Intellectuals: What Are the Drums Saying, Booker?," Adolph Reed compares the role of black public intellectuals to that of "native" translators for colonial interests. They speak, Reed suggests, "on the metaphorical boundary of the bantustan, but facing outward" toward whites (34). Underlying the role of black cultural translator are the assumptions by some whites that every black individual is fluent in the exotic language of a mysterious black subculture and that the primary contribution of black intellectuals to the nation is their ability to translate that language into "white American."

The role of interpreter also reflects the implicit assumption that each black intellectual is a specialist in the same area of expertise: blackness. In "Intellectuals and the Persisting Significance of Race," William Banks reports the compelling testimony of one black scholar, a specialist in Middle Eastern affairs, who describes the disheartening effect that white expectations have on his ability to communicate his work: "If I start talking abut the Arab-Israeli conflict, nobody wants to hear me. I have spent six of the last ten years on the ground researching, studying the problem. Now, intellectually, I want to pursue this issue. But when I stand up they want me to tell them why Jesse Jackson said so and so. I don't know why Jesse Jackson said anything! Because of this racial reality in the mind of Whites, I am not allowed to talk about the Middle East. All they think I know is what Jesse Jackson thinks" (85). In "The Role of the Black Public Intellectual" Johnson analyzes a related problem. He points out that in the Modern Library's "List of 100 Best Non-Fiction Books of the 20th Century," only seven are by black authors.[12] While emphasizing that these books are "seminal" for "any and all discussions of race," Johnson notes that books by white authors range over subjects from mathematics to history to philosophy, while the work of black intellectuals is "confined to race alone" (85). Johnson also observes that doctoral degrees awarded to black students fall heavily within a single field, education, and that their representation in fields such as geophysics, biomedical engineering, microbiology, and accounting is small or nonexistent. The lack of black participation in specialties such as these suggests to Johnson that rather than being encouraged to engage the "mysterious, inexhaustible world at large," blacks are expected to address a "smaller province of meaning" (85). In response, he argues that blacks should pursue the intellectual freedom to study any and all subjects, "for their *own sake*" (92).

Finally and significantly, new black intellectuals have been criticized for their identification with intellectual positions that have come to be grouped under the rubric of "cosmopolitanism." This debate is particularly important to critics of Johnson's fiction, because his writing over time has been increasingly identified with the cosmopolitan position. Other new black (and mixed-race) intellectuals frequently associated in particular with cosmopolitanism include Henry Louis Gates Jr., Kwame Anthony Appiah (who in 2006 published *Cosmopolitanism*), bell hooks, Randall Kennedy, Gerald Early, and Paul Gilroy. Called "one of the most important intellectual trends in the world today" by Don Robotham, "one of the most prevalent terms in the discussion of social identity in the twenty-first century" by Simon Gikandi, and the "Next Big Thing" by Eric Lott, cosmopolitanism attempts to rearticulate older conceptions of world citizenship and human rights (such as those offered by the Stoics or by Kant) in ways that will make them effective tools for advancing human rights in late modernity (Robotham 561, Gikandi 609, Lott 108). In part a reaction to the postmodernist rejection of grand narratives in favor of the particular and local, and in part a response to the essentialist claims of some versions of so-called identity politics, the new interest in cosmopolitanism reflects a resurgence of critical focus on the normative power of universals. This new interest in universals, however, is allegedly tempered by a respect for cultural, local, and ethnic specificity. Many cosmopolitan intellectuals hope that deference to multiple allegiances will enable them to avoid, for example, the unifying but proscriptive nationalism that often accompanies conservative critiques of multiculturalism. Recent attempts to articulate a cosmopolitanism that maintains an interplay between universals and particulars—or that puts them into dialogue—has led to a proliferation of designations at least as numerous as those used to describe new black intellectuals themselves, including critical cosmopolitanism, democratic cosmopolitanism, rooted cosmopolitanism, situated cosmopolitanism, discrepant cosmopolitanism, actually existing cosmopolitanism, postcolonial cosmopolitanism, working-class cosmopolitanism, wounded cosmopolitanism, patriotic cosmopolitanism, strategic cosmopolitanism, and vernacular cosmopolitanism.[13]

Critical debate over the new cosmopolitanism has centered especially on its complex relationships to nationalism and to ethnicity. Does cosmopolitanism's revitalized appeal to universal human rights provide a basis for progressive social reform, or does it promote abstract loyalties at the expense of actually existing ethnic, racial, and national communities? Does the new cosmopolitanism's rearticulation of cosmopolitan citizenship provide a position from which to criticize overzealous nationalism, or may it constitute, as Timothy Brennan warns, a "reckless American expansion" on a global scale? (682).[14] If cosmopolitanism seeks to reclaim the normative force of appeals to universal human rights—an appeal whose strategic potential was powerfully illustrated during the early civil rights era—can that normative force be deployed without promoting the sorts of totalizing social identities that have often served in the past as a pretext for white colonial interests? Questions like these suggest that what is at stake in the recent debate is whether

cosmopolitanism can achieve its universalizing, normative force without subverting the vigor of local cultures, cultural or ethnic, and whether cosmopolitan citizenship has the organizational structures that will enable it either
to resist state interference with human rights or to prove as effective as state
structures in defending such rights.

One criticism of cosmopolitanism's relationship to ethnicity that has
special significance for the study of Johnson's fiction is the judgment that cosmopolitanism tends to privilege a hybrid or mongrelized social identity at the
expense of allegiances to more inclusively ethnic communities. Reed argues
that by trying to inhabit a metaphorical boundary *between* white and black
cultures, some black intellectuals may end up turning their backs on the black
community. By contrast, Homi Bhabha observes that many black intellectuals effectively "rid[e] the boundary" (or use their cultural hybridity) in such
a way that it becomes "a transformative, double-edged thing" ("Black" 17).
As Bhabha contends, "Toni Morrison's exploration of the Africanist discourse
in the 'white' American novel is a testimony to hybridity; Anna Deavere
Smith's disquieting bricolages of the fear, force, and powerlessness that constitute Crown Heights or the L.A. riots is a performance of hybridity; . . .
Henry Louis Gates' refusal of Afrocentricity is the courage of hybridity;
Cornel West's African-Jewish dialogue is the sanity of hybridity" (114, 116).
Perceiving in Reed's argument an "either/or-ism" that understands cultural
difference as an "impassable frontier," Bhabha instead proposes a "vernacular cosmopolitanism" that recognizes both cultural specificity and transcultural complexity ("Unsatisfied" 191). Recent work on black cosmopolitanism
by Posnock and the historian Wilson Moses further complicates appeals to
binaries that would oppose cultural particularism to cosmopolitanism.
According to Posnock, today's cosmopolitan thinkers, both white and black,
were preceded by a long line of African American thinkers, from W. E. B. Du
Bois forward, who were themselves interested in exploring the possibilities for
a complex, ethnically and culturally responsive cosmopolitanism. In *Color
and Culture* Posnock argues that earlier black intellectuals were not only *cosmopolitan* black intellectuals but also the very intellectuals who provided the
model for *white* American cosmopolitan intellectuals. At the same time,
Moses argues persuasively that the opposition frequently assumed between
nationalist and cosmopolitan intellectuals is itself historically incorrect. (Early
black nationalist thinkers such as Alexander Crummell and William Ferris
were themselves cosmopolitan figures.) Other recent work on cosmopolitanism also suggests that critiques of black cosmopolitanism often fail to
recognize the degree to which black American intellectual and social culture
has historically "always already" been a cosmopolitan culture.[15]

Since the 1990s Johnson's fiction has been increasingly identified with the
cosmopolitan wing of black intellectualism. In part this identification fol-

lowed Posnock's brief discussions of Johnson's work in *Color and Culture*. There Posnock places Johnson with Samuel Delaney as contemporary writers related in some fashion to a long line of cosmopolitan African American writers in the nation's history (60). That such an identification is amenable to Johnson is suggested by the enthusiastic endorsement he wrote for the back cover of Posnock's book, where he praises the study as one that he had been "waiting to read for thirty years." Subsequently William Gleason, William Nash, and Rudolph Byrd each discussed Johnson in relation to the cosmopolitan position as it is articulated in *Color and Culture*. Gleason suggests that Johnson shares with many of the writers discussed by Posnock an interest in "critical pragmatism," while Nash points out that many of the "anti-race race men" and women identified by Posnock as black cosmopolitans were significant influences on Johnson's art.[16] In addition, Nash points to Johnson's willingness to "draw outside the African American canon" as reflective of his cosmopolitan ethos (*Charles* 13). Byrd also indicates that Johnson's "willingness to draw upon a pantheon of literary ancestors that include both American and English authors" reflects his "cosmopolitan vision" (*Charles* 196). In "Thinking in Public," Johnson elaborates on this point by explaining, "Personally and professionally, I feel that as a human being all the intellectual and artistic traditions of mankind—our predecessors' efforts to make sense of the world—are my inheritance, and they are there for me to draw upon when called to create or critically evaluate phenomena" (37). Johnson's frequent and enthusiastic endorsements of intellectual and creative hybridity clearly link him to the black thinkers discussed by Bhabha. Like Gates, Johnson has also criticized Afrocentricity in both his fiction and prose, and like West, he has contributed to the Jewish–African American dialogue (which chapter 5 discusses in more detail).

More important, Johnson frequently enunciates a position that resonates with attempts to articulate a cosmopolitanism that reclaims the normative force of the universal while recognizing multiple, overlapping allegiances. He says, "We must see ourselves as belonging to both a human and an ethnic community, and keep these balanced" ("Thinking" 37). Johnson's comment seems both to endorse Diogenes' well-known cosmopolitan credo "I am a citizen of the world"—a phrase echoed by King in 1967 and by Barack Obama in 2008—while he simultaneously modifies that sentiment.[17] This double gesture is characteristic of recent attempts to conceptualize a vernacular or democratic cosmopolitanism. Johnson's claim that one's commitments need to be "balanced" is significant because it suggests that one must undertake an ongoing process of negotiation among allegiances.[18] In addition, Johnson has moved self-consciously toward a more cosmopolitan position in his work over the course of his career. In discussing the development of his thinking, he explains that he has decided increasingly to "profile" in his fiction the more cosmopolitan or more "unitive, integrative dimensions of our lives" over racial difference ("Thinking" 37). In amplifying on the reasons for this progression, Johnson historicizes his own writerly project by explaining that he has begun to emphasize the importance of an identification with a larger cosmopolitan community over a more exclusively ethnic community because he believes that at the present historical moment these two commitments are *already* out of balance. After the death of Martin Luther King, the "ideals of universal brotherhood, of 'the beloved community,'" were replaced by the claims of "racial separatists, cultural nationalists, and Afrocentrists like Louis Farrakhan, who have dominated our discussion of race and American identity since 1968" (38). In response to such racial "balkanization," Johnson has increasingly chosen to profile the cosmopolitan values that he believes were too hastily discarded after King's assassination.

Johnson's use of the word "profile" is revealing because it captures some of the difficulty faced by cosmopolitans who attempt to place the particular and the universal in dialogue. The origins of the phrase lie in phenomenology's assertion that because individual positions on a subject render only a partial "profile," one must assume multiple perspectives in order to obtain a more comprehensive understanding—an argument Johnson endorses both in his essay "Whole Sight" and in his book on black fiction, *Being and Race*. If each profile is partial, however, that position nonetheless brings into sharp relief an important perspective on a subject. Thus, not only has Johnson increasingly chosen to profile cosmopolitan values that he believes are on the decline in discussions of race, but also he does so with a polemical intent: to address what he perceives as an already existing imbalance. At the same time, Johnson recognizes that the profiles he offers, as moments in a larger process of cultural negotiation, are necessarily provisional, incomplete, and liable to further interpretation. Indeed, the attempt to dramatize both the temporary stability provided by individual profiles and the continuing need for further negotiation between competing allegiances is itself an important characteristic of his complex cosmopolitan vision—and one important to *Middle Passage*.

## Johnson and the 1990 National Book Award

Johnson's winning the National Book Award in 1990 was an event of some significance in the history of new black intellectuals. At the time Johnson was only the second black male to receive the award in its forty-year history, and the first since Ralph Ellison was honored in 1953 for *Invisible Man*, published the previous year. The thirty-seven-year hiatus between these two awards speaks to the event's significance in helping to mark the generational shift between black intellectuals that was occurring across the nation, as did Gates's appointment as head of Harvard's Black Studies program in the same year. This generational shift was brought into sharp relief at the awards ceremony, where the seventy-seven-year-old Ellison was in attendance. The specific historical and institutional context of the 1990 awards helps to illustrate certain changes in the public sphere that contributed to the rise of black public intellectuals while simultaneously dramatizing the complex social position that they continue to occupy in American culture. Finally, the National Book Awards ceremony strengthened Johnson's ties to the more cosmopolitan wing of black intellectualism.

The announcement of the National Book Awards for 1990 was preceded by a minor controversy. On November 27, the day the selection committee was to cast its final vote, the *New York Times* published an article titled "Ideology Said to Split Book-Award Jurors." The piece highlighted the "climate of unusual divisiveness" surrounding that year's award committee (Cohen, "Ideology" C15). Paul West, one of five judges, spoke publicly about "deep ideological division" and "acute dividedness over nearly everything." The five finalists for the award were *Chromos* by Felipe Alfau, *Paradise* by Elena Castedo, *Dogeaters* by Jessica Hagestrom, *Because It Is Bitter and Because It Is My Heart* by Joyce Carol Oates, and *Middle Passage* by Charles Johnson. Of these authors, *Times* reporter Roger Cohen pointed out, two were Spanish born, one was born in the Philippines, one is African American, and only Oates, "a white American, has a wide reputation in the United States." The reporter's gloss on the ethnicity of the various finalists, which might strike readers as odd, in fact picks up on West's own characterization of the ideological split on the awards committee in decidedly racial terms: "Ethnic concerns, ideology, and moral self-righteousness," he asserted, had trumped aesthetic merit" (C15). After a final vote the next day awarded the prize for fiction to *Middle Passage*, the committee chair, Catherine Stimpson, revealed her own disagreement with West's assessment by emphasizing, Cohen reports, that the "selection process was based entirely on considerations of literary merit" ("*Middle*" C22).

West's interpretation of the voting for the award as driven by ideology would, of course, be anathema to Johnson, who by 1990 had forcefully and consistently positioned himself against certain traditions of African American literature, such as the Black Arts and social realist movements, for being themselves overtly ideological. Instead, Johnson was working toward what he called a "new black fiction" that would be characterized by what he termed "whole sight"—the title of an introduction to a special collection on "New Black Fiction" that Johnson guest-edited for *Callaloo* in 1984. In that introduction Johnson approvingly quotes Clayton Riley's comment that "the artist's first allegiance is to the imagination, as opposed to any prevailing dogma" ("Whole" 87). Two years before the awards, Johnson published *Being and Race*, in which he criticized naturalistic literature for holding "the imagination close to the ground" (6).[19] At the awards ceremony itself Johnson identified Ellison as the progenitor of a lineage of cosmopolitan black fiction separate from the prevailing genealogy established by the Black Arts movement. Whereas BAM urged writers "to control their images," said Johnson, Ellison inspires them to "expand their images" ("National" 209).

Johnson's acceptance speech can be read as a response to a call set forth in Ellison's own acceptance speech given thirty-seven years earlier. There Ellison also defines his project against naturalism and against an emphasis on victimization which he finds characteristic of naturalism. In order to "see America with an awareness of its rich diversity and its almost magical fluidity and freedom," Ellison states, he was "forced to conceive of a novel unburdened by the narrow naturalism which has led after so many triumphs to the final and unrelieved despair which marks so much of our current fiction." Johnson ends his own acceptance speech with a call for a new black fiction that is "Ellisonesque in spirit, a fiction of increasing intellectual and artistic generosity, one that enables us as a people—as a culture—to move from narrow complaint to broad celebration" (209). Given Johnson's self-conscious attempt to move black fiction in a different direction from the more overtly ideological schools pioneered by the social realist and Black Arts movements, West's comments to the *Times* are especially ironic (and more so given the fact that some critics of Johnson's work fault his fiction for not being ideological *enough*). The controversy surrounding the 1990 awards sheds light on the complex social position occupied by many new black intellectuals, whose achievements seemed fated to be read by others through an ethnic lens—even when their projects attempt to dismantle such expectations.

The 1990 National Book Awards also reflect in miniature certain material changes that were taking place in the American public sphere at the end of the twentieth century. In 1987 Larry Heinemann's first novel, *Paco's Story*, won over Philip Roth's *Counter Life* and Toni Morrison's *Beloved*, which later that year would receive the Pulitzer Prize for fiction. The passing over of *Beloved* sparked a major public outcry among black intellectuals and creative artists.[20] The following year it was reported in the *Times* that the National Book Foundation's awards committee would be increasing its panel of judges from three to five to "reduce the possibility of any individual judge casting a swing vote" (McDowell, "Book" C19). As the 1990 vote demonstrates, expanding the committee did not end debates about its selections, although it did broaden the selection process. Given West's comments, it is not inconceivable that the long absence of black male writers among National Book Award winners might have continued past 1990 if the three-person committee had been left in place. Other changes were made as well. At the same meeting in 1988 the board also decided "to broaden the award selection process" by considering more books from small houses (McDowell, "Nominees" C34). Although *Middle Passage* was an Atheneum imprint from Macmillan, the works of more small publishing houses were nominated for the 1990 awards than in previous years, and many of them received prizes.[21] Such institutional changes reflect the importance of greater access to awards for all books of merit. Early has argued that the expression "intellectual" became popular in the United States at the end of the nineteenth century with the rise of mass communications, which enabled a mass audience to come into being. Similarly, changes in the public sphere in the late twentieth century created an important context for the rise of new black intellectuals. The 1990 National Book Awards capture in miniature the increased access to national media culture that is one distinctive benefit enjoyed by this generation of intellectuals.

Most important for purposes of this discussion, the 1990 award cemented Johnson's identification with the cosmopolitan wing of black intellectualism. At the awards ceremony Johnson recognized Ellison as what Nash has aptly termed a literary "forebear."[22] Previously Johnson had often paid tribute to Ellison in his writings on the African American literary tradition, identifying him as an important influence on his work as a practitioner of black philosophical fiction and as a writer dedicated to technical excellence. Johnson used the occasion of the awards to define precisely what he meant in calling for a new black fiction that was "Ellisonian in vision" by quoting and commenting on statements by Ellison from the introduction to the thirtieth-anniversary edition of *Invisible Man*. There Ellison remarks that in that novel he wanted to "create a narrator who could think as well as act. . . . [G]ive him a consciousness in which serious philosophical questions could be raised, provide him with a range of diction that could play upon the richness of our readily shared vernacular speech and construct a plot that would bring him in contact with a variety of American types as they operated on various levels of society" (quoted by Johnson, "National" 208). Ellison's emphasis on the black intellect is striking. To Johnson these goals further suggested that Ellison understood black identity as complexly hybrid, or as "multisided, and synthetic as the American society that produced it" (209). Moreover, Johnson interprets Ellison's statement that "the human imagination is integrative" to mean that the black artist lays claim to a rich, specifically *cosmopolitan* inheritance: as Johnson elaborates in his acceptance speech, "all of human history—all of the effort mankind has put into making sense of the world—is our inheritance" (209). After Johnson's speech, Ellison, author of one of the most celebrated novels of the twentieth century and two landmark collections of essays on American culture, would respond, "I thought I had been forgotten" (Johnson, "Novel Genius" 19–20).

While Ellison had not been forgotten, his work had become a contested site in American literary studies, in large part because of his identification with a hybrid cosmopolitanism that appeared to some critics to undermine his racial authenticity. If Ellison's reputation seemed secure in 1952 with the publication of *Invisible Man*, a novel that interjected into American culture one of its most influential tropes for the black experience in America, he was nevertheless criticized by some white critics (famously Irving Howe) and by leading figures in BAM (notably Larry Neal and Amiri Baraka) for being overly enamored of and excessively influenced by Western literary and intellectual traditions. Neal's early criticism centered specifically on Ellison's cosmopolitan appropriation of Western artistic, philosophical, and critical forms. According to Neal, such cultural borrowings rendered Ellison a servant to "forms imposed from without" ("Black Writer" 22). Instead, Neal argued for a black aesthetic with a "separate symbolism, mythology, critique, and iconology" ("Black Arts" 272). By 1970, however, Neal demonstrated a greater appreciation for Ellison's in his essay "Ellison's Zoot Suit," where he acknowledges Ellison's mastery of African American folk and musical traditions and reconsiders his earlier criticism of Ellison's artistic adaptation of Western aesthetic traditions. Comparing Ellison to black musical greats who invented jazz on European instruments, Neal praises Ellison for the artistry he demonstrated in adapting Western forms for his own artistic purposes. Imaginatively addressing Ellison in his essay, Neal comments, "That trumpet you got in your hand may have been made in Germany, but you sure sound like my Uncle Rufus whooping his coming-home call across the cotton fields" (103).

In spite of Neal's change of heart, however, Ellison's status as an African American intellectual has continued to be controversial, and his cosmopolitan vision has remained the subject of forceful criticism. In "Failed Prophet and Falling Stock: Why Ralph Ellison Was Never Avant-Garde" (1999), Houston Baker criticizes *Invisible Man* for precisely the features that Johnson praises in his acceptance speech, arguing that Ellison pays little "studied attention to the intimate horrors of racism in the United States, . . . relinquish[ing] such analysis for a mess of Eliotian or Hemingwayesque allusions." Drawing on the biblical account of Esau, who foolishly trades his birthright for a mess of pottage (Genesis 25:34), Baker stresses the contradiction he perceives between the legacy of black suffering in America and the heritage of Western literary forms. Baker thus stakes out a position opposed to Johnson's cosmopolitan claim that "all of the effort mankind has put into making sense of the world—is our inheritance."[23] By publicly celebrating his intellectual allegiance to Ellison at the 1990 book awards,

Johnson interjected his own artistic project into the continuing debate over Ellison's cosmopolitan aesthetic.

Johnson's analysis also anticipates other trends in the current reconsideration of Ellison's work. While the critique of Ellison continues in works such as Arnold Rampersad's biography (2007), since the mid-1990s critics sympathetic to cosmopolitanism have undertaken a reexamination of the relationship of the aesthetic and the political in Ellison's prose and fiction (a revision inspired in part by the new materials by Ellison available in print since that time, including the selected letters between Ellison and Albert Murray). In "Ralph Ellison's Constitutional Faith," Gregg Crane argues that although critics repeatedly "wish that Ellison would choose between art and politics, high culture and folklore, universal themes and the particularities of black experience," Ellison "steadfastly refuses this choice" (104). Posnock's defense of Ellison's cosmopolitan position is stronger still. In a 2005 essay, "Ellison's Joking," he argues that "of all American writers, Ellison most forcefully took up the challenge of thinking beyond the imprisoning reductiveness of race and of liberating the cosmopolitan energies of democracy" (1). Against the earlier critiques of Ellison's artistic vision, Posnock suggests that only with the recent recognition of the "renewed promise of cosmopolitan democracy [that] has emerged as an animating ideal of popular, political, and academic culture" are we now "beginning to catch up with Ralph Waldo Ellison" (1). By the time of the 1990 National Book Awards, however, Johnson had already "caught up with" Ellison, for in writing the novel that was honored at the event, *Middle Passage*, he had just completed a sustained inquiry into *both* the dangers and the emancipatory potential of cosmopolitanism.[24]

## The Varieties of Cosmopolitanism and Charles Johnson's Middle Passage

Traditionally associated with an elite, urbane sophistication that seeks to transcend local, ethnic, and national identifications, cosmopolitanism would hardly seem an appropriate ethos to animate a neo-slave narrative that begins in antebellum America in 1830, follows the misadventures of its recently emancipated black protagonist, Rutherford Calhoun, as he makes his way as a cook's assistant on a slaver called the *Republic*, and charts a journey through the perilous waters of the Middle Passage that includes by the novel's conclusion both a mutiny and a slave revolt. Often identified with populations who travel by choice, cosmopolitanism is commonly understood to express a different kind of mobility, what Craig Calhoun has called the "class consciousness of frequent travelers" (897) and what James Clifford has criticized as the birthright of those who have the "privilege of standing above cultural particularism . . . , a privilege invented by a totalizing western liberalism" ("Review" 211). Similar assumptions of elitism and privilege are reflected in the traditional identification of cosmopolitanism with certain historical moments, including the effort by Alexander the Great (356–323 BCE) to unify the eastern Mediterranean, the attempt by medieval Christianity to establish a universal church, and the promotion by Enlightenment thinkers of universal humanism. Such cosmopolitan moments suggest that the universal claims asserted by cosmopolitanism may function primarily as a tool for the expansion of empire, for the evangelizing (or civilizing) of heathen others, or for what one critic has called the "Hegelian urge to homogenize" (Van Der Veer 165).

One of the most significant features of the late-twentieth-century theorization of cosmopolitanism, however, has been the effort to rethink both the history of and grounds for cosmopolitanism in ways that complicate its relation to non-elites, including immigrants, the poor, and the enslaved. That revision stems in part from the development of a more complicated picture of the history of cosmopolitanism. Cosmopolitan thinking in the West, it is now believed, predated Alexander's conquests and originated not in the upper class or even among Greek citizens but in the thinking of *metics*, or outsiders and immigrants who were interested not in expanding but in changing the status quo.[25] As the historian Paul Brown argues, cosmopolitanism originated "among the struggling lower classes seeking broader horizons" (60). In the West the development of cosmopolitan thought is often traced through the Greek Cynics, many of whom were themselves outsiders. (For example, when Diogenes is reputed to have made his famous claim to world citizenship, he was living in Athens as an exile from Sinope, in present-day Turkey.) According to Robert Fine and Robin Cohen, it was largely because of their outsider status that the Cynics were especially determined in advocating for the principle of *universal* equality under the law (139). Others have emphasized that a focus on Western forms of universalism, such as Christianity, can lead to the mistaken impression that cosmopolitan universalism is a Western phenomenon and to a concomitant failure to recognize both the extent and the impact of other forms of universalism, such as Hindu spirituality (Van Der Veer 174) or Middle Eastern cosmopolitanisms (Zubaida 32).

Cosmopolitanism is also being revised by the current reevaluation of Enlightenment thought. By turning from thinkers such as Kant and Locke to others like Pierre Bayle, Diderot, and Abbé Raynal, scholars are recovering a radical tradition of Enlightenment thinking that has been characterized by Jonathan Israel as "egalitarian, secularist, Spinozaist, and anti-colonial" (523). Finally, cosmopolitanism has attempted to give a better account not simply of the travels of elites but also of the movements of seamen, immigrant laborers, and slaves, a development resulting in part from a shift in diaspora studies from an earlier concentration on roots and origins to the more recent investigation of routes and movements. To Paul Gilroy, for example, it is Olaudah Equiano, the ex-slave, sailor, and composer of one of the world's most influential slave narratives, who is the exemplar of cosmopolitanism understood in terms of "the fluidity of relocation, displacement, and the forced transition between cultural codes and traditions, languages, and reform" (*Against* 117). Increasingly such a "cosmopolitanism from below," one that is the result of forced exile or slavery rather than of privileged mobility, has come to be understood not as the rare exception but rather as a defining characteristic of modernity.

An important consequence of the growing appreciation for the *varieties* of cosmopolitanism is the recognition that the normative force it espouses has been historically put to a variety of different, even conflicting, purposes. If cosmopolitan ideals have served imperial designs and the globalization of capital, they have also supported arguments for the greater civic participation of marginalized peoples. If cosmopolitan attitudes can be judged to weaken attachments to kith and kin, such values may also work to strengthen moral obligations that transcend the boundaries of caste or country. In *Middle Passage* Johnson puts into play several varieties of cosmopolitan thought on board the *Republic*, the dynamic meeting place of seamen, Allmuseri tribesmen, and the African American Rutherford Calhoun, in order to probe the conceptual limits of cosmopolitan thought and, finally, to develop an understanding of identity that is based on cosmopolitan competence rather than on birthright. By setting the primary action of the novel aboard a ship that is in "process" and in constant danger of "flying apart" (35–36), Johnson deliberately depicts the vessel as an unstable synthesis of ideas. At the same time, by anachronistically juxtaposing events that unfold on the *Republic* in 1830 with those occurring in twentieth-century America, Johnson dramatizes the transformation of one conceptual framework of cosmopolitanism into another, as his novel attempts to answer an overarching question: How does one recuperate a future out of the wreckage of the past?

A number of intellectuals from diverse backgrounds come into contact aboard the *Republic*, including the ship's captain and certain individuals drawn from both the crew and the Allmuseri people. Captain Ebenezer Falcon's intellect is signaled by a "thinker's brow," which Rutherford describes anachronistically as "the kind [that] fantasy writers put on spacemen far ahead of us in science and philosophy" (29). Rumored to be able to learn any language in two weeks' time, Falcon has mastered seven African dialects, although the unquestionably Western character of his mind is confirmed by the fact that he thinks "simultaneously" in French, Latin, and Greek (51). Peter Cringle, the ship's first mate, has almost "total recall of everything he'd read" (25). An educated easterner out of place among the rest of the *Republic*'s rough-and-tumble crew, Cringle reminds Rutherford of the type of woman who hides the fact that she knows "Leibnizian logic or Ptolemaic astronomy" in order not to "frighten off suitors" (25). Ngonyama, an African Allmuseri who is made a majordomo on board ship, is a repository of the knowledge that his tribe has gathered on their "globe-spanning travels" (77). From the first he is described by Rutherford as "studying everything—everything—we did" in order to learn all that he can about the ship (including how the steering works [75]). Rutherford himself received an education in theology and philosophy from his master, the Reverend Pegleg Chandler, who hoped that his pupil would become a Negro preacher—a calling for which Rutherford's commitment to the pleasures of the flesh makes him remarkably unsuited. Peppering his narration with allusions that range across African American folklore, classical literature, and Eastern religion, Rutherford provides Johnson's novel with an emphatically cosmopolitan voice. Significantly, Rutherford assumes that the readers of the ship's log in which he records the action of the novel share with him a broadly ranging, multicultural expertise. Finally, the narrative's anachronistic allusions suggest that in bringing these various intellectuals into contact aboard the *Republic*, Johnson is less interested in dramatic realism than in setting different conceptual positions against one another in order to probe the complex relationship of cosmopolitanism to ethnicity and nation.

Through the textual trope of piracy Captain Falcon represents what Peter Van Der Veer calls "colonial cosmopolitanism" ("Colonial" 165). With his name recalling a bird of prey, Falcon is associated with a rapacious nationalism from his birth, which occurred when "the nation was but a few hours old" (49). The form of citizenship that he practices is a predatory consumption that defines cultural goods in purely materialistic terms as plunder. Falcon's cosmopolitan travels, which range from South America and Africa to the Far East, enact the imperial designs of nation and the ventures of a "patriot whose burning passion was the manifest destiny of the United States to Americanize the entire planet" (30). Born at a time when the country was "buzzing with talk of what the new social order should be" (49), Falcon is in fact national history written as personal saga, or, as Rutherford calls him, "living history" (30). Falcon's piracy, then, is one answer to the question of what form the new social order will take both aboard the *Republic* and in the American Republic. Becoming disillusioned with the utopian dreams of "El Dorado and the Fountain of Youth" on which he was raised, Falcon, "like the fledgling republic," becomes "expansive, . . . bullying others and taking . . . what was not offered" (50). He represents, then, precisely the sort of predatory universalizing impulse that Timothy Brennan fears—an "imperial cosmopolitanism" that operates through "conquest" (669, 674).

Falcon's transformation of cultural goods into plunder reveals the operation of a decadent aesthetics of cosmopolitan consumption. Described as a "polyhistor" who wears a "Tyrian robe" and practices "esoteric Chinese jointlocks he'd learned . . . in King Miu village" (94, 55), Falcon in his cosmopolitan travels has been able to accumulate a treasure trove of cultural goods from around the globe: "Etruscan vases, Persian silk prayer carpets, and portfolios of Japanese paintings on rice paper" (48). In *Faith and the Good Thing*, Johnson details the transformation of value under capitalism whereby objects lose their use value and become commodities in a proliferating system of exchange. In *Middle Passage* a similar transformation of value is suggested by a pattern that emerges from Falcon's cultural looting: his piracy reduces the spiritual and cultural value of "goods" to consumables that satisfy his taste for the exotic. After living among the Hottentots for a month, for example, Falcon "plunder[s] their most sacred religious shrines" (30). He similarly translates the Bardo Thodol, the Tibetan Book of the Dead, not out of respect for Tibetan Buddhism but to demonstrate his own linguistic expertise—and not before he steals "the only scroll from a remote temple in Tibet" (30). Falcon reduces goods to mere plunder, then, by stripping them of the sacred, spiritual, or cultural meanings they originally carry, and his cabin is a repository for goods that are in the process of being similarly transformed, from "church boxes from sacked coastal towns" to prayer carpets and temple scrolls (142). That Falcon is unable to conceptualize goods in other than material terms is confirmed by the Bible that he keeps on his writing desk, which is "gilded" and purely "ornamental" (27). As Rutherford observes, most of the goods that Falcon accumulates on his travels are destined to fill a "standing order" for exotic objects that New Englanders will use to decorate their homes or to stock "Yankee museums" (48). Falcon's taste for the exotic, tied to that of the New Englanders in the United States, delineates an aesthetics of cosmopolitan consumption operating in the novel across individual, national, and international boundaries.

In "Eating the Other" bell hooks argues that in "commodity culture, ethnicity becomes spice" (21). The aesthetic consumption of the exotic Other becomes a way to enhance one's life by incorporating the rare, the exotic, and the new. In *Middle Passage* hooks's trope of cultural cannibalism is literalized by Falcon, who recounts to Rutherford at their first meeting his own act of cannibalism: "The sea does things to your head, Calhoun, terrible unravelings of belief that aren't in a cultured man's metaphysic. We ate tallow first, then sawdust, stopped up our noses and slurped foul water from the pumps before barbecuing that Negro boy. . . . He was freshly dead, of course, crushed by a falling mast. He tasted . . . stringy" (33). Listening to Falcon, Rutherford is immediately struck by the realization that the captain takes pleasure in telling others about his scandalous exploit:: "Cannibalism at sea was common enough, I knew, but he *enjoyed* telling this tale—enjoyed as I did, any experience that disrupted the fragile, artificial pattern of life on land. Once at home, I realized, he would probably boast of his 'experiences' at sea, use them to pull rank on those more timid and less vital than himself, interrupting a dinner with his wife's parson—some psalm-singing milquetoast—to say, 'I've no taste for chicken dumplings tonight after eating cabin boy, dear,' and they would be forced to look at him in both horror and fascination" (33). Falcon's cannibalism becomes the "spice" at his dinner table in the States, a way to make ordinary life more thrilling. By recounting the incident, Falcon also practices what hooks calls "imperialist nostalgia"—the "re-enacting and re-ritualizing in different ways [of] the imperial, colonizing journey as narrative fantasy of power and desire" ("Eating" 25). Both Falcon's act of cannibalism *and* his recounting of the event therefore enable him to indulge his aesthetics of cosmopolitan consumption, a form of cultural cannibalism that turns the Other and its goods into consumables, nourishes the self, and sustains the status quo.

By describing the sensational incident to Rutherford in their first interview, Falcon also polices racial borders. As Rutherford is aware, cannibalism was not unknown on actual voyages, and in fact was common enough historically to be named "the custom of the sea." Moreover, black crewmen were in fact often cannibalized before whites.[26] In his interview with Rutherford, Falcon draws on his cosmopolitan travels to reinforce the racial hierarchy and to put Rutherford, a Negro stowaway, in his place. To reinforce race privilege, Captain Falcon first calls Rutherford's intelligence into question by remarking that in his own travels among "the Lotophaghi," he learned that blacks "don't think too well, or too often" (30). Second, Falcon explains that he seldom includes black crewmen on his voyages because they are not good enough to meet his "standards of excellence":

> But no ... not on my ship, Mr. Calhoun. Eighty percent of the crews on other ships, damn near anywhere in America, are *incompetent*, and all because everyone's ready to lower standards of excellence to make up for slavery, or discrimination, and the problem ... the *problem*, Mr. Calhoun, is, I say, that most of these minorities aren't ready for the titles of quartermaster or first mate ... ready to be mediocre mates, I'll grant you that, or middlebrow functionaries, or run-of-the-mill employees, but not to *advance* the position, or make a lasting breakthrough of any kind. O 'tis a scandal on the ships I've seen, and hardly the fault of the poor, half-trained Negro who hungers like anyone else these days for the glamour of titles and position. (32)

Falcon's anticipation of late-twentieth-century conservative critiques of affirmative action programs is one of the moments in which the novel evokes multiple time frames. Falcon's observations, supposedly based on a wealth of cosmopolitan experience, work to reinforce racial borders by promulgating a universal norm that is a thinly disguised apologetics for the existing order. His pontifications about black crewmen lead him to recall the black cabin boy, ironically named Fortunado, whom he cannibalized. From denigrating the black intellect, to self-serving appeals to excellence, to actual cannibalism, Falcon practices a form of cultural cannibalism designed to police the borders of ethnic difference. As hooks writes, "It is by eating the other that one asserts power and privilege" ("Eating" 36).

Falcon's act of cannibalism also serves as a textual trope for the slave trade, a system of cosmopolitan consumption enacted on a global scale, as is emphasized by the African slave fort and port town of Bangalang. An international meeting place populated by Africans, Arab traders, and sailors from around the globe, Bangalang, we are told, was originally established as a slave fort in 1685 by the English Royal African Company, which fought with the Dutch and the French for control of the African population. The cosmopolitan history of Bangalang is embodied in its leader, the mixed-race Owen Bogha, son of a "brutal slave trader from Liverpool" and a "black princess" (44). As Falcon oversees the *Republic*, so Bogha "oversee[s] from his great hilltop home the many warehouses, bazaars, harems, and Moslem caravans" of Bangalang (44). Significantly, when Falcon is in port, he stays with Bogha rather than on board the ship with his men, where together the two "consum[e] stuffed fish and raisin wine" while discussing the news of "civilization" back in England and America (45). Sophisticates Bogha and Falcon both enjoy similar international pleasures—such as exotic cuisine and playing at the same "gaming tables in Paris" (44). Through Bangalang, a cosmopolitan center and slave port, *Middle Passage* provides an exemplum of what a city becomes when it is founded, developed, and organized by the principles that Captain Falcon espouses. It is here that Falcon begins his attempt to transform the Allmuseri people into consumables by listing them in his logbook immediately after "40 tons of rice" and just before "6 bullocks, sheep, goats, vegetables, and butter" (64–65).

Before his life-altering experiences aboard the *Republic*, Rutherford Calhoun is also motivated primarily by the pleasures promised by an aesthetic of cosmopolitan consumption. Immediately upon being emancipated, he sets out from Makanda, Illinois, for the "world port" of New Orleans, a city that functions as an American counterpart to African Bangalang. New Orleans, remarks Rutherford, "was a city tailored to my taste for the excessive, exotic fringes of life" (1). The cosmopolitan history of New Orleans is also inscribed in the bodies of its citizens, from the high-toned Creoles who control the more elite downstream sections of the city to the mixed-race women offered for sale at the Cabildos, "the fancy-dress quadroon balls and

slave auctions" held at the city's Exchange Market (7). In fact, the entire port
city of New Orleans can be understood as an exchange market where cultural goods are transformed into consumables: "To the newcomer she was an
assault of smells: molasses commingled with mangoes in the sensually damp
air . . . , the odor of Brazilian coffee and Mexican oils. And also this: the
most exquisitely beautiful women in the world, thoroughbreds of pleasure
created two centuries before by the French for their enjoyment. Mulattos
colored like magnolia petals, quadroons with breasts big as melons—women
who smelled like roses all year around" (2). From molasses to mangoes,
Brazilian coffee to Mexican oils, New Orleans is brimming with consumables, including for Rutherford the exotic women whose breasts he compares
to "melons" (2). Like the French who created mixed-race women "for their
enjoyment," Rutherford admits that he has "hungered—literally *hungered*—
for life in all its shades and hues" (3). Not surprisingly, he initially finds himself at "home" amid the multiethnic abundance of the city, where he supports himself as a "petty thief" (3). By spending his recently realized freedom
as a thief in this cosmopolitan port town, Rutherford practices a form of
piracy himself. Moreover, by "pilfering food" from others, he engages in a
version of cannibalism, or in a "life of living off of others" (3, 2).

The life that Rutherford makes for himself in New Orleans, moreover,
clearly takes the form of a cosmopolitan detachment that rejects ties to the
local and the familial. He comes to New Orleans in part because he prefers
the lush attractions of the city to an impoverished life with his brother
Jackson and the other recently emancipated slaves in Makanda. Rutherford
believes that Jackson has betrayed him by cheating him of an inheritance. As
Master Chandler's favorite and likely heir, Jackson had the opportunity to
ask that the plantation be split between the two brothers on Chandler's
death. Instead he requested that it be divided among all the "servants and
hired hands" who worked the plantation, denying Rutherford the inheritance for which he had hoped. Significantly, Rutherford imagines the fruits
of his would-be inheritance specifically in terms of cosmopolitan consumption: "That very next morning [he] figured on starting off the day with a
breakfast of egg bread; of sleeping until noon, hunting until dark, wearing a
pair of skilts and a stylish cap, then dining on potted salmon from England
and preserved meats from France" (116). A similar desire to consume "new
experiences" leads Rutherford eventually to run from marriage in New
Orleans, where Isadora Bailey, a schoolteacher from the eastern seaboard,
falls in love with Rutherford, pays off his growing debts, and attempts to
blackmail him into marrying her with the help of Papa Zerinque, a "Creole
gangster" who controls the black underworld of the city (10). Rejecting both
the life in Makanda represented by his brother and the shackles of "mortgage
and marriage" offered by Isadora, Rutherford goes to sea (10). Moreover,

he lands on the *Republic* in part because of the cosmopolitan attractions of seafaring: trying to escape Isadora, he finds himself in a pub filled with sailors from around the globe, "Chinese assassins, scowling Moors, English scoundrels, Yankee adventurers, and evil-looking Arabs" (18). Among such a group Rutherford feels "right at home" (18). But his travels on board the *Republic*, and especially his contact with the African Allmuseri people who are taken on board in Bangalang to be sold as slaves, will lead him over the course of the narrative to revise both his understanding and his practice of cosmopolitanism.

From the first the Allmuseri are the subject of wild speculation among the sailors on board the ship. These speculations are based on rumors, hearsay, and the report of one Raphael García, an explorer said to be the only European to escape alive from the Allmuseri village, who now resides in "an institution for the incurably insane in Havana" (43). Drawing on such unreliable sources, Cringle tells Rutherford that the Allmuseri are a "whole tribe — men, women, and tykes — of devil-worshipping, spell-casting wizards" (43). He also declares that the Allmuseri are "an old people . . . older . . . than the planet — the galaxy, even" (43). Such fabulously exaggerated reports, which include the assertion that the Allmuseri have a second brain at the "base of their spines" (61), recall the embellished accounts of exotic peoples and places produced by early European adventurers. They also undermine Falcon's previous statements about black people's lack of intelligence by revealing that such judgments are shot through with mystification — as are the captain's reported travels among "the Lotophagi." Fabled lotus eaters from North Africa described in book 9 of the *Odyssey*, the Lotaphagi on whom Falcon bases his opinion of blacks are themselves the creation of the Western imaginary.

As in the case of the Allmuseri people, the sailors also project their fears and desires onto the mysterious creature that is taken aboard in a "crate big enough to carry a bull elephant" (65). Squibb, the ship's cook, speculates that the crate holds a creature that is the "Missing Link between man and monkey"; Cringle guesses that it is a "nearly extinct lizard," whose discovery will rewrite natural history; while Meadows, a sinister crewman, frightens the men by reporting that he has heard that the creature fell from the "sky near the Allmuseri villages . . . and had been protected by them for centuries" (67–68). Identifying Allmuseri culture with natural history or with the supernatural unknown, the sailors project onto the creature their own colonial fantasies of discovery and their fears that the cultural Other represents an enigmatic power that is not completely in their control. (In the latter, they are right.) The creature also represents the fear of cultural contamination. Cringle warns his shipmates, "It belongs to the Allmuseri and has no business in our world" (63). Such a fear differentiates Cringle from Captain

Falcon, who confidently believes in his ability to control the Africans. That confidence extends to believing that he can manage the mysterious creature in the crate, which he reveals to Rutherford to be an Allmuseri god. Falcon intends to turn a god into plunder, a feat that he anticipates will win him a place "in the history books" (102). By consistently conceiving of the Allmuseri in terms of natural history, the supernatural unknown, or simply as plunder, the whites on board the *Republic* expose their inability to conceive of the Africans in terms of a shared humanity. Their predatory cosmopolitanism is thus the opposite of a form of ethical cosmopolitanism that would provide a basis for a cross-racial identity. Indeed the narrative's presentation of predatory cosmopolitanism is designed to point to the lack of, and to emphasize the need for, a different variety of universalism from the one practiced on board Falcon's *Republic*—a cosmopolitanism that would recognize norms or moral obligations that cut *across* the boundaries of continents, cultures, and races.

Although Rutherford perceives a broader range of possibilities in the Allmuseri than the other sailors do, his conjectures about the Africans are also the result of speculation and rumor. Rutherford learns about Allmuseri culture from Ngonyama, but the accuracy of that history is suspect both because Ngonyama has his own designs in his conversations with Rutherford and because the story that he relates is an "official history, the story of themselves they stuck by"—and one that Ngonyama unfolds before Rutherford "like a merchant's cloth" (76). Unlike the other sailors, however, Rutherford identifies the Allmuseri not with natural history but with past human civilizations, or "cities lost when Europe was embryonic" (61). In the Allmuseri Rutherford thus locates a nonproprietary cosmopolitanism that passes judgment on the "civilizing mission" implicit in Falcon's appeal to manifest destiny. A "seafaring people" who do not believe in private property, the Allmuseri through their travels define cosmopolitanism as a dynamic transfer of culture, as when they took their culture to Central America and introduced "their skills in agriculture and metallurgy" to the Olmec (76). Other cultural exchanges are suggested by the fact that the Allmuseri practice a form of martial arts that resembles Brazilian *capoeira* and that they wear white robes that are "similar to Greek chitons" (61). Allmuseri history as related by Ngonyama thus inverts the terms of civilization and barbarity assumed by Falcon, redefines cosmopolitanism as cultural exchange, and restores the tribe to its place in human, rather than natural, history.

Rutherford's understanding of the Allmuseri, however, is itself complicated by his own desire as a black American and former slave to locate in the Allmuseri an alternative personal history to the one he traces through his father in Makanda, a runaway slave whom Rutherford resents for "abandoning" him in slavery. For Rutherford the Allmuseri play a different representative role than they do for the white sailors, though one that is still shaped by processes of projection and mystification. In his case the Allmuseri take on mythic proportions far beyond the characteristics of a single people. As their name suggests, the Allmuseri come to represent for Rutherford "all" of the African (and perhaps the human) past. Even their bodies suggest to him a "synthesis of several tribes, . . . a biological repository of Egyptian and Sub-Saharan eccentricities" (61). Rutherford wonders if they might be the "Ur-tribe" of humanity itself, or "in the Hegelian equation—a clan distilled from the essence of everything that came earlier" (61). Rutherford's speculations expose his desire to reduce the diversity of Africa's peoples and cultures to a unitary inheritance that he can claim as his own. In other words, as singular heritage or as cultural essence, the Allmuseri offer Rutherford the possibility of grounding his identity in a (seemingly) less complex history than his own African American genealogy. "I wanted their ageless culture to be my own," he says (78). The Allmuseri as Rutherford initially perceives them are therefore part official history, part rumor, and part projection. Nevertheless, their presence on board the *Republic* raises the possibility of an alternative to Falcon's hegemonic pretensions to standards of excellence. Less a realistic African nation than a conceptual trope, the invented Allmuseri tribe enables Johnson to investigate the limitations inherent in the perspectives offered by Rutherford, the captain, and the other sailors on board, while introducing the potential for a new form of cosmopolitanism that would be based on shared ideals: the Allmuseri, as Rutherford will later realize, are "less a biological tribe than a clan held together by values" (109). Yet as Rutherford's changing perception of the Allmuseri will demonstrate, this understanding of cosmopolitanism itself is complicated by Johnson's narrative.[27]

As can be seen through the actions of Ngonyama, the presence aboard of the Allmuseri people also unsettles the "slaving formulas" that Falcon uses to oversee the *Republic*. In order to maintain order on his ship, Falcon places one out of every ten Africans in the position of "major-domo," giving them better food and clothing than the other Africans and some shipboard tasks, such as "pick[ing] old ropes apart." Falcon maintains, "The best way to control a rebellious nigger . . . is to give him some responsibility" (74). But as Rutherford points out, "Few slaving formulas worked with Ngonyama" (74). The African's resistance to Falcon's "formulas" is signaled by the text's ironic allusion to the "rope pickers" in "Benito Cereno." In Melville's novella the naïve Captain Delano believes the rope pickers to be contented workers, but he later discovers them to be elders who are helping to control an unfolding revolt on board ship. Ngonyama's motives are similarly opaque to Rutherford, who calls him "easily the most mysterious" of all those he encounters (75). Early on, Ngonyama's intelligence is clear, reflected by his ability to learn English quickly and to master various jobs on the ship. He also has other, more mysterious abilities which he reveals to Rutherford and to Squibb when he assists them in the kitchen. There Ngonyama displays an unusual skill at carving that enables him to "sli[p] metal through meat as if it wasn't there . . . until the pig fell apart magically in his hands. He left no knife tracks. Not a trace" (76). Although Rutherford claims that Ngonyama carves the meat "without doing harm," his skill with the blade clearly carries other implications, especially given the text's earlier allusion to "Benito Cereno." In spite of the fact that the two men teach each other their language, Ngonyama remains a mystery to Rutherford. His speech, in particular, seems "coded" in what Rutherford calls "Universal Native"—"the high-flown, inscrutable way whites made the Cherokees talk in dime novels, or the Chinese in bad stage plays" (83). Ngonyama's cosmopolitan performance of "Universal Native," which clearly includes an element of self-referentiality, serves both to denaturalize white representation and to demonstrate his capacity to adopt Falcon's formulas to his own ends.

In *Faith and the Good Thing* the African American folktale tradition becomes powerful evidence of the failure of even so repressive a regulatory system as chattel slavery to control the cultural Other completely. In *Middle Passage* a similar power is figured by a destructive storm that strikes the *Republic* and by the strange role that Ngonyama seems to play in its occurrence. As the storm begins to build, Rutherford describes the ocean as "a monster of energy" that spawns "form . . . upon form" (79). As Jonathan Little has observed, the ocean functions in terms of Buddhist metaphysics to represent a cosmic, creative force (*Charles* 142). But this "monster of energy" also contains explicitly cosmopolitan cultural forces. With waves that rise "in ranges like the Andes or the Rockies," the ocean reflects the disparate continents that its waters unify (80). It is in fact composed of "a hundred kinds of waters, if one could but see them all" (79). These different waters that compose the ocean in fact represent specific cultural energies, as is suggested by Rutherford's description of "waves the color of root medicine" (45). Furthermore, there is much to suggest that the storm which strikes the *Republic* may itself be a bit of root medicine conjured, or at least anticipated, by Ngonyama.[28] As the storm approaches, Rutherford notes that while others on board begin to panic, Ngonyama appears to be "waiting" (75). And once the storm unleashes its fury on the ship, he is the only one on board who remains dry, for "not a drop" of water touches him (82). As Rutherford marvels, it is almost as though Ngonyama had "known the storm was coming" (83).

Significantly, one effect of the storm is to loosen Falcon's hold on his plunder, as tools, animals, foodstuffs, and "half of the Allmuseri women and children" are thrown overboard. While Rutherford and critics of *Middle Passage* commonly read this event as an unmitigated tragedy, certain narrative details indicate that another, more hopeful reading of the event is possible:

> What came upon us next was not clear. . . . [T]he ship swung around with her face to the west, plunging into a trench, as if into Hell, below water columns that broke over us to the height of the crosstrees—two solid walls on either side, held still as when Moses parted the Red Sea. The sun stood still. The moon stayed. My heart stopped. It has never worked exactly right since, because when the roily waves spanked back, shaking the ship to her ribs, I saw two boys catapulted overboard to drown instantly in the shoal. Therewhile, half the Allmuseri children and women—Baleka's mother among them— five of Falcon's sheep, his hogs and fowl, were swept from the deck. The larboard quarterboat was torn away to disappear into the swell. (81)

Thrown overboard with the captain's quarterboat—a large boat capable of holding a fair complement of a ship's crew—is a group of Allmuseri women and children, with enough foodstuffs, one notes, to maintain them. When the storm abates, Rutherford comments, "Miraculously . . . we were through it as though it all had been a conjurer's trick" (81). Later still, Cringle exclaims that the storm came up as though "sky and sea were torn for a spell" (157). In Rutherford's first interview with the captain, Falcon's voice is described as sounding like that of "a genie in a jug" (27). One could say that Falcon performs various feats of social sorcery on board the *Republic*: he attempts to "materialize" objects out of thin air by reducing all value to plunder. The possibility that Ngonyama performs (or at least has prior knowledge of) a counter-spell worked in order to save a remnant group of Allmuseri is lent additional credence by the observation that the storm divides the ocean as "Moses parted the Red Sea"—the miracle that helped the enslaved Israelites escape from the Egyptians.

Whether it was the result of root medicine or not, the effect of the mysterious storm is to undermine Falcon's command on board ship, and especially to call into question the legitimacy of his profession to be upholding the universal norm of "excellence." During the storm Falcon's position as captain is forcefully undercut. He is "stewed to the gills" when it breaks out and to his embarrassment must call upon Cringle to take his place at the helm (80). "The men saw this," observes Rutherford (80). With his drunken movements resembling those of a "mime mocking normality," Falcon's ineptitude exposes his earlier appeals to "excellence" as a mere caricature of *norms*, or as predatory self-interest masquerading as universalism (80). The storm temporarily upsets the hierarchical order Falcon has established among the sailors in other ways as well, imposing among those on board a momentary accord. As Rutherford describes it: "Without speaking, we all clapped our

hands together as one company—thirty-two sopping-wet cutthroats black-
toothed rakes traitors drunkards rapscallions thieves poltroons forgers clot-
polls sots lobcocks sodomists prison escapees and debauchees simultaneously
praying like choirboys, our heads tipped, begging forgiveness after this brush
with death in Irish, Cockney, Spanish, and Hindi for a litany of collective
sins so long I could not number them" (82). Bringing the diverse sailors together in a moment of cosmopolitan concord as "one company," the storm
temporarily unites their diverse languages in a single prayer that speaks not
to cultural purity, race privilege, or class hierarchy but to their shared condition and frailties. "In mist-softened light," says Rutherford, "mutineers,
Africans, and able seamen could not be distinguished. Brief as this moment
might be, no stations were evident among the ship's company. . . . Just for a
spell the sea had swept some of that away" (106). The altered scene enables
Rutherford to consider values that are normally unrealized aboard Falcon's
*Republic*, as the ship is momentarily shaken, eliminating rank and revealing
a "concord" inclusive of both the particulars of cultural specificity (the men's
different languages) and the universals of their shared frailty and condition.
An unanticipated development that dislodges Falcon's plunder, destabilizes
the hierarchy on board, and points to cosmopolitan norms that differ from
Falcon's, the storm is a trope for cultural forces whose far-reaching effects
cannot be controlled.

## Negotiating Local and Cosmopolitan Identities

In *African American Servitude and Historical Imaginings* (2004), Margaret
Jordan suggests that Johnson's developing appeal to universal "*human*
values" in *Middle Passage* holds black and white characters to different standards of judgment (157). While black characters like Rutherford are seen as
responsible for their actions even under abject conditions of racism and
slavery, Jordan suggests, the racist behavior of white characters like Falcon
is "minimalized or explained away" (172). Jordan judges Falcon's presentation in the novel to be the "most extreme example in *Middle Passage* of a
complex yet ultimately benign white character in the slaving business" (168).
In particular, she suggests, Rutherford "clearly admires Falcon's exploits,
and in their first interview "rhapsodizes and even gushes" over Falcon's
achievements in a manner that is "without irony and completely genuine"
(168). Furthermore, Falcon develops "an intimacy with Rutherford that appears to disregard race," as is suggested, for example, by the fact that he
shares food with Rutherford "with the same fork" (168). But Rutherford's
descriptions of Falcon in their first interview are decidedly ironic, and even
satiric. Indeed, immediately before entering Falcon's room, Rutherford notes
that Falcon belongs to that "special breed of empire builder, explorer, and

imperialist that sculptors loved to elongate, El Greco–like, in city park statues until they achieved Brobdingnagian proportions" (29). Similar impulses
of exaggeration, projection, and mystification are at play, the narrative here
pointedly suggests, in the celebration of national heroes as in the degradation of its abject others. As Rutherford observes, even Falcon's "miscarried
exploits" have "made him raw material for myths spun in brandy and
Cavendish smoke in clubs along the eastern seaboard" (30). Rutherford's
comments make clear that even before he meets the captain in person, he is
aware that Falcon's exploits have been suspiciously exaggerated by those
with no real knowledge of the larger world. Furthermore, Rutherford's
allusion to Swift serves as an explicit textual invitation to read his comments
satirically. Falcon later shares his meal with Rutherford not out of any sense
of intimacy but because he believes that the black kitchen assistant's life is
expendable: afraid of being poisoned, Falcon has Rutherford taste his food
before eating it himself. Although Johnson does attempt to recuperate
"human" or cosmopolitan values in *Middle Passage*, that recovery does not
entail an endorsement of Falcon's particular brand of cosmopolitan consumption. Instead, the narrative is explicitly designed to juxtapose different
varieties of cosmopolitanism in order that the different principles on which
they operate may be weighed and judged.

Over the course of the narrative, the aesthetics of cosmopolitan consumption prove to be increasingly unsatisfying, even to Falcon himself, as is signaled by Falcon's diminished gustatory pleasures:

> He finished carefully arranging a plate of fresh prawns, earthapples,
> and kale he'd bought special for Captain Falcon in Bangalang. No
> French chef could have better composed the meal to seduce a hungry
> man's eye and mind. To my way of thinking, that's pretty much what
> you paid for in fancy-dress New Orleans restaurants anyway: a skimpy
> meal that left you famished hours later but laid out oh so beautifully, as
> Tintoretto might prepare a still life in eye-catching colors and forms.
> Added to that, Falcon insisted on the best silver and a freshly lighted
> candle with his supper. The funny thing was that while he demanded,
> like the rich, meals served in ever more inventive aesthetic configura-
> tions that took the poor steward hours to prepare, the skipper, after a
> second of appreciation, approached the act of eating like a task, falling
> to it with silent, single-minded determination, seldom looking up from
> the table, glopping it down with efficient, steady forklifts that favored
> a farmer baling hay. (93)

In spite of their "ever more inventive aesthetic configurations," Captain
Falcon's meals become increasingly unfulfilling. Although allusions to French
chefs, Italian painters, African foodstuffs, and American restaurants explicitly

tie the captain's repast to cosmopolitan sophistication, the satisfaction that he receives from his elaborate meals is ultimately reduced to the questionable, and decidedly rural, pleasure of "baling hay." What was formerly a source of enjoyment for the captain thus takes on the quality of work. Served on the best silver, Falcon's dinners are identified with the sumptuous commodities with which he fills his cabin. But because Falcon rates all goods, even food, in terms of their exchange value rather than their qualities, his meals are the sort that "leave you famished." Rutherford's comments on Falcon's dinner, which explicitly associate the captain's meals with those he himself sometimes enjoyed in New Orleans, demonstrate his growing awareness of the limitations of cosmopolitanism understood as a sophisticated taste for exotic consumables.

In *Middle Passage* Johnson presents Falcon as a reductio ad absurdum for the position of predatory cosmopolitan consumption. As a satirist with a philosophical background, Johnson often deploys a narratological version of this philosophical argument in his works. The reductio ad absurdum is form of argument that is used to undermine a proposition by extending it to its logical extreme or by demonstrating that absurd consequences follow from its acceptance. *Middle Passage* repeatedly uses the technique to undermine the "limits and premises" on which Falcon posits his *Republic* (143). His standing is reduced, most obviously, by the fact that the captain—the "man known for his daring exploits and subjugation of the colored races from African to the West Indies"—is described in the novel as a "*dwarf*" (29).[29] The captain is small in other ways as well: he "keeps a list of personal affronts, insults and abuses he's received . . . and *dates* them" (63); in all but rank, Captain Falcon is an extremely petty officer.

More important, as the novel elaborates on his claims to fame as an explorer, inventor, and patriot, Falcon is repeatedly cut down to size. As an explorer, Falcon fails notably in his attempt to discover the source of the Nile (30). As an inventor, he contributes to civilization the ridiculous contraption of "sock suspenders," which "ran from your shirttail to your socks so you never had to pull them up and always had a shirt that looked crisp, smartly starched, and capable of passing military inspection, including after a battle" (145). The captain's claim to uphold the standard of "excellence" is revealed during the storm to be no more substantial than a mime's exaggerated motions. Most tellingly, the captain is not a patriot. As he confides to Rutherford, "Fact is, down deep, no man's democratic" (97). From the first Falcon's intentions are imperial; he intends to redeem the Allmuseri deity for a "*king's* ransom" and to purchase land so that he can establish "the personal *empire* he had dreamed of since the Revolution" (103, emphasis added). In short, *Middle Passage* repeatedly tests the "premises" by which Falcon oversees the *Republic* and judges them predatory, self-destructive, and absurd. Although he is a "polyhistor," the narrative exposes Falcon to be nothing but a "pseudo-genius" whose mind is incapable of conceiving of value in any terms other than as plunder (94, 143).

Recent cosmopolitan thinkers have attempted to move beyond an "empty" cosmopolitanism that turns from the particulars of nation, caste, and kin in its advocacy for universal norms to one that is "full" or that takes into account the particulars of cultural location. In *Middle Passage* Johnson participates in the effort to delineate a universalism that avoids the twin traps of abstract universalism or cultural relativism. At the beginning of *Middle Passage* Rutherford epitomizes the "empty" form of cosmopolitanism, in which cosmopolitan identity is based precisely on a detachment from local affiliations, as is reflected in his pursuit of an aesthetics of cosmopolitan consumption in New Orleans. At first a life at sea seems to Rutherford the perfect choice for facilitating an escape from the local, especially since the sea, as a force of teeming variety, has the ability to disrupt, as Rutherford suggests, "the "fragile, artificial pattern of life on land" (33). Once at sea, however, Rutherford learns that such power is potentially both constructive and destructive. The sea has the power to destabilize organizing structures, as the storm unsettles Falcon's *Republic*. Afterwards Rutherford anticipates a change not simply "in the roles on ship but a revolution in its very premises" (126). By destabilizing the ship's hierarchy, the storm exposes Falcon's appeals to universalism as an extension of a particular regionalism, an imperial nationalism that is itself contingent, provisional, and makeshift. Yet the destabilization of structures that organize variety can carry its own dangers, including that of sinking into pure relativism. Such a danger is hinted at when Rutherford first boards the ship and finds that his "center of gravity" has left him (24). Later still he becomes "deprived of such basic directions as left and right, up and down" (45). If Falcon's ship embodies the dangers of an unbridled Western imperialism, the ocean, with its hundred different kinds waters, represents at times the dangers of a multiplicity unstructured by *any* norms, a roiling "chaosmos" (183). On board the *Republic*, Rutherford's cosmopolitan detachment reflects such a risk in the form of an almost complete moral relativism. "In waters strange as these," Rutherford asserts, "any allegiance looked misplaced, [and] I could no longer find my loyalties. All bonds, landside or on ships, between masters and mates, women and men, it struck me, were a lie forged briefly in the name of convenience and just as quickly broken when they no longer served one's interests" (92). In the novel the ability to navigate successfully serves as a trope for the successful negotiation of particular and universal. Rutherford's lack of direction thus demonstrates his failure, as Johnson says, to "see ourselves as belonging to both a human and an ethnic community, and keep these balanced" ("Thinking" 37).

Rutherford's lack of direction contrasts in important ways with the moral reasoning of the group of mutineers who plot to save the ship by taking it over from Falcon. Ironically, the men's unsophisticated exchange aptly illustrates an interplay between universal norm, local attachment, and nation. As they debate the wisdom of mutiny, the men clearly differentiate their own stance from Rutherford's position of moral relativism. To them Rutherford is simply a "stowaway" with "no stake" in what happens on board (86). The crew members, however, have no difficulty identifying general norms behind their own mutinous actions. As Cringle says: "We're here to decide the best way to put this ship back on a steady course. A crew has to trust its captain" (86). He elaborates further: "Mutiny. . . doesn't bother me. . . . God knows, to *be* a Yank is to be mutinous. The goddamn country was born out of rebellion" (89). Cringle's comments tie the men's action to the need for directions that will provide a "steady course" to a general norm for how a crew *should* relate to its captain, and to certain democratic principles in the republic at large. By doing so, the men's rough debate indicates that the nation's normative potential is not exhausted by Falcon's imperial designs. Moreover, although the crewmen are at sea, they clearly weigh their actions in relation to landside commitments. As one crewman, McGaffin, points out, Rutherford may be simply "along fer the ride," but the rest of the plotters "got to think about our future and families" (86). In an attempt to ascertain whether he is trustworthy, the mutineers quiz Rutherford about his own landside commitments: "You got a family? . . . You got a gel?" (86). In answering, Rutherford denies or remains silent about his relationships with both Isadora and Jackson. Through their colloquial exchange the crew members therefore effectively clarify their own moral reasoning as they also accurately identify Rutherford's condition of moral relativism: "He's driftwood, this one" (87). Driftwood is a perfect metaphor for cosmopolitanism understood in terms of a mobile detachment from local roots. As McGaffin predicts, "Calhoun'll go his own way, like he's always done, believin' in nothin', belongin' to nobody, driftin' here and there and dyin', probably, in a ditch without so much as leavin' a mark on the world—or as much of a mark as you get from writin' on water" (88). Because he has abandoned both local ties and the directions that would be provided by overarching norms, Rutherford is morally adrift.

Far more important to Rutherford's development, however, is his recognition of the depth of Allmuseri suffering, a realization that is powerfully impressed upon him when he is enlisted against his will in helping to throw overboard the rotting corpse of a youth brought up from the ship's hold. The boy's corpse, significantly, is itself described through the trope of consumables:

The underside of his body had the squishy, fluid-squirting feel of soft, overripe fruit. If you squeezed his calves, a cheeselike crasis oozed through the cracks and cuts made in his legs by the chains. . . . I cannot say how sickened I felt. The sight and smell of him was a wild thing turned loose in my mind. . . . Judging by what little was left of his face, hard as wood on one side and melting into worm-eaten pulp on the other as rigor mortis began to reverse, he was close to my own age, perhaps had been torn from a lass as lovely as, lately, I now saw Isadora to be, and from a brother as troublesome as my own. His open eyes were un-alive, mere kernels of muscle. . . . I gripped the boy from below, slipping my right hand behind his back, my other under his thigh, so cool and soft, like the purple casing of a plum, that my ragged, unmanicured nails punctured the meat with a hiss as if I'd freed a pocket of air. (122–23)

With an underside like "soft, overripe fruit," thighs like "the purple casing of a plum," eyes like "kernels," and skin with an "orange underlayer," the boy's body provides a visceral lesson in the results of Falcon's practice of cosmo-politan consumption. As the captain reduces goods to plunder, his slaver turns boys into "pulp" or "meat" to be consumed by worms or devoured by sharks "circling the hull" (22, 123). Realizing that the Allmuseri boy had likely been "torn away" from "a lass as lovely as Isadora . . . and a brother as troublesome as [his] own," Rutherford reads in the Allmuseri's forced sep-aration from nation, family, and loved ones a reproach for his own voluntary separation from Isadora and Jackson, a detachment that he now understands as a devastating loss. As he handles the body, it begins to fall apart in his hands, "disconnected like a doll's" (123)—a palpable illustration of slav-ery's severing of individuals from the relationships that make a human being whole. Afterwards, using a knife to scrape the boy's flesh from his palm, Rutherford momentarily considers slicing his own wrist and throwing his hand into the ocean after the boy's body, a consideration that confirms Rutherford's feeling of identity with the boy "about his own age," exposes his guilt for venturing on board a ship designed to transform living boys into a "clump from the butcher's block," and comments on his own cosmopolitan detachment (123). As Ngonyama challenges Rutherford: "We were forced onto this ship. Why have *you* wandered so far from your home?" (163). Alone in his berth afterwards, Rutherford demonstrates a new recognition of the importance of local affiliation, of the need "to belong somewhere and to someone" (126).

Rutherford's experience handling the corpse of the Allmuseri boy also leads him to adjust his earlier, overly romantic views of the Allmuseri. "Stupidly," he realizes, "I had seen their lives and culture as timeless product, as a finished thing, pure essence or Parmenidean meaning I envied and wanted to embrace, when the truth was that they were process and Heraclitean change, like any men, not fixed but evolving and as vulnerable to metamorphosis as the body of the boy we'd thrown overboard" (124). Rutherford's initial conception of the Allmuseri was shaped by rumor, the "official history" he receives from Ngonyama, and by his own desire to locate in the African's history both a civilized alternative for Falcon's cosmopolitan consumption and a less complicated personal genealogy than the one comprising his own past in Makanda. In his idealizations of Africa Rutherford resembles his father, who would recount to other slaves stories about their glorious past, tales that include the assurance, "We was kings once" (170). What his father fails to include, Rutherford notes, is the fact that "his own family was not royalty but instead the equivalent of Russian serfs or Chinese coolies" (170).

In remembering this story, however, Rutherford reveals that he himself fails to recognize the revolutionary potential that resides not in royalty or kings but precisely in the disadvantaged, such as Russian serfs, Chinese coolies—or slaves. Somewhat like his father, Rutherford exhibits a tendency to conceptualize the Allmuseri in the form of an idealized past, although his projection takes the form of a purified cosmopolitanism that is responsible for seeding civilization across the entire globe. Significantly, at the same time, Rutherford presents the Allmuseri as having romanticized characteristics that make them superior slaves: "Compared to other African tribes, the Allmuseri were the most popular servants. They brought twice the price of a Bantu or Kru. . . . Eating no meat, they were easy to feed. Disliking property, they were simple to clothe. Able to heal themselves, they required no medication. They seldom fought. They could not steal. They fell *sick*, it was said, if they wronged anyone. As I live they so shamed me I wanted their ageless culture to be my own, if in fact Ngonyama spoke truly" (78). Rutherford's handling of the boy's corpse demonstrates powerfully that the "ageless culture" he attributes to the Allmuseri is largely his own projection. No culture is ageless or ahistorical, and to so conceive of the Allmuseri is to translate them into an abstraction. More important, Rutherford fails to recognize that the attribution of idealized characteristics, such as the ability to heal oneself, to the Allmuseri can itself serve as a rationalization for their enslavement. Rutherford's mystifications, then, like the crew's association of the Africans with natural history, deny the Africans their full humanity. The Allmuseri suffer as much from scarcity, deprivation, and abuse as all other people—and on board the captain's *Republic*, as in the American Republic at large, they suffer more. In fact, the Allmuseri are easily captured by the slave traders in the first place because their culture has already been weakened by drought. Supposedly able to "heal themselves," the Allmuseri in reality prove susceptible to the diseases that run rampant on Falcon's ship. They suffer from scarcity and hunger, as the efforts of the child Baleka's mother to obtain food for her daughter make clear. Even the assertion that the Allmuseri "could not steal" is undercut by the fact that their society has a punishment for stealing (the chopping off of a hand), and that a one-handed Allmuseri has already suffered this penalty *before* he is exposed to the crew. Rutherford is initially attracted to the Allmuseri partly because he imagines them as the expression of a pure, idealized cosmopolitanism. After handling the Allmuseri boy's corpse, however, he revises the grounds for his cosmopolitan identification, recognizing through the fate of the boy the depth of the Allmuseri's suffering.

Early in the voyage Rutherford also fails to recognize the Allmuseri's revolutionary potential.[30] Only after his contact with the boy's corpse does he come to see the Allmuseri as something other than he had imagined them, "no longer Africans, but not Americans either," forever altered by their contact with the crew and their experiences on board the *Republic* (125). At this point Rutherford wonders of "what were they now capable?" (125). Rather like Captain Delano in "Benito Cereno," Rutherford earlier tends to overlook or minimize the potential for resistance and violence that others might detect in the Africans. Yet from the first the Allmuseri resist being taken captive; one African man attacks Cringle with a "belaying pin" (65). Later an Allmuseri "accidentally" kicks a sailor in the stomach as he walks by (122). In addition, the Allmuseri's own official history contains evidence of a violent past, since the Africans' "prowess as warriors" was immortalized in the songs of the Olmec (77, 76). Even the form of martial arts that the Allmuseri practice is suggestive of their capacity for resistance: they practiced *capoeira* when they were previously enslaved because it enabled them to fight even when they were chained. Finally, when Rutherford observes Ngonyama's mysterious skill in carving, an expertise that causes the pig to "magically fall apart," he suggests that the Allmuseri carves "without hacking or rending— doing no harm" (76).[31] Nevertheless, one notes, the pig is dead. Rutherford fails to see the destructive potential latent in such a skill until after the slave revolt, when crewman Daniels is "skivered from navel to nose quick as a butcherin'" by an unnamed Allmuseri (127). Rutherford's identification of the Allmuseri with an idealized or historically "empty" form of cosmopolitanism thus initially keeps him from understanding that there is, as Bruce Robbins suggests, "no room for purism here"—or no pure cosmopolitanism that remains untouched by time, location, and condition (*Feeling* 75).

The Allmuseri revolt completes the collapse of Captain Falcon's reign that was initiated by the mysterious storm. From the first Falcon believes that he can indulge in cosmopolitan consumption with impunity, feeding himself on the cultural Other without being changed himself. But as Falcon recognizes at last, he "underestimated the blacks," who were "smarter than [he] thought" (146). The "limits and premises" by which Falcon governs the ship ultimately prove self-destructive, as is suggested when Rutherford finds Falcon in his cabin after the revolt, his legs pinned under his own plunder and "contraptions" (143). His command overturned, Falcon commits suicide, an event precipitated in part by an apocalyptic vision of the future:

> "It came to me as I lay here, a nightmare that this was the last hour of history. Nothing else explains it. The breakdown. I mean, how *thorough* it is, from top to bottom, like everything from ancient times to now, the civilized values and visions of high culture, have all gone to hell in fine old hamlets filled high with garbage, overrun with Mudmen and Jews, riddled with viral infections and venereal complaints that boggle the mind and cripple whole generations of white children who'll be strangers, if not slaves, in their own country. I saw families killing each other. People were living in alleyways. Sexes and races were blurred. I saw riots in cities and on clippers.... Crazy as it seems, I saw a ship with a whole crew of women. Yellow men were buying up half of America. Hegel was spewing from the mouths of Hottentots. Gawd!" His whole body shuddered from stem to stern. "I was dreaming, wasn't I?" (144–45)

Constituting another moment in the text when the multiple time frames of the novel suggest that a new cosmopolitan order will emerge, Falcon's vision describes not the end of history but the emergence of a contemporary republic in which some of the democratic potential of the nation has been realized, although that new order is by no means itself perfect or untouched by time and condition. Falcon's vision comments explicitly on his own predatory nationalism, as the foreign nations that he once plundered for exotic artifacts and consumables are themselves envisioned as "buying up half of America." Similarly, the "natives" among whom Falcon traveled are recognized as cosmopolitan themselves and discussing Hegel. Falcon's earlier attempt to make relics of other cultures assumes that under his command those cultures will become obsolete. But as his vision makes clear, it is his own command that will be superseded. With the emergence of a new cosmopolitan order, Falcon's entire world will become unmoored. Not surprisingly, when Rutherford enters the captain's cabin, the objects he notices seem to be undergoing a process of transformation. Coming upon a "whale lamp," Rutherford observes that it "might as well have been a Phoenician artifact for all the sense that it made to me" (142). Later, in the narrative's final representation of the ship, Falcon's *Republic* has clearly become obsolete, itself transformed into relic or artifact, "a carcass suspended like an antique bark hung from a museum's ceiling" (184).

## A New Cosmopolitan Ethic

After the slave revolt, the unstable synthesis that was Captain Falcon's *Republic* comes apart. The new cosmopolitan order that begins to emerge is—at its best—one that transforms the aesthetics of cosmopolitan consumption into an ethics of cosmopolitan competence. The unlikely exemplar of the emerging order is, surprisingly, Squibb, the ship's cook. An alcoholic since "the age of eleven" and a mate who was always "slow, useless except in the kitchen," Squibb is at the outset of the novel both a physical and a moral wreck (37, 38). He rationalizes his condition to Rutherford by explaining: "I've *seen* some things, laddie. Reason I look so bad is 'cause I've been livin" (38). But Squibb's appeal to "livin'" is but another form of living off others. As Rutherford observes earlier in the narrative: "Like Captain Falcon, like me . . . he seemed to hunger for 'experience' as the bourgeois Creoles desired possessions. Believing ourselves better than that, too refined to crave gross, physical things, we heaped and hived 'experiences' instead, as Madame Toulouse filled her rooms with imported furniture, as if *life* was a commodity, a *thing* we could cram into ourselves" (38). Squibb's pursuit of exotic experiences, compared explicitly to the accumulation of imported international goods for well-to-do Creoles, betrays his own appetite for cosmopolitan consumption.

Through Squibb's position as the ship's cook, however, the narrative hints at his potential for positive change. As cook, Squibb is responsible in shipboard society for feeding the others on board. Rather than simply living off others, then, Squibb also has the opportunity, on a daily basis, to nurture others (though he, like Falcon, is sometimes too drunk to perform his duties competently). Feeding the Other, a reversal of eating the Other, is the novel's textual trope for a reconceptualized cosmopolitan ethic, one that responds to *both* universal norm and specific need. Earlier, when the mutineers are planning their revolt, Squibb evokes a cook's code of honor in refusing to poison the captain as they request: "I believe in what you're doin', but don't ask me that. . . . Say what yuh want. I ain't doin' it" (91). Squibb's refusal flows not from any affection that he harbors for Falcon but from a recognition that such an action would violate his duty as cook in shipboard society. After the slave mutiny, however, Squibb breaks his own code when, as conditions on board the ship become desperate, he steals rations from the Allmuseri children, "snatching food from the mouths of infants." Squibb is so shamed by his action—which he judges to be worse than "murder and man-eating"—that he is driven to reform. The overweight one-legged cook becomes, like Rudolph in Johnson's short story "China," physically and spiritually renewed. Afterwards he focuses his attention completely on a single question: "What must he do next?" (175). Squibb thus revises an aesthetic of cosmopolitan consumption into an ethic of cosmopolitan competence, as he draws on the techniques of various cultures in order to complete the work at hand: he climbs to the topmasthead to work in "Bristol fashion," learns "conversational Allmuseri," and works the lancet like Ngonyama (176). Rutherford observes, "I felt perfectly balanced crosscurrents of culture in him, each a pool of possibilities from which he was unconsciously drawing, moment by moment, to solve whatever problem was at hand" (176). Significantly, Squibb is not included among Johnson's description of intellectuals on board the *Republic* at the outset of the novel. But by the end of the narrative he has become a cosmopolitan intellectual by learning to negotiate the ocean's crosscurrents of a "hundred different kinds of waters."

The emergence of a new cosmopolitan order is also suggested by transformations in Cringle and Rutherford. After the revolt, scarcity on the ship reduces those on board to eating "shoes, barnacles, 'n' the buttons off . . . shirts" (173). Diseased and near death, Cringle offers his body as food to the others, a reiteration of the captain's earlier act of cannibalism that is designed to revise its significance. Cringle feeds the others on board, if in a manner far more macabre than Squibb. As in the case of the cook's reformation, however, Cringle's renovation can also be seen in part as a development of a certain potential in his character. Earlier Cringle is invited as an officer to reside and eat at Bogha's, but he refuses, partly because he detests "flesh merchants" and partly because he prefers to spend nights with the crew "on deck" (45). Cringle's refusal to dine in Bangalang with Falcon and Bogha suggests that he is never so attracted as they are to the pleasures of cosmopolitan consumption. In addition, his preference for staying with the men indicates that he is at least partially motivated by a democratic ethos that Rutherford associates with nurturing others: Cringle was, as Rutherford points out, "the sort of quartermaster given to rising at night to pull back the covers on those who'd kicked them off when sleeping" (70). Yet Cringle, like the other seamen on board, initially conceptualizes the Allmuseri in terms of natural history. After the revolt, however, Cringle revises his attitudes toward the Allmuseri. Working with them, he recognizes the Africans as "better shipmates," and he praises in particular the competence demonstrated by the Allmuseri women in their ability to perform their "full share as bluejackets" (173). The identification of Allmuseri as "bluejackets" suggests that the blurring of categories in the captain's vision is already beginning to take place, and Cringle's recognition of the Africans as good shipmates corrects the captain's earlier opinion of the inferiority of blacks as crew members. Significantly, in memorializing Cringle after his death, Rutherford describes the first mate not in the overblown terms of Falcon's self-serving appeal to "excellence" but in the everyday terms of a quiet competence: Cringle "gave hope, steadied the ladder for others, and solved more problems than he created" (174).

Like Cringle and Squibb, Rutherford also begins to practice an ethics of cosmopolitan competence after the revolt. In spite of his own appetite for the exotic, Rutherford's potential for such a transformation is suggested earlier in the narrative by the fact that he also has responsibility for feeding others as the "cook's assistant." In particular, Rutherford is assigned the role of feeding the Allmuseri. Especially important in this regard is his relationship to the eight-year-old Allmuseri girl Baleka. After Rutherford casually tosses a moldy biscuit to the child one day, her mother inspects the offering and hands it back to him, making clear to Rutherford that her daughter deserves better. "To square things," Rutherford begins sharing his dinner with Baleka (79). In doing so he recognizes a norm that cuts across the borders of nations and culture, demonstrates an appreciation for the Africans' immediate need, and begins to develop a genuine bond with them. "Her expectation," says Rutherford, "and that of Mama, for sharing my *every* pan of food became an unspoken contract no less binding between us than a handshake" (79). Functioning as an "unspoken contract," Baleka's expectations call for an ethical response that begins the moral education through which Rutherford's stance of detachment will be transformed into one of cosmopolitan competence.

Significantly, this relationship also helps to heal Rutherford's relationship to his brother in Illinois. As a boy, Rutherford himself was "always hungry," and, as he says, "if you have never been hungry, you cannot know the *either/or* agony created by a single sorghum biscuit—either your brother gets it or you do. And if you *do* eat it, you know in your bones you have stolen the food straight from his mouth, there being so little for either of you. This was the daily, debilitating side of poverty that no one speaks of, the perpetual scarcity that, at every turn, makes the simplest act a moral dilemma" (47). Comparing conditions of scarcity on board the *Republic* to those on the plantation, Rutherford begins through his relationship with Baleka to act more like his older brother, who in Makanda "often skipped meals secretly so I could have a little bit more" (47). Rutherford's cosmopolitan experiences on board the *Republic* thereby help him to revise and deepen his relationship to the local. He thus moves toward a form of cosmopolitan practice that is built not on a rejection of the familial but on an understanding of the connections between *multiple* attachments and affiliations.

Rutherford's account of scarcity on the plantation also provides insight into the motivations that lay behind his own earlier commitment to cosmopolitan consumption. Those conditions of scarcity make nurturing others a practical impossibility. Even something so basic as eating becomes equated with stealing food "straight" from your brother's mouth.[32] Such consumption, although it may be a matter of survival, necessarily leaves one psychologically wounded and morally unsatisfied, and Rutherford not surprisingly

suffers from an almost complete lack of self-esteem. His thievery is therefore
motivated in part by the need to feed his self-respect, which is, like his body,
"always hungry." Rutherford's lack of self-worth is compounded by his relationship to his father, since, as we have seen, he interprets Riley Calhoun's
attempt to escape from slavery as abandonment. (In *Beloved*, Morrison
traces through several generations a similar tendency for female characters
to read their mothers' attempts to escape slavery as maternal abandonment.)
As ex-slave and orphan, Rutherford believes that he has inherited nothing,
is worth nothing, and consequently has nothing to offer others.

As conditions become more desperate aboard the *Republic*, however,
Rutherford is prompted by the suffering of those on board—and especially
that of the Allmuseri children—to reconsider his own inner resources:

> To comfort the weary on the *Republic* I peered deep into memory and
> called forth all that had ever given me solace, scraps and rags of lan-
> guage too, for in myself I found nothing I could rightly call Rutherford
> Calhoun, only pieces and fragments of all the people who had touched
> me, all the places I had seen, all the homes I had broken into. The "I" that
> I was, was a mosaic of many countries, a patchwork of others and ob-
> jects stretching backward to perhaps the beginning of time. . . . What I
> felt, plainly, was a transmission to those on deck of all I had pilfered, as
> though I was but a conduit or window through which my pillage and
> booty of "experience" passed. (162–63)

Unlike Falcon, who hoards plunder in his cabin until it comes crashing down
on him, Rutherford learns to feed others from his accumulated "booty." His
ability to do so clearly comes in part from what Ross Posnock defines as a
"cosmopolitan recognition"—the recognition that one "lives as 'a mixed-up
self in a mixed-up world,' where ancestral imperatives do not exert a preordained authority" (*Color* 3).

Earlier in *Middle Passage* both Cringle, the white quartermaster, and
Rutherford, the black stowaway, demonstrate that they feel bound by
"ancestral imperatives." Cringle believes that he will always be a failure because he will never satisfy the expectations set for him by his astoundingly
successful father, a poor immigrant who rose to wealth in America. Rutherford, meanwhile, believes that he is a failure because he has no paternal expectations to fill. Both men therefore define their competence—or lack of
competence—in terms of ancestral imperatives that they believe to exert a
preordained authority. Cringle ultimately escapes that authority by coming
to think of legacy less in terms of a singular descent, of being "Papa's heir,"
and more in terms of cosmopolitan bequest: "having no inheritance to leave
[his] family in America," he leaves his body to the mixed group of Allmuseri

and seamen on the ship (159, 173). Similarly, Rutherford begins to comprehend his own potential less in terms of a birthright (which he believes that he failed to receive from his missing father) or a lost inheritance (which he failed to receive from Master Chandler) than in terms of his own cosmopolitan endowments: recognizing in himself abilities that he has gathered from a "mosaic of many countries," Rutherford draws on that knowledge to console the children. Turning from a concentration on consumption and inheritance to a focus on cosmopolitan bequest, Rutherford stops worrying about feeding his own self-worth and concentrates on feeding or nurturing others. By doing so, he begins to turn from an absorption with questions of personal identity to questions of citizenship—of how he can best contribute to the larger society—a question at the heart of Johnson's next novel, *Dreamer*.

In *Middle Passage* Rutherford is challenged to develop the ability to ascertain "directions" that will enable him to navigate between the twin dangers of cultural relativism and abstract universalism, or to see himself as "belonging to both a human and an ethnic community, and keep these balanced" (Johnson, "Thinking" 37). The difficulty of performing such a negotiation successfully is dramatized after the revolt in the contrasting responses of the two Africans Diamelo and Ngonyama, who each prove ineffective in establishing a new order on board the *Republic*, but for very different reasons. Coming to power after the revolt, Diamelo attempts to establish a new order of Allmuseri cultural purity.[33] He requires that the seamen speak Allmuseri in their dealings with the Africans, use Allmuseri maps, learn Allmuseri stories, and dine on dishes prepared in the Allmuseri manner (154–55). But Diamelo's identification with Allmuseri cultural traditions is itself problematic. In Africa, Ngonyama points out, Diamelo was the "village wastrel," a "soger who drank palm wine and drifted indifferently from one occupation to another" (153). As his drinking suggests, Diamelo was more focused on indulging in personal consumption than on mastering cultural practices. He was in fact "cool toward his tribe's culture" and "impatient with the painstaking years required to master one of the complex Allmuseri crafts" (154). Diamelo's new interest in Allmuseri culture is thus positioned primarily as a response to Falcon's rule, and he uses the Allmuseri's hatred for Falcon to exert power over others. Diamelo has "but to breathe one two-syllabled iambic word, *Falcon*, to hold their ear and magically control their emotions" (154). Diamelo's magic, which brings to mind the earlier description of Falcon as a "genie in a jug," suggests that by attempting to organize the ship solely on the basis of hatred for Falcon, he may exercise Falcon's magic rather than his own. Furthermore, because he attempts to navigate only by his hatred for Falcon, Diamelo is "spun leeward" when Falcon dies, and becomes "as "directionless . . . as a soldier after a war" (152, 154). He finally goes "the wrong side of the buoy," and because he has demonstrated no interest in learning about seaman's culture, misfires the canon and sets the *Republic* ablaze (182).

Similarly, if more surprisingly, Ngonyama—who once provided a model of cosmopolitan competence for the Americans on board—also proves ineffective after the revolt. An "orthodox Allmuseri," Ngonyama comes to believe that the diseases that multiply on the ship are a "moral plague" sent because the Allmuseri broke their own ethical code (163). "This evil," he suggests, "is visited upon us . . . for the crewmen we killed" (163). Having broken his own moral norms, Ngonyama "slip[s] into relativity" and despair (164, 163). Earlier Ngonyama had always seemed to Rutherford to be "waiting," anticipating something in the future. Focusing now only on the past, on the principle that has been broken rather than on their current situation, Ngonyama can no longer navigate: he cannot "move forward" (163). Although Ngonyama dies heroically, having lashed himself to the wheel in an effort to save the ship, his efforts, thanks in part to Diamelo's actions, prove futile. By itself, Ngonyama's idealism, his concern for universal law, is noble but ineffective. The clear implication is that one must undertake a negotiation between the particular and the universal in order to "navigate" competently.

## Ancestral Imperatives and Cosmopolitan Inheritance

According to Margaret Jordan, the change in Allmuseri culture that occurs on board the *Republic* indicates that Johnson believes that the African cultural heritage was lost to blacks during their enslavement in the Americas. She contrasts this view to that of Henry Louis Gates Jr., who maintains that the "complete annihilation" of African culture during slavery would have been "far more remarkable than its preservation" (quoted in Jordan 177). To support her interpretation, Jordan draws on a statement in "The Second Front," where Johnson writes: "Culture and civilization are both one generation deep. Yes, they can be lost in a mere twenty years. The blink of an eye. They are not givens" (182). In context, however, Johnson's comment focuses less on an inevitable *loss* of culture than on the concentrated *effort* that is required for culture to be preserved, for example, the "painstaking years" of practice" that Diamelo refuses to devote to learning Allmuseri crafts. The problem of cultural transmission is crucial to "The Second Front," an essay in which Johnson considers how he can best teach his children the values his father taught him, and which Johnson's father learned from his own father, "a farmer and blacksmith" (180). The problem of transmitting culture has become especially acute, Johnson writes, with the rise of ubiquitous media that present black people as "welfare cheats, criminals, incompetent parents, ex-cons, [and] poor students" (178). To counter such representations, Johnson repeatedly reminds his children of the lessons passed on to him by his elders: "I repeat it, mantra like, as much for my own benefit as for theirs, and primarily to remind myself that culture and civilization are but one generation deep. Yes, they can be lost in a mere twenty years. The blink of an eye. They are not givens. And if I do not tell the story of their grand- and great-grand elders, my progeny—weaned on the less than responsible media—may forget" (182). In context, then, Johnson's comments imply not that cultural inheritance cannot survive challenge—even so great a challenge as the Middle Passage and slavery—but that culture is never simply a matter of inheritance, or "a given." Culture itself involves *competence*—a mastery that must be taught and learned so that it will not be forgotten.

Johnson does, however, privilege in "The Second Front" his African American heritage over what he believes to be that of an idealized African past. To teach his children values, he need not turn to "mythic references to the glorious triumphs of African civilization shrouded in the dim mists of pre-history," but must look to a more immediate heritage provided by his father, "a far better man," Johnson asserts, "than I'll ever be" (178). Johnson does not mean to denigrate actual African history but instead wants to interrogate what he sees as the too easy practice of some who, like Rutherford, attempt to escape a complicated local African American lineage by identifying with an idealized African past. Other African American writers offer a similar critique. For example, Dee, in Alice Walker's frequently anthologized short story "Everyday Use," changes her name to Wangero Leewanika Kemanjo to honor her African heritage. But the change of name strikes her mother as disrespectful—and as especially disrespectful of the actual African American women in the family after whom Dee has been named. Johnson's analysis of Rutherford's actions in *Middle Passage* and his comments about inheritance in "The Second Front" are similarly designed to critique the act of granting one's allegiance to a more distant African cultural heritage *at the expense* of the legacy offered by a more immediate African American past. Johnson's dedication of his National Book Award acceptance speech to Ellison can be understood as a related act of paying respect. "It seemed to me," says Johnson, "the very least I could do in the presence of an elder who had forged a place in American culture for the possibility of the fiction I dreamed of writing" ("Singular" 111).

Significantly, Johnson also argues in "The Second Front" that a long-standing respect for learning—or for black intellectualism—is an important part of the African American heritage. Johnson's motivation in writing the essay stems in part from his concern that an earlier generation's reverence for education, which led them to make innumerable sacrifices so that their children could become educated, is at risk. Such a legacy is threatened in part, Johnson suggests, by a growing anti-intellectual black youth culture such as the one described by Nathan McCall in *Makes Me Wanna Holler*. In his autobiographical account of growing up in Portsmouth, Virginia, McCall speaks of the peer pressure that encouraged him to abandon his academic aspirations as an honor roll student in order to fulfill certain cultural expectations for black masculinity. After hooking up with a group of "hard dudes," says McCall, "I didn't want to be seen carrying an armload of books, and I felt too self-conscious to join in discussions. I sat in the back of the room . . . laughing, playing, and jonin' the nerds" (35). Against such developments, Johnson recalls the long-standing African American association of freedom and literacy, and he points to the historical examples of black intellectualism provided by figures such as Douglass, who studied Roman orators, and King, a student of "intellectual history from the Presocratics through Personalism" (184). As these references suggest, Johnson understands the African American intellectual heritage itself in terms of a dynamic cosmopolitanism. In "Whole Sight" he asserts, "Black American culture is not all of a piece, but instead a tissue of history, interwoven with all the diverse, global contributions that make the Republic a web of European, African, eastern, and classic influences" (80). To Johnson, then, African American culture has always already been a cosmopolitan culture, one in which African values were not lost but transformed, as African Americans created hybrid cultural forms in new languages, locations, and combinations precisely in order that their values might be passed on.

Similarly, in *Middle Passage* Rutherford's revised understanding of cosmopolitanism should not be read as a rejection of his African American and African past. Although cosmopolitanism is often pitted against the particulars of local culture, Rutherford's emerging practice of cosmopolitanism, performed properly, has the potential to reconnect him with familial, ancestral, and national traditions, as his experience at sea with Baleka enables him to strengthen his relationship to his brother Jackson in Makanda. Rutherford's growing appreciation for the multiple attachments that constitute cosmopolitanism is seen in particular when Baleka tells Rutherford that it is his turn to feed the African god. Earlier the cabin boy Tommy had been lowered into the hold by the crew to satisfy their curiosity about the contents of the mysterious crate—including their curiosity about what the creature might eat. Pulled up ten minutes later, Tommy has forgotten "where he was and why he had come," a transformation described by Rutherford as a "sea change nicer than any of us knew" (69). Seeing the result of the god's "brainrinsing song," one deck hand observes: "Blimey. . . . It eats people, that's what it eats" (69). Johnson thus relates Tommy's encounter with the Allmuseri god to the captain's practice of cultural cannibalism. Because Tommy can suddenly speak "a slabber of Bantu patois, Bushman, Cushitic, and Sudanic tongues" after he is pulled from the hold, the suggestion is that the deity also exercises the power to overturn cultural hegemony (68). As a "genie in a jug," Falcon attempts to materialize objects out of thin air by reducing all value to plunder. As a shape shifter, however, the Allmuseri god represents forces that resist such reification. Furthermore, as Falcon notes, the god attempts to trick people "into Heaven. It's Loki and Brer Rabbit together" (102). Associated with spiritual powers and with trickster figures drawn from different cultures that similarly defy the status quo, the shape-shifting Allmuseri god represents an ongoing process of struggle through which value is both "materialized" and "dematerialized" — or made and remade through an unfolding dialectical interplay of universal and particular. The powers of the deity suggest, like the novel's multiple time frames, that Falcon will not eat the Other with impunity.

Through his own encounter with the Allmuseri god, Rutherford is able to tie his new understanding of his cosmopolitan identity as a "mosaic of many countries" to his personal and ancestral past. Previously Rutherford had understood his African American heritage as a lack — as an empty patrimony that he had attempted to fill with an imagined African past. When he is lowered into the hold to feed the god, the shape-shifting deity appears to him in the form of the "one man with whom [he] had bloody, unfinished business": his father, Riley Calhoun. Throughout the novel Rutherford's lack of self-worth is tied to paternal abandonment. The Allmuseri god presents his father's life as one that is connected to countless other events: "Like a griot asked one item of tribal history, which he could only recite by reeling forth the entire story of his people, [the god] could not bring forth this one man's life without delivering as well the *complete* content of the antecedent universe to which my father, as a single thread, belonged" (169). As the Allmuseri god contains "whole cultures" of beings in its body, the deity invites Rutherford to understand himself as part of a larger, cosmopolitan whole (168). Comparing the deity to a griot, Rutherford connects his father's history to "his people's," to a larger process of cultural transmission, and, significantly, to his own transmission of what he had learned to the Allmuseri children. If earlier Rutherford had recognized in himself "a mosaic of countries," he now hears in the deity "a mosaic of voices within voices, each one immanent in the other" (171). In other words, Rutherford comes to understand his own cosmopolitan identity as an extension of the griot's. "Suddenly," he says, "I knew the god's name: Rutherford. And the *feel* of the ship beneath the wafer-thin soles of my boots was different. . . . [S]he seemed to *sing* like the fabled *Argo*" (171). In their ability to recount or to pass on what they have learned, griots transmit culture through their competence. By extension, Rutherford's confrontation with the Allmuseri god invites readers to understand Rutherford's narration — and Johnson's novel — as also participating in the griot tradition, a tradition that is now, after the African diaspora, performed in new languages, new countries, and new combinations (as Rutherford's allusions to both "Brer Rabbit" and the *Argo* attest). The Allmuseri god thus serves to ground the African cultural diaspora not in an unchanging, "ageless" homeland—or in a *static* cultural heritage—but in the dynamic practice of cosmopolitan competence.[34]

The collapse of Falcon's command, Rutherford's identification with the griot tradition, the cultural change that is intimated by the narrative's multiple time frames, and especially the evolving practice of cosmopolitan competence—all these promise that a new cosmopolitan order will emerge from the wreck of the *Republic*. It is important to note, however, that such an order is not firmly established by the conclusion of the novel either at sea or on land. The *Republic* has not been able to navigate properly since the mysterious storm. "The world tilted because of it," says Cringle, "or someone switched the sky on us" (158). Cringle's claim that there had been a change in the very stars that the ship navigates by emphasizes the potential that new cultural particulars have to reshape existing paradigms and guiding principles. Johnson's understanding of universals as "concrete universals," as we saw in chapter 2, asserts that they are themselves historical and, moreover, that they evolve under pressure from new particulars. Similarly, the movement of Africans to America, Johnson suggests, will realign the nation's guiding principles.

The ship's lack of direction parallels Rutherford's increasing vertigo, which is "like the vortices that suck ships to the bottom of the briny" (178). The implication is that neither society nor ships nor individuals can navigate without "directions" or overarching norms, which Rutherford needs in order to avoid the twin dangers of relativism on the one hand and hegemonic self-interest masquerading as universalism on the other. Confined to his berth and overcome by exhaustion and illness, Rutherford falls out of bed and, somewhat like Falcon, has a prescient vision of nation:

> Nay the States were hardly the sort of place a Negro would pine for, but pine for them I did. Even for *that* I was ready now after months at sea, for the strangeness and mystery of black life, even for the endless round of social obstacles and challenges and trials colored men faced every blessed day of their lives. . . . If this weird, upside-down caricature of a country called America, if this land of refuges and former indentured servants, religious heretics and half-breeds, whoresons and fugitives—this cauldron of mongrels from all points on the compass—was all I could rightly call *home*, then aye; I was of it. . . . Do I sound like a patriot? Brother, I put it to you: What Negro, in his heart (if he's not a hypocrite), is not? (179)

Like the captain's nightmare vision, Rutherford's evocation of nation is complexly cosmopolitan, inhabited by "mongrels" who hail "from all points on the compass." Also as in Falcon's premonition, Rutherford's description evokes a multiple time frame that invites us to read the horrors of the nineteenth-century America past as a trope for the challenges faced by contemporary African Americans. Significantly, however, it is Rutherford, not Falcon, who emerges as the novel's "patriot." Earlier Rutherford had insisted that he had "no family traditions to maintain," and he traded his life in the American Republic for his cosmopolitan adventures on Falcon's *Republic* (160). Believing that he had received no African American inheritance, he longed for the imagined purity of an ageless African culture. Now, however, Rutherford accepts the complexity of an African American heritage that is *both* "battlefield" and "home." Here Rutherford expresses something close to what Kwame Anthony Appiah has named "patriotic cosmopolitanism," a cosmopolitanism that is not defined against nationalism, but one that attempts to uphold cosmopolitan values while simultaneously honoring national forms of belonging.

The complicated heritage of the larger republic is also figured by the *Juno*, the ship that pulls Rutherford, Squibb, and three Allmuseri children from the ocean after their ship finally breaks apart, sending all others on board to their watery grave. The nation's "motley Crew" is reflected in the sea chantey sung by the passengers on board, "Have You Even Been in New Orleans?," which celebrates a range of American characters, including Negroes, priests, robbers, pirates, soldiers, and sailors (189). While it is tempting to read the carnivalesque celebration of national hybridity that is captured in the chantey at face value, it is important to note that the cosmopolitan nationhood represented by both the *Juno* and her port of origin, New Orleans, is problematic and, moreover, tied explicitly to an aesthetics of cosmopolitan consumption. A pleasure boat out of New Orleans, the ship carries among its passengers well-to-do Creoles, one of whom peers at Rutherford through a "lorgnette" (185). The passengers, who have set out on a cruise to the "West Indies," enjoy the privileged pursuit of exotic experiences. The *Juno* itself is a "floating gin palace," with "gold plates in the galley and Royal Wilton carpets that cost five dollars a yard" (186). Associated with democratic energies through Andrew Jackson, the *Juno* is also associated with royalty through its adornments, and by being named after the queen of the gods.[35]

Not surprisingly, then, Rutherford finds that the passengers' celebratory chantey fails to lift his spirits; it "didn't help" (189). His alienation from the other passengers is partly explained by the physical and psychological trauma that Rutherford has sustained. With his hair now turned completely white and all his teeth having fallen out, he is indeed, as he calls himself, "a wreck of the *Republic*" (190). More significantly, however, Rutherford's alienation from the other passengers serves to contrast their aesthetic of cosmopolitan consumption to his revised practice of cosmopolitan competence. Unlike the others, Rutherford is unable to enjoy the "trays of food" that are brought to his cabin each morning, partly because he now finds that he "cannot *eat*" until he knows that Baleka has "eaten first" (195). Similarly, he discovers that he is no longer attracted to the same pleasures as the other passengers, pleasures such as "getting a good-looking woman into bed" or "making a Big Killing" (188). To Rutherford, the *Juno* clearly represents American citizenship in terms of an aesthetic of consumption that leaves no room for ethical choice: when asked to choose between "white bedspreads or blue," he finds that he can "see no difference between the two choices" (187). While a new cosmopolitan order is emerging at the end of the novel, Johnson nevertheless makes clear—as he writes in "An American Milk Bottle"—that "American democracy is still a 'work-in-progress'" (175). Nevertheless, Rutherford exercises his own developing cosmopolitan competence on board ship by using both the *capoeira* that he learned from the Allmuseri and the contents of the captain's logbook to rescue Isadora from marriage to Papa Zeringue. Significantly, however, here—as elsewhere in *Middle Passage*—the conclusion does not simply celebrate cultural hybridity; it asks its readers carefully to evaluate different varieties of cosmopolitanism that comment on, modify, and interrogate one another.

Some critics of Johnson's fiction, and of *Middle Passage* in particular, have raised questions about the relation of universal and particular in Johnson's thought. In "*Beloved* and *Middle Passage*: Race, Narrative, and the Critic's Essentialism," Molly Travis suggests that Johnson equates universality with whiteness or uses a "European literature and culture as the universal standard" (83). In "Black Skin, White Tissues: Local Color and Universal Solvents in the Novels of Charles Johnson," Richard Hardack similarly identifies in Johnson's fiction a rejection of the local. Connecting Johnson's rejection of the naturalist school of writing to a rejection of "local color" in the sense of cultural particularity, he identifies in the thematics of novels such as *Oxherding Tale* and *Middle Passage* a repudiation of particularity (1032). There is, Hardack suggests, an implied "incommensurability between all particulars and the universal" in Johnson's thinking (1032). But while Hardack's criticism may seem plausible when directed at *Oxherding Tale* (a novel in which, after all, the narrator passes for white), *Middle Passage* figures a more complicated representation of the relation of universal to particular through its investigation of different ways in which the universal and local are related in a variety of forms of cosmopolitanism. Falcon's understanding of cosmopolitan consumption is condemned as an expression of universal capital that is revealed to be the tool of a particular localism, American imperialism. The inability of Diamelo and Ngonyama to navigate after the slave revolt demonstrates the necessity of negotiating between the universal and the particular. Rutherford's own projection of a pure cosmopolitanism onto the Allmuseri people is itself criticized for being a mere abstraction or idealization. Finally, Rutherford's initial practice of detachment, one shorn of both local affiliations *and* shared norms, is exposed as an "empty" cosmopolitanism, one that leaves him afloat like "driftwood."

But by the end of novel Rutherford recognizes that there is no pure cosmopolitanism. Instead he discovers that one exercises cosmopolitan competence only from a particular location. Such a recognition is confirmed by his new appreciation for multiple—but specific—attachments, which he demonstrates by stating his intention to return to Makanda, committing himself to raising the orphaned Baleka, revising his relationship to his brother, and proposing to Isadora. Johnson refuses to choose between universal and particular in the novel, partly because he refuses what Posnock calls the "dichotomous logic" which requires that one choose "between identity and difference, the universal and particular, as if such a choice is logically possible, as if the very capacity to think, judge, and communicate did not demand combining both sets of terms" ("Dream" 804). Such a logic, as Johnson argues in "Philosophy and Black Fiction," fails to recognize that "universals are not static . . . but changing, historical, *evolving* and enriched by particularization" (81). By putting into play *multiple* forms of cosmopolitanism that interrogate one another in *Middle Passage*, Johnson's novel joins in contemporary efforts to conceptualize a cosmopolitanism that takes into account both particular and universal. The novel's final cosmopolitan position fuses several of Johnson's intellectual and spiritual interests, including his philosophical interests in the phenomenological concept of intersubjectivity, his spiritual interest in the Buddhist understanding of inter-being, and his creative interest in the artistic practice of intertextuality. In *Middle Passage* Johnson expresses a cosmopolitanism that offers a fresh combination of these interests—and anticipates the more difficult synthesis that he will achieve in *Dreamer*.

As a new black cosmopolitan intellectual, Johnson makes his own contribution to the recent efforts by intellectuals, both black and white, to probe the dangers and the democratic potential of cosmopolitanism. Teeming with allusions to the world's varied artistic and historical traditions and evoking multiple time frames that provide the novel with an expansive spatial and temporal canvas, *Middle Passage* requires its readers to perform their own acts of cosmopolitan competence. This obligation relates, I would suggest, to Rutherford's scattered addresses throughout the narrative to his reader as "Brother." In part the term calls to mind Rutherford's brother Jackson, suggesting perhaps that Rutherford may be addressing his tale to his brother in an effort to heal their relationship by enabling Jackson to understand the

transformation that he has undergone. The focus on brotherhood also resonates with other characters and events, including the mutineer's oath that
binds them as blood brothers and Ngonyama's reference to the Allmuseri as
Rutherford's "brothers" (131). But Rutherford's address is also designed to
evoke a more cosmopolitan sense of universal brotherhood. Chapter 3 mentioned one of Johnson's intellectual influences, the Swami Vivekananda, a
representative of Vendantic Hinduism who traveled in 1893 to Chicago's
Parliament of Religions. Vivekananda evokes such a value when he states,
"Here I am, trying to understand on what grounds we may always remain
brothers" (quoted in Van Der Veer 177). The importance of establishing such
a cosmopolitan brotherhood is also emphasized by Martin Luther King Jr.,
the inspirational center of Johnson's next novel, *Dreamer*. In "Remaining
Awake through a Great Revolution" King urges his listeners to "develop a
world perspective": "Through our scientific and technical genius," he argues,
"we have made of the world a neighborhood and yet we have not had the
ethical commitment to make of it a brotherhood" (207). As the significance
of Rutherford's use of the address "brother" expands over the course of the
novel, Johnson issues a challenge to his readers to consider the principles by
which they might *all* become brothers.

   *Middle Passage* records the wreck of the *Republic* and considers the possibilities for the emergence of a new, more democratic cosmopolitan order.
Although, as Marc Conner points out, the work has "a paradigmatic comic
conclusion" ("To Utter" 71), the novel does not end with the carnivalesque
celebration of national hybridity on board the *Juno* or with the consumma-
tion that Isadora and Rutherford, long separated, might be expected to enjoy.
Instead it concludes as Isadora lowers her head to Rutherford's shoulder "as
a sister might" (209).[36] While Rutherford has been transformed by his experiences, and his relationship with Isadora will now be expanded to include
an appreciation for their figurative brother- and sisterhood, *Middle Passage*
offers no guarantee that a more liberating variety of cosmopolitan citizenship
will be incorporated into national structures. Both the difficulty of such a
transformation and the sacrifice it may require are the subject of *Dreamer*.
Although temporary syntheses are achieved, nation and culture are, like
everything else in a world characterized by a "hundred different kinds of
waters," inherently unstable. All is liable to change, and all is at risk. Only
in fiction can one hope that a cultural remnant will be spared by a spell. In
life, Johnson's novel and prose writings on cosmopolitanism suggest, cultural
inheritance is a matter of competence, not merely of descent, and therefore
must be earned by effort—and maintained through determination—if a
future is to be reclaimed out of the wreckage of the past.

# 5

---

## The Return of the King
## and the Logic of Conversion
## in *Dreamer*

Be ye not conformed to the world, but transformed
by a renewing of your mind.

*Romans 12:2*

Only through an inner spiritual transformation do we
gain strength to fight vigorously the evils of the world.

*Dr. Martin Luther King Jr., "Transformed
Nonconformist"*

By putting into play multiple forms of cosmopolitanism
on board a single ship in *Middle Passage*, Johnson joins in the efforts of late-
twentieth- and early-twenty-first-century thinkers to reconsider cosmopolitanism in ways that reclaim the normative force of universals while honoring
more local allegiances—including national, ethnic, and family bonds. In his
1998 novel *Dreamer*, Johnson complicates his analysis of the relationship
between universal norms and local commitments by entering a different cultural conversation: a newly invigorated debate that unfolded among public
intellectuals beginning in the 1990s over the legacy of Dr. Martin Luther
King Jr. Through his participation in this debate the various facets of
Johnson's intellectual and spiritual development have become crystallized
and powerfully focused. Johnson has identified King as one of the nation's
"greatest moral and political philosophers" ("The King We Need" 42). He
also identifies King's philosophy of nonviolence as an inspiration for the
development of an engaged Buddhist practice. Finally, Johnson identifies
King as a leading cosmopolitan intellectual whose greatness is determined

in part by his willingness to assume the burdens of national *and* international leadership—as a "man obligated to promote his belief in the 'beloved community' and peace on the world stage" ("The King" 49). Embodying in a single figure the black philosopher, religious leader, and cosmopolitan intellectual, King provides an especially fitting subject for Johnson's novel—and for the conclusion to my own book. For it is by entering a larger deliberation about the nature of King's legacy in his prose and in his fiction that Johnson develops a particular resolution to the tension between private conversion and civic action that is evident from the first in his fiction.

In the twenty-four years that span the 1974 depiction of a neo-Marxist paradigm of productive subjectivity in *Faith and the Good Thing* and the 1998 delineation of King's complex negotiation of ideal and practice in *Dreamer*, Johnson's fiction constitutes an evolving attempt to illuminate the relationship between personal transformation and social action. As we saw in chapter 2, Johnson's dramatization of a neo-Marist argument in favor of the subversive power of fiction generates a narrative tension in *Faith* between the crushing economic determinism that permeates the Chicago sections of the novel and an imaginative realm of freedom represented by the Swamp Woman's home in Georgia. A Marcusean revision of Marx leads the way from Johnson's master's thesis in philosophy to his first novel and intensifies his commitment to writing "philosophical fiction." In *Oxherding Tale* Johnson then turns more purposefully from Western deterministic philosophies as he fictionalizes a Mahayana Buddhist soteriology of sudden illumination and an ethics of personal altruism. But Johnson's attempt to assimilate ancient Eastern philosophical thought into the African American literary tradition, as my discussion in chapter 3 indicates, leads to a number of narrative dislocations that result in the displacement of the sphere of national concern—except insofar as that realm can be addressed by the positive ripple effects of individual acts of altruism over time. Therefore, although Faith's desire for the world is marvelously reborn at the end of the first novel, and although Andrew experiences Moksha, or sudden illumination, at the end of the second, both narratives leave unresolved the question of just how such aesthetic and spiritual transformations relate to national forms of belonging and action. Contributing to a larger debate about the dangers and democratic potential of cosmopolitan thought, Johnson moves in *Middle Passage* toward an ethic that recognizes both universal norms and local allegiances, including those of family, ethnicity, and nation. In that novel he thus begins the difficult intellectual task of putting back together the realms of concern that were separated in his first two narratives and thereby lays the conceptual groundwork for the book that would follow, *Dreamer*.

By contributing to larger cultural conversations about Buddhism, intellectualism, and the nature of Martin Luther King's legacy in the period between the appearance of *Faith* and the publication of *Dreamer*, Johnson develops a fresh, more finely articulated understanding of the relationship between personal conversion and civic action. That understanding is given dramatic form in *Dreamer*, though Johnson's depiction of King as a "transformed nonconformist," a figure drawn from a sermon that King preached at the Ebenezer Baptist Church in Atlanta in 1966, shortly before he left for Chicago to begin his troubled northern campaign.[1] In his sermon King develops the trope of the transformed nonconformist as a regulative ideal that enables him to critique both a citizenship of conformity that fails to challenge the troubled nation to improve and a citizenship of indulgent nonconformity that too easily degenerates into mere self-gratification. What is needed for effective citizenship, King argues, is a "*transformed* nonconformity." By depicting King as a transformed nonconformist in *Dreamer*, Johnson develops a sophisticated account of how personal transformation and civic engagement are related dialectically and offers his most compelling social vision (and his most profound spiritual reflections) as a black philosopher, Buddhist, and public intellectual. Johnson's complex depiction of King melds the divided material and imaginative realms of *Faith and the Good Thing*, reclaims forms of civic engagement that were intentionally displaced from *Oxherding Tale*, and deepens the analysis of citizenship that is broached in *Middle Passage*.

That Johnson is profoundly interested in interpreting the particular intellectual, spiritual, and social legacy of King is reflected by both the number and the diversity of his creative works that reflect on King's words, actions, example, and even his physical image. Several of Johnson's essays focus on King: "The King We Left Behind" (1996); "Searching for the Hidden Martin Luther King, Jr." (1996); "The King We Need: Teachings for a Nation in Search of Itself" (2005); "Mindfulness and the Beloved Community" and "A Sangha by Any Other Name," both collected in *Turning the Wheel* (2003); and "Blueprints of Freedom" (2008). With Bob Adelman, Johnson also published *King: The Photobiography* (2000), a lengthy collection of photographs spanning King's career, accompanied by Johnson's written commentary. Johnson also frequently talks about King in the interviews he grants; and he discussed that legacy in January 2008 on Michael Eric Dyson's nationally syndicated radio program.[2] Most important, of course, King is the inspiration for *Dreamer*, a novel that follows a fictionalized King through the challenges and disappointments of his Chicago campaign and the increasingly difficult final two years of his life, from 1966 to 1968. Johnson prepared for writing *Dreamer* by "studying [King's] sermons, history, speeches, even his college papers in order to capture something of his life and to understand . . . the elder we left behind" ("The King We Left" 198). By researching King's life, Johnson performs the sort of labor that he identifies in *Middle Passage* and in "The Second Front" as essential to the transmission of cultural inheritance. In addition to joining a larger debate about King's legacy and immersing himself in King's writings, Johnson also incorporated King into his private Buddhist practice by making him the subject of his meditation "for five years" ("The King We Left" 198). Given the number of Johnson's publications on King since the mid-1990s, one can legitimately say that Johnson's work since then constitutes an extended public deliberation on the significance of King's legacy to the nation.

In chapter 3 I analyzed Johnson's engagement with King explicitly in relation to a form of engaged Buddhism that emerged in the United States in the last half of the twentieth century. As documented there, many Buddhists detect a resonance between King's civil rights efforts and a socially engaged Buddhist practice, and many black Buddhists in particular find in King's nonviolent civil rights advocacy a catalyst for their own conversion to Buddhism. Certainly what could be termed the "Buddhification" of King is a distinguishing feature of Johnson's own engagement with the civil rights leader. In *Turning the Wheel* Johnson associates King explicitly with the Mahayana bodhisattva ideal and calls King's understanding of the Beloved Community a "*Sangha* [Buddhist religious community] by another name" ("Sangha" 52). In that collection and in "The King We Need," Johnson also identifies King's ethic of *agapic* love with the Buddhist ethic of loving kindness; and in "Be Peace Embodied" and "Buddhism Is the Most Radical and Civilized Choice," he compares King's understanding of human interrelatedness to Buddhist metaphysics. Several Johnson scholars develop these ideas in their readings of Johnson's fiction in general and of *Dreamer* in particular.[3] In this chapter I complement that work by placing the Buddhification of King into a different context: a larger cultural debate about King's legacy that by the turn of the twenty-first century had already evolved through several different stages.

After King's death some black thinkers—including some of the black philosophers discussed in the chapters 1 and 2—established a particular reading of King as being insufficiently radical in his methodology and too closely aligned with whites. In later years, however, several black thinkers, including black philosophers, black Buddhists (such as bell hooks and others discussed in chapter 3), and black public intellectuals (such as Dyson)—set out consciously to recover aspects of King's legacy that they believed had been lost, and the debate over that legacy entered a distinctively new stage. This contemporary recovery project provides an important cultural context for Johnson's *Dreamer*. In the first section of this chapter I consider the overall shape of this larger debate, especially as it entered the 1990s; I then compare and contrast two specific interpretations of that legacy, one offered by Johnson and one presented by Dyson in his popular *I May Not Get There with You: The True Martin Luther King, Jr.* (2000). Contrasting these two interpretations of King helps to clarify the questions at issue in the larger cultural conversation and to specify more specifically what is at stake for Johnson as he enters those deliberations. By joining the larger contemporary debate about King's legacy, Johnson finds a focal point for his participation in philosophy, Buddhism, and black intellectualism; a particular resolution to the tension between personal conversion and civic duty; and a conceptual architecture for his novel *Dreamer*.

## Debating King's Legacy

On June 8, 2006, the *New York Times* headline "King Archives Will Be Sold at Auction" once again brought to the front page of one of the nation's leading newspapers an ongoing debate over the significance, nature, and ownership of King's legacy to the nation. Only five months after the six-hour funeral of Coretta Scott King was televised nationally, Sotheby's had announced that it would be managing the auction of a historical treasure trove: a collection of King's papers that included a draft of his Nobel Peace Prize acceptance speech and an exam bluebook from Morehouse College described as his "earliest surviving theological writing" (Dewan A18). As the Pulitzer Prize–winning historian Taylor Branch pointed out, what was at stake in the potential auction of the King archive was nothing less than the nation's access to the civil rights leader's legacy (Dewan A18). The proposed auction raised questions both about the increasing commodification of the civil rights leader's memory and about the level of commitment to the shared national heritage that his papers represent. In the words of David N. Redden, the vice chairman of Sotheby's: "It does set a challenge for American institutions to decide whether or not they want to save and preserve the King legacy for posterity. This is a very important story that needs a very appropriate conclusion" (Goldman C4).

But whether the debate over King's legacy will ever reach "an appropriate conclusion" is doubtful. Certainly the high drama of the reported auction is only one aspect of the ongoing commercialization of King's legacy that also takes place in less rarefied venues. For example, the continuing interest in King as a cultural icon is reflected in the three hundred–plus items of King memorabilia listed for sale through what is perhaps the nation's (and the planet's) largest auction house, eBay. For sale are issues of national magazines such as *Life* and *Jet*, autographs, books, photographs, and posters (the overwhelming majority of which portray King at the 1963 March on Washington). One photograph for sale purports to be of King "at a Communist training school" (no doubt Highlander Folk School in Monteagle, Tennessee); another is described as "a picture of King and Gandhi" (in fact a picture of

King and *Arun* Gandhi, Mahatma Gandhi's grandson). King's image can be
purchased on plates and mugs, on commemorative decanters, on funeral
fans, on postage stamps (one from Samoa), and on statues in plastic, glass,
and ceramic. One figurine, in the form of a "pot bellied" King jar, is something of a curiosity: when King's head is removed, a "dove of peace" is discovered inside—a strange ceramic fusion of King's legendary appetite for
soul food and his commitment to nonviolent direct action. The auction of an
occasional street sign for "Martin Luther King Jr. Boulevard" reminds buy-
ers of the manner in which King's name has since his death multiplied across
the American landscape on streets, bridges, and public buildings. One of
the most unusual items at auction—and one that might appeal to Charles
Johnson—is an envelope from India. In its upper-right-hand corner is
a Martin Luther King postage stamp, and in its lower-left-hand corner is a
large image of Gandhi kneeling in front of the loom that became the national
symbol of Indian economic independence. Although eBay did not come into
existence until 1995, decades after King's tragic death on April 4, 1968, his
image now proliferates across cyberspace, providing a virtual register of the
public's desire both to appropriate and to memorialize his legacy.

As a repository for the projected hopes and fears of the nation, King was
well aware of his function as the national "symbol" of the civil rights movement. He was also aware that such symbols could be interpreted in many
different ways: as he once declared, "I am many things to many people."[4]
Baptist minister, charismatic civil rights leader, public intellectual, King was
a complex and multifaceted individual. Even before his death he was already
serving as an occasion for highly charged debates over integration, voting
rights, and social equity. But his elevation to the status of national icon ensured that the nature and significance of his legacy would continue to be a
matter of controversy. As Johnson has remarked: "We have canonized King.
He is both the creator and the creature of a moment in history. He is the
American symbol for the struggle against segregation, and the ideal of integration wears his face. But I think it's clear that the private man over time has
become a cultural object difficult to grasp" ("Searching" B5). Mrs. King's
battles with Boston University over the ownership of the archive housed
there, concerns about the management of the King Center in Atlanta, and
fears about the increasing commercialization of King's voice, image, and
words (including a multimillion-dollar deal signed between the King family
and Time-Warner in 1997) seemed by 2000 to have put King's legacy, as one
commentator suggested, "up for grabs" (Neal, review).

In fact the trajectory of King's career as a national icon had passed
through several different identifiable phases by the time Johnson was composing *Dreamer* in the 1990s. Even during King's lifetime his elevation to
the status of Black Messiah was already being undermined by several factors,

including failures in Albany, Chicago, and Memphis that suggested he was no longer the unifying leader he had once been. A generational shift from integrationist civil rights values to Black Power ideology further undercut King's standing in the African American community, while the growing backlash against previous civil rights gains and rioting in the nation's major cities together eroded support for his agenda among many whites. His increasingly outspoken criticism of the war in Vietnam and of economic exploitation further alienated many of King's foes—and a good number of his supporters.

Significantly, during the 1960s and 1970s the critique of King was led in part by black intellectuals who found his methods too conservative and who were suspicious of the ease with which white America had seemed to identify King as the black leader of choice. An essay by the black philosopher William R. Jones is representative of the thinking of many black intellectuals from the period. In chapter 2 I outlined the leadership that Jones provided to the Committee on the Black Experience for the American Philosophical Association and discussed the landmark publication of the first collection of essays by African American philosophers, *Philosophy Born of Struggle*. In 1983, the same year that the King holiday was signed into law, Jones published in that collection an essay highly critical of King. Analyzing the different reform strategies of King, Mao Tse-tung, and Malcolm X, Jones positions King's strategy for nonviolent protest in direct opposition to Mao's contention that "political power grows out of the barrel of a gun" (61; quoted in Jones, "Liberation" 230). Summarizing Mao's position as "only the gun" and King's position as "never the gun," Jones presents Malcolm X's strategy—famously summarized by the phrase "by any means necessary"—as a flexible alternative to the other extremes. To critique King, Jones draws upon an argument made by Mao that the oppressed cannot appeal to the conscience of the oppressor because the oppressor's conscience is destroyed by the practice of oppression itself. Force must be an option because the oppressor cannot be morally transformed: as Mao contends, the imperialists "will never lay down their knives. . . ; they will never become Buddhas, till their doom" (68; quoted in Jones, "Liberation" 230). Jones thus charges King with misidentifying the root cause of oppression by claiming that it is the conscience of the oppressor—rather than the oppressor's power—that is the problem which reform must address.

Jones's essay also reveals the degree to which the growing white appropriation of King's legacy was already a concern to black intellectuals in the 1980s. According to Jones, King was accorded the status of "black saint" largely because he had been exploited as "a guardian of white interests"; to a disturbing degree, King's elevated position was due to "the exalted status that whites have given him" ("Liberation" 233). Jones explains, "Like the role assigned to Jesus, King has become the Black Messiah, the singular and exclusive pattern for blacks to slavishly follow to imitate in their ethical models" (233). Rejecting both King's reform strategy and his elevation by whites to the status of Black Messiah in an argument that positions King's religious motivations as a rough equivalent to a black opiate of the masses, Jones ends his essay with an appeal to blacks to "scrutinize carefully the black heroes that white America seeks to force upon us" (239). Given Jones's preference for Malcolm X over King, his critique of King's radicalism, and his fears about the appropriation of King's legacy by whites, his article provides a good summary of a particular phase in the interpretation of King as a national symbol, an interpretation that would later be challenged by many "new" black intellectuals—including figures such as Cornel West, Dyson, and Johnson. Johnson's work on King is an important part of a larger revisionist project by a new generation who returned to King for intellectual and moral inspiration and who also worked to restore complexity to King's cultural representation.

Worries about white appropriation of King's legacy seemed to be increasingly borne out in the 1980s, however, as the proliferation of King holiday celebrations in the nation's public schools fostered a view of King as the new standard-bearer of America's civil religion. As Peter J. Albert pointed out in 1990, "Martin Luther King was as vulnerable as any other dead leader to the processes of co-option, canonization, and commercialization that conspire to replace with a more comfortable legend the stark truth of a courageous life cut short by an act of cowardice and bigotry" (Albert and Hoffman 3). Johnson would agree with this assessment. As he observes, although at present King's image has never been "more ubiquitous," his vision "suffers from the curse of canonization" ("The King We Left" 194). During the eighties King came to be increasingly reduced to his well-known "I Have a Dream" speech at the 1963 March on Washington and its oft-repeated phrase that individuals should be judged "by the content of their character" rather than the "color of their skin."[5] Several commentators have suggested that King's identification with this single speech creates a one-sided picture of the civil rights leader, a portrait that avoids a confrontation with the more controversial aspects of his thought. By 2000 Dyson offered in exasperation a "modest proposal" that a "ten-year moratorium" be called on reading the speech so that other King works could be studied (*I May* 15). The attenuated presentation of King's thought also led in the 1980s to an increasing appropriation of King's words and image by conservatives (white and black) working for policies and programs that King himself would have assuredly not supported.[6] The ease with which King's legacy was appropriated by varied and seemingly opposed camps led Johnson in 1996 to ponder what becomes of King's vision when "Louis Farrakhan and even pro-gun advocates in Washington

State . . . cite his words to support their vastly different political agendas?" ("The King We Left" 194).

The evolving appropriation of King's legacy by the white American mainstream and by conservatives did not go unaddressed, however. Historians were among the first to make a conscious effort to recapture the complexity of King's life, although much of their work did not enter more popular forums until many years after it was completed. Scholarly studies of King have now reached such a number and complexity that the relative merits of individual histories of King can be evaluated and a historiography of King criticism can be constructed.[7] Through this body of work the critique of King raised by Jones—namely that he was not radical enough and that his strategy for reform was too closely identified with the interests of whites—has been specifically engaged. A major focus of the recovery of King's complexity has been the attempt to clarify his relationship to African American intellectual, religious, and reform traditions, largely but by no means exclusively by black scholars. Work that clarifies King's ties to black theology, to the black social gospel tradition, and to the organizational, ministerial, and preaching traditions of the black church has been undertaken. Other studies focus on his function as an "organic" black public intellectual and on his continuation of a black tradition of nonviolent protest with roots in nineteenth-century America.[8] In reconsidering King's radicalism, historians have pointed to his willingness to put his life at risk on the front lines of protest in southern towns filled with hostile whites and administered by racist police. Attention has also been focused on the radical roots of King's thinking and the organizations with which he was associated, his early criticism of the Vietnam War, and his developing critique of American capitalism.[9] Finally, issues concerning King's plagiarism and his reputed sexism have been raised and analyzed. In short, against an increasingly narrow, commercialized image, scholars and public intellectuals have worked to present a fuller and more accurate assessment of King's achievements, leadership, and legacy.

As the nation approached the millennium, however, new developments seemed to threaten that legacy. Many scholars, fearing a retrenchment in King studies, publicly questioned the increased commercialization of King's legacy. Responding to escalating restrictions and fees imposed by the King family for the use of King materials, African American scholar Manning Marable has commented, "It's very disturbing for historians and scholars," especially so given that "Martin . . . cared very little about material wealth or gain. . . . He turned over the money from his Nobel Prize to the [civil rights] movement. He had very modest needs, and in that sense he devoted himself to the movement" (Christensen).[10] Ironically, the concern about the increased commercialization of King's legacy took place at precisely the moment when the interpretation of King was entering a new phase, as new research completed by historians was being disseminated through more popular forums. For example, many of the issues synthesized so passionately and so effectively by Dyson in his 2000 book had in fact been raised previously in historical studies. (Dyson's book on King includes over sixty pages of single-spaced endnotes.) Reviewed under headlines such as "Repoliticizing a Political Hero" and "Best We Get Comfortable with King the Radical, Too," Dyson's popular volume helped to counter earlier perceptions about King's lack of radicalism. In the preface to his 1998 novel about King, Johnson lists several historians whose work was especially important to his own writing of *Dreamer*, including David Garrow's *Bearing the Cross: Martin Luther King, Jr., and the Southern Leadership Conference*, winner of the 1987 Pulitzer Prize in biography. While preparing to write, Johnson also visited the Martin Luther King Papers Project at Stanford.[11] Another effect of the dissemination of King scholarship in more popular forms is the growing recognition on the part of conservatives that King is *not* the best poster boy for anti–affirmative action and other conservative causes, and Web sites have begun to spring up warning that in appropriating King to their causes, conservatives have seriously misunderstood his legacy. The conservative blogger Marcus Epstein notes, "Today, the official conservative and libertarian movement portrays King as someone on our side" rather than facing "the truth about King's views."

The cultural debate over the legacy of Martin Luther King Jr. has thus itself evolved through several different stages. King's identification as the symbol of the civil rights movement practically guaranteed that a good portion of his complexity and individuality would be lost to his representative function. If before his death King's symbolic meaning was already fracturing—from Black Messiah and black Gandhi to "Rev. Dr. Chickenwing" and "Martin Loser King"—after his assassination King's symbolic function seemed to take on a life of its own, inspirited by ongoing commercial processes and mobilized by both mainstream and conservative agendas.[12] At the same time, however, another process was taking form: the attempt to redraw a more detailed picture of King's intellectual and social bequest to the nation. Although this recovery project does not free itself from the processes of commercialization, it emerges nonetheless from a serious encounter with the diversity of King's own writings, made possible by access to the King archives. Today some of the same scholars who were involved in that recovery define the present moment in the preservation of King's legacy as a precarious one. One hopeful sign that his legacy will be preserved, however, is the June 24, 2006, announcement that Morehouse College, King's alma mater, would purchase the archive that had been slated for auction by

Sotheby's. At the same time, the recovery work of the 1980s and 1990s continues to make its way into more popular forums.

Recent reconsiderations of King's legacy such as Johnson's prose writings on King and Dyson's *I May Not Get There with You* are significant contributions to this larger recovery project. Both of these "new" black intellectuals write out of a profound belief that King's legacy has been so misunderstood that, as Johnson remarks, the nation has "left King behind," or as Dyson expresses it, King is "disappearing right before our eyes" (*I May* x). In addition, both writers position themselves as entering a larger national debate specifically in order to recover a lost heritage. According to Dyson, "the nation needs a King who can lead us to today. . . . I hope to resurrect that King" (x); or, as the subtitle to his book somewhat optimistically suggests, he intends to present the "*true* Martin Luther King." In "The King We Left Behind" Johnson similarly issues a call for the nation to return to the lost values that he finds to constitute King's heritage. A frequent contributor to Buddhist publications since the 1990s, Johnson offers what he calls "teachings" or lessons that he has learned "from fictionalizing King" ("The King We Need" 42). Similarly, Dyson, himself a minister, notes in the preface to *I May Not Get There with You* that he preached on King for years before writing his book. Both writers, then, identify—and emphasize in quasi-religious terms—a particular *historical* moment that seems to call for the return of King, and both consciously position the composition of their texts as responses to that larger social moment.

## Converting to King

Capturing Johnson's thinking about King in the mid 1990s, "The King We Left Behind" takes the form of a sermon. The essay is divided into four sections, and the first introduces a biblical passage for exegesis, Luke 2:41–52, a passage that focuses on Mary and Joseph's departure out of Jerusalem after Passover as they leave for their home in Nazareth. After discovering that they have inadvertently left their son behind, they return to Jerusalem to discover Jesus debating the doctors of law in the Temple. As Johnson indicates, the passage is one that King preached about in "Rediscovering Lost Values," a sermon he delivered in the Second Baptist Church in Detroit on February 25, 1954. While the scriptural narrative is often interpreted as a marker of Mary and Joseph's growing recognition of their son's divine vocation, in King's hands the family story becomes a homely trope for the inadvertent loss of something valuable—something as valuable as a lost child to an adoring family—and of the urgent need for its rediscovery. In the scramble for material goods, King suggests, the nation has left spiritual values behind. The intertextual relationship Johnson develops between King's sermon and his essay achieves several effects. First, it helps to elevate Johnson's essay to the level of a "lesson" or a "teaching." That is, by incorporating, expanding, and applying in the 1990s King's earlier interpretation of the gospel from the 1950s, Johnson assumes the position of a scribe or scriptural commentator who explains and amends an earlier reading of a text, simultaneously preserving and adding to a legacy. Johnson adds new meaning to the biblical passage specifically by developing an analogy between the loss of the Christ child and the loss of King from the national scene. Just as Mary and Joseph left Jesus behind, Johnson suggests, the nation is "guilty of the same forgetfulness with Martin Luther King" (194). Johnson also develops the intertextual relationship between his essay and King's sermon to identify a national fall from grace, which is elaborated in the second section of the essay, a jeremiad on the state of the nation. Finally, and most important, Johnson's essay reclaims King's legacy in order to intervene in a particular historical moment.

In the three "racially tempestuous decades" without King, Johnson contends in the second section, the nation—and especially the black community—has fallen into a "crisis" (194). To Johnson, this crisis developed in large part because King's call for a "beloved community" degenerated into Black Power's advocacy of "identity politics" (196). As William Nash has pointed out, Johnson's essay establishes a cultural genealogy that traces much of the nation's ills to the replacement of King as spiritual father by those whom Johnson refers to as "streetwise, ex-rapists like Eldridge Cleaver or Huey Newton," who over time became "the true spiritual fathers of today's Crips and Bloods" (195). As Johnson develops this cultural genealogy, the loss of King and the development of black nationalism lead inexorably to ethnic balkanization.[13] What the nation needs to heal, Johnson suggests, is to "rediscover the lost values" represented by King that it has left behind. In the third section of the essay Johnson describes his personal return to King's thinking. Finally, in section four he imagines that King himself has returned to the present moment to deliver a "sermon for the nineties." Placing King before a "forest of microphones," Johnson has him deliver a sermon from Proverbs 29:18, "gently yet emphatically reminding us that brotherhood was our goal, love our method, generosity and forgiveness our rule, peace our way of life, and finally, that where there is no vision, the people perish" (199). It is of course not King but Johnson himself who here offers a "sermon for the nineties" by imaginatively resurrecting King. In a 2000 interview with Rob Trucks, Johnson suggested that the narrative style of *Dreamer* was influenced by the gospel form. In this essay, Johnson assumes through its relationship with King's sermon the position of scriptural commentator two years before his novel on King is published.

But Johnson's essay also enters the cultural moment in a more specific manner than this general description of a generational fall from grace suggests. In fact, Johnson's discussion of King's legacy is properly read as an attempt to intervene in both a growing national dispute and in specific events unfolding at Howard University. In the early 1990s certain anti-Semitic statements by some black nationalist leaders had in fact led to a series of charged events. First among these was the firestorm of public reaction in 1990 and 1991 to statements by Leonard Jeffries. Chairman of the Black Studies Department at the City College of New York at the time, Jeffries was initially reported in the *New York Times* to have characterized whites as unfeeling "ice people" and blacks as compassionate "sun people."[14] In 1991 the *New York Post* reported comments made by Jeffries at the Empire State Black Arts and Cultural Festival blaming "rich Jews" for the slave trade. Similar statements were attributed to Nation of Islam (NOI) leader Louis Farrakhan and to then NOI spokesman Khalid Abdul Mohammed. In February 1994, when Mohammed appeared at Howard University, his speech was preceded by a chant led by a student organization associated with the NOI. In answer to questions such as "Who caught Nat Turner?" and "Who killed Nat Turner?" the audience responded in call-and-response fashion, "Jews!" This event was followed by the cancellation of the planned April 4 visit of Yale's David Brion Davis, a well-known Jewish scholar of slavery, out of fears that his presence might create unrest. Finally, on April 19 Mohammed returned to campus and delivered a speech in which he called Jews "dirty, low-down bastards" and praised Colin Ferguson, a black man who in December 1993 had killed six white people in a Long Island Railroad car.[15]

"The King We Left Behind" was written specifically as an attempt to bring King's legacy to bear on these unfolding events. Johnson's essay was published in *Common Quest*, a journal established as a joint effort of Howard University and the American Jewish Committee in 1996, two years after Mohammed's visit to Howard. The purpose of the journal, which had one black and one Jewish editor, was to deliberate on the state of black-Jewish and other racial relationships in the nation. Johnson's essay memorialized King's legacy in order to establish a regulative ideal that could be applied to the deteriorating relationship between blacks and Jews and its effects at Howard. Under King's leadership, writes Johnson, "the alliance of blacks and Jews of good will was formed, producing thirty years ago this country's finest (yet fragile) attempt at brotherhood, one that some of our present 'leaders' have fractured by singling out Jews as their adversaries" (196). It was only "a short step," he argues, "from Karenga's cultural nationalism in the 1960s to Professor Leonard Jeffries . . . describing Europeans as cold, individualistic 'ice people' (in contrast to the warm, communalistic 'sun people' of Africa)" (195). Given this specific cultural context and journalistic outlet,

Johnson's intertextual relationship with King's sermon can be seen to serve purposes other than those already discussed: by beginning his essay with a scriptural passage describing Mary and Joseph's trip to Jerusalem to celebrate Passover, for example, Johnson subtly introduces a shared Judeo-Christian, Jewish-black heritage against the separate lineage emphasized by many black nationalists.

The features of King's legacy that are important to Johnson stand out in sharper relief when they are contrasted with those identified by other contemporary public intellectuals such as Dyson. Interestingly, in their respective analyses of King, both Johnson and Dyson incorporate accounts of a personal conversion that the civil rights leader effected in their lives, but these transformations reveal important differences between the two writers. Dyson begins *I May Not Get There with You* by describing the moment when, as a boy of nine, he first learned of King's assassination, "the moment that changed [his] life" (3). Dyson's awakening, however, is not to a transcendent religious truth but to a cultural reality that is nonetheless saturated with spiritual significance: the reality of race in America. He writes, "The bullet that shattered King's jaw ended his life; its shrapnel lodged deep in my psyche and burned me awake to race in America" (3). It was King's assassination, and not the riots of the year before that left forty-three people dead in Dyson's hometown of Detroit, that first introduces him to the nation's racial complexity. By beginning his study with an account of his personal response to King's assassination, Dyson achieves several effects. First, he focuses the reader's attention on the supreme sacrifice King made as a civil rights leader: the assassination serves as the book's primary argument against those who would question King's commitment. Second, by beginning with this event, Dyson locates the moment of origin of the book that he would publish over thirty-two years later in the personal "awakening" that is occasioned by King's death: "This book is the most recent symbol of my awakening and the product of my attempt to interpret King's life and meaning in a new way" (3). Finally, by tracing his current attempt to "resurrect" King through his personal transformation as a young boy, Dyson positions himself, like Johnson, as a convert to King who is working to pass on a legacy to a new generation.

In his varied prose writings on King, Johnson also presents a personal conversion narrative, one that both recapitulates and reinforces the national fall from grace that he recounts in "The King We Left Behind." Growing up as a "child of integration" in a home that displayed King's picture, Johnson reports, he somewhat unconsciously imbibed a belief in integration. But Johnson was also part of a generation that matured after King's great civil rights victories. When President Lyndon Baines Johnson signed the Civil Rights Act on July 2, 1964, with King standing behind him, Charles Johnson was "living not in the south but in a Chicago suburb where many young black men viewed nonviolence as unmanly and listened with greater interest to the speeches of Malcolm X" than to those of King (197). At this stage he knew King only through "reflections and refractions" and was more impressed by black nationalism (197). It was not until he had children of his own and observed the difficulty they experienced in negotiating a "social minefield" that Johnson returned to King's writings in an attempt to understand the "genesis" of the social conditions faced by the present generation. After immersing himself in King's writings, Johnson undergoes what might be described as a second conversion. Earlier his introduction to black nationalism had replaced the ideal of integration, as Johnson says, "before I fully had the chance to subject the black American goal of integration to philosophical examination" ("Searching" B5). Reflecting on his own personal history and the nation's decline, Johnson judges, "We are all apostates" (196). But King's writings restore and deepen Johnson's faith in integration and in nonviolence. Johnson's personal conversion narrative, then, recounts *two* transformations, first a "false," unexamined conversion to black cultural nationalism, a transformation that leads him to devalue King, and then a second "true" conversion to King's message as he comes to understand it through a firsthand encounter with King's own writings. Thus while Dyson's conversion narrative underscores the reality of race in America, Johnson's emphasizes the ideals of integration and nonviolence.

Interestingly, if both Johnson and Dyson incorporate a personal conversion narrative into their analyses of King, both also emphasize a conversion in King's own life. Dyson's book is predicated on the thesis that King underwent a radical shift between the early and later parts of his public career, a shift that fundamentally altered his ideas and methods. Indeed, a failure to recognize "the radical message" of King's later life, Dyson suggests, is the primary cause of the nation's misunderstanding of his legacy (ix).[16] While the public is aware of Malcolm X's conversion to traditional Islam after his trip to Mecca and his separation from the Nation of Islam, most people are not aware, according to Dyson, that King experienced a conversion in many ways "more startling and consequential than Malcolm's" (31). First, Dyson suggests, King executed "a stunning about-face on his earlier belief in the inherent goodness of whites" (38)—a result of his northern campaign, which showed King a more intractable and devious face of white racism than the one he had confronted in the South. Second, King was later converted to what Dyson calls "an enlightened black nationalism" (20), a transformation in King's thinking that he attributes to the influence of Malcolm X (31). Third, these changes led King to shift his methods of reform to a more aggressive posture, inspiring him to speak out against the Vietnam War and motivating him to shift his focus to economic oppression. In emphasizing this dramatic shift in King's attitudes, Dyson enters the larger cultural conversation by responding directly to earlier charges made by black intellectuals like William Jones, who criticized King's radicalism. Dyson "resurrects" King's legacy, then, by turning the public's attention away from King the "great pacifist" to the "hard-nosed critic of economic injustice" (xv).

While Johnson's prose writings also define a decisive conversion in King's life, he locates that transformation early in King's career and reads the civil rights leader's later views as a development, expansion, and deepening of his earlier positions rather than an abrupt shift in beliefs and strategies. Johnson too defines different stages in King's public career. During the first, which culminates in King's acceptance of the Nobel Peace Prize in 1964, King converts to a distinctive method of social reform that incorporates a firm commitment to nonviolence, an understanding of *agapic* love with deep roots in the African American church, and a conviction that "interdependence is the life's blood of our being" ("The King We Need" 49). It is the radical depth of King's commitment to these principles, Johnson believes, that results in his emergence as the national leader of the civil rights movement. To the question why that leadership position was not filled by better-known black leaders such as Congressman Adam Clayton Powell or the NAACP's Roy Wilkins, Johnson notes that "the answer to that question can be found on the night of January 30, 1956" ("The King We Need" 47), when King's house was bombed during the Montgomery campaign while his wife and his infant daughter Yolanda were at home. Learning of the attack, King returned home to find his family unharmed inside, while outside an explosive situation was setting armed white policemen against an armed crowd of blacks who had arrived to protect King's family. By persuading those present that "we cannot solve this problem through retaliatory violence," King defused the situation. To Johnson, this event, by demonstrating the depth of King's commitment to nonviolence, confirms his unique fitness for leadership: "His Gandhi-esque stance, his *agapic* vision, was heard round the world as something uniquely redemptive" (48).

What Johnson calls "the second stage of King's evolution" began on the day the civil rights leader received the Nobel Peace Prize, an event that crystallized for King his own evolving status as an international figure: King "now understands himself not merely as a Southern civil rights leader, but instead as a man obligated to promote his belief in the 'beloved community' and peace on a world stage" (49). It is thus King's changing perception of his leadership role, and especially his growing perception of being part of an international peace and human rights movement, Johnson suggests, that leads to his increasingly vocal opposition to the Vietnam War. Citing the speech King delivered at the Nobel awards ceremony, Johnson emphasizes King's assertion that "nonviolence is the answer to the crucial and moral question of our time." Johnson points out that King saw the antiwar Buddhist monk Thich Nhat Hanh as the natural successor for his award—and indeed, King nominated the monk for a subsequent Nobel Prize in 1967. For Johnson, then, the decisive factor was King's coming to understand himself as being called to a *cosmopolitan* leadership position that was global in scope. Thus while Dyson attributes to the later King a deepening *racial* identity as he converts to an "enlightened black nationalism," Johnson focuses on King's assumption of a cosmopolitan leadership position in what King himself described as "a world-wide fellowship that lifts neighborly concern beyond one's tribe race, class, and nation" (*Where* 190). To Johnson, King is not only "one of America's greatest moral and political philosophers" ("The King We Need" 42) and a dedicated spiritual leader, but also the leading representative of a new form of cosmopolitanism citizenship, a fact that proves important to *Dreamer*.[17]

In his prose writings about King, Johnson also engages critics of King such as Jones, but in a very different manner from Dyson. In developing his critique of King, Jones treats the religious aspects of King's reform strategy as a sort of "opiate of the masses," a tool that can be manipulated by white America. Johnson's analysis of King, in contrast, asserts that a deep spirituality is central to King's civil rights practice, and furthermore that a commitment to nonviolence is a key component of his legacy. In order to emphasize the centrality of nonviolence to King's spiritualized practice, in "The King We Left Behind" Johnson draws on the authority of John Lewis (congressman from Georgia, former chairman of the Student Nonviolent Coordinating Committee [SNCC], and one of the original Freedom Riders): "If King could speak to us today he would say, in addition to doing something about guns, he would say there needs to be a revolution of values, a revolution of ideas in the black community. He would say we need to accept non-violence not simply as a technique or as a means to bring about social and political change, but we need to make it a way of life, *a way of living*" (198). Elsewhere, in "The King We Need," Johnson echoes Lewis, his capitalization giving certain phrases a noticeable Buddhist inflection: "Nonviolence—in words and actions—must be understood not merely as a strategy for protest, but as a Way, a daily praxis people must strive to translate into each and every one of their deeds" (48). While Dyson contrasts an apparently "soft" pacifism with a "hard-nosed" economic reform (*1 May* 3), Johnson argues that King's advocacy for nonviolence is itself a "tough-minded message"—one that opposes a "racial mythology" that Johnson dismisses as too "easy" an intellectual and moral position ("The King We Left" 194, 96). As a black Buddhist and cosmopolitan thinker, Johnson fears primarily not that the public identifies King too strongly as the "nonviolent messenger of integration" but rather that the nation is too quick to assume that pacifism can no longer be effective—or that "Gandhi-esque nonviolence died at the Lorraine Hotel" ("The King We Left" 195).

Finally, in their analyses of King, both Johnson and Dyson identify potential heirs to King's legacy. In one of his more controversial claims, Dyson suggests that "King is a man who had as much in common with Tupac Shakur as he does with Rev. Ralph Abernathy" (*I May* x). Attempting to bridge a historical divide between the hip-hop generation and King, Dyson suggests that we must "meet youth where they are"; this means that King's legacy will necessarily have to be "adapted, translated, and reinterpreted" (310). In "The King We Left Behind," however, Johnson effects such a translation by positioning Buddhism as King's potential successor—a claim that may strike readers as even more controversial than Dyson's identification of King with Shakur. Later, in *Turning the Wheel*, he will repeat this association by identifying Buddhism as "the logical extension of King's dream of the 'beloved community'" (xvi).

Johnson elaborates on this position in an interview titled "Buddhism Is the Most Radical and Civilized Choice." Given the historical denigration of people of color as "uncivilized," Johnson's choice of "most civilized" to describe Buddhism may strike readers as incendiary. But Johnson's idea of "civilization" has its own genealogy and social resonance. Indeed, Johnson traces his use of the word explicitly to King's statement in his Nobel address that "violence and civilization are antithetical concepts" (quoted in Johnson, "Buddhism" 34). This understanding of civilization informs Johnson's approach to citizenship in *Dreamer*. King consistently argued that some means are more likely to bring about a civil society than others. Understanding civil conduct and the realization of a more just society to be dialectically related, he advocated for nonviolent direct action as a civilized means to a civilized end. In *Stride toward Freedom*, for example, King specifically set out to unsettle racist usages of the terms "civilized" and "citizenship" by contrasting the nonviolent tactics of the boycotters to the barbaric tactics of their opposition (108–32). In that work the threats, bombings, and attacks on innocent men and women establish without a doubt that it is the boycotters who best represent American citizenship rather those who belong to White Citizens Councils.[18] It is this use of "civilization" that Johnson wishes to appropriate for Buddhism when he describes it as the "most civilized" choice.

It is in *Dreamer*, however, that Johnson would most powerfully represent the complex, dialectical nature of King's vision of citizenship. King understands ideology and morality, spirituality and practice, to be mutually reinforcing aspects of power, each of which has a role to play in the creation of a more just society. In order for civil action to be effective, King argues, it must be carried out under a "regulating ideal"; at the same time, such action itself contributes to the amplification of value in the civic sphere ("Non-

Aggression," 326). By dramatizing the injustice of current laws and by interrupting the system, civil protest works to make new laws a reality. Those
laws then govern future behavior, which over time transforms a nation's cit-
izenry. As King argues, by regulating behavior, the law "plays an indirect part
in molding public sentiment" (*Stride* 216). But as King also argues, "the laws
need help." For citizens to obey laws, they "must believe they are right"
(*Stride* 216). King's underlying claim, then, is that nonviolence is effective
because it wields *related* forms of power: the power to interrupt the system
and the power to "reach men where the law cannot reach them" (*Stride* 215).
King thus understands nonviolence as a force for personal *and* national conversion that unfolds under a regulative ideal (the discipline of love) as it
works to implement ideals (or just laws) at the national level.

Like many other intellectuals of his generation, Johnson joined in a larger
recovery project aimed at correcting a popular, attenuated representation of
King that had been established in the decades since the great civil rights
leader's death. Reexamining King's writings in the 1990s, Johnson drew on
his philosophical training to assess anew the social and ethical goal of integration. As an increasingly committed and outspoken Buddhist, Johnson felt
a deep resonance between King's dedication to nonviolence and Buddhist
values. As a black public intellectual, Johnson mobilized King's legacy to address specific historical events in the 1990s. Finally, by returning to King,
Johnson arrived at a fresh understanding of the importance of a transformed,
civil, or "converted" citizenship, an understanding to which he gives potent
dramatic form in *Dreamer*. There Johnson responds to the national crisis of
leadership that he identifies in "The King We Left Behind" by locating the
genius of King's "civil" war leadership in the properties of the transformed
nonconformist.

## Dreamer, *Citizen King, and the Transformed Nonconformist*

In *Oxherding Tale*, Johnson deemphasizes the political struggles of the Civil
War in order to privilege an ethics of altruism over other models of social engagement. The war that is minimalized in that narrative, however, resurfaces
full-blown in *Dreamer*, where warfare becomes the primary trope for nation
in 1960s America. In "Searching for the Hidden Martin Luther King, Jr.,"
Johnson argues that the popular view of the sixties is often "nostalgic." The
decade should be remembered instead, he suggests, as a time when "the level
of violence was so great . . . that the government was considering what to do
in the event of civil war—specifically, race war." In *Dreamer* Johnson defines King's legacy by dramatizing the nature of the leadership King provided
during this time of emergency. Before the historical Martin Luther King
moved to Chicago in January 1966, rioting had broken out after an errant

fire truck killed a young black girl, a tragedy that served to highlight long-standing racial tensions in the highly segregated northern city, where fewer than 4 percent of blacks lived in integrated neighborhoods. After the riots of 1965 King announced that he would take his battle against unfair housing, employment, and educational practices to the North. But shortly after he succeeded in leading a nonviolent march from Soldier Field to City Hall, rioting broke out again on Chicago's west side when police shut off a fire hydrant being used by residents for relief from a heat wave. Although it was unrelated to King's planned protest, the riot nonetheless seemed to signal the beginning of a new, tragic stage in his civil rights leadership.

Introducing King as a new breed of American war general, *Dreamer* opens with a prologue designed to describe the state of the union and the specific difficulties that he encounters as King leads his northern campaign into the troubled streets of an overheated Chicago in the summer of 1966. While King's movement from South to North replicates the trajectory of Faith's journey in *Faith and the Good Thing*, the young woman's assumption of the role of storyteller in that novel contrasts sharply with King's concentrated efforts in *Dreamer* to establish "a beachhead" for nonviolent resistance in the North (16). In his willingness to engage "the enemy" (15), King also differs from the otherworldly Reb, who in *Oxherding Tale* defines a type of reclusive leadership opposed to the public governance provided by Lincoln. Instead, more like Lincoln than opposed to him, King is dramatized in *Dreamer* as leading a campaign during a conflict of national proportions, when "families [are] divided," "brothers [spill] each other's blood," and the country is "as divided as it had been during the Civil War" (13, 14).

Against the backdrop of racial strife on the home front and the Vietnam War abroad, the novel introduces King at a decisive moment in his public career, when his command is under assault both from those who oppose his efforts to desegregate the nation and from those who support equal rights but find his methods "outmoded" (16). Ten years after his stunning "Montgomery victory," it has been many months since King has won a campaign (16). With his reputation tarnished and many of his former supporters arguing that his "day of leadership is done" (17), King as he enters the novel is setting up headquarters in a flat at 1550 South Hamlin Avenue in the slum of West Lawndale, with nothing less than the governance of the civil rights movement at stake: as the omniscient narrator comments, King "need[s] a victory here" (16).

By figuring King as a military leader in a new "civil" war, *Dreamer* in fact replicates the historical King's own framing of his public ministry. King routinely referred to the civil rights movement in terms of campaigns and battles, and he called Montgomery "one of the glowing epics of the twentieth century" (*The Autobiography* 136). More to the point is King's use of Ulysses

S. Grant's famous phrase to announce the goals he hoped to achieve by taking his civil rights movement to Chicago: "Our primary objective will be to bring about the *unconditional surrender* of forces dedicated to the creation and maintenance of slums" (quoted in Oates 387; emphasis added). Some critics have concentrated on King's representation in the novel primarily as a bodhisattva or Black Messiah. Certainly King's character fulfills both functions; as John Whalen-Bridge observes, "Neither a strictly Christian nor a strictly Buddhist interpretation of the novel will work" ("Waking" 514).[19] But the Christian and Buddhist elements are fused in Johnson's compelling presentation of King as a leader in a special kind of "war." While both Johnson and King understand warfare to be a trope for psychological, spiritual, and philosophical struggle, both also take seriously the proposition that the civil rights movement was a literal battle for equality, as significant as other wars fought in the nation's history. King was committed to the goal of creating a more perfect union, and the elaboration of a specific conception of his wartime leadership is central to Johnson's interpretation of King's legacy in *Dreamer*.

The omniscient narrator of the prologue is one of the two alternating narrators in the novel. Most of the book is the first-person narrative of Matthew Bishop, a twenty-four-year-old follower in the civil rights movement who records events as they unfold. A philosophy major at Columbia College, Matthew describes himself as someone who "lived best as a witness" (110). His narrative position in the novel is reminiscent of Nick Carraway's in *The Great Gatsby*: Matthew observes, weighs, and attempts to comprehend King's greatness within a narrative that also seeks to define an American decade and to investigate a version of the American Dream. In Johnson's scheme, however, Matthew also serves the same function for a second character, Chaym Smith, King's doppelganger. A down-and-out black man with a violent past who is described as "the kind of Negro the Movement had for years kept away from the world's cameras" (33), Chaym appears one day at the flat from which King directs his campaign and asks to be hired as King's stand-in. While the omniscient narrator focuses on King's history, Matthew's first-person narration focuses both on King and on Chaym's preparations to double for King. In other words, Matthew has *two* Gatsbys to observe, and the nature of Chaym's enigmatic, potentially dangerous, but conceivably admirable character is another puzzle that Matthew attempts to unlock, as is the relationship between the two forceful personalities that he recounts.

There are good reasons, however, to speculate that the entire narrative is the composition of a mature Matthew, who returns to his earlier first-person account after the main events in the novel have taken place, amending, expanding, and redoubling his reflections on King's career by assuming the position of a disciple who turns secular history into sacred history. This dual function is suggested when Matthew describes himself as "recording the Revolution" with "no idea at the time that just possibly I was composing a gospel" (102). Matthew's name of course identifies him as both the author of a gospel and a church leader, and his anticipation of composing a gospel and his highly suggestive name in fact support the interpretation that the italicized sections of the novel are the record of a transformed, more deeply dedicated Matthew, who, after recording the events he narrates in his first-person account, has answered the call to take up the task of writing what is paradoxically both war epic and "social gospel." The voice of the novel's omniscient narrator also resonates with the scribal voice that Johnson adopts in "The King We Left Behind." In this regard it is significant that the narrative's many scriptural passages draw heavily not only from the New Testament but also from the Pentateuch—the five books of the Hebrew Bible that recount the epic history of the Israelites and establish the prophetic voice of the jeremiad form. The *five* italicized sections of the novel are in dialogic relationship with the *Penta*teuch as well as with the gospels, emphasizing King's role as the black Moses.[20] Finally, while he was writing the novel, Johnson incorporated meditations on King into his personal Buddhist practice, and several of the italicized sections of the novel consist of meditations on King's legacy. Fusing Buddhist devotion, holy writ, King's own sermons, and historical studies of King and the civil rights movement, then, *Dreamer* is part jeremiad, part gospel, part Buddhist teaching, and part war epic.

Johnson draws his own battle lines clearly in the novel, positioning King in opposition to the two camps that contest his ideal of racial integration. The first camp is made up of white segregationists. In the North, King's white opponents run the gamut from "average" white homeowners who become "hysterical" when blacks attempt to integrate neighborhoods, to George Lincoln Rockwell and other extremist members of the American Nazi Party who flock to Chicago to oppose a planned march through the white enclave of Cicero, to Richard Daley's democratic machine which threatens protesters with the loss of jobs and other reprisals, and finally to the "faceless institutions: banks, real estate agents, insurance companies, and landlords" that fight King's suggestions for meaningful reform (118, 16). In the South, King's white opponents range from the inept Bull Conner, who falls easily into the "bully-buffoon role" that the movement "script[s] for him" (15), to the sinisterly effective Virginian John Sutherland, who wears a Confederate colonel's cap, displays a rebel flag proudly in this home, and belongs to the "covert Southern group with deep pockets" that posts the $50,000 bounty on King's head, leading to his assassination (189).

The second camp that King attempts to outmaneuver is composed of the black nationalist and Black Power advocates who also challenge his leadership. The novel elaborates on the position Johnson takes in "The King We

Left Behind" by attributing the crisis in King's command partly to the rise of Black Power styles of leadership, as when the narrator asserts that Stokely Carmichael's "cry for Black Power during [the] Mississippi march . . . opened a Pandora's box of rage and rang deeper into black hearts than any appeal for love" (16). Incorporating Malcolm X's critique of his experiences in the Nation of Islam from a February 1965 conversation with Gordon Parks, the novel calls the followers of the NOI "zombies." Describing his experience as a "foot soldier" in Elijah Muhammad's national forces, Malcolm X declared, "I was a zombie—like all the rest of them. I was hypnotized, pointed in a certain direction and told to march" (437). *Dreamer* thus positions King as a beleaguered general who has dedicated twelve years of his life to leading a national battle for civil rights against rabidly segregationist whites only to find himself labeled a "traitor, an Uncle Tom," by black separatists who have entered into their own "frail, forced confederacy" (17, 55).

While King is called by many names in *Dreamer*, one that is repeated is "Citizen King." This paradoxical sounding title is suggestive of the complex nature of his leadership, a "transformed nonconformity" that Johnson develops in his fictional presentation of King's legacy. On January 16, 1966, King delivered his "Transformed Nonconformist" sermon at Ebenezer Baptist Church in Atlanta—only ten days before he moved into the Lawndale flat. In that sermon, which Matthew refers to explicitly at one point, King could be said to theorize citizenship as he defines the specific form of "dual citizenship" that the transformed nonconformist exercises. With his imminent northern campaign in mind, King identifies the present moment in American history as one that calls for a particular kind of civic practice: the transformed nonconformist is a "citizen of two worlds, the world of time and the world of eternity" (9). To explain what it might mean to exercise such citizenship, King refers to the example of Roman citizens who established small colonies in far-off lands while remaining loyal to Roman values and to early Christian communities who lived among nonbelievers but held faithfully to Christian ideals. In the words of Saint Paul, "Be not conformed to this world, but be ye transformed by the renewing of your mind" (Romans 12:2). King's sermon thus suggests that in a certain sense both *nonconformity* and *conversion* are essential elements of dual citizenship.

King's definition builds on the dialectical understanding of the relationship between ideal and practice that he had developed since Montgomery. In the sermon, the transformed nonconformist functions as a "regulative ideal" that enables King to critique both a citizenship of conformity that fails to challenge the nation to improve and a citizenship of self-indulgent nonconformity that too easily degenerates into mere "exhibitionism" (13). For King, the complacent American Christian Church has too often practiced a dangerous conformity: "Called to combat social evil," King argues, the church has "remained silent behind stained glass windows" (11). On the one hand, because a "constructive nonconformity" is needed to undermine existing inequities, churches need to heed the call of a higher morality than simply that of the imperfect state of affairs. On the other hand, nonconformity runs its own risks if it takes the form of mere self-expression. Nonconformity becomes "creative" precisely when, King asserts, it is "controlled and directed by a transformed life" and "embraces a new mental outlook" (13). Nonconformity therefore requires conversion, the "renewing of mind" to which Saint Paul refers. Put in terms of his or her dual citizenship, the transformed nonconformist, "living in the colony of time," is called to be "responsible to the empire of eternity" (9). The two realms of time and eternity, practice and ideal, are captured in the dual citizenship implied by the name "Citizen King."

## Reasoning Vertically and Acting Historically

As it is developed in *Dreamer*, dual citizenship implies both a way of thinking and a way of acting. One must be a citizen of "eternity" in order to develop the regulative ideals that make it possible to critique nation and nationalism for the sake of a more perfect union, but one must also be a citizen *in* time in order to take effective action in the national sphere. The thinking of the transformed nonconformist is dramatized skillfully in chapter 4 of the novel, which follows King on a 4:30 AM flight from Chicago back to Atlanta, where he intends to continue to preach his Sunday sermons to his congregation even as he sustains the Chicago campaign. Boarding the plane, King notes with some dismay that the stewardess, who recognized his name on the passenger list, has purchased over forty copies of *Stride toward Freedom* for him to autograph during the flight. King had been hoping to prepare his sermon and, if possible, to catch some much-needed sleep. As he settles into his seat, he muses that airplanes "piqued his anagogic and analogical side, the old student of Aquinas who enjoyed reasoning vertically from the natural world toward the heaven, which these flying machines came close to bumping into" (76). The chapter is carefully designed to illustrate the form of "reasoning vertically" that the transformed nonconformist brings to history, a kind of *metaphoric* logic that perceives more than one meaning simultaneously. King's reference to Aquinas's theory of analogical reasoning anticipates Matthew's later training of Chaym in Saint Augustine's four levels of scriptural interpretation: the literal, analogical, tropological (i.e., moral), and anagogic (i.e., eschatological). Flying high above Lake Michigan, King perceives that the lake beneath him appears frozen, "as if someone had called time out on all motion in the world below" (77). King's position in the plane thus provides the opportunity for him to practice the perspective of eternity.

From this point of view King reflects on his relationship to the pilot of the plane, relaxing when he hears the pilot's voice over the intercom. Realizing that "someone he couldn't see or talk to had control over his destination and whether he lived or died, and most likely that person was trustworthy because his own life depended upon his doing his job well," King rests, turning over responsibility for his life momentarily to someone else (77). From an analogical perspective, King's relationship to the pilot provides a concrete illustration of humanity's dependence, as King frequently expressed it, on a "web of mutuality." King then expands his thinking anagogically by reflecting: "It wasn't easy to be an atheist on an airplane. No sooner had you strapped in than you had to believe in something beyond yourself" (77). As his logic unfolds, the composition of place with which this meditative chapter begins—the description of the plane trip—gives way, somewhat in the fashion of Augustinian meditation, to memory's recreation of the past, as King next recalls the night of his kitchen conversion.

King's thoughts first turn to his early, "half-hearted" conversion at Ebenezer when, as a young boy, he followed his sister forward in church, and his later negative reaction to witnessing the conversion of a young girl, to whom he had been attracted, in a "moment of epilepsy and seizure" (78). From there King's thoughts shift to the kitchen conversion in the midst of the Montgomery campaign. Calling on God for the strength to continue his civil rights leadership, King hears a voice saying, "Stand up for righteousness, stand up for the truth, and God will be at your side forever" (83). Vertical reasoning thus leads King's thoughts from the airplane flight, to the mutual interdependence of humankind, to the moment when King first becomes a "transformed nonconformist." Figured in the specific historical context of the crisis he experienced over his leadership of the Montgomery campaign, King's conversion is presented in *Dreamer* in terms of a dual citizenship that entails both spiritual and civic obligations, as he is charged to take up his civil rights leadership and "stand up for the truth." King's kitchen epiphany, like his pilgrimage to nonviolence, takes place in a highly fraught, exceedingly dangerous racial context. That spiritual experience was occasioned by his practice of nonviolent direct action, and it enabled him to return to that practice. Personal conversion and social conversion are vitally connected.

At the same time, Johnson describes the moment of King's kitchen conversion in language that evokes a Buddhist conception of meditative practice: "Then it came quietly, unbidden. He was traveling light again, for the long, lurid dream of multiplicity and separateness, the very belief in an 'I' that suffered and strained to affect the world, dissolved, and for the first time he felt like a dreamer gently roused from sleep and forgetfulness" (82). Structured as a meditation that draws on several spiritual traditions, the chapter is designed to dramatize the transformative potential of reasoning vertically. As in Augustinian meditation, it starts with a composition of place, continues through the application of memory, and ends with the exercise of will in the present, as King begins to dedicate personally and to autograph individually the books bought by the flight attendant, Stephanie. Although he knows from experience that by the time he finishes the task, the joints in his fingers will be throbbing so badly that he will have to soak his hand in hot water (and knows that his sermon will not be written), King takes up the books willingly, recognizing after his meditative reflection that "there was nothing inside the blue coat and skirt Stephanie was wearing except Allah" (84). The airplane flight thus provides an everyday example of the vertical reasoning required by dual citizenship, a reasoning that leads to morally informed action.

In developing the idea of dual citizenship in his sermons, King discusses the ability to reason vertically in different ways, most frequently in explicitly Christian terminology, but also in the language of a power of abstraction that recalls Marx's famous passage about human creativity which I discussed in chapter 2.[21] In *Strength to Love*, King explains that man lives on "two levels": "He can do creative things that lower animals could never do. Man can think a poem and write it; he can think a symphony and compose it, he can think a great civilization and produce it" (90). At other times King employs civic values in order to express vertical reasoning, most frequently the principle expressed in the Declaration of Independence that "all men are created equal." Commonly, however, King freely *combines* religious, creative, and civic ideals, as he does when explaining the significance of his own historical period: "When future generations men look back upon these turbulent, tension-packed days through which we are passing, they will see God working through history for the salvation of man. They will know that God was working through those men who had the vision to perceive that no nation could survive half slave and half free" ("Our God" 104). Joining phrases from Abraham Lincoln's description of the nation during the Civil War with the particular historical exigencies of the 1960s and with Christian eschatology, this passage captures well the complex standpoint of the transformed nonconformist. Significantly, the various levels of meaning that King brings to bear here — religious, creative, and civic — are presented not as mutually exclusive but as mutually reinforcing. If dual citizenship suggests that one must be a citizen of eternity in order to develop the perspective that enables one to critique nation rather than to conform blindly, it also suggests that one must be a citizen of time in order to act effectively. The transformed nonconformist is therefore foremost a *citizen*. *Dreamer* thus completes the turn from a focus on issues of subject identity to a concentration on the duties of citizenship that was begun in *Middle Passage*. Without a commitment to acting historically, the insights achieved by reasoning vertically cannot be realized. The sort of dual citizenship required by transformed nonconformity is not that of the reclusive monk or even that of the householder occupied with familial obligations (the ethical focus in *Oxherding Tale*). Instead, as King writes in his sermon on transformed nonconformity, what is needed are "men and women who will courageously *do battle* for truth" (15; emphasis added).

It is precisely from the standpoint of the transformed nonconformist that King in *Dreamer* confronts the difficult challenges of the final two years of his career. These challenges take two primary forms in Johnson's narrative. First, there is the challenge to King's "most cherished" faith in the equality of all men that is posed by his encounter with Chaym Smith. Second is the dispiriting challenge to his leadership that is posed by the increasingly more fractious engagements of his later civil rights campaigns. The challenge posed by Chaym's sudden appearance in his life is generated by the fact that although he resembles King closely in physical appearance, Chaym is King's negative in fortune. In contrast to King, with his deep roots in the African American community, comfortable middle-class upbringing, and loving family, Chaym is orphaned, destitute, and outcast. Although King is used to countering the arguments of opponents who question the validity of the principle of equality, he finds that all the "standard apothegms" that he would normally use to explain the existence of injustice are "suspended" by the "ineluctable presence of this man who could have been his brother" (45).

Chaym is not an abstract argument to be countered but the living presence of suffering. During the sleepless night that King spends after refusing to hire Chaym, King draws on the dual perspective of the transformed nonconformist to respond to the crisis of belief that Chaym's presence elicits. From the perspective of time, Chaym reveals to King in an irreducibly personal manner the reality of inequality and suffering. King reflects: "The idea of justice in his life and Chaym's was a joke. Not only was the distribution of wealth in society grossly uneven . . . but so was God-given talent. Beauty. Imagination. Luck. And the blessing of loving parents. They were the products of the arbitrariness of fortune. You could not say they were deserved" (47). Reasoning as a citizen of eternity, King is assured that Chaym has an inherent worth beyond the limitations of his present condition. Merging civic and spiritual ideals in a manner characteristic of the historical King, Citizen King recognizes that "in the realm of the spirit evoked by the Founders, in God, there were no defensible social distinctions, for all creatures, great and small, black and white, were isomers of the divine Person" (46). Or as the historical King writes, "Every human being has etched in his personality the indelible stamp of the Creator" (*Where* 97). When he first gazes into Chaym's face, King exclaims, "Sweet Jesus!" As Whalen-Bridge has beautifully elaborated, King's exclamation expresses both his surprise that Chaym is a dead ringer for himself and the recognition that Chaym also mirrors the divine presence ("Waking" 508).

In other words, Chaym functions as a *revelation* to King—a revelation of the lived reality of injustice, but also a revelation of the divine, which is not just transcendent but, through Chaym, *immanent*. Never simply material or transcendental, the perspective of dual citizenship shares something of the paradoxical qualities of the "concrete universal" discussed in chapter 2, qualities constituted through tensions between the historical and the suprahistorical, the concrete and the abstract, the personal and the social. As the omniscient narrator points out, King's position is that of a "tightrope walker straddling two worlds. One of matter. One of spirit" (18). King's response to Chaym's dual revelation illustrates the proper exercise of a committed citizenship. Although he initially rejects Chaym's proposal, after reflection King reconsiders, realizing that "they could share one another's fate. They could—and, in fact, should—rearrange the social world to redress the arbitrary whims of contingency, accident, and chance" (49–50). In other words, Chaym's "ineluctable presence" is a *call to action*—both to action that will aid Chaym as an individual and to actions that are designed to fulfill the committed citizen's obligation to work for justice in the national sphere.

It is also precisely from the unique existential standpoint of dual citizenship that King in *Dreamer* faces the growing challenges to his embattled leadership of the civil rights movement, as the narrative follows King from his difficult urban campaign in Chicago to his agonizing final march in Memphis. Influenced by David Garrow's Pulitzer Prize–winning history of King, *Bearing the Cross*, which Johnson cites in the preface to the novel, *Dreamer* is structured in part as "the passion of Martin Luther King Jr."[22] With reference to the central metaphor of Garrow's history of King and to King's own frequent discussions of the spiritual, personal, and social redemption that derives from bearing the cross, Johnson designs his novel to counter treatments of King's career that include less sympathetic assessments of his religious motivations, such as the one offered by William Jones. Significantly, King ends his sermon on the transformed nonconformist by comparing the willingness to act in history to the readiness to carry a cross. Exercising dual citizenship is demanding, King warns, precisely because it requires that one "take up the cross, with all its difficulties and agonizing and tragically-packed content, and carry it until that very cross leaves its marks upon us and redeems us" (14).

Through its presentation of the gathering forces arrayed against King, then, *Dreamer* powerfully dramatizes the "tragedy-packed content" of King's final days as he bears the cross of his civil rights leadership in Chicago,

Atlanta, and Memphis. In Chicago, King endures the personal taunts of racist whites and the ridicule of fellow blacks. He suffers the pain of watching his philosophy of nonviolence being rejected by former supporters, and he agonizes over his inability to redress quickly enough the plight of the poor who suffer in Chicago's slums. Stumbling to his knees after he is struck by a brick while marching from Gage Park to the Halvorsen real estate agency, King recalls the moment when Christ stumbles under the weight of his cross. In Atlanta another form of sacrifice is dramatized, as a poignant visit home clarifies the sacrifices that King's leadership has required in relation to the "roles he cherished the most," those of father and husband (187). As the increasing seriousness of the death threats he faces becomes apparent and King consequently feels the moment of his death drawing nearer, it is for his imperfections as a husband and father that he asks forgiveness. King's agonies, however, become most fully realized at his engagement in Memphis.

King undertakes the Memphis march for several reasons. First, the striking sanitation workers need a "nationally visible champion" to bring attention to their plight. Alluding to Marx, the narrative comments that the sanitation workers provide the "'socially necessary labor' without which the city would sink in its own sludge" (200). Like King in *Stride toward Freedom*, Johnson subverts the traditional usage of the terms "civilized" and "uncivilized" by pointing out that the suffering of the sanitation workers sustains the "so-called civilized life" of the wealthy (220). At the same time, King reasons that the plight of the sanitation workers will shine a national spotlight on the economic issues that he plans to address at the upcoming Poor People's March on Washington. Finally, as a campaign with identifiable goals, and as one in the southern territory with which he was more familiar, the protest is one that King hopes will achieve a much-needed victory for nonviolence. He decides to join the March 28, 1968, march, knowing, then, that in "Memphis nonviolence was being tested—he was on trial" (224).

Rather than a victory, however, King suffers a crushing defeat as the protest disintegrates into violence shortly after it begins. (Historically the Memphis demonstration is notable as the only protest march that King had to leave because of violence.) Two weeks before, on an earlier visit to Memphis, Citizen King had mused that the garden outside his hotel window reminded him of the "Garden of Gethsemane" (217). If Memphis serves as King's Gethsemane in *Dreamer*, it is Black Power that plays the role of Judas, cast as the disruptive force that causes the march to degenerate into rioting. By the time King arrives late in Memphis because of a delayed flight, the march is already under way. Disturbed by the organization of the protest, he observes that the crowd resembles a "mob" more than a disciplined "line of protestors" and notes with some uneasiness placards in the crowd reading "Black Power is Here" (221, 222). While King states that he will not lead "a violent march," before he has advanced three blocks, rioting breaks out. The Memphis march has become "a bona fide catastrophe, one with his name attached to it" (215, 216).

The protest in fact results in the death of a sixteen-year-old black boy. Immediately after the Memphis disaster King sinks into a depression that is partly caused by a feeling of responsibility for the boy's death. Memphis has made clear to King the "perennial dilemma of his public ministry, how to end evil without creating evil" (224). His depression takes a racialized form in *Dreamer*, since he momentarily loses faith in the ability of nonviolence to heal the breach of racial division. As Citizen King confides to his colleague Ralph Abernathy, "If we believe in peace, maybe we should get out of the way and let the separatists and segregationists, the Invaders and racists, black anti-Semites and Klansmen, go at each other in a full-scale war" (223). But he is able to overcome his cynicism by deploying the logic of dual citizenship. Realizing that "no piety from the scriptures could ever justify the fact that the world's suffering poor in the modern era were predominantly black and brown, women and children" (218), King decides to act. "Men of conviction were required to act," King concludes, "though always on the basis of partial information, blindly forging ahead and hoping for the best. The word for this from time immemorial, he knew, was faith" (223). Characteristically, King's definition of faith demonstrates a dedication to both ideal and practice. Battling through his despair, King decides to rejoin the protest the following week to demonstrate that he can lead a truly nonviolent march, a decision that leads to his tragic appointment with destiny. The historical King gave his last public appearance in Memphis on April 3, 1968, at the Mason Temple (see figure 5), and on the following day was assassinated.

Although the focus here is on the transformed nonconformist as an analytical lens for examining the representation of King's legacy in *Dreamer*, the model of citizenship the figure represents also helps to illuminate the characters of Chaym and Matthew. At the beginning of the novel Chaym represents a particular form of nonconformity—the nonconformist as outcast rather than as citizen. After King agrees to hire Chaym as his double, Chaym, Matthew, and Amy Griffiths (a young woman volunteer in the Coordinate Council of Community Organizations to whom Matthew is attracted) set out for an isolated farmhouse near Makanda in southern Illinois, owned by Amy's grandmother, which they refer to as "the Nest." While Matthew and Amy begin to train Chaym to act, speak, and dress like King, however, Chaym sets out to convert Matthew to his own philosophy of "second-class citizenship" (67), as opposed to King's conception of transformed citizenship.

Recognizing Matthew as a fellow orphan (because he was also abandoned by his father), Chaym instructs Matthew: "We're outcasts. And outcasts can't

*5. Martin Luther King Jr. at his last public appearance, Memphis, April 3, 1968.*
AP Images/Charles Kelly.

ever create community" (65). Because he ascertains in the standpoint of outcast a certain epistemological and psychological power, Chaym urges Matthew to adopt his own alienated position: "I've been on the outside long enough to know that hatred is healthy—even holy—and that until you step away, or they cast you out, you can't see nothin' clearly" (66). Shaped partly by his own tragic destiny, partly by his envy of King's accomplishments, and partly by a legitimate critique of conformists who practice a stultifying form of "group think," Chaym's estranged epistemological position is designed to reflect both the potential and the danger inherent in the nonconformist's stance. Extolling the merits of nonconformity, Chaym commends it to Matthew as a "blessing" and a necessity, if you have any creative spark at all" (66). Chaym's critique of the "obedient, psalms-singing herd" and of "Christians, Communists, and Cultural Nationalists" disturbs Matthew, but at the same time it reminds him of a sermon in which King rails against the "mass mind"—the sermon called "Transformed Nonconformist" (67).

While Chaym's alienated position offers the distance required for him to critique a complacent conformity, his nonconformity tends toward the self-indulgent form of which King's sermon warns. Specifically, Chaym lacks a stabilizing transformation and thus an inspirited commitment to a historical project. If the potential for identities to be disrupted and transformed is a vital component of the logic of conversion, that logic also suggests that identities can become stabilized: the insights gained, convictions achieved, or projects chosen can be so profound in their effects that they continue to influence identity over time. In other words, the logic of conversion, as David Leighty states in *Circuitous Journeys: Modern Spiritual Autobiographies*, "provides an anchor for intelligibility" (10). Chaym is described by Matthew as a "constantly mutating soul," and accordingly his nonconformity tends toward changeability rather than commitment, as is dramatized when Amy gives Chaym an SCLC commitment blank to sign when they arrive at the Nest. Rather than signing the pledge, he takes the form to the outhouse to use as toilet paper, "emptying his bowels loudly, with trumpeting flatulence" as he "rail[s] against conformity and convention" (93). As Chaym's confusion of scatology and eschatology emphatically suggests, his practice of nonconformity inclines toward exhibitionism.

Despite a jealousy of King that is intensified by a physical resemblance that serves only to accentuate their differences in ability and fortune, however, Chaym is perceptive enough to recognize something uniquely valuable in King's leadership. Contrasting King to those who practice "group think," Chaym tells Matthew, "There's not a real individual in the bunch . . . nobody who . . . bear[s] the cross of a unique, singular individuality . . . except for him" (67). Chaym thus demonstrates a nascent recognition of the paradoxical position of dual citizenship in which leadership is exercised through service to others and freedom is realized in the vigorous taking up of one's fate. As suggested earlier, the "metaphoric logic" of dual citizenship requires the ability to hold two different interpretations simultaneously. As King says in *Strength to Love*, "The strong man holds in a living blend strongly marked opposites" (136). Practicing the perspective of dual citizenship on his airplane flight, King recognizes that in every position there is something of its opposite: "in fame the fear of humiliation, in strength the fear of enemies, in social stature the fear of slander" (82). Such a paradoxical perspective shapes the historical King's understanding of freedom as a form of "finite freedom," or a freedom that is realized within limitations. In suggesting that King had to make a "choice to be chosen" to dedicate himself to his leadership role, Richard H. King identifies a similar paradox at the center of King's leadership (131). The "singular individuality" that Chaym recognizes in King is thus paradoxically realized when King *chooses* his fate and takes up the burden of his civil rights leadership.

The concept of transformed nonconformity also informs the narrative's appropriation of the biblical tale of Cain and Abel. On one level King clearly represents Abel and Chaym, as his name suggests, Cain. But as Matthew points out, King is also a "rebel Messiah, the almost paradoxical fusion of Cain and Abel" (125). As critics have noted, various characters in the novel represent different mixtures of Cain and Abel.[23] What is important here is that the categories of Cain and Abel themselves should also be understood, paradoxically, to include qualities of each other. That is, it is not simply that being an Abel is constructive while being a Cain is destructive, for the position of the Abelite can tend toward a passive conformity, while the practice of the Cainite can provide an epistemological independence, as King's sermon on the transformed nonconformist suggests. Paradoxically, each position, Cainite or Abelite, requires some of the other in order for it to realize its fullest potential in the transformed nonconformist. Indeed, part of Chaym's problems stem from the fact that he erroneously *reifies* the categories of Cain and Abel. In describing the advantages of the outcast's perspective, Chaym demands of Matthew, "You ever thought we might be second-class citizens because we *are* second-rate?" (65). Adopting the explanation for the oppression of black people advanced by some white racists, Chaym attributes the cause of his own misfortunes to the mark of Cain: "We are, as a tribe, descended from the first of two brothers whose best just couldn't hack it. . . . We got the stain, the mark. Nothing else really explains our situation" (66). In other words, Chaym refuses to historicize his own situation, accepting his outcast position as a fait accompli rather than assuming the obligation of acting historically. While recognizing that King is different from others, Chaym does not at first comprehend the paradoxical position of finite freedom. The members of the congregation at Calvary AME Church who were themselves "initially outcasts" successfully migrated to the Chicago area and built a community (125). Furthermore, as Matthew notes, King's father once described their family as descended from "nowhere" (63). Over time, however, that family has been able to produce a King. Rather than acting on the historical possibilities in his own situation, Chaym essentializes the categories of Cain and Abel, partly to avoid the obligations that dual citizenship entails.

Although Matthew serves in King's army, he represents the dangers of a reserved conformity at the beginning of the novel. Attracted to both King and Chaym, Matthew in fact requires the tutelage of both to reach his full potential as a transformed nonconformist.[24] Describing himself as a "shy, Victorian personality," Matthew characteristically goes to "great lengths not to call unnecessary attention to [him]self" (164, 25). While such circumspection might be judged to be an admirable alternative to Chaym's exhibitionism, Matthew's reticence also betrays an insecurity that leads him to retreat to positions of relative safety. Furthermore, Matthew's admiration for King's talents cause him further to discount his own abilities as a "nobody" in the movement, "merely a face in the undifferentiated mass of Movement people who dutifully did what our leaders asked . . . replaceable like . . . placards"

(26). Matthew's comments reveal that he subscribes to a top-down understanding of leadership that serves, like Chaym's reified categories, in part as a rationalization to diminish his own obligations. Like King, Matthew is an idealist who is not satisfied with the world as it is, but his idealism tends toward reflection rather than action, toward "Socratic doubts, interiority, and always having an afterthought" (109). In other words, Matthew's idealism runs the danger of devolving into a mere formalism, like the slogans written on placards, or like the Bible which he continues to carry even though he can no longer "breathe life" into its system of meaning (54).

Through his relationships with both King and Chaym, Matthew begins to develop more fully the dual characteristics of transformed nonconformity that are latent in his personality. Coming into Chaym's "orbit," Matthew discovers that the possibility of seeing from Chaym's perspective—"the oblique angle of alienation"—is both "fascinat[ing] and frighten[ing] . . . at the same time" (164, 85). Chaym's influence is both potentially liberatory and potentially dangerous. On the one hand, Chaym's instruction leads Matthew to question the virtues of "group think," a lesson that Matthew effectively applies when he visits the Black People's Liberation Library, where he echoes Chaym's arguments about "kitsch" in criticizing the library's founder, Yahya Zubena. On the other hand, Chaym's philosophy of second-class citizenship can be as detrimental to effective action as Matthew's reticence. Rather than being challenged further to transform himself, under Chaym's influence Matthew becomes more "comfortable" with the "sad inevitability of [him]self" (109). At the outset of the narrative, then, Matthew needs instruction from Chaym in nonconformity and instruction from King in order to achieve a *transformed* nonconformity.

Matthew's development is captured in the novel in two separate scenes. In both he attempts to "reason vertically" by praying to God. The first scene dramatizes the moment when Matthew loses his faith. Having prayed desperately for his mother's life as she lay dying, Matthew concludes after she dies that the "offering" of his prayers has been rejected, as Cain's offering was rejected by God. King addresses the difference between effective and ineffective prayer in a sermon suggestively titled "God Is Able," where he argues dialectically that "the belief that God will do everything for man is as untenable as the belief that man will do everything for himself" (123). Instead, God is able *because* he works through history and through humankind to achieve his ends. To expect God to do everything, King asserts, is not "faith, but superstition" (123). Similarly, Matthew previously has demonstrated a top-down understanding of leadership and a willingness simply to follow.

Expecting God to save his mother miraculously, Matthew interprets her death as a sign of his own unworthiness. Rather than indicating a concern for personal purity, however, King's sermon suggests that it would be more appropriate for Matthew to ask in his prayers how God might work histor-ically *through* him. This is precisely the stance that Matthew adopts in Reverend Littlewood's church at the end of the novel, when he prays, "*Thy will be done*" (214). As Gary Storhoff has explained, two paintings hang in Littlewood's church, one illustrating the Garden of Gethsemane, the other de-picting Simon the Cyrene, an African, carrying Christ's cross (*Understanding* 214). By reflecting on Simon, Matthew is able to revise his understanding of the relationship between the exalted (Christ and King) and the outcast (Simon the Cyrene, Chaym, and Matthew himself): "I felt I knew him. Was him. No man could equal the Nazarene. But Simon? I was thinking that here was a black man I might measure myself against, a standard I could attain" (212). As a "black man from the most despised tribe on earth" who was "given the priceless gift of easing the suffering of a savior," Simon the Cyrene models for Matthew the possibilities that reside in a finite freedom that is achieved by taking up one's cross (212).

## Critiquing Black Nationalism

Dual citizenship also provides a standard that explains *Dreamer*'s extrava-gant critique of black nationalism and Black Power. If the transformed non-conformist undergoes a transformation that enables him to reason vertically and act historically, *Dreamer* suggests that black separatists undergo a *false* conversion that leads them to reason poorly and engage history ineffectively. While a critique of various forms of black separatism appears throughout the novel, the distinction between black nationalism and the dual citizenship proposed by a transformed nonconformity is developed most comprehen-sively in chapter 9, when Matthew and Amy visit the Black People's Libera-tion Library in Chicago. The practice of establishing alternative libraries for black and white people began before the Civil War, when education was systematically denied to black Americans. Frederick Douglass, for example, helped to establish a library above the press that published his newspaper, the *North Star*, a library that Harriet Jacobs used to expand her education after her own escape from slavery. As Nash points out, the Black People's Libera-tion Library in *Dreamer* is based on the Black People's Topographical Insti-tute, a headquarters for revolutionary thought established in Chicago in the 1960s (*Charles* 186). Unlike Douglass's antislavery reading room, the Black People's Revolutionary Library in *Dreamer* is a separatist institution, and it functions in the narrative specifically as a metaphorical archive for black nationalist thought.

At the library, Matthew and Amy meet Yahya Zubena, the ex-convict who established the library and who functions as a composite of several different Black Power and black nationalist leaders. Like Eldridge Cleaver, Yahya

admits to having raped black women "as practice" for raping white women
(171); like Leonard Jeffries, he espouses a theory of whites as "ice people"
and blacks as "sun people" (173); like Mulana Karenga (whom he also resembles physically), he espouses cultural nationalism; and like Amiri Baraka,
he composes liberation verse.[25] Significantly, Yahya also functions in the narrative as an "apostate" who has experienced a false conversion: while in
prison for a series of crimes that include the brutal murder of a black gas
station attendant, he was reborn by being "baptized in blackness" (168).
Johnson here signifies on the jailhouse conversions of figures such as Eldridge
Cleaver. It is important to note that rather than enabling him to "reason vertically," however, Yahya's conversion leads him to adopt a faulty method of
reasoning: as Matthew observes, "The way he reasoned, with racial politics
as every syllogism's major premise, led all his thoughts to the same termi-
nus" (174). Because Yahya does not reason well, the episode suggests, he fails
as a historian, producing a analysis that is "one-dimensional" rather than
one that exhibits the twin dimensions of dual citizenship (173).

Johnson's belief that black separatists produce a distorted record of history is illustrated at several points in *Dreamer*—from the interjection of
Elijah Mohammed's history of the creation of the white race by an evil sci-
entist, to Floyd McKissick's announcement after King's assassination that
"nonviolence is a dead philosophy" (226), to Jeffries's anthropological arguments about "ice people" and "sun people" which Yahya purports to find
"in the history books" (173). When Amy attempts to complicate Yahya's history by mentioning the whites who "risked their lives" on the Freedom Rides
and pointing to the deaths of Andrew Goodman and Michael Schwerner
(murdered with black civil rights activist James Chaney in Mississippi on
June 21, 1964), Yahya derides her racial authenticity, identifying her and
Matthew—supporters of King and adherents of integration—as "house
niggers" and "Uncle Tom Nigguhs" (173, 175). Wearing a dashiki in the
colors of Marcus Garvey's red, black, and green flag, Yahya suggests that it
is to Africa rather than to America that black Americans owe their allegiance
as citizens (a position that, as we saw in chapter 4, is rejected in *Middle
Passage*).

In *Dreamer*, Johnson deploys Yahya's one-dimensional interpretation of
history to critique nationalist models of citizenship and nation. In an essay
titled "Black Power," the historical King criticizes the concept of a separate
black nation within the United States. "Few ideas," King writes, "are more
unrealistic" (48). Yahya's lecture on nation in *Dreamer* is in fact drawn from
fiction—the "King Alfred Plan" developed in John A. Williams's novel *The
Man Who Cried I Am*.[26] Serving as a separatist representation of nation, the
walls of the inner room from which Yahya lectures are covered with "huge
colored maps of every major city in America" (170). These are designed to

illustrate Yahya's thesis, drawn from the King Alfred Plan, that blacks have been strategically placed in commercial areas so that "tanks and trucks and the National Guard troops" will easily be able to round them up when they revolt (172). According to Herb Boyd in "The Plan and the Man: Conspiracy Theories and Paranoia in Our Culture," Williams took sections of his novel, which describes an international conspiracy to exterminate black people, and distributed copies in subway trains across Manhattan in order to promote the book. "The ploy worked so well," notes Boyd, "that soon after, black folks all over New York City were talking about 'the plan,' a fictitious plot that many thought was true" (38). Because of his reliance on fiction as history, the novel suggests, Yahya is not able to attack as effectively as King the real causes of segregation. The model of conversion that Yahya preaches, reflected in the title of his most popular poem, "Nigger, Nigger, Wake Up!," is one mistakenly based on the reality of the King Alfred Plan conspiracy and "the necessity of revolutionary violence" (173). Rather than being the leader of a revolutionary future, Yahya actually belongs to the "frail, false confederacy" described elsewhere in the novel, a coalition opposed to King and one whose understanding of history will not survive the test of time. Black Power and black separatists' most serious misreading of history, *Dreamer* repeatedly implies, is their failure to understand the principles and practice of King's leadership.

Lecturing from his hidden headquarters behind the Black People's Liberation Library where he tries to enlist recruits, Yahya functions as a counterfeit commander who battles a fictive conspiracy, unlike Citizen King, a true "civil" war general who courageously directs his troops in the face of real threats and actual conspiracies against his life. Like the false nonconformity that King warns against in "Transformed Nonconformist," Yahya's revolutionary stance is presented as a form of exhibitionism. As Matthew observes, Yahya is "one of the darlings of the white media," and his headquarters is as "flimsy as constructions of pasteboard and papier-mâché" (171). Behind the false front of the library, Yahya exercises a form of "group think" that offers a false nonconformity and an ineffectual citizenship. From false front to faulty logic to fictitious conspiracy, the Black People's Liberation Library seeks not to liberate Matthew and Amy but to lock them into flawed forms of reasoning—as Yahya locks Matthew and Amy into his hidden headquarters before beginning his lecture.

Significantly, the education offered at the Black People's Liberation Library also contrasts to the one provided by black churches in Johnson's narrative. The congregants of the Calvary AME in Evanston, for example, pool their resources to send students to "Morehouse and Fisk" (134). The novel's juxtaposition of the schooling provided by the black church community with that offered by the Black People's Liberation Library resonates with

Cornel West's charge in "The Paradox of the African American Rebellion" that Black Power failed to maintain an organic relationship with the organizational, intellectual, and social traditions of the black church (286). Similarly, in *Dreamer*, the Black People's Liberation Library appears as a threat to the social gospel tradition of education that produces Citizen Kings. In southern Illinois, Reverend Littlewood's library and the classrooms at Bethel AME are unfinished, the novel suggests, partly because their congregations dwindled "after the rise of Black Power" (156). Through his depiction of the Black People's Liberation Library, Johnson offers his strongest condemnation of Black Power and black separatism to date, building on the analysis he presented earlier in "The King We Left Behind." As his commitment to Buddhism deepened in the 1980s and his immersion in King's writings in the 1990s intensified his commitment to nonviolence, Johnson's criticism of Black Power and black separatism became more bold, if often monolithic in its failure to draw distinctions among the various tactics and philosophies advocated by different Black Power and black nationalist leaders. With his portrait of Yahya and the Black People's Liberation Library in *Dreamer*, Johnson's novel draws its own metaphorical line in the sand.

## *The Analogical Structure of* Dreamer

A conversion in Chaym's character begins to take place while he is in training at the Nest to stand in as King's double. As part of his preparation, Matthew instructs Chaym in the "broad themes and tropes in the minister's speeches," and specifically in "the four levels of meaning in the Bible (literal, allegorical, tropological, and anagogic)" (105). In other words, part of Chaym's preparation take the form of exercises in the "vertical reasoning" of dual citizenship. Analogous to the composition of place that begins King's meditative reflections on his airplane trip, Chaym's training involves the use of photographs of places and people important in King's life, which Chaym studies as "monks do with mandalas" (105). In particular, Chaym works to bring the photographs to life by placing himself in the photos and by filling their forms with his own emotions, as he does when he examines photographs of King's birthplace at 501 Auburn Avenue in Atlanta: "With th[e] pictures spread out before him on the farmhouse floor, he imaginatively climbed the four steps to the door and worked to *feel* everything in the images, bringing forth an emotional association for the umbrella box, high-backed chair, and table with a bouquet of flowers in the entryway" (105). By inspiriting the stiff paper forms of the photographs, Chaym enters King's world—and perhaps replicates Johnson's own meditative practice.

Significantly, Chaym's exercises lead him to develop a new sense of history that enables him to revise his essentialist conception of the classes of Cainites and Abelites. As he imaginatively relives life in the King household and feels, for example, "the height of the second-floor ceiling which Daddy King, who was only five-six, touched with his fingertips when he learned of Martin's birth and literally jumped for joy" (106), Chaym begins to understand in more depth the factors that have contributed to their respective fortunes. That night his dreams are peopled with King's family members, "loving folks such as Smith himself had never known" (107). By reliving history, or rather by enlivening the material traces of history with his own spiritual, intellectual, and emotional resources, Chaym practices a nascent form of vertical reasoning. He also begins to historicize his own situation, to revise his understanding of the categories of Cain and Abel, and to evaluate critically the shortcomings of the epistemological perspective of outcast. As Chaym tells Matthew, "I woulda given anything for a loving, decent childhood like that. . . . Bishop, it ain't right not having anybody who cared" (107).

In *Mystery and Manners* Flannery O'Connor writes that "the kind of vision the fiction writer needs to have, or to develop, in order to increase the meaning of his story is called anagogical vision, and that is the kind of vision that is able to see different levels of reality in one image or one situation" (72). It is important to note that Matthew's exercises for Chaym are similar in structure to those that Johnson creates for his reader, as is seen in chapter 4 of *Dreamer*, which invite the reader to participate in King's meditative reflections in flight, or in chapter 10, which invites readers to participate imaginatively in King's home life before he leaves for Memphis, as he "wrest[les] with his children" on the living room floor with "the rugs rolled back into a corner and furniture pushed to one side" (186). Reasoning vertically can also be understood, then, as a metafictional trope for the processes of writing and reading themselves, or for the incarnation required to bring black marks on the page to life through acts of interpretation and identification. Finally, it is also a trope for a way of understanding history, as Johnson says, as "imagination." Elaborating on Aristotle's claim that "poetry is truer than history," John Dewey argues that history "only tells us that certain things happened," while literature "presents to us the permanent passions, aspirations, and deeds of men which are behind all history, and which make it" (*Early* 172). This is precisely the "truer" form of history that Johnson attempts to provide for King's legacy in *Dreamer*, a uniquely creative contribution to the recovery project of his generation.

From larger thematic and organizational structures to smaller elements of language use, Johnson's narrative technique in *Dreamer* is in fact designed carefully to evoke the paradoxical perspective of dual citizenship. The juxtaposition of different levels of meaning is one effect of the novel's doubling of narrative structures, including its two alternating narrators. While Matthew's narrative functions to "record" or "chronicle" the history of the movement, the omniscient narrator more consistently presents the same history in mythological and prophetic terms, or as "gospel," a narrative juxtaposition that itself recreates the standpoints of time and eternity. Other structures, such as the explicitly meditative patterns through which some scenes deliberately unfold, also exhibit a similar architecture. Narrative evocations of the metafictional practices of interpretation, the Buddhist conception of interbeing, or the Christian understanding of incarnation also evoke this dual standpoint. *Dreamer* has a highly articulated analogical structure.

One distinctive feature of Johnson's narrative technique is the multilevel development of tropes in the novel, such as those of the theater, architecture, war, marks, and the Cain and Abel myth. Over the course of the novel these tropes form and transform in a dialectical interplay to reinforce the emphasis on the need for both change and stability, nonconformity and commitment. The trope of the theater, for example, functions at times to capture nonconformity's negative potential for exhibitionism, as is seen periodically through the character of Chaym. The trope plays a similar role in the depiction of Jesse Jackson's apparently self-serving actions after King's assassination, described as an "act of theatre and falsity . . . [that] would define the spirit of the black struggle for decades after the minister's demise" (233). The period of the 1960s is itself described in similarly critical terms as "the first truly *theatrical* decade. A moment when role-playing and how things appeared took primacy over reality" (164). But as the trope of theater transforms and transmutes in the novel, it also conveys the possibilities for achieving a transformative stability. By playing the role of King, Chaym begins a process of conversion. Roles also function as stabilizing structures that preserve meaning, as is seen in the respective roles of student and priest, "thousands of years old," in which Chaym participates at the *zendo* in Korea (97). The potential for roles to function as stabilizing structures is dramatized most forcefully in the novel through King's acceptance of his public roles of black Moses, black Buddha, and Black Messiah, and in its most exalted form, in his willingness to "bear the cross." Through King's various speaking engagements, the stage itself becomes a site where the paradoxical standpoint of the transformed nonconformist is enacted. As Matthew says, in King "man and mask were fused" (138). Unlike Chaym, King has found the conviction that provides stability to his identity over time. Johnson's unusual elaboration of tropes in *Dreamer*, through which he captures brilliantly an unfolding interplay between change and stability, is one of the novel's most distinctive narrative features.

Chaym undergoes a more substantive conversion when, substituting for King, he is mistakenly shot by a disturbed elderly black man. By taking the bullet for King, Chaym begins to share King's fate and becomes, like Matthew, a type of Simon the Cyrene. His long convalescence at the Nest provides a refuge from "the social crises and catastrophes" of Chicago, a temporary respite that enables Chaym to heal (154). His recovery is signaled and strengthened by his serving as a carpenter and gardener for Reverend Littlewood's Bethel AME church. Always "under construction," the church is a stabilizing structure that is nonetheless itself in process. Since each generation acts to finish the work of its "predecessor," the church represents a gradualist form of constructive action (155).[27] By working to repair the church, then, Chaym gains practice in building structures that help to stabilize value. Matthew says of the church in Evanston, "So much of value was preserved, meaning made manifest in the minutest details by black people who came to this place" (133). As he labors on the church, Chaym brings to mind both Matthew's statement and Johnson's analysis of productive labor in *Faith*. Simultaneously, Chaym's own physical and spiritual architecture undergoes renovation. Most significantly, as he adds his labor to the work of generations of black families who lie buried in the cemetery plot that he helps to clear of weeds, Chaym begins to act constructively while he establishes through his labor ties to a lineage *other* than Cain's.

Chaym's ultimate fate in the novel remains unknown. Blackmailed by two federal agents who have the Nest under surveillance for much of the novel, he goes with the "Wise Guys" under the threat of being jailed. It is clear that the agents intend to use his resemblance to King to ruin the minister's reputation and to damage his leadership, but Chaym's moral culpability in going with them is left unclear. Chaym explains to Matthew that he doesn't "have much choice"; he has to go, since he could not stand to be jailed (213). Yet he hands Matthew a signed commitment blank before he leaves, suggesting that he will resist the agents' designs. Whether Chaym participates in a plot against King or whether he himself is a victim of the agents is uncertain, and it is only after his disappearance that Matthew realizes the danger that Chaym himself may be in: if King is assassinated, Matthew reasons, the existence of a double becomes a liability, putting Chaym's life in danger. Chaym's decision to leave with the agents has been the subject of considerable critical debate. Nash finds his signing of the commitment blank "specious at best" and entertains the possibility that Chaym's action contributes "to the minister's doom" (*Charles* 176). Whalen-Bridge suggests that Chaym's "*struggle* for the good" and King's "*achievement* of the good" are both admirable ("Waking" 515). To Bryd Chaym becomes the novel's central figure of transformation, "underg[oing] a marked alteration in his consciousness" (185). In his "Qualifying Exam in Systematic Theology," the historical King stated that "no one is ever converted *all at once*" (231). This observation is borne out in Chaym's character: his conversion progresses in stages in the novel as he begins to think vertically, to share King's fate, to historicize his own position, and to undertake constructive action. That conversion is cut short, however, before Chaym can obtain the stabilizing commitment and comprehensive social vision characteristic of dual citizenship (143).

Such a comprehensive vision, however, is precisely what Johnson achieves in his presentation of King as part Black Messiah, part black Buddha, and part "civil war" leader. By creating narrative structures equal to the difficult task of representing King's complex fusion of personal conversion and civic activism, Johnson offers his most compelling contribution to the contemporary debate over the significance of King's legacy. By revising "unconditional surrender Grant" to "total surrender" King (111), Johnson delineates a new kind of national leader, the transformed nonconformist, whose ability to reason vertically and to act historically melds inner transformation to outer engagement. Johnson's complex depiction of King fuses the material and imaginative realms that were divided in *Faith and the Good Thing*, reclaims an emphasis on direct civic engagement that was missing in *Oxherding Tale*, and deepens the analysis of the national sphere that is introduced in *Middle Passage*. By returning to King—by considering his philosophical ideas, spiritual practice, and public leadership; by entering a larger debate about King's legacy to the nation; and by applying the lessons he gathered from King to current events—Johnson discovers a unifying focus for his multiple intellectual and cultural commitments. And in *Dreamer* Johnson offers King's legacy to his readers as an unsurpassed regulative ideal for the nation's unrealized future.

Johnson's representation of King as a national leader in *Dreamer* completes an intellectual and aesthetic journey that he began as an undergraduate student studying philosophy in the 1960s. As I argue in chapter 1, Johnson's fiction makes an important contribution to the larger efforts of black philosophers to bring a new social and phenomenological immediacy to the traditional practice of Western philosophy. Johnson began the study of philosophy at a pivotal moment in the history of the nation's university system and at time of crisis for blacks in the discipline. In response to the academy's entrenched practice of analytic philosophy, he committed himself to a more capacious philosophical and creative project: the writing of "philosophical fiction." Over a long writing career Johnson has maintained his early faith in the revitalizing and clarifying power of art, a faith for which he first found philosophical validation in the neo-Marxist argument that the critical function of literature rests in its ability to construct alternatives to an imperfect reality, a position that anticipates his interest in phenomenological variation. Johnson's narrative strategy of connecting art to social action through a neo-Marxist paradigm in *Faith and the Good Thing*, however, generates a tension in his first novel between a realm of imaginative freedom and one under the sway of a strict economic determinism.

In his next novel, *Oxherding Tale*, Johnson structured his narrative according to a particular Buddhist understanding of personal enlightenment and civic engagement that reflected his growing interest in Buddhist thinking and practice. Written at a time when he was immersing himself in Eastern thought but before he began, with other black Buddhists, to interpret Buddhism more consistently through the lens of the civil rights movement and thereby to revise an ancient inheritance from an explicitly African American location, *Oxherding Tale* gains its conceptual structure from traditional Mahayana Buddhism, a school that tends to advocate for social action in the form of personal altruism rather than collective activism. Because of the particular point in Johnson's development as a Buddhist at which it was written, *Oxherding Tale* is the novel in which the dramatic tension between a personal and a collective understanding of social engagement is most striking. Most important, as I show in chapter 3, in order to assimilate Mahayana thought into the slave narrative genre, Johnson displaces the national realm of civic engagement from his own narrative. His first two experiments in enunciating a comprehensive account of the relationship between personal transformation and social action thus do not incorporate national forms of action or belonging. But the striking ideological tensions and narrative disruptions apparent in his first two novels prove constructive: they stimulate Johnson's thinking and lead to the expansion of his art.

Joining with other "new" black intellectuals in an effort to rethink cosmopolitanism in ways that make it more responsive to the claims of the particular and the local, however, Johnson recuperates the arena of national concern in his third novel, *Middle Passage*. By placing into contention characters who represent different forms of cosmopolitan thought, he dramatically tests the assumptions that undergird *multiple* cosmopolitan positions. Although cosmopolitanism is often defined in opposition to local or national bonds, public intellectuals have recently attempted to reclaim the normative power of universals while maintaining a respect for cultural and local specificity. In *Middle Passage*, Rutherford Calhoun is able to reestablish his bonds to familial ancestral, and national traditions precisely by acting on his newly achieved cosmopolitan education. Contributing to a larger cultural debate about the dangers and democratic potential of cosmopolitanism, Johnson moves in his novel toward an ethic that recognizes the importance of action guided by both universal norms and local allegiances, including especially those of family and nation. Finally, Johnson's participation in the renewed cultural debate over Martin Luther King's legacy provokes his deepest deliberations about how value is tested and amplified in the civic sphere. By confronting questions over the nature of King's legacy to the nation, Johnson discovers a unifying focal point for his evolving intellectual and spiritual interests.

In assessing the status of African American literature in "Black American Literature at Year 2000," Robert B. Stepto identifies Johnson as a leading figure in a generation of writers who, by the turn of the millennium, had elevated African American literature to a new position of national prominence. While offering a strikingly original synthesis of literature, philosophy, and Buddhism, Johnson's creative work also vigorously participates in, advances, and helps to define larger directions in American intellectual and cultural life. In his fiction and prose Johnson joins with other philosophers who have been working since the 1960s to open academic philosophy to new forms of intellectual inquiry and narrative vitality, with Buddhists who are interpreting anew an ancient religious tradition, and with intellectuals who are currently articulating a reformed cosmopolitan ethic. Johnson's fiction is both aesthetically compelling and culturally important. His creative work provides insight into a period in the nation's history when black Americans set off in exciting new directions and encountered fresh opportunities and challenges: they enjoyed increased participation in American institutions, including universities, but labored to change the terms of that participation; they joined in an exciting global exchange of ideas but worked to translate those ideas into an African American idiom; they commanded in growing numbers the national stage but had to navigate a radically altered public sphere. Illuminating the paths taken by many who set off in new directions in the 1960s, Johnson's fiction simultaneously traces his own intellectual and aesthetic journey as black philosopher, Buddhist, and public intellectual.

# NOTES

## 1. From Philosophy to Black Philosophical Fiction

1. Somewhat like the fictional Andrew, Johnson has also received the attention of accomplished artisans in the tradition of Reb—critics who over the course of the last several years have worked to delineate the distinctive features of his fiction. Since Little's study *Charles Johnson's Spiritual Imagination* was published in 1997, three other book-length studies of Johnson's fiction have appeared: Nash's important *Charles Johnson's Fiction* (2003); Storhoff's insightful analysis focused primarily on the Eastern religious ideas in Johnson's work, *Understanding Charles Johnson* (2004); and Byrd's wide-ranging elaboration of the intertextual character of Johnson's novels, *Charles Johnson's Novels: Writing the American Palimpsest* (2005). Scholars of Johnson's fiction also benefit from three edited collections of Johnson materials: Byrd's collection of materials written by or about Johnson, *I Call Myself an Artist* (1999); McWilliams's compilation of interviews with Johnson, *Passing the Three Gates* (2004); and Conner and Nash's collection of scholarly essays, *Charles Johnson: The Novelist as Philosopher* (2007). In addition, in 1996 Boccia and Beavers edited a special edition of the *African American Review* focused on Johnson's work. My thinking on Johnson has been influenced by all of these scholars and by important single articles or book chapters on Johnson's work, especially those by Rushdy, Gleason, and Whalen-Bridge.

2. One uses the adjective "black" before an analysis of Johnson's work with some apprehension. As an intellectual who freely claims the cultural production of all those who have come before him as his rightful heritage, as a writer who argues for an expansive understanding of literary tradition based on "whole sight," as a Buddhist who is suspicious of conceptual abstractions, and as a phenomenologist who attempts to strip away calcified modes of vision, Johnson is a thinker for whom race is a problematic category. Yet from his early essay on phenomenology and the black body, to his book *Being and Race*, to his numerous short stories and four novels, to his more recent essays on the deteriorating situation of many black Americans in twenty-first-century America, Johnson has consistently used fiction, Buddhist reflection, and philosophical acumen to investigate the lived experience of black Americans. As genetic phenomenology emphasizes, perception is not a "view from nowhere" but a view from a particular location with its own distinctive genealogy. It is therefore with trepidation but also with conviction that I relate Johnson's fiction to these broader cultural projects of black Americans.

3. I do not mean to suggest that Johnson's work has not received careful analysis, particularly in relation to *literary* history. In regard to cultural history, however,

Johnson's work has been analyzed most extensively in relation to the Black Power and Black Arts movements. For a complex analysis of that relationship, see especially Rushdy (*Neo-Slave*). For a discussion of Johnson's critique of the black cultural nationalists' intellectual and aesthetic positions through his cartoons and through specific characters in his fiction, including George Hawkins in *Oxherding Tale*, Diamelo in *Middle Passage*, and Yahya Zubena in *Dreamer*, see especially Little (*Charles*) and Nash (*Charles*). A collection of essays by Conner and Nash develops positions more closely related to the cultural analysis I attempt here. See Gleason's "Go There" for an essay on critical pragmatism that is richly situated in relation to the tradition of Jamesian pragmatic pluralism, and Nash's "Application" for an essay that interprets *Turning the Wheel* in relation to Johnson's goals as an African American Buddhist seeker. Finally, see Byrd's analysis of the political context for King's Chicago campaign in *Charles*.

4. Citations to this collection of seventeen interviews with black philosophers are indicated by interviewer George Yancy's last name, short title, and page number in parenthesis.

5. Both Johnson's autobiographical "I Call Myself an Artist" and his "Northwestern Acceptance Speech" can be found in Byrd's *I Call*. Johnson also contributed an essay to the *Contemporary Authors: Autobiography* series. The interviews collected by McWilliams — the first from 1978 and the last from 2003 — are also important sources of information. For other biographical material, see especially Whalen-Bridge ("Charles"), Nash (*Charles* 15–25), and Storhoff (*Understanding* 1–6).

6. Johnson has had a long and varied personal relationship with Northwestern. A Northwestern literary magazine published his first piece of fiction, later to become the first chapter of *Faith and the Good Thing*. Afterwards, however, the university turned down his graduate school application.

7. After passing his doctoral examinations, Johnson left Stony Brook for the position at Washington without completing the Ph.D. Stony Brook awarded Johnson a Ph.D. in philosophy in 1999, although it was backdated to 1988, the year he completed *Being and Race* (see Nash, *Charles* 197 n. 1).

8. See, for example, Banks, *Black Intellectuals: Race and Responsibility in American Life* (1996); James, *Transcending the Talented Tenth: Black Leaders and American Intellectuals* (1996); Posnock, *Color and Culture: Black Writers and the Making of the Modern Intellectual* (1998); and Carby, *Race Men* (1998).

9. For example, see conservative critic David Horowitz's attack on Cornel West, "Cornel West: No Light in His Attic" (1999).

10. For scholarly studies, see especially Wiese. See also Cashin and Winerap on the barriers of race and class that remain in supposedly integrated suburbs.

11. Wiese contends that pre–World War II blacks living in suburbs were predominantly working class (15.).

12. Posnock discusses Johnson briefly in relation to what he calls an "unappreciated pragmatist cosmopolitan tradition" of black intellectuals who oppose racism from a universalist perspective (24, 262). See Gleason ("Go There") and Storhoff (*Understanding* and "Pragmatic"). See also Brown, Nash (*Charles* 13, 14), Byrd (*Charles* 196 and 197), and my discussion in chapter 5.

13. Boxill, born in 1937, completed his Ph.D. at UCLA in 1965.

14. Patrick Francis Healy is the first known U.S. citizen of African descent to receive a Ph.D. in philosophy (from the University of Louvain). Beginning in 1866, he

taught philosophy at Georgetown University and later became its president. For recovery work on Baker and Jones, see "Jones" and "Baker" by Yancy.

15. See, for example, Williams, "W. E. B. DuBois" (14).

16. On Locke, see Harris, *Philosophy* (xv). In "The Horror of Tradition," Harris complicates the idea of a "black philosophical tradition."

17. *Proceedings of the American Philosophical Association* 61 (1987): 357–60. Mills suggests that the figure remained at 1 percent through 1998 (*Blackness* 205 n. 3).

18. See Lott and Pittman, *A Companion to African American Philosophy* (2003); Ward and Lott, *Philosophers on Race: Critical Essays* (2002); Mills, *Blackness Visible: Essays on Philosophy and Race* (1998); Lee and Hord, *I Am Because We Are: Readings in Black Philosophy* (1995); Outlaw, *On Race and Philosophy* (1996); Appiah, *In My Father's House: Africa in the Philososphy of Culture* (1992); and Gordon, *Existentia Africana: Understanding Africana Existential Thought (Africana Thought)* (2000), *Existence in Black: An Anthology of Black Existential Philosophy* (1996), and *Bad Faith and Anti-Black Racism* (1995).

19. See Mills's discussions in *Blackness Visible* of Ellison (8ff.) and Douglass (167ff.).

20. That overview, however, does not include an analysis of Johnson's early attraction to Marxist critique.

21. For Johnson and Eastern thinkers, see especially Gleason ("Liberation"), Whalen-Bridge ("Waking Cain"), Storhoff (*Understanding*), and Byrd (*Charles*); for Husserl, see Rushdy ("Phenomenology"), Coleman, Nash (*Charles*), and Selzer ("Genesis"); for Hegel, see McCumber, Selzer ("Master"), and Byrd (*Charles*); for Plato, see Griffiths ("Sorcery") and Byrd (*Charles*); for Marx, see Selzer ("Charles"), Coleman ("Charles"), and Rushdy (*Neo-Slave*); for Kant, see Selzer ("Genesis"); for Berkeley, see Storhoff ("Artist"); for Whitehead, see Byrd ("It Rests" and *Charles*).

22. According to an unpublished interview with Whalen-Bridge, Slaughter first noticed Johnson as an undergraduate student in a section of his Introduction to Logic course at Southern Illinois. One day when he was passing back an exam, he noted that a black student—Charles Johnson—had earned one of the few As in the class. E-correspondence with Whalen-Bridge, March 17, 2005.

23. Johnson also studied under well-known pragmatist philosopher Justus Buchler (e-correspondence with Johnson, March 19, 2005), in addition to taking a course on Hinduism with Doug Allen and a course on Taoism with a visiting Asian professor at SIU (e-correspondence with Johnson, January 7, 2007). Johnson's graduate education in philosophy thus represents well the major lines of his continuing philosophical interests.

24. E-correspondence, March 3, 2005.

25. This article is often discussed in relation to *Oxherding Tale*, in which the main character, Andrew Hawkins, contends that the worst thing about slavery is "the fact that men had epidermalized being" (52).

26. See Selzer, "Master-Slave Dialectics in Charles Johnson's 'The Education of Mingo.'"

27. For Aristotle, see the *Politics*, 1.5.1254a, 18–24 and 29–33. For an evaluation of the racial and racist views of these philosophers and others, see Ward and Lott, *Philosophers on Race*; Outlaw, "The Future of 'Philosophy' in America," in *On Race and Philosophy* (183–204); and Mills, "Non-Cartesian Sums," in *Blackness Visible* (1–19).

28. Mills argues that the theoretical whiteness of philosophy is more responsible for

the small number of blacks in the discipline than is explicit racism among leading philosophers ("Non-Cartesian Sums," 3). See also Gordon, *Existence in Black*;
and Harris, "Believe It or Not."

29. Johnson's complex position on universals evolves partly out of his experiences
with a philosophical discipline that had historically defined black experience as
*sub-universal*. Aware of the "theoretical war" over the problem of reconciling
universals with the particulars of black life, as he puts it in "Philosophy and Black
Fiction," Johnson is often concerned with legitimating black experience as a
source of universal knowledge. His writings on the universal in both "Philosophy
and Black Fiction" (1980) and "Where Fiction and Philosophy Meet" (1988) are
best understood in this specific historical and oppositional context. Johnson was
not led by the failure of philosophy to grant universal significance to black
experience to reject universals themselves—a position that he refers to as the
"dull" understanding of universals as a "static mold that violates Black life"
("Philosophy" 82). Johnson's thinking on universals includes both a defense of the
universality discoverable in black particulars and an argument that universals are
not static but changeable. In chapter 2 I argue that Marcuse played an important
role in shaping Johnson's understanding of universals as necessarily social, situated, and changeable, an understanding established by the early 1970s.

30. Little, Nash, and Rushdy provide descriptions of this visit and of Johnson's rela-
tionship to the BAM. Rushdy offers a sophisticated analysis of the importance of
BAM to the emergence of the slave narrative genre in general and to *Middle
Passage* in particular (*Neo-Slave*). Little discusses Baraka's visit in relationship to
the ambivalent attitude toward black nationalism and the BAM detectable in
Johnson's cartoons (*Charles* 17–53). Nash discusses the BAM in relation to
Johnson's cartooning and offers an especially detailed description of Baraka's
visit as it relates to the political climate on the SIU campus (*Charles* 17–29).

31. For an excellent analysis that uses West's conception of "prophetic pragmatism"
to read *Dreamer*, see Storhoff (*Understanding* 186–88).

32. My analysis builds on the work of Little (*Charles*), Nash (*Charles*), and Storhoff
(*Understanding*).

33. For philosophers on Kant's attitudes toward the emotions, see Sullivan and Schott
(*Cognition* and "Gender").

34. As translated and quoted by Frings (41).

35. Scheler lost his academic appointment in the German university system as a result of scandals after his first divorce. He found work afterwards as a Catholic
educator, but lost that position after his second divorce when students and clergy
were forbidden to attend his classes. See Staude.

36. Schott discusses the consequences of such repression in *Cognition and Eros*,
especially chap. 8 (101–14). In "The Gender of Enlightenment," she also points
out that in attempting to exclude the erotic from rationality, Kant's claims of a
position of objectivity is "already an emotional posture" (329), a critique with
which Johnson's phenomenological orientation would lead him to agree.

37. See also Nash (*Charles* 93).

38. This is one translation of Kant's famous dictum. See "What Is Enlightenment"
(54).

39. The professor's abandonment of rationalism also resonates with Zen Buddhism's
call to put aside one's attachment to one's thoughts and "let be" what appears be-

fore consciousness without judging it, which can be related, perhaps, to the early state of "irrealization" in the Husserlian *epochē*

40. Although at times Johnson can sound as though he rejects black particulars in favor of a deracialized universal—as when he suggests in "Philosophy and Black Fiction" that "aspects of the Black world become, after the *epochē*, only the occasion for universal reflection"—it is important to note that this bracketing (or ir-realization) is only a single step in a process, one designed to aid thought in overcoming not particulars but *presuppositions about those particulars*. Misreadings of Johnson's understanding of universals often result from a failure to understand their role in a phenomenological method that unfolds over time. In other words, Johnson understands the bracketing of particulars—in this tale Wendy's specificity, and by extension, that of the black community—as an *initial* step in a process. The goal is not to abandon the particulars but to prepare to see them afresh, and by doing so to arrive at new universals (concepts). The appearance of the universal is then "anchored" in the particular. Or as Johnson explains, "From the fibrous particulars of Black life a perception anchored in racial experience is bodied forth, and we come to understand somewhat how new seeing—revitalized vision—occurs in black fiction" ("Philosophy and Black Fiction" 57).

41. For the importance of "de-symbolization," see Staude (21ff.) and Spiegelberg (241ff.).

42. See Spiegelberg (241). In *Being and Race* Johnson refers to Spiegelberg's essay "Phenomenology through Vicarious Experience" in explaining how fiction can fling readers, in Johnson's words, "toward revelation and unsealed vision" (36, 33).

43. See also Griffiths.

44. It is tempting to compare the professor to Johnson in other ways. Like the professor, Johnson read Plutarch's *Lives of the Noble Grecians* as a boy ("Charles" 226). He also once worried if he were "caring enough and loving enough and responding enough with the heart" (*Passing* 146). Johnson is frequently put in the position of defending his interest in philosophy. Some of his comments, therefore, defend philosophy even in the face of its traditions of racism. Johnson's passion for philosophy is sincere; it is not, however, a-critical or blind to the problems that he satirizes in "Alēthia" or elsewhere.

45. From Du Bois's "My Evolving Program for Negro Freedom" (quoted by Williams, "W. E. B. Du Bois: Afro-American Philosopher of Social Reality," 16).

46. I am aware that Johnson himself sometimes speaks of his decision to write philosophical fiction in this fashion. Nevertheless, an examination of Johnson's early work shows that he was very aware both of the disciplinary constraints of academic philosophy and of a tradition of philosophical inquiry within African American literature.

47. I do not mean to imply that Johnson's and Rorty's views are identical. Ironically, the "writer" Johnson maintains a stronger belief in the efficacy of philosophical critique than does the "philosopher" Rorty.

## 2. From Marx to Marcuse in *Faith and the Good Thing*

1. Some historians read the New Left as a marker of the disintegration of Marxism since World War II. Anderson's standard history critiques the aesthetic Western

tradition of Marxism in comparison to a classical tradition; and Kolakowski offers a blistering estimation of New Left Marxism as a sort of "pablum" that has not "produced any intellectual results worth the name" (488). Rather than looking to Russian and eastern European models, he argues, the New Left looked for its "heroes" to "leaders of the third world and western ideologues interested in its problems" as well as "Negro leaders in the United States who advocated violence and black racialism" (488). Kolakowski's comments suggest that he is suspicious of racial analysis and the possibilities that it may offer theory. Mills argues instead that racial analysis has led to developments in "political science, history, sociology, and legal theory" ("Prophetic" 216).

2. Johnson arrived at SIU in 1966, the same year that Carmichael took over the leadership of SNCC from John Lewis and James Forman, moving the organization toward a black separatist position. Subsequently Forman joined the League of Revolutionary Black Workers in Detroit (organized by the members of Detroit's Uhuru, with the advice of James and Grace Lee Boggs). Carmichael was voted out of SNCC in 1968. Afterwards he joined the Black Panthers, but in 1969 he left to protest their association with white groups. He subsequently went to West Africa.

3. Important recent studies on these movements include Smethurst (*The Black Arts Movement*); Brown (*Fighting for Us*); Ture [Stokely Carmichael] (*Ready for Revolution*); Woodward (*A Nation within a Nation*); and Bush (*We Are Not What We Seem*).

4. Histories of Southern Illinois University include Koplowitz and Harper. See also Nash (*Charles* 18–22). For a more personal memoir of the protests, see Keith.

5. E-correspondence, February 16, 2008.

6. E-correspondence, October 19, 2001.

7. E-correspondence, February 16, 2008.

8. This chapter draws from papers presented in 2002 and 2003 (at the yearly ALA and MELUS conferences) that focused on the treatment of Marx and Nietzsche in the novel, especially in relation to the character Issac Maxwell. See also Byrd (*Charles* 45–48). For an analysis of Faith in relationship to Gardner and to Wright, see Little (*Charles* 54–79). For an analysis of the philosophical allusions in the novel as revisions of Hegel, see McCumber. For an analysis of Faith's quest as an effort "to overcome a narrow, racialized vision of identity, through her pursuit of a universal good"—an analysis that also compares the novel to works by Hurston, Du Bois, and Drieser—see Nash (*Charles* 51–78). For an analysis of conjuring in the novel, in relation to classical myth and to Johnson's first short story collection, see Griffiths. For an analysis of *Faith* in relation to the fairy-tale tradition, see Chandler ("Dreaming"). Critical analysis of Johnson's engagement with Marxist thought has focused primarily on the appearance of Marx as a comic character in *Oxherding Tale*; see Coleman; Little (*Charles*); Spaulding; and Rushdy (*Neo-Slave*). With the exception of Rushdy, these critics emphasize Johnson's "rewriting of Marx in order to undercut pre-established assumptions about Marxism (Little, *Charles* 100). Others detect a more substantive engagement with Marx. Rushdy argues that Marxism is important to both *Oxherding Tale* and *Middle Passage* (*Neo-Slave* 211), and I have written on Johnson's engagement with Marx ("Exchange Value"). Compared to other Johnson novels, critical work on *Faith* is limited.

9. Robinson argues that an apprenticeship in Marxism led these thinkers to enunciate a black radical position critical of Marx for not considering American slavery

seriously enough in his theories, for identifying slavery with feudal agrarianism rather than understanding its role in the emergence of modern capitalism, and for providing a class theory that failed to account for race.

10. For a short survey of black Marxist thought, see Marable ("Black"). For more detailed analyses, see Robinson (*Black Marxism*) and Dawson (*Black Visions*). In his influential work *The Crisis of the Negro Intellectual*, Cruse judges the relationship of the CPUSA with blacks to be manipulative. Dawson identifies characteristics that may account for this difficult relationship: a predisposition toward dogmatism, a dependence on authoritative regimes, a tendency to separate black members of the party from the black community, and a reliance on foreign models that did not always correspond to political realties in the United States (*Black Visions* 236–37). Other, more recent studies, however, challenge the cold war account of manipulation. Wald (*Exiles from a Future Time*), Hutcheson (*The Harlem Renaissance in Black and White*), Maxwell, (*New Negro, Old Left*), Solomon (*The Cry Was Unity*), Mullen (*Popular Fronts*), and Smethurst (*The New Red Negro*) all complicate that account, often by drawing on Soviet sources not available until after the 1991 collapse of the USSR. These scholars dispute whether a firm color line existed in the party.

11. For an analysis of the schools of Marxism, see Kolakowski. I follow Mulhern in the use of the term "critical classicism" (*Contemporary* 12).

12. See *For Marx* and *Lenin and Philosophy*.

13. Johnson's attraction to Marx's early writing is part of a long-standing disagreement among scholars over the early writings. While some detect a radical break in Marx's thought between the earlier and later writings, others perceive a continuation of thought. This disagreement is partly attributable to the late publication of the early writings, especially in English. The first German edition of *The 1844 Manuscripts* did not appear until 1932, and the first English translation was not available until 1959 (in Great Britain). The first popular translation did not appear in the United States until 1961, when Erich Fromm presented a translation by T. B. Bottomore. Much of Marx's early work was thus published *after* canonical interpretations of Marxism had already been established. Where the early texts seem at odds with these interpretations, scholars were divided over whether those differences meant that Marx had changed his mind or that the standard interpretation should be changed. The weight given to the early writings divides critical from critical classicist scholars. Like the critical Marxists (and like black philosophers such as Outlaw), Johnson valorizes the early work. He quotes Marx's *1844 Manuscripts* in his master's thesis from Fromm's 1970 edition. Where possible I also quote from that edition. Where not possible (because Fromm did not include the entire document), I quote from *Karl Marx and Frederick Engels: Collected Works* (hereafter *CW*).

14. See, for example, my analysis of being and having in Johnson's story (Selzer, "Charles").

15. The phrase is from Schiller, *The Aesthetic Education of Man.*

16. Meszaros uses the example of a piano player to illustrate Marx's point. For one to be even *potentially* a great piano player requires the existence of "a socially produced musical instrument," and a "highly complex social activity of discriminative musical enjoyment" (175).

17. Johnson frequently offers versions of this figure, which was inspired by the naturalist Guy Murchie, to illustrate intersubjectivity; see "Whole Sight" (19).

18. For biographical information on Reich, Johnson draws upon Cattier. For a more recent biocritical study, see Corrington.

19. For passages from Reich included in Johnson's thesis, I quote from Johnson to provide the clearest picture of his thinking. For other passages I include parenthetical documentation.

20. Johnson describes completing his fifty-page master's thesis in one week ("Charles" 239).

21. See Little (*Charles*) on the novel in relation to Wright's Chicago and Ellison's New York.

22. Here Faith echoes the words of Marx's daughter to her father, "Tell me another mile," as recounted in her biographical essay on her father (included in the Fromm collection from which Johnson quotes Marx).

23. See also McCumber for a positive reading of Todd Cross's "lies."

24. Gordon identifies alienation as of special significance to black philosophers (*Existentia*).

25. See, for instance, "Wilhelm Reich" (27, 38).

26. Johnson read *Beyond Good and Evil* in his second summer of college ("I Call" 17).

27. For a reading of this name in relation to Christian symbolism, see Nash (*Charles* 70).

28. In the *Symposium*, Diotima describes the education of Eros as a process of transcendence that leads from desire for the lover to love of beauty as an ideal. She thus implicitly judges the things of the world as lesser goods. In reversing this process, the Swamp Woman shares similarities with Wendy in "Alēthia" (529). See also Griffiths. On the Swamp Woman as an agent of "Africanist spiritualism and magical powers," see Little (*Charles* 58). For an analysis of her as "phenomenological good faith," see Nash (*Charles* 58). Nash interprets the parable to suggest that desire is divisive (133), while I read it as endorsing a multifaceted desire.

29. E-correspondence, July 25, 2002.

30. E-correspondence, October 22, 2001.

## 3. The Emergence of Black Dharma and *Oxherding Tale*

1. For a discussion of this photo in relation to the Soka Gakkai group, see Chappell 194–95.

2. A 2007 essay by Nash, "The Application of an Ideal," also moves in this direction by analyzing how the essays in Johnson's *Turning the Wheel* propose a means by which "an African American seeker" can serve the ideal of the beloved community (173).

3. Since Gleason's 1991 article, several critics have written on the influence of Buddhism in the novel and of Johnson's allegiance to an engaged Buddhist practice. Critics typically contrast Mahayana Buddhism to an older, monastic form of Theravada Buddhism and to read Mahayana as successfully incorporating the social, as does Little (*Charles*). By reading Mahayana Buddhism of engagement against forms of twentieth-century Buddhism, I see its incorporation of the social as more limited by comparison. For the distinction between traditional Mahayana and twentieth-century understandings of engagement, see especially Queen (*Engaged*).

4. As Fields points out, by the 1860s Chinese immigrants made up as much as one-tenth of the population of California, and as early as 1853 the first Buddhist tem-

ple in the United States had been established in San Francisco (How 70–71, 55). The founding of the Theosophical Society in 1875 by Helena B. Blavatsky and Colonel Olcott was also an important event in East-West exchange, in spite of the unusual nature of the spiritualists' beliefs. Literate blacks in the United States may have also been exposed to Buddhism through various translations, commentaries, and literary works produced in the nineteenth century, including those by Emerson and Thoreau, and by the circulation of the popular English poem "The Light of Asia," published by Sir Edwin Arnold in 1879.

5. The religions were Buddhism, Christianity, Confucianism, Hinduism, Islam, Jainism, Judaism, Shintoism, Taoism, and Zoroastrianism. For the most detailed history of the Parliament, see Seager, *World's Parliament of Religions* and *The Dawn of Religious Pluralism*. For a Foucauldian study of how the representation of religion at the World's Parliament staged various colonial projects, see Burris.

6. For an analysis of the importance of Carus to the Americanization of Buddhism, see Verhoeven.

7. In addition to the active missionary efforts of various Buddhist organizations, two other factors contributed especially to the dissemination of Buddhism in the twentieth-century United States: the return of servicemen from overseas with wives who carried their devotional practices with them; and the liberalization of immigration laws in 1965, which led to a new influx of immigrants from Sri Lanka, China, Thailand, Cambodia, Laos, Burma, Taiwan, and Vietnam (Seager, "Buddhist" 252). Today Asian immigration to the United States is second in numbers only to Hispanic immigration.

8. Well-known white literary figures such as Jack Kerouac, Allen Ginsberg, and Gary Snyder admired Suzuki's writings, and all of them met him in person (although Suzuki criticized Beat Zen for being poorly disciplined). In an essay on Johnson's 1998 novel, *Dreamer*, Whalen-Bridge argues that Johnson's "cross-cultural philosophical and religious exchange" is important for having "imaginatively integrated the largely white male Beat tradition in American literature" ("Waking" 511). Suzuki also influenced Alan Watts, who produced a series of books on Buddhism popular on college campuses in the sixties and seventies. His work was of interest to Bob Kaufman and to LeRoi Jones (Amiri Baraka), and may have influenced the selection of the name *Yugen* for the Beat literary magazine that Jones edited with his first wife, Hettie Cohen, a Jewish woman whom he married in a Buddhist temple in New York in 1958.

9. Suzuki was a Renzai Zen Buddhist. Johnson originally registered with a Diago-ji temple (Renzai Zen) in Osaka but did not take vows, in part because Martin Hughes, the abbot, died in the early 2000s while working with street children in the Philippines (e-correspondence, August 16, 2005). He afterwards made Buddhist vows in the Soto Zen tradition at the Dai Bai Zan Cho Bo Zen temple in Seattle with Claude AnShin Thomas on November 14, 2007.

10. The precise number of black people participating in Buddhism is extremely difficult to ascertain. The scholarly study of American Buddhism is itself a young discipline. Prebish points out that Buddhist Studies did not begin to emerge as a "significant discipline in the American university system" until the 1960s ("Academic" 186). Because the study of American Buddhism took time to establish itself as a legitimate field, the secondary literature was modest through the 1980s. Information on black Buddhists in the United States was especially limited until people of color began writing about their Buddhist practice.

11. For information on black Buddhism, see especially *Turning Wheel* (Spring 1993, Fall 2000, Spring 2001, and Summer 2003); *Tricycle* (Fall 1994); and the edited collections and books by people of color discussed here. Internet resources for black Buddhists have grown rapidly to include the Spirit Rock Web page; an Internet list serve for black Buddhists (blackbuddhists-subscribe@yahoogroups.com); the Rainbow Dharma Web site (www.rainbowdharma.com) established by Choyin Randgröl (an African American lay teacher in the Tibetan Buddhist tradition and author of two booklets, *Buddhist Meditations for African Americans* and *Black Buddha: Living Without Fear*); a Web site for the racially diverse Soka Gakkai organization (www.sgi_usa.org); and one specifically for black practitioners of Nichiren Soshu Buddhism (www.proudblackbuddhist.org), among others.

12. For an analysis of the story suggesting that difference is instead lost in the universal, see Bill Brown.

13. See Queen's work; Rothberg; and Ken Jones, *The New Social Face of Buddhism*.

14. Outreach to the imprisoned has expanded to such an extent that Joseph Jarmen has suggested that the "vast majority" of black Buddhist practitioners in the United States today may in fact be prison inmates (quoted by Pintak 4).

15. For an argument that Queen may misread the tradition in order to emphasize the West's contributions to engaged Buddhism, see Yarnall, "Engaged Buddhism: New and Improved?"

16. See Harvey, *An Introduction to Buddhist Ethics* 34.

17. The Buddha was initially unwilling to accept women in the *sangha* until he realized that this exclusion did not follow from his own precepts. Even so, rules for orders of monks subordinate female to male monks. See Barnes, "Buddhist Women and the Nuns' Order in Asia" (261).

18. For *Oxherding Tale*'s relation to the Oxherding pictures, see Gleason, "The Liberation."

19. See Whalen-Bridge, "Now That I Am Old and Have the Words for It."

20. Rushdy admits that he doesn't want to "stress the point too much, for it is accurate only to a degree." Nonetheless he raises the comparison in his chapter on *Oxherding Tale* (*Neo-Slave* 170–71).

21. This is not to imply that the relationship between Dharmapala and Olcott was not important: Dharmapala's conversion to Buddhism was inspired by Olcott, who established the Theosophical Society in India, which would provide an organizational base for many of Dharmapala's reform efforts.

22. For more information, see the notes to Dharmapala's letters in the Washington papers. I thank Mike Mucci for his help in locating these letters.

23. For a different view, see Nash's comment that the novel "lacks some of the tensions that mark Johnson's earlier and later work" (*Charles* 129).

24. For other discussions of the significance of the Platform Sutra, see Nash (*Charles* 106); Storhoff (*Understanding* 53); and Byrd (*Charles* 61–62).

25. See also Rushdy, who defines the "palimpsest imperative" of neo-slave narratives in *Remembering* (1–33).

26. For different readings of the significance of disease in the novel, see Ouiment and Chandler ("In-Itself").

27. See especially Rushdy, *Neo-Slave*; Little, *Charles*; and Nash, *Charles*.

28. See especially Coleman (638), Little ("Charles Johnson's Revolutionary *Oxherding Tale*"), Jablon, Scott, and Spaulding on Johnson's use of defamiliarization. See also Storhoff's analysis of parodic homage (*Charles*).

29. See Hayward for an analysis of eighteenth-century narrative strategies in the novel.

30. See Selzer, "Master-Slave Dialectics in 'The Education of Mingo'" and "Signifying on Marx." For a summary of criticism on the novel in relation to Marxism, see chapter 2, n 8.

31. See also Hardack's observation that the "civil war" in the novel is a "metaphysical" conflict (1035).

32. For other interpretations of the function of gender in Johnson's fiction, see especially Nash ("I Was"), Hayward, Muther, and Whalen-Bridge ("Invisible").

33. Since he has just witnessed a slave auction at which seemingly congenial white people undergo a terrifying nighttime transformation, one is tempted to wonder how Andrew's paranoia is "self-induced."

34. The function of the householder in Hindu thought has been elaborated by Little (*Charles*), who stresses the social efficacy of the role and its importance in Johnson's fiction. See also Storhoff (*Understanding*) and Byrd (*Charles*).

35. Althea's paralysis may also signal Ezekiel's own impotency.

36. For Bannon as Shiva, see Little, *Charles*. For Bannon as Maya, see Byrd, *Charles*.

37. Reb is a figure, like other elements in the narrative, who combines Buddhist and Hindu spiritualism, as Little (*Charles*) and Byrd (*Charles*) emphasize. Nash discusses Reb in relation to other father figures in Johnson's work ("I Was"). Coleman and Byrd (*Charles*) emphasize Reb's role in Andrew's escape from the Soulcatcher; whereas Little (*Charles*) and Storhoff (*Understanding*) emphasize Andrew's activities as a householder.

38. Johnson's essay first appeared in *Ju-Ju* (1976) and was later collected by Byrd (*I Call*). Slaughter's appeared in 1977 in *Man and World* and was later included in Harris's collection, *Philosophy Born of Struggle* (1983).

39. Cited in Little, *Charles* (80).

## 4. The Rise of the New Black Intellectual and the Varieties of Cosmopolitanism in *Middle Passage*

1. Both Boynton (54) and Reed (32) identify Jacoby as renewing interest in the fate of "public" intellectuals. Boynton and Bérubé define these intellectuals largely in relation to the New York intellectuals; Reed analyzes them against a black intellectual tradition.

2. Rutherford Calhoun in *Middle Passage* is educated by his master in the hope that he will become a "Negro preacher"; Andrew Hawkins, the son of the plantation owner and an enslaved black woman in *Oxherding Tale*, is educated by a private tutor and later becomes a teacher himself; and Matthew Bishop is a college philosophy major in *Dreamer*, a novel that also features the learned Dr. Martin Luther King Jr.

3. See, for example, Bérubé, "Public Academy"; Bhabha, "Black and White and Read All Over"; Boynton, "The New Intellectuals"; Chametzsky, "Public Intellectuals—Now and Then"; Early, "Black Like Them" and "Partisanship, Race, and the Public Intellectual"; Gates, "Black Demagogues and Pseudo-Scholars"; Hanchard, "Cultural Politics and Black Public Intellectuals"; Neal, "Lifestyles of the Rich and Tenured"; Rivers, "Black Intellectuals"; Reed, "What are the Drums Saying, Booker?"; Spillers, "The Crisis of the Negro Intellectual: A Post-Date"; and West, "The Dilemma of the Black Intellectual."

4. See Carby's *Race Men* and hooks's contribution to *Breaking Bread*. As a contributor to the *Village Voice*, Davis has often referred to the "dominance" of black males in discussions of black intellectuals; see especially "Spinning Race at Harvard." For another reading of the event she discusses, see Chametzky.

5. See Neal, "Hip-Hop," and Farred, *What's My Name?*

6. Reid Pharr uses this term in reference to research that challenges the supposed divide between Afrocentric and cosmopolitan intellectuals, such as the work of Moses and Posnock.

7. For an excellent overview of these developments by social scientists, see Parsi and Geraghty. See also Dawson ("Black Counterpublic") and Spillers.

8. Dyson sees such a divide in Bill Cosby's controversial comments at the 2004 NAACP commemoration of the *Brown v. Board of Education* decision, where the entertainer remarked that "the lower economic and lower middle economic people are not holding their end in this deal. In the neighborhood that most of us grew up in, parenting is not going on." Although some see Cosby's comments as in line with a long tradition of intracommunity rhetoric, Dyson suggests that they reflect the attitude of a growing "Afristocracy" toward a "Ghettocracy" (*Is Bill* 110).

9. I should point out that Neal is younger than most of the intellectuals discussed here.

10. See Nash's discussion of punditry and black intellectuals in "Application."

11. See "Interview by Mike Wallace" of King, June 25, 1958. Asked if integration will lead to "mass intermarriage," King responds, "Races don't marry, people do" (436).

12. *Up from Slavery* by Booker T. Washington, *Black Boy* by Richard Wright, *Notes of a Native Son* by James Baldwin, *The Souls of Black Folks* by W. E. B. Du Bois, *The Autobiography of Malcolm X* by Alex Haley and Malcolm X, *Why We Can't Wait* by Martin Luther King Jr., and *Shadow and Act* by Ralph Ellison. Johnson was the sole black member of the committee.

13. For critical cosmopolitanism, see Mignolo; for vernacular cosmopolitanism, see Bhabha, "Unsatisfied"; for patriotic cosmopolitanism, see Appiah, "Cosmopolitanism"; for rooted cosmopolitanism, see Hollinger; for discrepant cosmopolitanism, see Clifford ("Traveling"); for actually existing cosmopolitanism, see Malcolmson.

14. Brennan discusses the repeated warnings that thinkers raise along such lines (682).

15. One thinks immediately of Gilroy's reorientation of Wright scholarship in The *Black Atlantic* (1993). More recently, Nwankwo analyzes how the Haitian revolution mobilized a cosmopolitan identity among African American, West Indian, and Afro-Latin peoples. See also Appiah (*Cosmopolitanism*), Posnock (*Color*), and Moses (*Afrotopia*).

16. Gleason's conference paper on this topic is cited by Nash (*Charles* 197 n. 1). More recently Gleason has published a rich discussion of Johnson's critical pragmatism ("Go There"), in which he discusses Johnson's cosmopolitanism in relation to the "universalist concerns of Jamesian pluralism" as they are refigured by the thought of Du Bois, Locke, and Ellison. Nash discusses "anti-race race men" in *Charles* (13–14, 23–24, 47–48). Byrd discusses Johnson's cosmopolitan vision in the final two pages of his study (*Charles* 196–97), but other parts of his analy-

sis are pertinent to the discussion here, especially his comments relating the novel to Appiah (124–25).

17. King's statement is from "Beyond Vietnam," delivered in New York City on April 4, 1967. Obama's statement is from a speech in Berlin, Germany, on July 24, 2008.

18. Not all critics agree that Johnson balances these allegiances successfully. See Hardack, Travis, and Jordan.

19. Johnson's critique of naturalism is directed less at individual writers than at its reliance on a flawed metaphysic. He writes, "I've always distinguished 'realism' . . . from 'naturalism,' which as a late nineteenth- early twentieth-century approach to fiction is informed by a metaphysic most writers never question, critically or philosophically" (e-correspondence, January 2, 2007).

20. Noting that Johnson won two years after Morrison was denied, Travis speculates that Johnson won because his work is "more accommodating to the white male reader" than Morrison's (70). In fact, at the 1990 awards two white males voted *against* Johnson, while two women on the committee—one white and one black—voted for him (along with Phillip Lopate). West's comments suggest that he identified Johnson more as an "ethnic" writer than as a fellow male. The history of the awards also demonstrates that in the years leading up to Johnson's win, more black women had been so honored than black men. Morrison's being passed over and Johnson's being awarded the prize are related materially, however, in that Morrison's case led to the structural changes discussed in the text.

21. Diane Olsen, in charge of press relations for the foundation, stated, "We made an effort [in 1990] to get in touch with small publishers across the land" (McDowell, "Nominees" C34). Many large publishers were not happy with the result. Noting that small presses did well in 1990, while some books from large presses—such as works by Thomas Pynchon, Kurt Vonnegut, and Tim O'Brien—were not included among the finalists, one anonymous senior publisher complained, "It's bizarre as hell." Such comments suggest that many large publishing houses felt threatened by increased competition from smaller presses.

22. Ellison's influence on Johnson has been widely recognized. For Johnson as Ellison's "spiritual heir," see Little (*Charles* 135–36, 155–58), Nash (*Charles* 27–28), Byrd, (*Charles* 102–3), Gleason, ("Go There") and Conner ("To Utter"). For a negative reading of Ellison's influence, see Hardack.

23. Baker quotes approvingly Watts's 1994 study (*Heroism*), which faults Ellison for his "political disengagement" (119). Johnson reviewed the same study negatively for the *New York Times* in a review titled "Race, Politics, and Ralph Ellison."

24. Although this chapter is related to earlier critical discussions that read *Middle Passage* as a celebration of multi-culturalism, I argue that the narrative is designed to interrogate the issues at stake in *multiple* cosmopolitan positions.

25. On the status of *metics*, see Sabine (5) and Fine and Cohen (138).

26. In *The Custom of the Sea*, Hanson discusses the cannibalism that took place after the shipwreck of the whaleship *Essex*, the incident that inspired Herman Melville's *Moby Dick*, which in turn served as a literary influence on *Middle Passage*. He concludes that social hierarchy played a major role in the order in which people were cannibalized at sea: "Slaves were eaten first, black men before white, women before men, passengers before crew, unpopular crew before the rest" (133).

27. See Rushdy's "Phenomenology of the Allmuseri" for an analysis of the tribe in relation to phenomenology and intersubjectivity. For their relation to Eastern thought, especially as embodying the concepts of the "unity of being" and "no self," see Little (*Charles*), Storhoff (*Understanding*), and Byrd (*Charles*). For a reading that ties the Allmuseri to Appiah's thinking, see Hardack, Travis, and Byrd (*Charles*).

28. Johnson attributes the inspiration for the Allmuseri to a space in African villages where magic was practiced (*Trucks* 8). The Allmuseri and their descendants in America are frequently identified with sorcery in Johnson's fiction. See Mingo in "The Education of Mingo," Allen in "The Sorcerer's Apprentice," Reb in *Oxherding Tale*, the Allmuseri and Santos (and possibly Jackson and Rutherford) in *Middle Passage*, and Chaym in *Dreamer*.

29. While Jordan acknowledges that the fact that Falcon is a dwarf might "be seen on some level to represent the moral and ethical statures of the masters and leaders" (168), she believes that this reading is "ultimately undermin[ed] as a possibility." Other narratological details, however, seem clearly to support the reading that Falcon's status is being purposefully undermined.

30. As a free black man aboard a slaver, Rutherford occupies an unusual position on board the *Republic*, which has been the subject of much critical commentary. See especially Fagel, Goudie, Travis, and Scott for analysis of his position "in the middle."

31. Little ties Ngonyama's carving to a parable from Chuang-tzu, a fourth-century Chinese Taoist (*Charles* 146).

32. See Rushdy's analysis of Rutherford as "phenomenological thief" ("Properties" 78–79).

33. Diamelo is commonly identified by critics with the nationalist ethos of the Black Power and Black Arts movements.

34. Evoking a related idea of intellectual inheritance, Spillers argues in "Crisis" that black intellectuals should adopt performative excellence—such as that achieved in black musical performance—as a model for black intellectual practice.

35. As in Little's *Charles* (141), most critics connect the pleasure ship's name with Juno's role as goddess of marriage, a foreshadowing of Rutherford's upcoming marriage to Isadora.

36. The novel's final line, which indicates that Isadora would remain all night resting "snugly" beside Rutherford while they "gently crossed the Flood, and countless seas of suffering," may be an allusion to the Platform Sutra discussed in chapter 3, which in developing its conception of personal enlightenment suggests that "although the sea of suffering is inexhaustible, a turning of the head is the other shore" (*Sixth Patriarch* 86).

## 5. The Return of the King and the Logic of Conversion in *Dreamer*

1. Most critics, including Nash, Whalen-Bridge, and Byrd, agree that *Dreamer* is Johnson's most politically engaged work, as is befitting a work inspired by the great twentieth-century civil rights leader. Conner, however, suggests that the novel demonstrates that Johnson's career moves "progressively into increasingly spiritual domains" ("Numinous" 170). The figure of the transformed nonconformist captures this dual trajectory in Johnson's career.

2. E-correspondence with the author, January 11, 2008.

3. In discussing the novel's focus on what it means to "do well," Nash expertly ties the novel to a project Johnson begins in *Oxherding Tale*, arguing that the novel "completes [Johnson's] own cycle of *Oxherding Pictures*, molding his enlightenment to serve his community through this process of social and aesthetic engagement" (*Charles* 190). Whalen-Bridge's groundbreaking essay on the novel's complex engagement with the Cain and Abel myth, "Waking Cain," identifies many of the Buddhist themes in the novel, arguing that the narrator "boldly reinterpret[s] King's life in recognizably Buddhist terms" (518); Storhoff interprets King as both bodhisattva and prophetic pragmatist (*Understanding*); and Byrd (*Charles*) also discusses the novel's analysis of doing well, the *Oxherding Pictures*, and the Cain and Abel biblical myth, tying each to Buddhist thematics.

4. King finished, "But in the quiet recesses of my heart, I am fundamentally a clergyman, a Baptist preacher" (quoted in Carson, "Martin" 173).

5. See Whalen-Bridge's observation that *Dreamer* provides an alternative to the "'canonized King' of American civic religion" ("Waking" 518).

6. These include attempts to use King's image in advertising for the passage of Proposition 209, a bill against affirmation action admissions policies in public colleges and universities in California; Operation Rescue's appropriation of King in its protests against abortion; and Ralph Reed's assertion that King provided a model for his Christian Coalition. See Dyson (*I May* 22–25).

7. For an overview of King historiography, see Carson, "Paradoxes" and "Reconstructing the King Legacy." See also Lawson, "Freedom Then, Freedom Now." Street also contains a helpful analysis of the stages of King scholarship. Through the 1970s work emphasized King's role as a charismatic leader and attributed the success of legislation both to King and to national organizations such as the Southern Christian Leadership Conference. During the 1980s research began to focus more on local organizations, recovering the contributions of grassroots efforts. Studies now strive to bring these two concerns together. Serving as a sort of capstone to these efforts is the 2007 publication of *At Canaan's Edge*, the final volume in Branch's award-winning trilogy.

8. See, for example, Lischer, *Preacher King*; Miller, *Voice of Deliverance*; Cone, "Martin Luther King, Jr"; West, "Prophetic Christian as Organic Intellectual"; and Carson, "Martin Luther King, Jr., and the African-American Social Gospel." Both Miller and Carson locate King's power in his ability, as Miller says, to "expertly blend" black and white traditions (9).

9. See the collection of essays on King published by scholars in 1990, *We Shall Overcome* (Albert and Hoffman).

10. By contrast, Carson argues that by licensing material the King family is attempting to bring the commercialization of King's legacy under control (Christensen).

11. Johnson's novel has found a receptive audience: at a 2006 appearance at Marygrove College in Detroit, for example, five hundred people showed up to hear Johnson read and to have copies of the novel autographed (Loretta Woodard, e-correspondence, August 25, 2006).

12. Malcolm X called King "Uncle Tom" and "Rev. Dr. Chickenwing"; Adam Clayton Powell called him "Martin Loser King." See Dyson (*I May* 110).

13. Johnson's opposed genealogies risk reinforcing the sort of dualism that he so often decries. There is a range among the positions of Black Power and black nationalist leaders—between an Eldridge Cleaver and a Stokely Carmichael—that is too easily elided.

14. It should be noted that Jeffries here echoes a position on Europeans that was put forward earlier by a Canadian author, Michael Bradley, in his 1978 *Iceman Inheritance*, a position subsequently popularized by Farrakhan's Nation of Islam.

15. Howard received considerable negative press coverage over the event. On April 24, 1994, three days after Mohammed's second speech—and one day before the university's board of trustees was to meet to consider whether to ask him to step down—President Franklyn Jenifer resigned to accept a position as president of the University of Texas at Dallas.

16. Identifying the shift from race to economic issues as a radical move is itself arguable. See Steinberg, *Turning Back*, which argues that the retreat from race is conservative.

17. Like Dyson, Johnson defines stage three in King's development as one primarily concerned with economic injustice. With the successes of the Civil Rights Act in 1964 and the Voting Rights Act in 1965 behind him, King advocated in the final two years of his life for a guaranteed income for all Americans and prepared to lead a 1968 Poor People's March on Washington. Unlike Dyson, Johnson positions this focus not as a dramatic shift in King's thought but as the logical outcome of "a conclusion [King] noted about our economic life as early as 1951" ("The King We Need" 50). At that time King wrote: "It is a well known fact that no social institution can survive when it has outlived its usefulness. This capitalism has done. It has failed to meet the needs of the masses" ("Notes on American Capitalism," 435; quoted in Johnson, "The King We Need," 50).

18. While Johnson's identification of Buddhism as "radical" may strike readers as exaggerated, it is worth pointing out that King identified the "unified Buddhist Church" as the "only un-Communist revolutionary force" in Vietnam ("Beyond Vietnam" 149).

19. Many critics have commented on the significance of transformation in the novel. Nash (*Charles*) and Storhoff (*Understanding*) underscore King's conversion process. Whalen-Bridge focuses on Matthew as the novel's changing character ("Waking"). Byrd emphasizes Chaym's transformation as the novel's central "figure of regeneration" (*Charles* 182). Conner suggests the novel reveals Johnson's realization that philosophy alone is not sufficient for renovated vision ("Numinous"). My focus is on how the conceptual figure of the transformed nonconformist provides a heuristic for understanding the novel's multilayered thematic and narratological focus on conversion.

20. See Whalen-Bridge's research on individual biblical passages in "Waking Cain." For a discussion of the novel's point of view as illustrative of Johnson's description of "first-person universal" in *Middle Passage*, see Byrd (*Charles* 148–50). For an analysis of ethical Christianity and of exile communities, see Conner ("Numinous").

21. In a famous passage Marx contrasts the work of animals, which create merely out of instinct, to the work of people, who create "universally": "What distinguishes the worst architect from the best of bees is that the architect raises his structure in imagination before he erects it in reality" ("Process," in *Collected Works* 1:187).

22. See also Storhoff (*Understanding* 214) and Byrd (*Charles* 189).

23. Nash identifies the redemptive possibilities in the position of Cain, although he believes that Chaym falls short of realizing that potential (*Charles*). Whalen-Bridge develops a reading of Chaym as a Cainite, who has at least "caught a

glimpse of the goodness of Abel" ("Waking" 515). Storhoff suggests that King also shares attributes of both Abel and Cain (*Understanding* 189). Byrd discusses these points in relation to Quinones's analysis of the myth, *The Changes of Cain*, which Johnson read while drafting *Dreamer*.

24. Nash points out that both King and Chaym serve as "father figures" (*Charles* 181).

25. See Nash's discussion of Cleaver in light of the development of Johnson's aesthetic (*Charles* 186ff.). See also Storhoff on Chester Himes (*Understanding* 193ff.).

26. See Nash (*Charles* 183ff.), Storhoff (*Understanding* 193), and Byrd (*Charles* 189).

27. For an analysis linking Chaym's labor to Whitehead's process philosophy, see Byrd (*Charles* 183).

# WORKS CITED

Adiele, Faith. *Meeting Faith: The Forest Journals of a Black Buddhist Nun*. New York: W. W. Norton, 2004.

Albert, Peter, and Ronald Hoffman. Introduction. *We Shall Overcome* 3–7.

———, eds. *We Shall Overcome: Martin Luther King, Jr., and the Black Freedom Struggle*. New York: Pantheon, 1990.

Althusser, Louis. *For Marx*. London: Allen Lane, 1970.

———. *Lenin and Philosophy*. London: New Left Books, 1971.

Anderson, Perry. *Considerations on Western Marxism*. New York: Verso, 1976.

Appiah, Kwame Anthony. *Cosmopolitanism: Ethics in a World of Strangers*. New York: W. W. Norton, 2006.

———. "Cosmopolitan Patriots." Cheah and Robbins 91–114.

———. *In My Father's House: Africa in the Philosophy of Culture*. New York: Oxford University Press, 1992.

Baker, Houston. *Betrayal: How Black Intellectuals Have Abandoned the Ideals of the Civil Rights Era*. New York: Columbia University Press, 2008.

———."Failed Prophet and Falling Stock: Why Ralph Ellison Was Never Avant-Garde." *Stanford Humanities Review* 7.1 (1999). www.stanford.edu/group/SHR/7-1/html /baker.html.

Banks, William. *Black Intellectuals: Race and Responsibility in American Life*. New York: W. W. Norton, 1996.

———. "Intellectuals and the Persisting Significance of Race." *Journal of Negro Education* 64.1 (1995): 75–86.

Barber, Michael. *Guardian of Dialogue*. Lewisburg, Pa.: Bucknell University Press, 1993.

Barnes, Nancy. "Buddhist Women and the Nuns' Order in Asia." *Engaged Buddhism: Buddhist Liberation Movements in Asia*. Ed. Christopher Queen and Sallie B. King. Albany: State University of New York Press, 1996. 259–94.

Barrett, William. *Irrational Man: A Study in Existential Philosophy*. New York: Doubleday Anchor, 1958.

Barrows, John H., ed. *The World's Parliament of Religions*. Vols. 1 and 2. Chicago: Parliament Publishing, 1893.

Baumann, Martin. "The Dharma Has Come West." *Journal of Buddhist Ethics* 4 (1997): 198.

Begley, Adam. "Black Studies' New Star." *New York Times*, April 1, 1990.

Bérubé, Michael. "Public Academy." *New Yorker*, January 9, 1995. 73–80.

Bhabha, Homi K. "Black and White and Read All Over: Homi Bhabha on the New Black Intellectual." *Artforum International* 34.2 (1995): 16–17, 114, 116.

———. "Unsatisfied: Notes on Vernacular Cosmopolitanism." *Text and Nation*. Ed. Laura Garcia-Moreno and Peter C. Pfeiffer. Columbia, S.C.: Camden House, 1996. 191–207.

Bilimoria, Purushottama. "The Reconciliation Sutras of Two Twentieth-Century Doctors of Non-Violence." www.emory.edu/ACAD-EXCHANGE/2001/decjan/bilmoria.

Boccia, Michael. "An Interview with Charles Johnson." 1966. McWilliams 192–205.

Boccia, Michael, and Herman Beavers, eds. *Charles Johnson Issue*. Spec. issue of *African American Review* 30.4 (Winter 1996): 514–694.

Bogues, Anthony. *Black Heretics, Black Prophets: Radical Political Intellectuals*. New York: Routledge, 2003.

Boyd, Herb. "The Man and the Plan: Conspiracy Theories and Paranoia in Our Culture." *Black Issues Book Review* 4 (March–April 2002): 38–40.

Boyd, Merle Kyoto. "A Child of the South in Long Black Robes." Gutiérrez Baldoquín 101–5.

Boynton, Robert. "The New Intellectuals." *Atlantic Monthly* (March 1995): 73–90.

Branch, Taylor. *At Canaan's Edge: America in the King Years, 1965–68*. New York: Simon and Schuster, 2007.

Brennan, Timothy. "Cosmo-Theory." *South Atlantic Quarterly* 100.3 (2001): 659–91.

Brentano, Franz. *Psychology from an Empirical Standpoint*. Ed. Oskar Kraus. London: Routledge and Kegan Paul, 1973.

Brown, Bill. "Global Bodies/Postnationalities: Charles Johnson's Consumer Culture." *Representations* 58 (1997): 24–48.

Brown, Scot. *Fighting for Us: Maulana Karenga, the Us Organization, and Black Cultural Nationalism*. New York: New York University Press, 2003.

Burris, John P. *Exhibiting Religion: Colonialism and Spectacle at International Expositions, 1851–1893*. Charlottesville: University Press of Virginia, 2001.

Bush, Rod. *We Are Not What We Seem: Black Nationalism and Class Struggle in the American Century*. New York: New York University Press, 2000.

Byrd. Rudolph P. *Charles Johnson's Novels: Writing the American Palimpsest*. Bloomington: Indiana University Press, 2005.

———, ed. *I Call Myself an Artist: Writings by and about Charles Johnson*. Bloomington: Indiana University Press, 1999.

———. "It Rests by Changing: Process in *The Sorcerer's Apprentice*." *I Call Myself an Artist* 333–52.

———. "*Oxherding Tale* and *Siddhartha*: Philosophy, Fiction, and the Emergence of a Hidden Tradition." 1996. Byrd, *I Call Myself an Artist* 305–17.

Calhoun, Craig. "The Class Consciousness of Frequent Travelers: Toward a Critique of Actually Existing Cosmopolitanism." *South Atlantic Quarterly* 101.4 (2002): 869–97.

Calhoun, Ramon. "Inside a Triple Parenthesis: Being a Black Buddhist in the U.S." *Turning Wheel* 12 (Summer 2003): 39–42.

Callinicos, Alex. *Marxism and Philosophy.* Oxford: Clarendon Press, 1983.

Carby, Hazel. *Race Men.* Cambridge: Harvard University Press, 1998.

Carson, Clayborne. "Martin Luther King, Jr., and the African-American Social Gospel." *African-American Christianity.* Ed. Paul E. Johnson. Berkeley: University of California Press, 1994. 159–77.

———. "Paradoxes of King Historiography." *Magazine of History* 19.1 (2005): 7–10.

———. "Reconstructing the King Legacy." Albert and Hoffman, *We Shall Overcome* 239–50.

Cartwright, Samuel. "Diseases and Peculiarities of the Negro Race." *De Bow's Review* 11 [New Orleans] (1851). Rpt. New York: AMS Press, 1967. www.pbs.org/wgbh/aia/part4/4h3106t.html.

Cashin, Sheryll. "Middle-Class Black Suburbs and the State of Integration." *Cornell Law Review* 729 (May 2001). www.antibiaslaw.com/biblio/Cashin.

Cattier, Michel. *The Life and Work of Wilhelm Reich.* Trans. Ghislaine Boulanger. New York: Horizon Press, 1971.

Chametzsky, Jules. "Public Intellectuals—Now and Then." *Melus* 29.3–4 (Fall–Winter 2004): 211–16.

Chandler, Gena. "Dreaming and Waking in Wonderland: *Faith and the Good Thing* and Charles Johnson's Fairy-Tale Fictions." *New Essays on the African American Novel.* Ed. Lovalerie King and Linda F. Selzer. New York: Palgrave, 2008. 75–91.

———. "'In-Itself-for-Me': Decomposition and Art in Charles Johnson's *Oxherding Tale.*" Conner and Nash 20–39.

Chappell, David W. "Racial Diversity in the Soka Gakkai." Queen, *Engaged Buddhism in the West* 184–217.

Cheah, Pheng, and Bruce Robbins, eds. *Cosmopolitics: Thinking and Feeling Beyond the Nation.* Minneapolis: University Press of Minnesota, 1998.

Chen, Viveka. "Finding True Freedom." Gutiérrez Baldoquín 111–15.

Christensen, John. "Scholars Fear King's Legacy Is Fading." CNN Interactive. April 5, 1999. www.cnn.com/SPECIALS/1999/mlk.legacy.

Clifford, James. Review of Edward W. Said's *Orientalism. History and Theory* 19.2 (1980): 204–23.

———. "Traveling Cultures." *Cultural Studies.* Ed. Lee Grossberg et al. London: Routledge, 1991. 96–116.

Cohen, Rodger. "Ideology Said to Split Book-Award Jurors." *New York Times,* November 27, 1990.

———. "*Middle Passage* and *Morgan* Win." *New York Times,* November 29, 1990.

Coleman, James W. "Charles Johnson's Quest for Black Freedom in *Oxherding Tale*." *African American Review* 29.4 (1995): 631–44.

Cone, James H. "Martin Luther King, Jr.: Black Theology—Black Church." *Theology Today* 40 (1984): 409–20.

Conner, Marc C. "'At the Numinous Heart of Being': *Dreamer* and Christian Theology." Conner and Nash 57–81.

———. "To Utter the Holy: The Metaphysical Romance of *Middle Passage*." Conner and Nash 57–81.

Conner, Marc C., and William R. Nash, eds. *Charles Johnson: The Novelist as Philosopher*. Oxford: University Press of Mississippi, 2007.

Cooper, Carol. "About Black Folks and Buddha Dharma: An Interview with bell hooks." 2001. www.carolcooper.org/iview/hooks-01.php.

Corrington, Robert. *Wilhelm Reich: Psychoanalyst and Radical Naturalist*. New York: Farrar, Straus and Giroux, 2003.

Cosby, Bill. "Pound Cake Speech." *American Rhetoric*. 2004. www.americanrhetoric.com/speeches/billcosbypoundcakespeech.htm.

Cotkin, George. *Existential America*. Baltimore: Johns Hopkins University Press, 2002.

Cox, Oliver Cromwell. *Caste, Class, and Race*. New York: Doubleday, 1948.

Crane, Gregg. "Ralph Ellison's Constitutional Faith." *The Cambridge Companion to Ralph Ellison*. Ed. Ralph Posnock. New York: Cambridge University Press 2005. 104–20.

Cruse, Harold. *The Crisis of the Negro Intellectual*. New York: William Morrow, 1967.

Cuomo, Chris J., and Kim Q. Hall, eds. *Whiteness: Feminist Philosophical Reflections*. Lanham, Md.: Rowman and Littlefield, 1999.

Davies, Linda. "Charles Johnson Interview." 1993. McWilliams 142–58.

Davis, Angela. "Unfinished Lecture on Liberation—II." Harris, *Philosophy Born of Struggle* 130–38.

Davis, Thulani. "Spinning Race at Harvard." *Village Voice*, January 16–22, 2006. www.villagevoice.com/news/0203,davis,31527,1.html.

Dawson, Michael. "A Black Counterpublic?" *Public Culture* 7.1 (1994): 195–223.

———. *Black Visions: The Roots of Contemporary African-American Political Ideologies*. Chicago: University of Chicago Press, 2001.

Deitrick, James. "Engaged Buddhist Ethics: Mistaking the Boat for the Shore." Queen, Prebish, and Keown 252–69.

Desmond, William. *Being and the Between*. New York: State University of New York Press, 1995.

Dewan, Shalia. "King Archives to Be Sold at Auction." *New York Times*, June 9, 2006.

Dewey, John. *The Early Works of John Dewey, 1882–1898*, Vol. 2: 1897, *Psychology*. Ed. Jo Ann Boydston. Carbondale: Southern Illinois University Press, 1967.

Dharmapala, Anagarika. "Criticism and Discussion of Missionary Methods." Barrows, *The World's Parliament of Religions* 2:1093.

———. Letter to Booker T. Washington. June 20, 1903. *The Booker T. Washington Papers Online.* Vol. 13. 507–8. www.historycooperative.org/btw/info.html.

———. Letter to Booker T. Washington. December 26, 1903. *The Booker T. Washington Papers Online.* Vol. 13. 508. www.historycooperative.org/btw/info.html.

———. "The World's Debt to Buddha." *The Dawn of Religious Pluralism.* Ed. R. H. Seager. La Salle, Ill.: Open Court, 1993. 410–20.

Du Bois, W. E. B. *Black Reconstruction in America.* New York: Harcourt, Brace, 1935.

———. "Karl Marx and the Negro." *W. E. B. Du Bois: The Crisis Writings.* Ed. Dan Walden. New York: Fawcett, 1972. 393–400.

Dyson, Michael Eric. *I May Not Get There With You: The True Martin Luther King, Jr.* New York: Free Press, 2000.

———. *Is Bill Cosby Right? Or Has The Black Middle Class Lost Its Mind?* New York: Basic Civitas Books, 2005.

Early, Gerald. "Black Like Them." *New York Times Book Review*, April 21, 1996. 7.

———. "Partisanship, Race, and the Public Intellectual." MIT Communications Forum. January 5, 2000. Para. 19. web.mit.edu/comm-forum/papers/early.html.

Ellison, Ralph. "National Book Award Acceptance Speech." *National Book Awards Acceptance Speeches.* NBA Foundation. www.nationalbook.org /nbaacceptspeech_rellison.html.

Epstein, Marcus. "Myths of Martin Luther King." http://www.lewrockwell.com /orig/epstein9.html.

Fagel, Brian. "Passages from the Middle: Coloniality and Postcoloniality in Charles Johnson's *Middle Passage.*" *African American Review* 10.4 (1996): 625–34.

Farber, David, and Beth Bailey. *The Columbia Guide to America in the 1960s.* New York: Columbia University Press, 2001.

Farred, Grant. *What's My Name? Black Vernacular Intellectuals.* Minneapolis: University of Minnesota Press, 2003.

Fields, Rick. "Confessions of a White Buddhist." *Tricycle: The Buddhist Review* 13 (Fall 1994): 54–65.

———. *How the Swans Came to the Lake: A Narrative History of Buddhism in America.* Boston: Shambhala Publications, 1981.

Fine, Robert, and Robin Cohen. "Four Cosmopolitan Moments." Vertovec and Cohen 137–62.

Freud, Sigmund. "Three Essays on Sexuality." *The Standard Edition of the Complete Works of Sigmund Freud.* Ed. and trans. James Strachey. 24 vols. London: Hogarth Press, 1966–74. 7:125–244.

Frings, Manfred S. *Max Scheler.* Milwaukee: Marquette University Press, 1996.

Fromm, Erich. *Marx's Concept of Man.* New York: Frederick Ungar, 1970.

Garrow, David J. *Bearing the Cross.* New York: William Morrow, 1986.

Gates, Henry Louis, Jr. "Black Demagogues and Pseudo-Scholars." *New York Times,* July 20, 1992.

Geller, Alan. "An Interview with Ralph Ellison." *The Black American Writer: Fiction.* Ed. C. W. E. Bigsby. DeLand, Fla.: Everett/Edwards, 1969. 153–68.

Ghosh, Nibir K. "From Narrow Complaint to Broad Celebration: A Conversation with Charles Johnson." *Melus* 29 (2004): 359–75.

Gikandi, Simon. "Race and Cosmopolitanism." *American Literary History* 14.3 (2002): 593–615.

Gilroy, Paul. *Against Race: Imaging Political Culture beyond the Color Line.* Cambridge: Belknap Press of Harvard University Press, 2000.

———. The *Black Atlantic: Modernity and Double Consciousness.* Cambridge: Harvard University Press, 1993.

Gleason, William. "'Go There': The Critical Pragmatism of Charles Johnson." Conner and Nash 82–105.

———. "The Liberation of Perception: Charles Johnson's *Oxherding Tale.*" *Black American Literature Forum* 25 (1991): 704–28.

Goldman, Adam. "Sotheby's to Auction Martin Luther King, Jr., Papers." *Washington Post,* June 9, 2006.

Gordon, Lewis. *Bad Faith and Anti-Black Racism.* Amherst, N.Y.: Humanity Books, 1995.

———. *Existence in Black.* New York: Routledge, 1996.

———. *Existentia Africana.* New York: Routledge, 2000.

Goudie, S. X. "'Leavin' a Mark on the Wor(l)d': Marksmen and Marked Men in *Middle Passage.*" *African American Review* 29.1 (1995): 109–22.

Griffiths, Frederick T. "'Sorcery Is Dialectical': Plato and Jean Toomer in Charles Johnson's *The Sorcerer's Apprentice.*" *African American Review* 30 (1996): 527–38.

Gutiérrez Baldoquín, Hilda, ed. *Dharma, Color, and Culture: New Voices in Western Buddhism.* Berkeley: Parallax Press, 2004.

Hanchard, Michael. "Cultural Politics and Black Public Intellectuals." *Social Text* 48 (1966): 95–108.

———. "Intellectual Pursuit." *Nation* 19 (February 1996): 22–25.

Hanh, Thich Nhat. *Going Home: Jesus and Buddha as Brothers.* New York: Riverhead, 2000.

———. *Living Buddha, Living Christ.* New York: Riverhead, 1997.

———. *Peace Is Every Step.* New York: Bantam, 1991.

Hanson, Niel. *The Custom of the Sea.* New York: John Wiley, 1999.

Hardack, Richard. "Black Skin, White Tissues: Local Color and Universal Solvents in the Novels of Charles Johnson." *Callaloo* 22.4 (1999): 1028–53.

Harper, Robert A. *The University That Shouldn't Have Happened, but Did.* Carbondale, Ill.: Devil's Kitchen Press, 1998.

Harris, Abram L. *The Black Worker.* Port Washington, N.Y.: Kennikat Press, 1931.

Harris, Leonard. "'Believe It or Not' or the Ku Klux Klan and American Philosophy Exposed." *Proceedings of the American Philosophical Association* 68 (1995): 133–37.

———. "The Horror of Tradition or How to Burn Babylon and Build Benin While Reading *A Preface to a Twenty-Volume Suicide Note*." *African-American Perspectives and Philosophical Traditions*. Ed. John P. Pittman. New York: Routledge, 1997. 94–118.

———, ed. *Philosophy Born of Struggle*. Dubuque: Kendall/Hunt, 1983.

Harvey, Peter. *An Introduction to Buddhist Ethics*. New York: Cambridge University Press, 2000.

Haywood, Jennifer. "Something to Serve: Constructs of the Feminine in Charles Johnson's *Oxherding Tale*." *Black American Literature Forum* 25 (1991): 689–703.

Hegel, G. W. E. Introduction to *The Philosophy of History*. New York: Dover, 1956. 91–99.

Heiferman, Marvin, and Carole Kismari. *Talking Pictures: People Speak about the Photographs That Speak to Them*. San Francisco: Chronicle Books, 1994.

Hollinger, David. *Postethnic America: Beyond Multiculturalism*. New York: Basic Books, 1995.

hooks, bell. "bell hooks Speaks to John Perry Barlow." *Shambhala Sun* 13: 1 (September 2005). www.shambhalasun.com/index.php?option=content-&task=view&id=2089.

"Eating the Other." *Black Looks*. Boston: South End Press, 1992. 21–40.

———. *Rock My Soul*. New York: Atria Books, 2003.

———. "Surrendered to Love: King's Legacy." *Shambhala Sun* 13.3 (January 2005): 51–53.

———. "Waking Up to Racism." *Tricycle: The Buddhist Review* 13 (Fall 1994): 42–45.

hooks, bell, and Cornel West. *Breaking Bread: Resurgent Black Intellectual Life*. Boston: South End Press, 1991.

Horowitz, David. "Cornel West: No Light in His Attic." Salon.com News, October 11, 1999. 1–2. www.salon.com/news/col/horo/1999/10/11/cornel/

Howard, Dick, and Karl E. Klare, eds. *The Unknown Dimension*. New York: Basic Books, 1972.

Hume, David. "Of National Characters." *The Philosophical Works of David Hume*. Vol. 3. Boston: Little, Brown, 1854. 217–36.

Hurst, Jane. "Nichiren Shoshu and Sokka Gakkai in America: The Pioneer Spirit." Prebish and Tanaka 80–97.

Hutcheson, George. *The Harlem Renaissance in Black and White*. Cambridge: Belknap Press of Harvard University Press, 1997.

Israel, Jonathan. "Enlightenment! Which Enlightenment?" *Journal of the History of Ideas* 67.3 (2006): 523–45.

Jablon, Madelyn. *Black Metafiction: Self-Consiousness in African American Fiction.* Iowa City: University of Iowa Press, 1997.

Jacoby, Russell. *The Last Intellectuals: American Culture in the Age of Academe.* New York: Basic Books, 2000.

James, C. L. R. *The Black Jacobins.* New York: Vintage Books, 1963.

James, Joy. *Imprisoned Intellectuals.* Lanham, Md.: Rowman and Littlefield, 2003.

———. *Transcending the Talented Tenth: Black Leaders and American Intellectuals.* New York: Routledge, 1996.

Jameson, Frederic. *The Prison-House of Language.* Princeton: Princeton University Press, 1972.

Jay, Martin. *The Dialectical Imagination.* London: Heinemann, 1973.

Jeffreys, Derek S. "Does Buddhism Need Human Rights?" Queen, Prebish, and Keown 271–85.

Jensen, Robert. "Best We Get Comfortable with King the Radical, Too." *Houston Chronicle,* January 14, 2001.

Johnson, Charles. "Alēthia." 1979. *The Sorcerer's Apprentice* 97–112.

———. "An American Milk Bottle." *Turning the Wheel* 169–76.

———. *Being and Race: Black Writing since 1970.* Bloomington: Indiana University Press, 1988.

———. "Be Peace Embodied." *Shambhala Sun* 12.6 (July 2004): 28–33.

———. *Black Humor.* Chicago: Johnson Publishing, 1970.

———. "Blueprints of Freedom." *Tricycle: The Buddhist Review* 17.3 (2008): 76–77.

———. "Buddhism Is the Most Radical and Civilized Choice: Interview with John Malkin." *Shambhala Sun* 12.3 (January 2004): 33–37.

———. "Charles Johnson." *Contemporary Authors: Autobiography Series.* Vol. 18. Ed. Joyce Nakamura. Detroit: Gale, 1994. 223–43.

———. "China." 1983. *The Sorcerer's Apprentice.* 61–95.

———. "Dr. King's Refrigerator." *Dr. King's Refrigerator and Other Bedtime Stories.* New York: Scribner, 2005. 21–31.

———. *Dreamer.* New York: Scribner, 1998.

———. "The Education of Mingo." 1977. *The Sorcerer's Apprentice* 1–23.

———. "The Elusive Art of 'Mindfulness'." *Turning the Wheel* 34–41.

———. "Exchange Value." 1981. *The Sorcerer's Apprentice* 25–40.

———. *Faith and the Good Thing.* New York: Viking, 1974.

———. *Half-Past Nation Time.* Chicago: Aware, 1972.

———. "I Call Myself an Artist." Byrd, *I Call Myself an Artist* 3–30.

———. Introduction to *Oxherding Tale.* New York: Penguin, 1995. ix–xix.

———. "Inventing Africa." Review of Kwame Anthony Appiah's *In My Father's House: Africa in the Philosophy of Culture. New York Times Book Review,* June 21, 1992.

———. "Keeping the Blues at Bay." Review of Albert Murray's *The Blue Devils of Nada and the Seven League Boots. New York Times Book Review,* March 10, 1996. 4.

———. "The King We Left Behind." *Common Quest* (Fall 1996). Byrd, *I Call Myself an Artist* 193–99.

———. "The King We Need: Teachings for a Nation in Search of Itself." *Shambhala Sun* 13.3 (January 2005): 42–50.

———. *Middle Passage.* New York: Atheneum, 1990.

———. "National Book Award Acceptance Speech." *TriQuarterly* 82 (Fall 1991): 208–9.

———. "Northwestern Commencement Address." 1994. Byrd, *I Call Myself An Artist* 141–44.

———. "Novel Genius." *The New Crisis* 109.2 (2002): 17–21.

———. "On the Books of Proverbs." *Turning the Wheel* 58–67.

———. *Oxherding Tale.* New York: Grove, 1982.

———. "A Phenomenology of the Black Body." 1976. Byrd, *I Call Myself an Artist* 109–22.

———. "The Philosopher and the American Novel." 1991. McWilliams 53–67.

———. "Philosophy and Black Fiction." 1980. Byrd, *I Call Myself an Artist* 79–84.

———. "Race, Politics, and Ralph Ellison." Review of Jerry Gafio Watt's *Heroism and the Black Intellectual: Ralph Ellison, Politics, and Afro-American Intellectual Life. New York Times*, February 5, 1995.

———. "Reading the Eightfold Path." 2003. Gutiérrez Baldoquín 127–55.

———. "The Role of the Black Intellectual in the Twenty-first Century." *Turning the Wheel* 83–93.

———. "A Sangha by Another Name." *Turning the Wheel* 46–57.

———. "Searching for the Hidden Martin Luther King, Jr." *Seattle Times*, January 14, 1996.

———. "The Second Front: A Reflection on Milk Bottles, Male Elders, the Enemy Within, Bar Mizvahs, and Martin Luther King Jr." *Black Men Speaking*. Ed. Charles Johnson and John McCluskey Jr. Bloomington: Indiana University Press, 1997. 177–88.

———. "Shall We Overcome?" 2005. *Society* 43.6 (July 2006): 13–14.

———. "The Singular Vision of Ralph Ellison." *Turning the Wheel* 105–11.

———. *The Sorcerer's Apprentice: Tales and Conjurations.* New York: Penguin Books, 1986.

———. *Soulcatcher and Other Stories.* New York: Harcourt, 2001.

———. "Thinking in Public." *American Literary History* 10.1 (Spring 1998): 1–83.

———. *Turning the Wheel: Essays on Buddhism and Writing.* New York: Scribner, 2003.

———. "Where Philosophy and Fiction Meet." 1988. Byrd, *I Call Myself an Artist* 91–95.

———. "Whole Sight: Notes on New Black Fiction." 1984. Byrd, *I Call Myself an Artist* 85–90.

———. "Wilhelm Reich and the Creation of a Marxist Psychology." Master's thesis. Southern Illinois University, 1973.

Johnson, Charles, and Bob Adelman. *King: The Photobiography of Martin Luther King, Jr.* New York: Viking, 2000.

Jones, Ken. *The New Social Face of Buddhism: An Approach to Political and Social Activism.* Somerville, Mass.: Wisdom Publications, 2003.

Jones, Marlene. "Moving toward an End to Suffering." Gutiérrez Baldoquín 43–45.

Jones, William R. "The Crisis in Philosophy: The Black Presence." *Proceedings of the American Philosophical Association* (1974): 118–25.

———. "The Legitimacy and Necessity of African American Philosophy: Some Preliminary Considerations." *Philosophical Forum* 9 (1977–78): 149–60.

———. "Liberation Strategies in Black Theology: Mao, Martin, or Malcolm?" Harris, *Philosophy Born of Struggle* 229–41.

Jordan, Margaret. *African American Servitude and Historical Imaginings.* New York: Palgrave, 2004.

Kant, Emmanuel. *Anthropology from a Pragmatic Point of View.* Trans. Victor Lyle Dowdell. Carbondale: Southern Illinois University Press, 1978.

———. *Foundations of the Metaphysics of Morals.* Trans. Lewis White Beck. Indianapolis: Bobbs Merrill, 1959.

———. *Observations on the Feelings of the Beautiful and the Sublime.* Trans. John T. Goldwaith. Berkeley: University of California Press, 1960.

———. "What Is Enlightenment?" *Kant's Political Writings.* Ed. Hans Reiss. Trans. H. B. Nisbet. Cambridge: Cambridge University Press, 1970. 54–60.

Karenga, Maulana. "Society, Culture, and the Problem of Self-Consciousness." Harris, *Philosophy Born of Struggle* 212–28.

Keith, Allan H. *SIUC'S Days of Dissent.* Mattoon, Ill.: Allan H. Keith, 2007.

Kennedy, Randall. "Forum: The Responsibility of Intellectuals in the Age of Crack." *Boston Review* 18.1 (1993). www.bostonreview.net/BR18.1/responsibility.html.

King, Martin Luther, Jr. *The Autobiography of Martin Luther King, Jr.* Ed. Clayborne Carson. New York: Grand Central Publishing, 1998.

———. "An Autobiography of Spiritual Development." *The Papers of Martin Luther King, Jr.* Vol. 1. *Called to Serve.* Ed. Clayborne Carson, Ralph E. Luker, and Penny A. Russell. Berkeley: University of California Press, 1992. 359–63.

———. "Beyond Vietnam." *A Call to Conscience: The Landmark Speeches of Martin Luther King, Jr.* Ed. Clayborne Carson et al. New York: Grand Central Publishing, 2001. 133–64.

———. "Black Power." *Where Do We Go from Here* 23–66.

———. "Non-Aggression Procedures to Interracial Harmony." *The Papers of Martin Luther King, Jr.* Vol. 3: *Birth of a New Age.* Ed. Clayborne Carson et al. Berkeley: University of California Press, 1997. 321–28.

———. "Notes on American Capitalism." *The Papers of Martin Luther King, Jr.* Vol. 1. *Called to Serve.* Ed. Clayborne Carson et al. Berkeley: University of California Press, 1994. 435–36.

———. "Paul's Letter to American Christians." *Strength to Love.* 127–42.

———. "Qualifying Examination in Systematic Theology." *The Papers of Martin Luther King, Jr.* Vol. 2. *Rediscovering Precious Values.* Ed. Clayborne Carson et al. Berkeley: University of California Press, 1994. 228–33.

———. "Rediscovering Lost Values." *The Papers of Martin Luther King, Jr.* Vol. 2. *Rediscovering Precious Values.* Ed. Clayborne Carson et al. Berkeley: University of California Press, 1994. 248.

———. "Remaining Awake through a Great Revolution." *A Knock at Midnight.* Ed. Clayborne Carson and Peter Holloran. Warner Books, 2000. 201–24.

———. *Strength to Love.* New York: Harper and Row, 1963.

———. *Stride toward Freedom.* San Francisco: Harper Collins, 1958.

———. "Transformed Nonconformist." *Strength to Love.* 8–15.

———. *Where Do We Go from Here: Chaos or Community?* Boston: Beacon Press, 1967.

King, Richard H. "Martin Luther King, Jr., and the Meaning of Freedom." Albert and Hoffman, *We Shall Overcome* 130–52.

Kolakowski, Leszek. *Main Currents of Marxism.* London: Clarendon Press, 1978.

Koplowitz, H. B. *Carbondale after Dark.* Carbondale, Ill.: Dome, 1982.

Kuklick, Bruce. *A History of Philosophy in America, 1720–2000.* New York: Oxford University Press, 2002.

Lawson, Steven. "Freedom Then, Freedom Now: The Historiography of the Civil Rights Movement." *American Historical Review* 96:2 (1991): 456–71.

Lee, Jonathan Scott, and Fred L. Hord. *I Am Because We Are: Readings in Black Philosophy.* Amherst: University of Massachusetts Press, 1995.

Lee, William Poy. "Black on Black: Interview with Lawrence Ellis with Introduction by William Poy Lee." 2002. 1–7. www.spiritrock.org/html/diversity_BlackonBlack_Ellis.html.

———. "Black on Black: Interview with Ralph Steele." 2001. 1–4. www.spiritrock.org/html/diversity_BlackonBlack_Steele.html.

Leighty, David. *Circuitous Journeys: Modern Spiritual Autobiographies.* New York: Fordham University Press, 2000.

Levasseur, Jennifer, and Kevin Rabalais. "An Interview with Charles Johnson." 2002. McWilliams 246–70.

Levine, Lawrence. *Black Culture and Black Consciousness.* New York: Oxford University Press, 1977.

Lischer, Richard. *The Preacher King: Martin Luther King, Jr., and the Word That Moved America.* New York: Oxford University Press, 1995.

Little, Jonathan. *Charles Johnson's Spiritual Imagination.* Columbia: University of Missouri Press, 1997.

———. "From the Comic Book to the Comic: Charles Johnson's Variations on Creative Expression." *African American Review* 30.4 (Winter 1996): 579–601.

———. "An Interview with Charles Johnson." 1993. McWilliams 97–122.

———. "Charles Johnson's Revolutionary *Oxherding Tale*." *Studies in American Fiction* 19 (1991): 141–51.

Lott, Eric. "The New Cosmopolitanism." *Transition* 72 (1996): 108–35.

Lott, Eric, and John P. Pittman, eds. *A Companion to African American Philosophy*. Malden: Blackwell, 2003.

Lowenstein, Jeff Kelly. "Marching On." *Chicago Reporter*, January 2006. www.chicagoreporter.com/2006/1-2006/king/current/htm.

Lukács, Georg. *History and Class Consciousness*. Trans. Rodney Livingstone. Cambridge: MIT Press, 1972.

Machery, Pierre. *The Object of Literature*. Cambridge: Cambridge University Press, 1995.

Mailloux, Steven. "Thinking in Public with Rhetoric." *Philosophy and Rhetoric* 39. 2 (2006): 140–46.

Malcolm X. *The Autobiography of Malcolm X: As Told to Alex Haley*. New York: Ballantine, 1964.

———. *By Any Means Necessary*. Ed. George Brietman. New York: Pathfinders, 1970.

Malcomson, Scott. "Varieties of Cosmopolitan Experience." Cheah and Robbins 233–45.

Mao Tse-tung. *Quotations from Chairman Mao Tse-tung*. Peking: Foreign Languages Press, 1972.

Marable, Manning. "Black Studies: Marxism and the Black Intellectual Tradition." *The Left Academy*. Ed. Bertell Ollman. New York: McGraw-Hill, 1982. 35–66.

Marcuse, Herbert. *Counterrevolution and Revolt*. Boston: Beacon Press, 1972.

———. *Eros and Civilization*. New York: Vintage Books, 1962.

———. *One-Dimensional Man*. Boston: Beacon Press, 1964.

Marx, Karl. "Debates." *Rhenische Zeitung*, no. 125 (May 5, 1942). Marx and Engels 1:174.

———. *The 1844 Manuscripts. Marx's Concept of Man*. Ed. Erich Fromm. Trans. T. B. Bottomore. New York: Frederick Ungar, 1970. 87–196.

Marx, Karl, and Frederick Engels. *Collected Works*. 47 vols. London: Lawrence and Wishart, 1975.

Maxwell, William J. *New Negro, Old Left*. New York: Columbia University Press, 1999.

McCall, Nathan. *Makes Me Wanna Holler: A Young Black Man in America*. New York: Vintage Books, 1995.

McClendon, John H. "Eugene Holmes: A Commentary on a Black Marxist Philosopher." Harris, *Philosophy Born of Struggle* 37–50.

McCumber, John. "Philosophy and Hydrology: Situating Discourse in Charles Johnson's *Faith and the Good Thing*." Byrd, *I Call Myself an Artist* 251–69.

McDowell, Edwin. "Book Notes." *New York Times,* July 27, 1988.

———. "Nominees for the National Book Awards." *New York Times,* October 19, 1990.

McKay, Claude. *Negroes in America.* Port Washington, N.Y.: Associated Faculty Press, 1979.

McWilliams, James, ed. *Passing the Three Gates: Interviews with Charles Johnson.* Seattle: University of Washington Press, 2004.

Meszaros, Istvan. *Marx's Theory of Alienation.* London: Merlin Press, 1970.

Michael, John. *Anxious Intellects: Academic Professionals, Public Intellectuals, and Enlightenment Values.* Durham: Duke University Press, 2000.

Mignolo, Walter. "The Many Faces of Cosmo-Polis: Border Thinking and Critical Cosmopolitanism." *Cosmopolitanism.* Ed. Carol A. Brackenridge, Homi Bhabha, and Dipesh Chakrabarty. Durham: Duke University Press, 2002. 157–88.

Miller, Keith. *The Voice of Deliverance.* New York: Free Press, 1992.

Mills, Charles W. "Alternative Epistemologies." *Blackness Visible* 21–39.

———. *Blackness Visible: Essays on Philosophy and Race.* Ithaca: Cornell University Press, 1998.

———. "Non-Cartesian Sums." *Blackness Visible* 1–19.

———. "Prophetic Pragmatism as a Political Philosophy." *Cornel West: A Critical Reader.* Ed. George Yancy. London: Blackwell, 2001. 192–223.

Moses, Wilson Jeremiah. *Afrotopia.* New York: Cambridge University Press, 1998.

Mudede, Charles. "The Human Dimension." McWilliams 236–70.

Mulhern, Francis. *Contemporary Marxist Literary Criticism.* White Plains, N.Y.: Longman, 1992.

Mullen, Bill. *Popular Fronts.* Champaign: University of Illinois Press, 1999.

Muther, Elizabeth. "Isadora at Sea: Misogyny as Comic Capital in Charles Johnson's *Middle Passage.*" *African American Review* 30.4 (Winter 1996): 649–58.

Nash, William R. "The Application of an Ideal: *Turning the Wheel* as Ontological Program." Conner and Nash. 171–81.

———. *Charles Johnson's Fiction.* Urbana: University of Illinois Press, 2003.

———. "'I Was My Father's Father and He My Child': The Process of Black Fatherhood and Literary Evolution in Charles Johnson's Fiction." *Contemporary Black Men's Fiction and Drama.* Ed. Keith Clark. Urbana: University of Illinois Press, 2001. 108–34.

Nattier, Jan. "Visible and Invisible: Jan Nattier on the Politics of Representation in Buddhist America." *Tricycle: The Buddhist Review* 17 (Fall 1995): 42–49.

Neal, Larry. "The Black Arts Movement." *The Black Aesthetic.* Ed. Allison Gayle, Jr. New York: Doubleday, 1971. 257–74.

———. "The Black Writer's Role: Richard Wright." *Liberator* 5.12 (1965): 20–22.

———. "Ellison's Zoot Suit." *Black World* 20 (1970): 31–50.

Neal, Mark Anthony. "Hip-Hop: Not Your Pop's Culture." *Duke Magazine* 92.4 (July–August 2006). www.dukemagazine.duke.edu/dukemag/issues/070806/hiphop1.html.

———. "Lifestyles of the Rich and Tenured." seeingblack.com, April 25, 2006. seeingblack.com/x042502/blackivory.shtml.

————. Review of Michael Eric Dyson's *I May Not Get There With You*. Popmatters.com. www.popmatters.com/books/reviews/i/i-may-not-get-there-with-you.shtml.

Nietzsche, Friedrich. *Nietzsche: The Anti-Christ, Ecce Homo, Twilight of the Idols, And Other Writings*. Ed. Aaron, Ridley. Cambridge: Cambridge University Press, 2005. 1–68.

————. *Beyond Good and Evil*. Trans. Walter Kaufmann. New York: Vintage Books, 1989.

Nwankwo, Ifeoma Kiddoe. *Black Cosmopolitanism: Racial Consciousness and Transnational Identity in the Nineteenth-Century Americas*. Philadelphia: University of Pennsylvania Press, 2005.

Oates, Stephen B. *Let the Trumpet Sound: A Life of Martin Luther King, Jr.* Harper Perennial, 1994.

O'Connell, Nicholas. "Charles Johnson." 1987. McWilliams 16–33.

O'Connor, Flannery. *Mystery and Manners*. New York: Farrar, Straus and Giroux, 1969.

O'Keefe, Vincent A. "Reading Rigor Mortis: Offstage Violence and Excluded Middles 'in' Johnson's *Middle Passage* and Morrison's *Beloved*." *African American Review* 30.4 (Winter 1996): 635–51.

Ouiment, Lorrain. "Freedom through Contamination: Collapsed Boundaries in Charles Johnson's *Oxherding Tale* and *Middle Passage*." *Canadian Review of American Studies* 30.1 (2000): 35–51.

Outlaw, Lucius. "Language and the Transformation of Consciousness." Ph.D. dissertation. Boston College, 1972.

————. *On Race and Philosophy*. New York: Routledge, 1996.

————. "Race and Class." Harris, *Philosophy Born of Struggle* 107–16.

Parsi, Kayhan P., and Daren E. Geraghty. "The Bioethicist as Public Intellectual." *American Journal of Bioethics* 4.1 (2004): W17–23.

Perry, La Vora. "Religion Is Deeper Than Culture: On Being an African-American Buddhist." *Cleveland Plain Dealer*, August 19, 2000.

Pierce, Lori. "Buddhism and the Body Problem: A Historical Perspective on African American Buddhism." *Turning Wheel* 12 (Summer 2003): 20–22.

Pintak, Lawrence. "'Something Has to Change.'" *Shambhala Sun* (September 2001). www.shambhalasun.com/Archieves/Features/2001/sept01/pintak.htm.

Pittman, John P., ed. *African American Perspectives and Philosophical Traditions*. New York: Routledge, 1997.

Posnock, Ross. *Color and Culture: Black Writers and the Making of the Modern Intellectual*. Cambridge: Harvard University Press, 1998.

————. "The Dream of Deracination: The Uses of Cosmopolitanism." *American Literary History* 12.4 (Winter 2000): 802–18.

————. "Ellison's Joking." *The Cambridge Companion to Ralph Ellison*. Ed. Ralph Posnock. New York: Cambridge University Press. 1–10.

Prebish, Charles. "The Academic Study of Buddhism in America: A Silent Sangha." Williams and Queen 183–214.

Prebish, Charles, and Kenneth Tanaka, eds. *The Faces of Buddhism in America.* Berkeley: University of California Press, 1998.

Queen, Christopher S., ed. *Engaged Buddhism in the West.* New York: Routledge, 2003.

Queen, Christopher S., Charles Prebish, and Damien Keown, eds. *Action Dharma: New Studies in Engaged Buddhism.* New York: RoutledgeCurzon, 2003.

Quinones, J. Richard. *The Changes of Cain.* Princeton: Princeton University Press, 1991.

Rabb, Christopher. "Blogging While Black." www.alternet.org/mediaculture /21301/.

Rangdröl, Choyin. "Black Buddha: Bringing the Tradition Home." *Turning Wheel* 12 (Summer 2003): 23–25.

Reed, Adolph. "What Are the Drums Saying, Booker? The Current Crisis of the Black Intellectual. *Village Voice*, April 11, 1995.

Reich, Wilhelm. *Character Analysis.* Trans. Theodore P. Wolfe. New York: Noonday Press, 1949.

———. *The Function of the Orgasm.* Trans. Mary Higgins. New York: Farrar, Straus and Giroux, 1973.

Reid-Pharr, Robert F. "Cosmopolitan Afrocentric Mulatto Intellectual." *American Literary History* 13.1 (2001): 169–79.

Rivers, Eugene. "Black Intellectuals in the Age of Crack." *Boston Review* 19.1 (1994): 19.

Robbins, Bruce. "Actually Existing Cosmopolitanism." Cheah and Robbins 1–19.

———. *Feeling Global: Internationalism in Distress.* New York: New York University Press, 1998.

Robinson, Cedric. *Black Marxism.* Chapel Hill: University of North Carolina Press, 2000.

Robotham, Don. "Cosmopolitanism and Planetary Humanism: The Strategic Universalism of Paul Gilroy." *South Atlantic Quarterly* 104.3 (Summer 2005): 561–82.

Rodberg, Simon. "The Content of His Character: Repoliticizing an American Hero." *Yale Review of Books* 3.2 (2000). www.yale.edu/yrly/summeroo /review4.html.

Rodriquez, Hector. "Ideology and Film Culture." *Film, Theory, and Philosophy.* Ed. Richard Allen and Murray Smith. Oxford University Press: 1999. 260–81.

Rorty, Richard. *Philosophy and the Mirror of Nature.* Princeton: Princeton University Press, 1979.

Rothberg, Donald. "Responding to the Cries of the World: Socially Engaged Buddhism in North America." Prebish and Tanaka 266–86.

Rowell, Charles H. "An Interview with Clarence Major." *Callaloo* 20.3 (1998): 667–78.

Rushdy, Ashraf H. S. *Neo-Slave Narratives: Studies in the Social Logic of a Literary Form.* New York: Oxford University Press, 1999.

———. "The Phenomenology of the Allmuseri: Charles Johnson and the Subject of the Narrative of Slavery." *African American Review* 26 (1992): 373–94.

———. "The Properties of Desire: Forms of Slave Identity in Charles Johnson's *Middle Passage*." *Arizona Quarterly* 50.2 (1994): 74–108.

———. *Remembering Generations*. Chapel Hill: University of North Carolina Press, 2001.

Sabine, George H. *A History of Political Theory*. New York: Holt, Rinehart and Winston, 1961.

Sartre, Jean-Paul. *Anti-Semite and Jew*. Trans. George Becker. New York: Schocken Books, 1995.

Schiller, Friedrich. *On the Aesthetic Education of Man*. Trans. Reginald Snell. New York: Dover, 2004.

Schott, Mary May. *Cognition and Eros*. University Park: Penn State University Press, 1998.

———. "Gender and the Enlightenment." *Feminist Interpretations of Immanuel Kant*. Ed. Mary May Schott. University Park: Penn State University Press, 1997. 319–37.

Scott, Daniel. "Interrogating Identity: Appropriation and Transformation in *Middle Passage*. *African American Review* 29.4 (1995): 645–55.

Seager, R. H. "Buddhist Worlds in the U.S.A.: A Survey of the Territory." Williams and Queen 238–61.

———. *The Dawn of Religious Pluralism*. La Salle, Ill.: Open Court, 1993.

———. *The World's Parliament of Religions: The East-West Encounter*. 1893. Rpt. Bloomington: Indiana University Press, 1995.

Selzer, Linda. "Charles Johnson's 'Exchange Value': Signifyin(g) on Marx." *Massachusetts Review* 42 (2001): 253–68.

———. "The Genesis of Charles Johnson's Philosophical Fiction." Conner and Nash 1–15.

———. "Master-Slave Dialectics in Charles Johnson's 'The Education of Mingo.'" *African American Review* 37 (2003): 105–14.

Selzer, Linda, and Lovalerie King, eds. *New Essays on the African American Novel*. New York: Palgrave, 2008.

Shklosky, Viktor. *Theory of Prose*. Normal, Ill.: Dalkey Archive Press, 1991.

*The Sixth Patriarch's Dharma Jewel Platform Sutra*. Trans. Buddhist Text Society. Burlingame, Calif.: Buddhist Text Society, 2001.

Slaughter, Thomas F., Jr. "Epidermalizing the World." Harris, *Philosophy Born of Struggle* 283–88.

Smethurst, James Edward. *The Black Arts Movement: Literary Nationalism in the 1960s and 1970s*. Chapel Hill: University of North Carolina Press, 2005.

———. *The New Red Negro*. New York: Oxford University Press, 1999.

Smith, Bardwell L. "Sinhalese Buddhism and the Dilemmas of Reinterpretation." *The Two Wheels of Dhamma*. Ed. Bardwell L. Smith. Chambersburg, Pa.: American Academy of Religion, 1972. 79–106.

Solomon, Mark. *The Cry Was Unity.* Oxford: University Press of Mississippi, 1995.

Spaulding, A. T. "Finding the Way: Karl Marx and the Transcendence of Discourse in Charles Johnson's *Oxherding Tale.*" *Sycamore* 1 (1997). www.unc.edu/sycamore/97.1/oxherd.html.

Spiegelberg, Herbert. *The Phenomenological Movement.* Vol. 1. The Hague: Martinus Nijhoff, 1978.

Spillers, Hortense J. "The Crisis of the Negro Intellectual: A Post-Date." *Boundary 2* 21.3 (Autumn 1994): 65–116.

Staude, John Raphael. *Max Scheler: An Intellectual Portrait.* New York: Free Press, 1967.

Steele, Ralph. "A Teaching on the Second Noble Truth." Gutiérrez Baldoquín 75–80.

Steinbach, Sara. "The Stories I Live With." Gutiérrez Baldoquín 89–90.

Steinberg, Stephen. *Turning Back: The Retreat from Racial Justice in American Thought and Policy.* Boston: Beacon Press, 1995.

Stepto, Robert. "Black American Literature at the Year 2000." *U.S. Society and Values* 5.1 (February 2000). usinfo.state.gov/journals/itsv/0200/ijse/stepto.htm.

Storhoff, Gary. "The Artist as Universal Mind: Berkeley's Influence on Charles Johnson." *African American Review* 30 (Winter 1996): 539–48.

———. "Pragmatic Ethics in Charles Johnson's Fiction." Conner and Nash 106–26.

———. *Understanding Charles Johnson.* Columbia: University of South Carolina Press, 2004.

Street, Joe. Review of John A. Kirk's *Martin Luther King, Jr.* July 8, 2005. www.history.ac.uk/reviews/paper/street.html.

Sullivan, Roger J. *Immanuel Kant's Moral Theory.* Cambridge: Cambridge University Press, 1989.

Taylor, Clarence. *Black Religious Intellectuals.* New York: Routledge, 2002.

Thomas, Paul. "Critical Reception: Marx Then and Now." *The Cambridge Companion to Marx.* Ed. Terrell Carver. Cambridge: Cambridge University Press, 1991. 23–54.

Thurman, Robert A. F. "The Emptiness That Is Compassion: An Essay on Buddhist Ethics." *Religious Traditions* 4:2 (1981): 11–34.

Travis, Molly. "*Beloved* and *Middle Passage*: Race, Narrative, and the Critic's Essentialism." *Reading Cultures.* Carbondale: Southern Illinois University Press, 1998. 68–88.

Troutt, David D. *After the Storm: Black Intellectuals Explore the Meaning of Hurricane Katrina.* New York: New Press, 2006.

Trucks, Rob. "A Conversation with Charles Johnson." *TriQuarterly* 107–8 (Winter–Summer 2000): 547–60.

Ture, Kwame [Stokely Carmichael], with Michael Thelwell. *Ready for Revolution.* New York: Scribner, 2003.

Van Der Veer, Peter. "Colonial Cosmopolitanism." Vertovec and Cohen 165–79.

Verhoeven, Martin J. "Americanizing the Buddha: Paul Carus and the Transformation of Asian Thought." Prebish and Tanaka 207–28.

Vertovec, Steven, and Robin Cohen, eds. *Conceiving Cosmopolitanism: Theory, Context, and Practice.* New York: Oxford University Press, 2002.

Vivekananda. "Hinduism." Barrows, *The World's Parliament of Religions* 2:968–78.

Wald, Alan. *Exiles from a Future Time.* Chapel Hill: University of North Carolina Press, 2002.

Walker, Alice. "Everyday Use." *In Love and Trouble: Stories of Black Women.* New York: Harcourt Brace Jovanovich, 1973. 47–59.

———. "This Was Not an Area of Large Plantations." Gutiérrez Baldoquín 189–200.

Ward, Julie K., and Tommy L. Lott, eds. *Philosophers on Race: Critical Essays.* Malden: Wiley-Blackwell, 2002.

Washington, Booker T. *Up from Slavery.* Ed. William L. Andrews. New York: Oxford University Press, 1995.

Watts, Jerry Gafio. *Heroism and the Black Intellectual: Ellsion, Politics, and Afro-American Intellectual Life.* Chapel Hill: University of North Carolina Press, 1994.

West, Cornel. "The Dilemma of the Black Intellectual." *Cultural Critique* 1.1 (1985): 109–24.

———. *The Ethical Dimensions of Marxist Thought.* New York: Monthly Review Press, 1991.

———. "The Paradox of the African American Rebellion." *Keeping Faith.* New York: Routledge, 1992. 271–91.

———. "Philosophy, Politics, and Power: An Afro-American Perspective." Harris, *Philosophy Born of Struggle* 51–59.

———. "Prophetic Christian as Organic Intellectual: Martin Luther King, Jr." *The Cornel West Reader.* New York: Basic Civitas Books, 1999.

———. "Race and Social Theory." *Keeping Faith: Philosophy and Race in America.* New York: Routledge, 1992. 251–70.

Whalen-Bridge, John. "Charles Johnson." *The Dictionary of Literary Biography: American Novelists since World War II.* Vol. 278. Ed. James R. Giles and Wanda H. Giles. Detroit: Gale, 2002. 201–11.

———. "Invisible Threads: Charles Johnson and Feminine Civility." Conner and Nash 127–49.

———. "'Now That I Am Old and Have the Words for It': Interview with Maxine Hong Kingston." *Shambhala Sun* 13.3 (January 2005): 60–66.

———. "Waking Cain: The Poetics of Integration in *Dreamer*" *Callaloo* 26.2 (2003): 504–21.

———. "'Whole Sight' in Review: Reflections on Charles Johnson." *MELUS:* 31.2 (2006): 244–67.

Wiese, Andrew. *Places of Their Own: African American Suburbanization in the Twentieth Century.* Chicago: University of Chicago Press, 2004.

Wiggershaus, Rolf. *The Frankfurt School.* Cambridge: MIT Press, 1994.

Williams, Angel Kyoto. *Being Black: Zen and the Art of Living with Fearlessness and Grace.* New York: Viking Compass, 2000.

Williams, Duncan R., and Christopher S. Queen, eds. *American Buddhism: Methods and Findings in Recent Scholarship.* Richmond, Surrey: Curzon, 1999.

Williams, John A. *The Man Who Cried I Am.* Boston: Little, Brown, 1967.

Williams, Robert. "W. E. B. Du Bois: Afro-American Philosopher of Social Reality." Harris, *Philosophy Born of Struggle* 11–20.

Willis, Jan. "Dharma Has No Color." Gutiérrez Baldoquín 217–24.

———. *Dreaming Me: An African American Woman's Spiritual Journey.* New York: Riverhead, 2001.

———. "You're Already a Buddha, So Be a Buddha." *Turning Wheel* 12 (Summer 2003): 31–33.

Winerip, Michael. "In the Affluent Suburbs, an Invisible Race Gap." *New York Times*, June 4, 2003.

Wood, Lewis. "From the Guest Editor." *Turning Wheel* 12 (Summer 2003): 2.

Woodward, Komozi. *A Nation within a Nation: Amiri Baraka (Leroi Jones) and Black Power Politics.* Chapel Hill: University of North Carolina Press, 1999.

Yancy, George. *African American Philosophers: Seventeen Conversations.* New York: Routledge, 1998.

———. "Gilbert Haven Jones." *African American National Biography.* Vol. 1. Ed. Henry Louis Gates Jr. and Evelyn Higgenbotham. New York: Oxford University Press, 2008. 237–38.

———. *The Philosophical I.* Lanham, Md.: Rowman and Littlefield, 2002.

———. "Thomas Nelson Baker, Sr." *African American National Biography.* Vol. 2. Ed. Henry Louis Gates, Jr., and Evelyn Higgenbotham. New York: Oxford University Press, 2008. 654–55.

Yarnall, Thomas Freeman. "Engaged Buddhism: New and Improved? Made in the USA from Asian Materials." Queen, Prebish, and Keown 286–344.

Zubaida, Sami. "Middle Eastern Experiences of Cosmopolitanism." Vertovec and Cohen 32–41.

# INDEX

Abernathy, Ralph, 228, 240
Adelman, Bob, 11, 213
Adiele, Faith, 110
affirmative action, 125, 180–81, 220, 269n.6
*African American Perspectives and Philosophical Traditions* (Pittman), 18
African American philosophy: African Americans in graduate programs in 1960s and 1970s, 3–4, 15, 17, 49; "Alēthia on black scholar in white academy, 30–44; black philosophers leave profession, 45–46; black philosophical fiction, 21, 22, 31, 44–50; and crisis of American philosophy, 23–30; early African American philosophers, 15–16; first African American to receive Ph.D., 256n.14; first African American woman to receive Ph.D., 16; Johnson as philosophy student, 3–4, 8–23; Johnson's philosophical interests, 14; legitimacy of, 17–19; literature seen as legitimate site for philosophy in, 19, 47; as pluralist, 19; as political, 25; roots in nonacademic forms of writing, 19
*African American Philosophy: Seventeen Conversations* (Yancy), 18
African Americans: anti-intellectualism in black youth culture, 204; "bread and butter" approach to education of, 24; Buddhists, 3, 5, 105–26; cosmopolitanism of, 204; doctoral degrees awarded to, 166; education sought by, 9, 203–4; Evanston, Illinois, community, 9, 10; explosion in black popular culture, 163; first-generation college students, 33; in higher education, 1940–70, 10, 15, 162; idealized African past versus heritage of, 203, 207; Jewish-black relations, 223–24; Marxism's influence on black reformers, 55–56; media representations of, 202–3; suburbanization of, 13–14, 164; widening class divisions among, 164; at World's Parlia-

ment of Religion, 107–8. *See also* African American philosophy; Black Arts Movement; Black Dharma; black liberation movement; black public intellectuals; civil rights movement; racism; slavery
African Blood Brotherhood, 56
Afrocentricity, 12, 168, 169, 170
Albert, Peter J., 218
"Alēthia" (Johnson), 30–44; allusions to books in, 41–42; ambivalence toward phenomenology in, 40–41; autobiographical elements of, 45, 259n.44; Baldwin's "Sonny's Blues" compared with, 43–44; dissatisfaction with tradition philosophical discourse in, 47; Kant in, 31–32, 34, 36, 38, 40, 41, 42, 43, 44; *Oxherding Tale* compared with, 143, 147; plot of, 31; primary locales of, 37; professor's first vision of Wendy, 34–35; professor's second vision of Wendy, 31, 37–40; Scheler in, 31, 34, 35, 36, 39, 40, 41, 42, 43; three moments of phenomenological insight in, 35; trope of homosexuality in, 39; Wendy's multiple roles in, 42–43
Alexander the Great, 176
Alfau, Felipe, 171
Allen, Anita, 15, 46
Allen, Doug, 53, 257n.23
Allen, Richard, 159
Althusser, Louis, 57
"American Milk Bottle, The" (Johnson), 207
American Nazi Party, 232
American Negro Academy, 159
American Philosophical Association, 17, 18, 23, 50
analytic philosophy: black philosophers' relationship to, 3, 23, 50; in crisis of American philosophy, 27–28; Johnson's work as response to, 21; Marcuse's criticism of, 100; Rorty's criticism of, 48–49
*Anxious Intellectuals* (Michael), 162